Legal Issues in Social Work Practice and Research

Sana Loue

Legal Issues in Social Work Practice and Research

Springer

Sana Loue
School of Medicine, Department of Bioethics
Case Western Reserve University
Cleveland, OH, USA

ISBN 978-3-319-77412-1   ISBN 978-3-319-77414-5 (eBook)
https://doi.org/10.1007/978-3-319-77414-5

Library of Congress Control Number: 2018936608

© Springer International Publishing AG, part of Springer Nature 2018
This work is subject to copyright. All rights are reserved by the Publisher, whether the whole or part of the material is concerned, specifically the rights of translation, reprinting, reuse of illustrations, recitation, broadcasting, reproduction on microfilms or in any other physical way, and transmission or information storage and retrieval, electronic adaptation, computer software, or by similar or dissimilar methodology now known or hereafter developed.
The use of general descriptive names, registered names, trademarks, service marks, etc. in this publication does not imply, even in the absence of a specific statement, that such names are exempt from the relevant protective laws and regulations and therefore free for general use.
The publisher, the authors and the editors are safe to assume that the advice and information in this book are believed to be true and accurate at the date of publication. Neither the publisher nor the authors or the editors give a warranty, express or implied, with respect to the material contained herein or for any errors or omissions that may have been made. The publisher remains neutral with regard to jurisdictional claims in published maps and institutional affiliations.

Printed on acid-free paper

This Springer imprint is published by the registered company Springer International Publishing AG part of Springer Nature.
The registered company address is: Gewerbestrasse 11, 6330 Cham, Switzerland

Introduction

Social workers are routinely confronted with legal issues, many of which are complex and not easily resolved. Indeed, it is difficult to conceive of any practice, research, or administrative setting in which social workers do not face a legal issue in some form.

This text is designed to serve as a reference for practicing social workers and for graduate students preparing for practice. However, because laws can change frequently, the reader is always urged to consult with the most recent relevant law in any situation. This book can serve as a first step, pointing the reader in the appropriate direction.

The first portion of the text addresses legal and ethical issues that are specific to the practice of social work and are relevant to clinical, research, and academic social workers alike. Chapter 1 explores the social worker-client relationship, with an emphasis on its fiduciary nature and violations of the relationship. The concept of informed consent and the social worker-client agreement are also addressed. Chapter 2 continues this discussion of legal and ethical responsibilities through an examination of the parameters of confidentiality and privacy. Licensure, gatekeeping, and disciplinary proceedings before professional boards are considered in Chap. 3, while Chap. 4 focuses on liability in the context of civil lawsuits and criminal prosecution.

Social workers who conduct research will be particularly interested in Chap. 5, which explores the legal and ethical responsibilities that arise specifically in the context of research. Individuals who interface with the judicial system, whether in the capacity of an expert witness, a case manager, a reentry social worker, a mediator, or in some other role, will find Chap. 6 on forensic social work to be of interest. Chapter 6 also reviews the process through which an idea may become legislation, important for social workers engaged in advocacy work.

Chapters 7, 8, 9, 10, and 11 focus on the many legal issues that arise in the context of providing services to individuals and families. On any given day, social workers may be asked to provide testimony in a proceeding to terminate parental rights (Chap. 7), assist a family to obtain needed services in the public school for their disabled child (Chap. 8), explain the potential use of a durable power of attorney for health care to a critically ill adult facing surgery (Chap. 9), weigh the pros and cons of referring a pregnant woman to substance use treatment or reporting her for child abuse (Chap. 10), or assess an elderly person's situation to determine whether his deteriorating health condition results from caregiver neglect (Chap. 11). Each such situation is complex in its human aspects; resolution is often made even more challenging when one considers the multiple ethical and legal dimensions.

Chapters 12 and 13 provide an opportunity to focus on legal issues arising in the international context. Chapter 12 discusses the structure of the U.S. immigration system and the roles that can be played by social workers in assisting clients with their efforts to immigrate family members to the U.S. and in representing clients in administrative proceedings. Chapter 13 examines internationalism in social work over time and investigates human rights as a basis for international social work.

Social workers are privileged nearly every day to be able to connect with others in their moments of joy, anguish, fear—indeed, in all of their humanity. An understanding of the interplay between law and social work practice, research, and administration can enhance our ability to serve our clients, our profession, and ourselves.

Contents

1	**The Social Worker-Client Relationship**	1
	The Social Worker and Client: A Fiduciary Relationship	1
	Defining the Fiduciary Relationship	1
	Violations of Fiduciary Responsibility	2
	Safeguarding the Social Worker-Client Relationship	5
	The Social Worker-Client Agreement	5
	Informed Consent	6
	References	13
2	**Confidentiality and Disclosure**	17
	Confidentiality and the Social Worker-Client Relationship	17
	Protecting Client Information	19
	The Health Insurance Portability and Accountability Act (HIPAA)	19
	The Confidentiality of Alcohol and Drug Abuse Patient Records Act and Regulations	23
	Social Worker-Client Privilege	25
	Disclosure of Confidential Communications	26
	Working with Minor Clients	36
	Client Consent	36
	Duty to Warn/Protect	37
	Reporting Abuse and Neglect	39
	Responding to Subpoenas	40
	References	41
3	**Licensing Issues**	45
	Licensure and Licensing Boards: Purpose and Scope	45
	Licensing Boards and Disciplinary Proceedings	46
	Bases for Disciplinary Action	46
	Gatekeeping and Licensure	49
	Disciplinary Proceedings	51
	References	53

4 Liability Issues for Social Workers in the Clinical Context: An Overview ... 57
Social Work and Legal Liability ... 57
Professional Malpractice ... 58
    Defining Malpractice ... 58
    Treatment Selection and the Standard of Care ... 59
    Internet-Based Services and Malpractice ... 62
    Supervisory Liability ... 64
Unintentional and Intentional Torts ... 65
    Breach of Confidentiality/Privacy ... 65
    Fraud ... 67
Breach of Contract ... 68
Federal Claims: Violations of Civil Rights and Constitutional Claims ... 69
The Legal Process Simplified ... 70
    Civil Lawsuits ... 70
    Criminal Prosecution ... 71
Strategies to Manage Risk and Reduce Potential Liability ... 72
References ... 76

5 Legal Issues in Social Work Research ... 81
Introduction ... 81
Legal and Ethical Obligations to Participants ... 81
    Respect for Persons ... 83
    Beneficence and Nonmaleficence ... 88
    Justice ... 89
Legal Issues Associated with Data ... 89
    Confidentiality and Its Limits ... 90
    Data Ownership, Storage, and Sharing ... 94
Authorship and Publication ... 96
References ... 98

6 The Social Worker and Forensic Social Work ... 103
Defining Forensic Social Work ... 103
Social Workers and Dispute Resolution ... 106
    Restorative Justice ... 106
    Therapeutic Jurisprudence ... 107
In the Courtroom: Social Workers as Expert Witnesses ... 108
    Court Structure ... 109
    The Basics of Court Proceedings ... 110
    Qualifying as an Expert Witness ... 111
    Determining the Admissibility of Expert Testimony ... 117
The Legislative and Policymaking Settings ... 119
    Evaluation Research ... 124
    Advocacy ... 124
Ethical Issues in Forensic Social Work ... 125
References ... 127

7 Working with Families ... 133
Defining "Family" ... 133
The Growing Family ... 135
    Marriage and Domestic Partnerships ... 135
    Adoption ... 136
Family Ruptures: Separation, Divorce, and Termination
    of Parental Rights ... 139
    Separation, Divorce, and Custody Proceedings ... 139
    Termination of Parental Rights ... 142
References ... 150

8 School Social Work ... 153
The Role of the School Social Worker ... 153
Social Worker Involvement in Access to School
    and School Services ... 154
    The Every Student Succeeds Act ... 155
    The Equal Access Act ... 156
    Title IX of the Education Amendment Act of 1972 ... 157
    Individuals with Disabilities Education Act ... 158
    Americans with Disabilities Act of 1990 ... 160
    Vocational Rehabilitation Act of 1973 ... 161
Intervention with Individuals, Groups, or Families ... 162
Considerations Relating to Confidentiality, Privacy,
    and the Release of Information ... 162
    The Family Educational Rights and Privacy Act (FERPA) ... 162
References ... 165

9 Social Work in the Context of Health Care ... 169
Documentation Issues ... 169
Patient Rights in the Health-Care Context ... 171
    The Right to Treatment and Access to Care ... 171
    Consent to and Refusal of Treatment ... 175
Health-Care Decisionmaking ... 177
    Surrogate Decisionmakers in the Absence
        of Advance Directives ... 177
    Advance Directives ... 178
References ... 180

10 Mental Health and Substance Use ... 183
Mental Illness and Involuntary Outpatient Civil Commitment ... 183
Mental Illness and Involuntary Emergency Inpatient Commitment ... 186
Pregnancy, Substance Use, and Law ... 186
Drug and Mental Health Courts ... 193
    Substance Use, Incarceration, and Drug Courts ... 193
    Mental Illness, Criminal Offense, and Mental Health Courts ... 196
    Social Workers in Drug and Mental Health Court Settings ... 198
Mental Illness and the Americans with Disabilities Act ... 200
References ... 201

11	**Abuse and Neglect Issues Across the Lifespan**	207
	Child Maltreatment	207
	Incidence	207
	Definitional Issues and Reporting Dilemmas	208
	Reporting Procedures	213
	Partner Violence	215
	Incidence and Consequences	215
	Definitional Issues and Reporting Dilemmas	216
	Legal Procedures for the Social Worker	217
	Elder Abuse and Neglect	218
	Incidence	218
	Definitional Issues and Reporting Dilemmas	219
	Reporting Procedures	223
	Other Roles for Social Workers in the Context of Abuse and Neglect	223
	References	225
12	**Legal Issues Working with Immigrants, Refugees, and Asylees**	233
	Immigrants in the USA	233
	Immigration Law: The Basics	234
	Nonimmigrants	234
	Immigrants	240
	Asylees and Refugees	241
	Removal Proceedings	242
	Immigration and Public Support	243
	Qualifying for Benefits	243
	Access to Benefits	244
	Public Charge Concerns	245
	Roles of the Social Worker in the Immigration Law Context	247
	Case Management and Public Benefits	247
	The Social Worker as Expert Witness	247
	The Social Worker as Accredited Representative	248
	References	250
13	**International Social Work**	253
	Social Work in an International Context: Preliminary Considerations	253
	Human Rights as a Basis for International Social Work	255
	Issues at the Intersection of Law, Ethics, and Systems	259
	References	261

Appendix A: State Laws Permitting Family-Related Discriminatory/Differential Treatment of LGBT Individuals on the Basis of Religious Belief 265

Appendix B: State Laws Related to Emergency Hospitalization for Observation 283

Index. 319

Index to Legal Cases. 325

List of Tables

Table 1.1	Sample of state statutory provisions related to provision of mental health services to minors absent parental consent.....	11
Table 2.1	Summary of conditions governing protected mental health information under HIPAA, as relevant to social workers.......	21
Table 2.2	Brief summary of Part 2 and HIPAA provisions compared	25
Table 2.3	Summary of state statutes related to client-social worker privilege........	27
Table 4.1	Summary of common grounds for social worker civil liability........	66
Table 4.2	Summary of discovery mechanisms	70
Table 4.3	Summary of suggested risk management strategies	73
Table 4.4	Domains and topics for ethics audit	75
Table 5.1	Provisions of the Nuremberg Code	82
Table 6.1	Definitions of forensic social work	104
Table 6.2	Summary of state requirements for reliance on expert witnesses	113
Table 7.1	Select state law provisions for emancipation of minors	145
Table 10.1	State laws relating to substance abuse reporting during pregnancy........	188
Table 11.1	Definitions of types of abuse (acts of commission) and neglect (acts of omission)........	211
Table 11.2	Categories and definitions of elder abuse and neglect..........	220
Table 12.1	Nonimmigrant visa categories, U.S........	235
Table 12.2	Categories for immigration on the basis of family relationship	240

Table 12.3	Categories for immigration on the basis of employment relationship.	241
Table 13.1	Definitions of international social work	254
Table 13.2	Comparison of provisions of NASW Code of Ethics and provisions of international human rights documents	256
Table 13.3	International instruments ratified by the United States	258

Chapter 1
The Social Worker-Client Relationship

The Social Worker and Client: A Fiduciary Relationship

Defining the Fiduciary Relationship

It has been suggested that the relationship between a social worker and his or her individual client is fiduciary in nature (Kutchins, 1971; Lawrence & Kurpius, 2000). As one court explained:

> In general, a fiduciary or confidential relationship exists where one person reposes trust and confidence another, who, as a result, gains an influence and superiority over the first. The existence of such a relationship prohibits the one trusted from seeking or obtaining any selfish benefit for himself during the course of the relationship. The therapist-patient relationship is one of great intimacy and trust, in which the therapist encourages the patient to confide in the therapist, and the therapist has a corresponding fiduciary responsibility to the patient. Psychiatrists, psychologists, and other mental health professions are required to exercise due skill and care in conformity with that ordinarily exercised by qualified professionals in their respective fields. (*Martino v. Family Service Agency of Adams County*, 1982)

A fiduciary relationship requires that the fiduciary, such as a social worker, acts primarily for the benefit of the individual(s) for whom the individual is serving as the fiduciary. The relationship is such, however, that the fiduciary, *by the very nature of the relationship*, has the potential to dominate and influence the client (Kutchins, 1991). This potential arises from the trust that is placed in the social worker by the client and the nature of the responsibilities and obligations placed on and assumed by the social worker as a function of their professional license and governing professional code of ethics.

It can be argued that status as a fiduciary necessarily requires that one acts in a manner that is consistent with the ethical principles of beneficence and nonmaleficence. Simply stated, the concept of beneficence requires that one acts for the welfare of others with whom one has a special relationship (Beauchamp & Childress, 1994). One is not required to do so for those with whom no such relationship exists. The social worker-client relationship would qualify as a special relationship because of the trust placed in the social worker by virtue of his or her position and role. This principle is reflected in Standard 1.01 of the *Code of Ethics* of the National Association of Social Workers (2008), relating to commitment to clients:

> Social workers' primary responsibility is to promote the well-being of clients. In general, clients' interests are primary. However, social workers' responsibility to the larger society or specific legal obligations may on limited occasions supersede the loyalty owed clients, and clients should be so advised. (Examples include when a social worker is required by law to report that a client has abused a child or has threatened to harm self or others.)

Nonmaleficence refers to the ideas that one is obligated not to intentionally cause harm to others (Beauchamp & Childress, 1994). It is possible that someone may be harmed by an unintentional act. Such circumstances would raise a question as to whether the harmful act, even if unintentional, comported with the ethical principle of beneficence. The principle of nonmaleficence can be seen in the social work profession's injunction against dual relationships, as discussed below in the context of violations of fiduciary responsibility.

Violations of Fiduciary Responsibility

Because fiduciary relationships involve unequal power and unequal responsibility of the parties, it is critical that this inequality does not permit exploitation of the client. Traditionally, it has been thought that the maintenance of boundaries between the social worker and the client would prevent or at least reduce the potential for such exploitation (Dietz & Thompson, 2004). The presence of various factors suggests the existence of a boundary violation. It has been suggested that four specific elements are indicative of a boundary violation: (1) role reversal, through which the client becomes the caretaker of the social worker, although the social worker remains in control of the relationship; (2) secretiveness, in that the social worker fails to disclose or advise the client of information that may be important to the client; (3) client's double bind, in that an attempt to resolve the situation will entail a loss of some kind; and (4) "indulgence in personal privilege," referring to the social worker's knowing or unknowing exploitation of his or her authority and power over the client (Dietz & Thompson, 2004, p. 4; see also Peterson, 1992). Yet another model identifies three elements as suggestive of a boundary violation: the professional's gratification of his or her own desires, the privileging of professionals' needs, and the objectification of clients (Brown, 1994).[1]

---

[1] Some writers have suggested that a therapist's unilateral decision to maintain boundaries may be perceived by a client as inauthentic, disempowering, and abusive. For additional information pertaining to this perspective, see Dietz and Thompson (2004) and Heyward (1993). Dietz and Thompson (2004, p. 20) have endorsed a practice characterized by "mutuality and safe connection" in lieu of one premised on "boundaries and distance." While this reframes the relationship in a less legalistic manner, "safe connection" requires the delineation of boundaries.

Dual relationships may also constitute or lead to a breach of the fiduciary relationship, depending on the nature and circumstances of the dual relationship. A dual relationship occurs when:

> a professional ... assumes a second role with a client, becoming social worker and friend, employer, teacher, business associate, family member, or sex partner. A practitioner can engage in a dual relationship whether the second relationship begins before, during, or after the social worker relationship. (Kagle & Giebelhausen, 1994, p. 213)

Dual relationships may reflect a boundary violation in that the relationship between social worker and client extends beyond those roles to encompass additional ones *and* the dual relationship is exploitative, manipulative, deceptive, or coercive of the client (Reamer, 2003). Boundary violations are to be distinguished from boundary crossings which, although involving dual relationships, are not exploitative, manipulative, deceptive, or coercive of the client. In many, if not most, instances of both boundary violations and boundary crossings, there also exists a conflict of interest because the social worker's obligations and responsibilities that are associated with one such role conflict with those associated with the other, potentially leading the social worker to disregard the responsibilities associated with one of these roles (Reamer, 2003).

The *Code of Ethics* of the National Association of Workers (2008) makes clear the inappropriateness of conflicts of interest and dual relationships. Paragraph 1.06 of the *Code* provides:

> (a) Social workers should be alert to and avoid conflicts of interest that interfere with the exercise of professional discretion and impartial judgment. Social workers should inform clients when a real or potential conflict of interest arises and take reasonable steps to resolve the issue in a manner that makes the clients' interests primary and protects clients' interests to the greatest extent possible. In some cases, protecting clients' interests may require termination of the professional relationship with proper referral of the client.
> (b) Social workers should not take unfair advantage of any professional relationship or exploit others to further their personal, religious, political, or business interests.
> (c) Social workers should not engage in dual or multiple relationships with clients or former clients in which there is a risk of exploitation or potential harm to the client. In instances when dual or multiple relationships are unavoidable, social workers should take steps to protect clients and are responsible for setting clear, appropriate, and culturally sensitive boundaries. (Dual or multiple relationships occur when social workers relate to clients in more than one relationship, whether professional, social, or business. Dual or multiple relationships can occur simultaneously or consecutively.) (National Association of Social Workers, 2008, Standard 1.06)

Social workers may be alleged and may be found to have breached their fiduciary responsibilities when, for example, they engage in sexual relations with a client or former client (*Doe v. Harbor Schools, Inc.*, 2005; *Martino v. Family Service Agency of Adams County*, 1982; *Noval v. Kaiser Foundation Health Plan*, 2012; *Weisbeck v. Hess*, 1994. See also *Roy v. Hartogs*, 1976) or disclose confidential client communications or information (see *MacDonald v. Clinger*, 1982). The social worker's misleading of clients by inappropriately relying on the authority of the profession may lead to client harm (Gambrill, 2001), raising the possibility that this, too, may constitute a breach of one's fiduciary responsibilities.

Although it is generally agreed that a friendship with a current client is an inappropriate dual relationship, there appears to be no consensus in the literature as to whether a friendship with a former client constitutes either an inappropriate dual relationship or a breach of fiduciary duty (Reamer, 2003). It has been argued both that a friendship with a current client is not inappropriate and that such a relationship reflects a nonhierarchical and more egalitarian approach to social work practice.

However, there is also disagreement with respect to the identification or definition of a former client. Three positions appear to exist: (1) that a client is always a client because he or she may return for services at some time in the future; (2) that a client becomes a former client after the passage of a defined period of time following the termination of services, e.g., a period of years; and (3) that a client is no longer a client once services are terminated (Mattison et al., 2002). The *Social Work Dictionary* seems to suggest that the termination of services may be definitive:

> The conclusion of the social worker-client intervention process: a systematic procedure for disengaging the working relationship. It occurs when goals are reached, when the specified time for working has ended, or when the client is no longer interested in continuing. (Barker, 1999, p. 483)

Accordingly, it is critical that the social worker and the system in which the social worker is employed, whether in private practice or with an agency or other entity, implement measures to reduce the likelihood of inappropriate influence over the client. Mechanisms that are widely used include the social worker-client contract, the ethical mandates of professional associations for social work, and the legal requirements and oversight provided by state licensing authorities. The remainder of this chapter focuses on the social worker-client contract and the concept of informed consent from both the legal and the ethical perspective. Issues related to licensing are addressed in Chap. 3.

The process by which social work services are terminated is relevant not only to a determination of whether a client is a former client but also to the issue of abandonment. Abandonment of a client may provide the basis for a malpractice action (Felton & Polowy, 2015) but also arguably constitutes a breach of the social worker's fiduciary responsibilities. The therapeutic relationship may end for any number of valid reasons including the identification of a conflict of interest after services have been initiated; the client's inability to make progress over a period of time; the therapist's inability to continue providing services, such as in the case of a protracted illness; lack of communication from the client; and nonpayment of agreed-upon fees for services, among others. The NASW *Code of Ethics* (2008) sets forth an ethical standard to guide social workers in terminating services:

> (a) Social workers should terminate services to clients and professional relationships with them when such services and relationships are no longer required or no longer serve the clients' needs or interests.
> (b) Social workers should take reasonable steps to avoid abandoning clients who are still in need of services. Social workers should withdraw services precipitously only under unusual

circumstances, giving careful consideration to all factors in the situation and taking care to minimize possible adverse effects. Social workers should assist in making appropriate arrangements for continuation of services when necessary.

(c) Social workers in fee-for-service settings may terminate services to clients who are not paying an overdue balance if the financial contractual arrangements have been made clear to the client, if the client does not pose an imminent danger to self or others, and if the clinical and other consequences of the current nonpayment have been addressed and discussed with the client.

(d) Social workers should not terminate services to pursue a social, financial, or sexual relationship with a client.

(e) Social workers who anticipate the termination or interruption of services to clients should notify clients promptly and seek the transfer, referral, or continuation of services in relation to the clients' needs and preferences.

(f) Social workers who are leaving an employment setting should inform clients of appropriate options for the continuation of services and of the benefits and risks of the options (National Association of Social Workers, 2008, Standard 1.16).

It has been suggested that social workers prepare for the termination of services to a client at the time those services are initiated (Felton & Polowy, 2015). The informed consent process and the written documentation of the process, discussed further below, should set forth the circumstances under which services may be terminated, whether voluntarily or involuntarily. Clients should be informed of the reason(s) for the termination at the time that it occurs, and the termination should be memorialized with a formal letter to the client. The letter should specify the client's name, the date on which services commenced, the effective date of service termination and the reasons for the termination, a summary of the treatment that was provided during the course of the services, and whether continued treatment is recommended. In situations in which additional treatment is suggested, the social worker should provide the client with the names and contact information for several suitable referrals.

Safeguarding the Social Worker-Client Relationship

The Social Worker-Client Agreement

A distinction has been drawn in the literature between a therapeutic contract and a personal services contract. A therapeutic contract has been defined as "a metaphor that has been used to discuss goal setting and related activities that are part of the treatment process" (Kutchins, 1991, p. 109). As an example, a social worker and his or her client might develop a behavioral contract to assist the client in achieving specified goals.

In contrast, a personal services agreement outlines the parameters of the relationship between the social worker and the client. A contract is:

> an agreement between two or more persons which creates an obligation to do or not do a particular thing. Its essentials are competent parties, subject matter, a legal consideration, mutuality of agreement and mutuality of obligation. (Black, 1979, pp. 291–292)

Key elements of a contract include an agreement as to what exactly constitutes the obligation and what is to be exchanged to secure that obligation (the legal consideration) and both the competence and willingness of each party to enter into the agreement (Croxton, 1988). As an example, a social work contract would set forth the obligations of the social worker, e.g., frequency of meeting, contact information, availability outside of appointment hours, and the legal consideration that will be exchanged for these services, i.e., how much and in what manner the client is to make payment.

Some writers, however, have conflated the two concepts, suggesting that the social worker-client contract should include the treatment goals and objectives, the techniques to be used, and the time limitations, as well as any administrative matters, such as the fees, the completion of forms, and the availability of agency resources (Seabury, 1976). One writer has suggested that, unlike a "static and binding" legal contract, a social work contract develops through various stages and is subject to ongoing negotiation and revision (Seabury, 1976, p. 17).

The evolution of the contract is said to progress through three distinct phases. During the initial phase, the target issue is identified, and the social worker and client define their obligations and expectations, ultimately deciding whether they will or will not continue to work together. The second phase has been termed the "preliminary contract phase" and involves a decision by both parties to test out the process. The "central phase" is characterized by an explicit agreement by the social worker and the client with respect to the goals, time limitations, and tasks to be accomplished. This mutual understanding of goals and processes may be a critical factor in a client's decision to continue with services (Mayer & Timms, 1969). The "final phase" focuses on the evaluation of the efforts that have been made and a decision to continue, renegotiate, or terminate the relationship (Seabury, 1976).

This conceptualization of a social worker-client contract is similar to some degree to the informed consent process. Both require agreement, an explicit statement of what is to be done during the course of the relationship, the goals of the treatment, and such administrative matters as the cost. However, the informed consent process differs in some significant ways from a contract, as can be seen from the discussion below.

Informed Consent

Ethical Foundations of Informed Consent The requirement of informed consent derives from the principle of respect for persons. This concept encompasses both a respect for the autonomy of the individual, which can be fully realized: liberty, meaning freedom from controlling influences, and agency, that is, having the capacity for intentional action (Beauchamp & Childress, 1994). This principle requires not only a respectful attitude toward a person but also respectful action. It is thought that individuals are owed such respect because of their unconditional worth (Kant, 1959, 1964) and in recognition of their right to develop their lives in accordance with their beliefs and desires, as long as they do not interfere with others (Mill, 1977).

The corollary of this ethical principle in social work is that of self-determination. The *Code of Ethics* of the National Association of Social Workers (2008) states as an ethical principle: "Social workers respect the inherent dignity and worth of the person." Standard 1.02 further provides:

> Social workers respect and promote the right of clients to self-determination and assist clients in their efforts to identify and clarify their goals. Social workers may limit clients' right to self-determination when, in the social workers' professional judgment, clients' actions or potential actions pose a serious, foreseeable, and imminent risk to themselves or others. (National Association of Social Workers, 2008)

Clearly, some individuals may lack the ability to act autonomously. As an example, children may not act autonomously because they often lack the knowledge and experience to make informed decisions. Minors are not recognized legally as having decisionmaking capacity for this reason. Individuals who are comatose, who are unable to distinguish reality from hallucinations, and who are severely intoxicated serve as additional examples of individuals lacking the ability to act autonomously. A client's lack of agreement with the social worker's perspective or advice or a refusal to adhere to a social worker's recommended course of action does not signify a lack of capacity to act autonomously.

Elements of Informed Consent Informed consent to treatment is both a legal and an ethical requirement. The *Code of Ethics* of the National Association of Social Workers (2008) provides:

> (a) Social workers should provide services to clients only in the context of a professional relationship based, when appropriate, on valid informed consent. Social workers should use clear and understandable language to inform clients of the purpose of the services, risks related to the services, limits to services because of the requirements of a third-party payer, relevant costs, reasonable alternatives, clients' right to refuse or withdraw consent, and the time frame covered by the consent. Social workers should provide clients with an opportunity to ask questions.
> (b) In instances when clients are not literate or have difficulty understanding the primary language used in the practice setting, social workers should take steps to ensure clients' comprehension. This may include providing clients with a detailed verbal explanation or arranging for a qualified interpreter or translator whenever possible.
> (c) In instances when clients lack the capacity to provide informed consent, social workers should protect clients' interests by seeking permission from an appropriate third party, informing clients consistent with the clients' level of understanding. In such instances social workers should seek to ensure that the third party acts in a manner consistent with clients' wishes and interests. Social workers should take reasonable steps to enhance such clients' ability to give informed consent.
> (d) In instances when clients are receiving services involuntarily, social workers should provide information about the nature and extent of services and about the extent of clients' right to refuse service.

(e) Social workers who provide services via electronic media (such as computer, telephone, radio, and television) should inform recipients of the limitations and risks associated with such services.
(f) Social workers should obtain clients' informed consent before audiotaping or videotaping clients or permitting observation of services to clients by a third party. (National Association of Social Workers, 2008, Standard 1.03)

The client's consent must reflect four basic elements to be considered valid: the client must (1) have the capacity to provide consent, (2) have been provided with the information necessary to make a decision, (3) have understood the information that has been provided, and (4) have a voluntarily consent. Indeed, a failure to obtain valid informed consent may lead to professional sanctions (see Chap. 3) and may constitute malpractice (discussed in Chap. 4).

In most cases, individuals are presumed to have capacity to consent.[2] Capacity is to be distinguished from competence. Capacity refers to an individual's mental ability to make a decision, whereas competence is a legal determination made by a court. In general, competency refers to an individual's ability to communicate his or her choices; to understand his or her current health-care situation, the options available for treatment, and the consequences of each treatment option; and to consider the information provided in a rational manner (Austin, 2007).

Minors are legally presumed to lack capacity due to their age, although clearly some minors may display greater thoughtfulness in their decisionmaking processes than some adults. The (in)ability of minors to provide consent is discussed further below. In some situations, a client's capacity to make a decision may be questionable, e.g., when a client is clearly intoxicated. However, a diagnosis of a mental illness alone, or institutionalization alone, is likely an inadequate basis for a determination that the client lacks capacity (Rozovsky, 2001).

Information refers to the information to be provided to a client to enable him or her to make a decision. Minimally, this should include an explanation of the processes and procedures that comprise the treatment, any treatment alternatives, the potential benefits of the proposed treatment, the risks associated with the treatment, the right to terminate or discontinue treatment at any time, and the right to all relevant information (Palmer & Kaufman, 2003). The social worker should also disclose the extent to which the proposed approach to treatment is evidence-based and potential alternatives to that approach (Loue, 2017; Loue & Parkinson, 2015). (Obligations related to confidentiality and the potential for disclosure are addressed in Chap. 2.) Relevant information may include the time frame during which services are to be provided, the duration of each session, the costs associated with the services, the (non)availability of insurance coverage and the extent to which the client will remain responsible for charges, and whether services will be provided via elec-

---

[2] Research suggests that social workers are more likely to underestimate clients' capacity to consent if the clients are of a lower socioeconomic status, are identified as members of a minority group, or have a disability (Davis & Proctor, 1989; Desselle & Proctor, 2000; Franklin, 1986; O'Donnell, 1999). This issue may also be present in social workers' interactions with nonheterosexual-identified clients (cf. Berkman & Zinberg, 1997).

tronic media and the risks and benefits associated with its use. It has been suggested that informed consent provided by clients in a managed care setting in which the social worker is prohibited by the health-care facility from providing complete information to the client about alternative treatments is not truly informed consent and may constitute a violation of the social worker's fiduciary responsibilities to the client (Strom-Gottfried, 1998).

It is not enough, though, that individuals be provided with the necessary information; they must also understand the information. This suggests that the language used in the explanation be at a level that is understandable to the client, both with respect to the specific language, e.g., Spanish instead of English, and that the sophistication of the language utilized be easily understandable. In addition to allowing sufficient time for the client to ask questions about what is to be done, the social worker may find it helpful in assessing the client's understanding of the information to ask the client to explain what he or she remembers about the information that was conveyed and to explain how that information will impact the client directly, e.g., the frequency with which the client will be coming to the office.

Informed consent cannot occur unless the client's consent is voluntary. However, some settings in which social workers provide services are themselves characterized by limited client control, e.g., when client attendance at treatment is court-mandated. Further, clients may defer to the social worker's authority, or the social worker himor herself may assert control on the basis of their position or claimed expertise (Gambrill, 2001; Miley et al., 2001; Purtilo & Allen, 1999).

Although these elements of informed consent are also prerequisites to a valid contract, informed consent differs from a contract in that it is an ongoing process. An informed consent form signed by the client evidencing his or her consent is a representation of the process, but it cannot stand alone in lieu of an ongoing process. The social worker and the client may engage in periodic reevaluations of the treatment approach, the frequency of sessions, and the cost of sessions. Client circumstances may change over time, potentially requiring revisiting the provisions relating to insurance, payments, and other details.

Informed Consent and the Provision of Services to Minors In many situations, informed consent to provide services to a minor can be obtained from the child's natural or adoptive parent (Vukadinovich, 2004). However, there are multiple situations involving children and adolescents in which the issue of informed consent can be challenging, complex, and even potentially contentious.

In some states, there is a legal presumption that divorced parents share custody of a child with some exceptions, such as where there is evidence of abuse by a parent (Polowy & Felton, 2015). This encompasses both physical and legal custody, so that either parent may legally consent to the child's treatment. However, even in these states, the court may impose different custody arrangements, or the parents themselves may have agreed to a different arrangement.

Accordingly, the social worker providing services to a child of divorced or separated parents is advised to request a copy of the temporary and/or final custody order in order to identify the rights of each parent with respect to mental health-care decisionmaking for the child and to ascertain who bears responsibility for the costs of the treatment. In situations in which the right of each parent to make such decisions is unclear, it is advisable to obtain from each parent a signed informed consent form authorizing the provision of treatment of their child. Failing that, the social worker should ask the consenting parent to sign an authorization that states that they have legal right to make mental health-care decisions for the child (Polowy & Felton, 2015). A failure to do so may potentially lead to disciplinary proceedings and the potential suspension or loss of one's professional license. (See, e.g., *Andrews v. Board of Social Worker Licensure,* 2005.)

In addition, the social worker should be aware that the specific situation may differ with different children of the same parents. He or she should not assume that just because a parent can consent for one child, the parent can also consent for all of the children born to the same parents.

A legally appointed guardian may or may not have the legal ability to consent to the provision of mental health treatment for the minor in their custody. Whether the guardian may do so depends upon the scope of the guardian's authority that has been granted by the court (Vukadinovich, 2004). In general, a licensed foster care parent may consent to the provision of routine medical care for a child that has been placed with him or her by court order or with the voluntary legal consent of the individual who has legal custody of the child.

There are circumstances in which a minor child may have a legal right to obtain social work services without parental consent. This may occur (1) when provided for by state statute under specified conditions, (2) when the child is considered to be an emancipated minor, and (3) when under the exception of mature minors.

Many states provide that children may obtain mental health services without parental consent upon attaining a specified age, when experiencing a crisis, and/or for a limited number of sessions. However, parents may generally not be held liable for any costs that would be associated with the provision of these services. Table 1.1 provides examples of these state provisions.

Minors may be considered to be emancipated within the term set forth by state statute and pursuant to court order. These may include marriage, pregnancy, parenting a child, or military service (Schlam & Wood, 2000). Statute may also require that the child have attained a specified minimum sage, e.g., 16, be living independently of their parents and/or be able to document economic self-sufficiency (Maradiegue, 2003; Wallach, 1999).

Although the doctrine of "mature minor" is generally premised on common law (judicial decisions), it has been adopted by statute in several states (Schlam & Wood, 2000). In order to determine whether a child falls within the mature minor exception to parental consent, the court will ascertain whether the individual is sufficiently mature to act in his or her own best interest and make an independent judgment to consent to treatment. (The status of emancipated and mature minors is addressed more fully in Chap. 7, which focuses on legal issues in the context of social work with families.)

Table 1.1 Sample of state statutory provisions related to provision of mental health services to minors absent parental consent

State	Statutory provision	Reference
Alabama	Any legally authorized medical, dental, health, or mental health services may be rendered to minors of any age without the consent of a parent or legal guardian when, in the physician's judgment, an attempt to secure consent would result in delay of treatment which would increase the risk to the minor's life, health, or mental health	Code of Alabama § 22-8-3 (2017)
California	(b) A minor who is 12 years of age or older may consent to mental health treatment or counseling on an outpatient basis, or to residential shelter services, if both of the following requirements are satisfied: (1) The minor, in the opinion of the attending professional person, is mature enough to participate intelligently in the outpatient services or residential shelter services (2) The minor (A) would present a danger of serious physical or mental harm to self or to others without the mental health treatment or counseling or residential shelter services or (B) is the alleged victim of incest or child abuse (c) A professional person offering residential shelter services, whether as an individual or as a representative of an entity specified in paragraph (3) of subdivision (a), shall make his or her best efforts to notify the parent or guardian of the provision of services (d) The mental health treatment or counseling of a minor authorized by this section shall include involvement of the minor's parent or guardian unless, in the opinion of the professional person who is treating or counseling the minor, the involvement would be inappropriate. The professional person who is treating or counseling the minor shall state in the client record whether and when the person attempted to contact the minor's parent or guardian, and whether the attempt to contact was successful or unsuccessful, or the reason why, in the professional person's opinion, it would be inappropriate to contact the minor's parent or guardian (e) The minor's parents or guardians are not liable for payment for mental health treatment or counseling services provided pursuant to this section unless the parent or guardian participates in the mental health treatment or counseling, and then only for services rendered with the participation of the parent or guardian. The minor's parents or guardian are not liable for payment for any residential shelter services provided pursuant to this section unless the parent or guardian consented to the provision of those services	California Family Code § 6924(b)-(e) (2017)

(continued)

Table 1.1 (continued)

State	Statutory provision	Reference
New York	(c) A mental health practitioner may provide outpatient mental health services, other than those treatments and procedures for which consent is specifically required by Section 33.03 of this article, to a minor voluntarily seeking such services without parental or guardian consent if the mental health practitioner determines that: (1) The minor is knowingly and voluntarily seeking such services (2) Provision of such services is clinically indicated and necessary to the minor's well-being (3) (i) A parent or guardian is not reasonably available (ii) Requiring parental or guardian consent or involvement would have a detrimental effect on the course of outpatient treatment (iii) A parent or guardian has refused to give such consent and a physician determines that treatment is necessary and in the best interests of the minor The mental health practitioner shall fully document the reasons for his or her determinations. Such documentation shall be included in the minor's clinical record, along with a written statement signed by the minor indicating that he or she is voluntarily seeking services. As clinically appropriate, notice of a determination made pursuant to subparagraph (iii) of paragraph three of this subdivision shall be provided to the parent or guardian (d) A mental health practitioner may provide a minor voluntarily seeking outpatient services an initial interview without parental or guardian consent or involvement to determine whether the criteria of subdivision (c) of this section are present	New York Consolidated Law Service Mental Hygiene §33.21 (c) (2017)
Ohio	(A) Upon the request of a minor 14 years of age or older, a mental health professional may provide outpatient mental health services, excluding the use of medication, without the consent or knowledge of the minor's parent or guardian. Except as otherwise provided in this section, the minor's parent or guardian shall not be informed of the services without the minor's consent unless the mental health professional treating the minor determines that there is a compelling need for disclosure based on a substantial probability of harm to the minor or to other persons and if the minor is notified of the mental health professional's intent to inform the minor's parent or guardian (B) Services provided to a minor pursuant to this section shall be limited to not more than six sessions or 30 days of services whichever occur sooner. After the sixth session or 30 days of services, the mental health professional shall terminate the services or, with the consent of the minor, notify the parent, or guardian, to obtain consent to provide further outpatient services (C) The minor's parent or guardian shall not be liable for the costs of services which are received by a minor under division (A)	Ohio Revised Code Annotated § 122.04 (A)–(C) (2017)

In situations in which a minor may not legally consent to the provision of social work services, it may be advisable to obtain his or her assent. Both the American Medical Association (Blake, 2012) and the Committee on Bioethics of the American Academy of Pediatrics (1995) suggest that children can assume increasing responsibility in medical decisionmaking, consonant with their age and level of understanding. The American Academy of Pediatrics has identified the following elements for inclusion in an assent process:

1. Helping the patient achieve a developmentally appropriate awareness of the nature of his or her condition
2. Telling the patient what he or she can expect with tests and treatment(s)
3. Making a clinical assessment of the patient's understanding of the situation and the factors influencing how he or she is responding (including whether there is inappropriate pressure to accept testing or therapy)
4. Soliciting an expression of the patient's willingness to accept the proposed care (Committee on Bioethics, American Academy of Pediatrics, 1995, p. 315)

Unfortunately, relatively little has been written regarding child assent in the context of social work practice, in contrast to the growing literature related to child assent in the contexts of medical care and research. At least one writer has suggested that social workers providing treatment to children may wish to obtain child assent in addition to parental consent, although parental consent is generally legally sufficient even in the absence of child or adolescent assent (Barsky, 2010). The social worker may, however, wish to consider the potential for progress and the advisability of continuing to provide services in situations in which the parents provide consent but the child or adolescent denies assent and consistently refuses to participate actively in the treatment process and in those situations in which the treatment may appear to be contrary to the best interests of the minor.

References

Austin, A. W. (2007). Medical decisions and children: How much voice should children have in their medical care? *Arizona Law Review, 49*, 143–169.
Barker, R. L. (1999). *Social work dictionary* (4th ed.). Washington, DC: NASW Press.
Barsky, A. E. (2010). *Ethics and values in social work: An integrated approach for a comprehensive curriculum.* New York: Oxford University Press.
Beauchamp, T. L., & Childress, J. F. (1994). *Principles of biomedical ethics* (4th ed.). New York: Oxford University Press.
Berkman, C. S., & Zinberg, G. (1997). Homophobia and heterosexism in social workers. *Social Work, 42*(4), 319–332.
Black, H. C. (1979). *Black's law dictionary* (5th ed.). St. Paul, MN: West Publishing Company.
Blake, V. (2012). Minors' refusal of live-saving therapies. *AMA Journal of Ethics.* http://journalofethics.ama-assn.org/2012/10/hlaw1-1210.html. Accessed 26 June 2017.
Brown, L. S. (1994). *Subversive dialogues: Theory in feminist therapy.* New York: Basic Books.
Committee on Bioethics, American Academy of Pediatrics. (1995). Informed consent, parental permission, and assent in pediatric practice. *Pediatrics, 95*, 314–317.

Croxton, T. A. (1988). Caveats on contract. *Social Work, 33*(2), 169–171.

Davis, L. E., & Proctor, E. K. (1989). *Race, gender, and class: Guidelines for practice with individuals, families, and groups*. Englewood Cliffs, NJ: Prentice-Hall.

Desselle, D., & Proctor, T. (2000). Advocating for the elderly hard-of-hearing population: The deaf people we ignore. *Social Work, 45*(3), 277–281.

Dietz, C., & Thompson, J. (2004). Rethinking boundaries. *Journal of Progressive Human Services, 15*(2), 1–24.

Felton, E. M., & Polowy, C. I. (2015). *Termination: Ending the therapeutic relationship—Avoiding abandonment*. http://naswcanews.org/termination-ending-the-therapeutic-relationship-avoiding-abandonment/. Accessed 26 June 2017.

Franklin, D. L. (1986). Does client social class affect clinical judgment? *Social Casework: The Journal of Contemporary Social Work, 67*, 424–432.

Gambrill, E. (2001). Social work: An authority-based profession. *Research in Social Work Practice, 11*(2), 166–175.

Heyward, C. (1993). *When boundaries betray us: Beyond illusions of what is ethical in therapy and in life*. San Francisco: Harper.

Kagle, J. D., & Giebelhausen, P. N. (1994). Dual relationships and professional boundaries. *Social Work, 39*, 213–220.

Kant, I. (1959). *Foundations of the metaphysics of morals*. L.W. Beck (trans.). Indianapolis, IN: Bobbs-Merrill Company.

Kant, I. (1964). The doctrine of virtue. In Kant, I. *Metaphysics of morals*, part II. M. Gregor (trans.). Philadelphia: University of Pennsylvania Press.

Kutchins, H. (1991). The fiduciary relationship: The legal basis for social workers' responsibilities to clients. *Social Work, 36*(2), 106–113.

Lawrence, G., & Kurpius, S. E. R. (2000). Legal and ethical issues involved when counseling minors in nonschool settings. *Journal of Counseling & Development, 78*, 130–136.

Loue, S. (2017). Strengths-based social work. In A. Sandu & A. Frunza (Eds.), *Ethical issues in social work practice* (pp. 62–81). Hershey: IGI Global. https://doi.org/10.4018/978-1-5225-3090-9.

Loue, S., & Parkinson, J. (2015). Special ethical considerations in sandplay therapy. In S. Loue (Ed.), *Ethical issues in sandplay therapy practice and research* (pp. 87–98). New York: Springer Science+Business.

Maradiegue, A. (2003). Minors' rights versus parental rights: Review of legal issues in adolescent health care. *Journal of Midwifery & Women's Health, 48*(3), 170–177.

Mattison, D., Jayaratne, S., & Croxton, T. (2002). Client or former client? Implications of ex-client definition on social work practice. *Social Work, 47*(1), 55–64.

Mayer, J., & Timms, N. (1969). Clash in perspective between worker and client. *Social Casework, 50*, 32–40.

Miley, K. K., O'Melia, M., & DuBois, B. (2001). *Generalist social work practice: An empowering approach* (3rd ed.). Boston: Allyn & Bacon.

Mill, J. S. (1977). On liberty. In *Collected works of John Stuart Mills*, vol. 18. Toronto: University of Toronto Press.

National Association of Social Workers. (2008). *Code of ethics*. https://www.socialworkers.org/pubs/code/code.asp. Accessed 11 February 2016.

O'Donnell, J. (1999). Involvement of African American fathers in kinship foster care services. *Social Work, 44*(5), 428–441.

Palmer, N., & Kaufman, M. (2003). The ethics of informed consent. *Journal of Ethnic & Cultural Diversity in Social Work, 12*(1), 1–26.

Peterson, M. R. (1992). *At personal risk: Boundary violations in professional-client relationships*. New York: W.W. Norton & Co..

Polowy, C. I., & Felton, E. (2015). *Working with children: The many layers of consent to treat*. https://www.socialworkers.org/assets/secured/documents/sections/courts/newsletters/SW%20and%20the%20Courts%202015-%20Fall.pdf. Accessed 26 June 2017.

Purtilo, R., & Allen, A. (Eds.). (1999). *Ethical dimensions in the health professions* (3rd ed.). Philadelphia: W.B. Saunders.
Reamer, F. D. (2003). Boundary issues in social work: Managing dual relationships. *Social Work, 48*(1), 121–133.
Rozovsky, F. A. (2001). *Consent to treatment: A practical guide*. Gaithersburg, MD: Aspen.
Schlam, L., & Wood, J. P. (2000). Informed consent to the medical treatment of minors: Law and practice. *Health Matrix, 10*, 141–174.
Seabury, B. A. (1976). The contract: Uses, abuses, and limitations. *Social Work, 21*(1), 16–21.
Strom-Gottfried, K. (1998). Informed consent meets managed care. *Health & Social Work, 23*(1), 25–33.
Vukadinovich, D. M. (2004). Minors' rights to consent to treatment: Navigating the complexity of state laws. *Journal of Health Law, 37*, 667–691.
Wallach, T. (1999). Rights of children: Statutory emancipation in California. Privilege or poverty? *Journal of Contemporary Legal Issues, 11*, 669–673.

Legal References

Cases

Andrews v. Board of Social Worker Licensure, 2005 WL (Me. Super. Ct. 2005).
Doe v. Harbor Schools, Inc., 445 Mass. 1101 (2005).
MacDonald v. Clinger, 446 N.Y.S.2d 801 (App. Div. 1982).
Martino v. Family Service Agency of Adams County, 445 N.E.2d (Ill. App. 1982).
Noval v. Kaiser Foundation Health Plan, Inc., (2012). http://www.thaddeuspope.com/images/Noval_v.Kaiser_complaint_02-2012_.pdf. Accessed 12 June 2017.
Roy v. Hartogs, 381 N.Y.S.2d 587 (1976).
Weisbeck v. Hess, 524 N.W.2d 363 (Sup. Ct. S.D. 1994).

Statutes

California Family Code § 6924(b)-(e) (2017)
Code of Alabama § 22-8-3 (2017)
New York Consolidated Law Service Mental Hygiene §33.21 (c) (2017)
Ohio Revised Code Annotated § 122.04 (A)-(C) (2017)

Chapter 2
Confidentiality and Disclosure

Confidentiality and the Social Worker-Client Relationship

Confidentiality has been defined as "an ethical standard that protects clients from disclosure of information without their consent" (Herlihy & Sheeley, 1987, p. 479). As such, it reflects:

> the human service worker's obligation not to disclose client information that is gained in the course of a professional human service relationship. Under the principle of confidentiality, personal or other information that is gained in the context of such a relationship cannot be used in a different context or for a different purpose by the human service worker. (Collingridge, Miller, & Bowles, 2001, p. 4)

Professional confidentiality additionally suggests four propositions. First, information includes not only information conveyed by the client to the social worker through writing or oral communication but also encompasses the social worker's opinions that he or she forms through observation, interaction, and application of professional judgment (Collingridge et al., 2001). Second, the duration of the confidentiality obligations extends beyond the cessation of the social worker-client relationship (Collingridge et al., 2001), including, in many cases, the death of the client (Felton & Polowy, 2015a; Morgan, Polowy, & Khan, 2010). The obligation to maintain confidentiality, however, can be overridden by ethical considerations under some circumstances and, additionally, is subjected to compliance with legal mandates (Collingridge et al., 2001).

The concept of confidentiality is often confused with that of privacy (Collingridge et al., 2001; Herlihy & Sheeley, 1987), which has been referred to as a "legal concept that recognizes individuals' rights to choose the time, circumstances, and extent to which they wish to share or withhold personal information" (Herlihy & Sheeley, 1987, p. 479). The concept of privacy rests on two assumptions: that privacy is "a fundamental moral right" and that it serves as the foundation for the concept of confidentiality in the realm of social services (Collingridge et al., 2001, p. 3). The Code of Ethics of the National Association of Social Workers

(2008) recognizes the distinction between confidentiality and privacy, advising social workers not to solicit private information from clients unless it is essential to the provision of services and noting that "once private information is shared, standards of confidentiality apply" (National Association of Social Workers, 2008, Standard 1.07(a)).

Research suggests that many social workers in direct practice frequently experience ethical dilemmas relating to confidentiality. A survey study involving 152 social workers found that more than one quarter of the respondents experienced ethical dilemmas related to collaboration on a treatment team; discussions with family members; client records; insurers; work with at-risk groups, e.g., clients involved in illegal activities or engaged in self-destructive behavior; specific client problems such as mental illness; specific age groups; and/or clients of a different culture from that of the social worker (Millstein, 2000).

Not only may social workers face ethical dilemmas relating to confidentiality, but they may also be confronted with legal issues related to confidentiality, the focus of this chapter. In the best case scenario, the social worker's ethical and legal obligations and the potential solutions will be consistent with each other. However, social workers may experience conflicting legal and ethical obligations. Similarly, the potential solutions for a situation may be compatible with the prevailing legal standard but inconsistent with the social worker's ethical obligations or vice versa (Reamer, 2005). The following exemplify circumstances in which a social worker may be faced with conflicting legal and ethical obligations and solutions.

> A young adult is residing in a residential therapeutic program for individuals dually diagnosed with a substance use disorder and a mental illness. His private health-care insurance requires periodic reports relating to his progress. The client has actually been doing well, but his treatment team believes that he requires additional treatment in order to reduce the likelihood that he will again use substances or cease taking his prescribed medications when he leaves the therapeutic community. The insurance company authorizes a specific number of days in treatment and will not extend its absent documentation of continuing necessity. The social worker has an ethical responsibility to ensure that the client receives appropriate care but a legal responsibility to accurately report the client's status to the insurance company. Here, there is a conflict between the social worker's ethical and legal obligations. The provision of an accurate report to the insurance company will fulfill her legal responsibility but will likely lead to the termination of the client's treatment.

Consider, as well, the following example. Wisconsin Section 905.04(4)(e)3 (2016) provides:

> There is no privilege in situations where the examination of the expectant mother of an abused unborn child creates a reasonable ground for an opinion of the physician, registered nurse, chiropractor, psychologist, social worker, marriage and family therapist or professional counselor that the physical injury inflicted on the unborn child was caused by the habitual lack of self-control of the expectant mother of the unborn child in the use of alcohol beverages, controlled substances or controlled substance analogs, exhibited to a severe degree.

This effectively means that a social worker may be compelled to testify regarding a client's substance use in a legal proceeding brought by child protective services to remove a newborn from his or her mother. While testifying would be consistent with the social worker's legal obligation, it would likely contravene his or her ethical obligation to the mother, who has consulted with the social worker for the express purpose of obtaining substance abuse treatment. Not only would the mother's information not remain confidential, but she would probably not receive the services that she needs and, additionally, could be prosecuted for child abuse and lose physical and/or legal custody of her child following his or her birth.

Protecting Client Information

The Health Insurance Portability and Accountability Act (HIPAA)

The Health Insurance Portability and Accountability Act (HIPAA) (1996) became effective for most "covered entities" on April 14, 2003 (Dunn, Rose, & Wieland, 2013) and on April 14, 2004 for small health plans (United States Department of Health and Human Services, Office for Civil Rights, 2013). "Covered entities" refer to health plans, health-care clearinghouses, and any health-care provider, regardless of size, who transmit health information in electronic form in connection with specified transactions. These transactions include claims, benefit eligibility inquiries, referral authorization requests, and other transactions for which the US Department of Health and Human Services has established HIPAA standards (United States Department of Health and Human Services, Office for Civil Rights, 2013).

The privacy rule is intended to protect individually identifiable information that is "held or transmitted by a covered entity or its business associate, in any form or media, whether electronic, paper, or oral" (United Sates Department of Health and Human Services, Office for Civil Rights, 2013). Information is considered to be individually identifiable if it identifies the individual or if there is a reasonable basis to believe that it identifies the individual and the information pertains to the individual's past, present, or future physical or mental health or condition, the provision of health care to the individual, or the past, present, or future payment by the individual for the provision of health care. The health-related information is termed "protected health information (PHI)." Examples of individually identifiable information include the individual's name, address, birth date, and Social Security number.

Some social workers in private practice do not engage in any activities that would fall within the parameters of transactions covered by the legislation, such as billing insurance companies or electronically transmitting client information to another provider. Many social workers who are employees of public or nonprofit agencies also likely do not become deeply involved with HIPAA provisions because the procedures are generally established by the agency and there may be other personnel in that entity who are responsible for setting practice standards and ensuring compliance. Nevertheless, a basic understanding of the law's provisions may be helpful.

There are only two situations in which the disclosure of protected health information is required: to the individual him- or herself if they request the information and to the United States Department of Health and Human Services in conjunction with a compliance investigation or review or enforcement action (45 Code of Federal Regulations § 164.502(a), 2013). HIPAA permits, but does not require, the disclosure of protected health information, without the client's consent, to the individual in connection with treatment, payment, and health-care operations for national security purposes that are delineated by regulation; for certain public health activities, when required by law and when necessary to prevent or reduce a serious and imminent threat to the individual or the public; for research, within the parameters delineated by law; for essential government functions; and for several other circumstances (United Sates Department of Health and Human Services, Office for Civil Rights, 2013). Specific provisions identify circumstances under which healthcare providers may release information about deceased clients without consent or authorization. However, because such disclosure is not mandated by law, it would be wise to obtain written consent from the deceased client's legal representative prior to complying with the request (Felton & Polowy, 2015a; Morgan, Polowy, & Khan, 2010).

In general, client authorization is required for the disclosure of psychotherapy notes. There are only two exceptions to this general rule: (1) the covered entity that originated the notes may rely on them for treatment; and (2) the covered entity may use the notes without client consent for its own training, to defend itself in legal proceedings brought by the individual, in connection with efforts by the United States Department of Health and Human Services to assess the entity's compliance with the provisions of HIPAA, to prevent a serious and imminent threat to public health or safety, to a health oversight agency for its lawful oversight, and for the lawful activities of a coroner or medical examiner as required by law (45 Code of Federal Regulations § 164.508(a)(2), 2002, as amended 2013). Table 2.1 provides a summary of the conditions outlined under HIPAA under which a mental health provider may disclose mental health information.

HIPAA provisions indicate that a client can consent to send the psychotherapy notes to different persons or places within the same consent, e.g., to his or her attorney and his or her primary care physician. If authorization is requested for psychotherapy notes and a general authorization or authorization for research is to be used, the authorization must specifically identify psychotherapy notes, e.g., by using a check mark or by using a separate form (Dunn, Rose, & Wieland, 2013). However, one writer has strongly cautioned against the use of an authorization to release both separately maintained psychotherapy notes and any other type of information and has recommended, instead, the use of separate authorizations (Wertheimer, 2016).

A valid client authorization for the disclosure of protected health information must be in plain language and include, at a minimum, the following elements:

- A specific and meaningful description of the information that is to be used or disclosed
- The name or specific identity of the person or class of persons that are to be authorized to use or disclose the information

Table 2.1 Summary of conditions governing protected mental health information under HIPAA, as relevant to social workers

Communication	Permitted?	Conditions
To client's family, friend, or others involved in his/her care	Maybe	Client has capacity to make health-care decisions, provider requests client's permission, and client does not object Client is not present or is incapacitated, and provider determines that it is in client's best interests to share information If person with whom information is to be shared is not client's friend or family member, provider must be reasonably sure that the client requested that the person be involved in their care or payment for their care *In all cases, information provided must be limited to that which is directly relevant to the person's involvement in the client's care or payment for care*
Psychotherapy notes	Rarely	"Psychotherapy notes" are notes recorded by a health-care provider who is a mental health professional documenting or analyzing the contents of a private counseling session or a group, joint, or family counseling session that are separate from the rest of the client's medical record. Psychotherapy notes do not contain information about medication, modalities of treatment, session frequency and length, clinical tests, diagnostic summaries, symptoms, treatment plans, prognosis, or progress Client written authorization generally required for disclosure. Exceptions include mandated reporting and, depending on state law, mandated duty to warn
Discussion of mental health information of adult client with capacity with parents or other family members	Maybe	Client is provided with opportunity and does not object, but only the information that the individual needs to know about the client's care or payment for care
To family and friends during periods of client incapacity	Maybe	Provider believes that the client cannot at the time meaningfully agree or object to sharing of information with family and friends Provider considers client's previously expressed preferences, if any, regarding disclosure of their information Provider believes it is in patient's best interest to disclose information Provider gives the client an opportunity to agree or object to disclosure of information once client regains capacity

(continued)

Table 2.1 (continued)

Communication	Permitted?	Conditions
To family members regarding client cessation of prescription medication	Maybe	Client has capacity and client does not object Provider believes based on professional judgment that client does not have capacity and sharing of information would be in client's best interests Client has capacity, client objects to sharing of information, provider's sharing of information is consistent with ethical standards and governing law, provider has a good faith belief that the client poses a threat to the health or safety of him-/herself or others, and family member is reasonably able to prevent or reduce the threat
To parents of minor child client about client's mental health status and needs	In general, yes	In general, parent is treated as minor child's personal representative and can receive information EXCEPT when: State law does not require the consent of a parent or other persons for the particular service Someone other than the parent is legally authorized to consent to treatment The parent agrees to a confidential relationship between the provider and the child client with respect to the specific health-care service The disclosure to the parent is prohibited by state law Note that the age of majority is determined by state law
Provide copy of psychotherapy notes about minor child's mental health treatment to parents	No	Disclosure of psychotherapy notes to client directly or his/her personal representative is permissive under HIPAA. Psychotherapy notes are considered to be for the personal use of the treating provider and not for other purposes
To client's family member despite client's capacity and objection	Maybe	Provider may disclose only if the provider perceives a serious and immediate threat to the health or safety of the client or others and the family members may be able to reduce the threat Provider may always listen to family members or other caregivers regarding the client's health
To client's physician or law enforcement	Maybe	Provider believes that client presents a serious and imminent threat to him-/herself or others Provider believes in good faith that such a warning is required to prevent or lessen the threat Communication is consistent with state law and ethical standards of conduct

Adapted from the United States Department of Health and Human Services, Office for Civil Rights, 2017

- The name or other specific information to identify the person(s) or class of persons to whom the covered entity will make the disclosure
- A description of each purpose of the requested use or disclosure
- An expiration date or event that relates to the individual or the purpose of the use/disclosure
- The signature of the client and the date on which he or she signed the authorization
- A statement indicating that the client has the right to revoke his or her authorization in writing
- Either a reference to the right of revocation and procedures or a statement indicating exceptions to the right to revoke and a description of the procedures that the client must utilize to revoke his or her authorization

In situations involving disclosure or use for research, the delineated time frame may indicate that the use or disclosure will occur at the end of the research study or "none."

Covered entities are required to provide clients with a notice of their privacy practices within specified time limits. The time limits depend on whether the entity has a direct treatment relationship with the client or has an indirect treatment provider or health plan. Those with a direct treatment relationship must attempt to obtain acknowledgment of receipt from the individual. A more complete discussion of HIPAA-required notices and forms is available in Chap. 9, which focuses specifically on legal issues arising in the health context.

HIPAA also requires that covered entities make efforts to safeguard the data that they have from intentional or unintentional use or disclosure. These measures may include administrative, technical, and physical safeguards, such as shredding documents prior to disposing of them and limiting access to the information with locks on doors and cabinets and passwords for computers and databases.

The Confidentiality of Alcohol and Drug Abuse Patient Records Act and Regulations

Congress promulgated this legislation in 1975 in recognition of the stigma that is associated with substance use and people's fear of prosecution for their substance use, which often prevented them from seeking appropriate treatment (Substance Abuse and Mental Health Services Administration, 2004; Ward, 2002). Regulations adopted to implement this law, often referred to as "Part 2" because they are set forth in Part 2 of title 42 of the Code of Federal Regulations, protect "any and all information that could be reasonable used to identify an individual" (Substance Abuse and Mental Health Services Administration, 2004); disclosures must be circumscribed to include on the information that is needed to carry out a specific disclosure (42 Code of Federal Regulations §§ 2.11, 2.13(a), 2017b). These regulations apply to any person who has applied for or who has received a diagnosis of treatment for drug or alcohol abuse at a federally assisted program (42 Code of Federal Regulations § 2.11, 2017b).

In many cases, there is consistency between the mandates of HIPAA and those of the regulations contained in Part 2. In many situations in which there is an inconsistency, covered entities, as defined under HIPAA, must adhere to the requirements of HIPAA. As an example, Part 2 does not consider an individual's medical record number to be "protected health information" unless it includes numbers that could be used to identify a patient reasonably accurately and quickly from external sources. Under HIPAA, however, the medical record number constitutes protected health information. Accordingly, entities that both fall with the programs encompassed by Part 2 and that are covered entities under HIPAA must follow HIPAA's privacy rules pertaining to protected health information.

Part 2 prohibits the disclosure or use of any information about any patient, absent the patient's written consent. A consent valid under Part 2 must contain:

- The name or general designation of the program or person allowed to make the disclosure
- The name or title of the individual or the name of the organization to which the disclosure is to be made
- The name of the patient
- The purpose of the disclosure
- How much of what kind of information is to be disclosed
- The signature of the patient (and guardian, if required by state law)
- The date of the patient's (and guardian's, if needed) signature
- A statement that the consent can be revoked at any time except to the extent that the program has already acted on the consent
- The date, event, or condition when the consent will expire if it not revoked

Part 2 permits oral revocation, whereas HIPAA requires written authorization or a revocation. It has been suggested that programs continue to honor oral revocations of consent but also document the revocation in the individual's record and/or also obtain written authorization for the revocation.

Table 2.2 below provides a brief summary of various other differences between HIPAA and Part 2 requirements relating to confidentiality. Differences also exist between Part 2 and HIPAA with respect to disclosures associated with research, audits and evaluations, and accreditation bodies. Accordingly, this summary is not comprehensive, but focuses instead on situations most likely to confront social workers providing services in the context of drug and alcohol diagnosis and/or treatment. Providers are urged to consult relevant sources and their agency administration and/or legal counsel for more detailed information.

Protecting Client Information

Table 2.2 Brief summary of compared Part 2 and HIPAA provisions

Focus	Part 2	HIPAA	Controlling provision
Child abuse	Permits compliance with state law to make initial complaint only, absent court order, or patient consent	Permits reporting	Part 2
Crime on program premises or against program personnel	May disclose limited information directly related to the crime or threat to commit the crime including only circumstances of the incident and patient status, name, address, and last known whereabouts	May disclose protected health information if there is a good faith belief that it constitutes evidence of the crime. Permits staff member who is a victim of the crime to report specified information	Part 2
Information within program	Limited to people who have need of information in connection with their responsibilities to provide diagnosis, treatment, or referral for treatment for alcohol or drug abuse	Similar to Part 2	Part 2
Medical emergencies	Disclosure permitted to those who need to know to the extent needed to treat a condition that poses an immediate threat to the health of any individual and requires immediate medical attention. The disclosing entity/individual must document the name and affiliation of personnel to whom the disclosure is made, the name of the individual making the disclosure, the date and time of the disclosure, and the nature of the emergency		Part 2
Subpoenas	Disclosure requires patient written consent or a court order that complies with Part 2	Disclosure permitted without patient consent under specified conditions	Part 2

Social Worker-Client Privilege

Privilege in the context of law refers to the legally recognized right to withhold certain information that is generated within and in the course of a protected relationship (Watkins & Watkins, 1983). The privilege is based on the supposition that trust is essential to the success of the relationship, that trust is engendered through a promise of confidentiality, and that society values specified relationships and seeks to foster them by ensuring in most cases that communications within those relationships can remain confidential. Traditionally, this privilege has existed between spouses, between clergy and penitent, and between physician and patient.

The client is the holder of the social worker-client privilege. This means that, in most cases, the social worker cannot waive the privilege and disclose confidential information without the consent of the client. However, in some situations, the client will be deemed to have waived the privilege. As an example, if a client sues a social worker for malpractice, he or she will be considered to have waived the privilege because the content of the social worker's records is the basis for the claim of malpractice.

The Supreme Court case of *Jaffee v. Redmond* (1996) established the social worker-client privilege in federal cases. That case involved a lawsuit by the administrator, Carrie Jaffee, of the estate of Ricky Allen, who had been shot and killed by the defendant, Mary Redmond, a police officer. Jaffee claimed that Redmond had used excessive force when she responded to a police call at an apartment complex, resulting in Allen's death. Redmond had sought counseling from a licensed clinical social worker following the shooting. Redmond refused to release her notes despite a court order to do so, claiming that her communications with Redmond were privileged under the psychotherapist-patient privilege.

The Supreme Court found it appropriate for federal courts to recognize a psychotherapist privilege pursuant to Rule of Evidence 501. The Court recognized that a psychotherapist's promise of confidentiality would have little meaning if the content of the client's communications could be disclosed in court. The Court specifically extended the privilege to licensed social workers providing psychotherapy, noting that social workers provide a significant amount of mental health treatment and that drawing a distinction between more costly psychotherapists and social workers would serve "no discernible purpose" (*Jaffee v. Redmond*, 1996, p. 17).

All 50 states, the District of Columbia, and all federal courts recognize such a privilege between psychotherapist and patient. However, exactly which professionals are encompassed within the term "psychotherapist" varies across jurisdictions. Table 2.3 provides a brief summary of state statutory provisions related to mental health professionals generally and social workers specifically.

Disclosure of Confidential Communications

The Code of Ethics of the National Association of Social Workers (2008) advises that confidential information may be disclosed only for "compelling professional reasons" (National Association of Social Workers, 2008, Standard 1.07(c)). Clients are to be advised about the nature of confidentiality, the limits of confidentiality, and, to the extent possible, prior to a disclosure, the potential consequences of that disclosure (National Association of Social Workers, 2008, Standard 1.07(d), (e)). Information relating to the extent to which confidentiality will be maintained and foreseeable exceptions can and should be conveyed to a client as part of the informed consent process (cf. Kutchins, 1991).

Disclosure of Confidential Communications 27

Table 2.3 Summary of state statutes related to social worker-client privilege

State	Provision relating to mental health professionals	Provision relating to social workers specifically
Alabama	Alabama Rule of Evidence 503A provides privilege for communication between a victim counselor and an individual seeking counseling services related to sexual assault or family violence. The victim counselor may not be associated with law enforcement or the prosecutor's office. The privilege extends to the client's guardian or conservator or the personal representative of a deceased client. Exceptions include hospitalization for mental illness; court-ordered examination of client's mental or emotional condition, when the client's condition is an element of the claim or defense; and breach of counselor duty	
Alaska		Alaska Statutes § 08.95.900(a) (2004); *Alfred v. Alaska* (1976). Statute provides that "A licensed social worker, and the social worker's employees or other persons who have access to the social worker's records, may not reveal to another person a communication made to the licensee by a client about a matter concerning which the client has employed the licensee in a professional capacity." It does not apply to "information revealed as part of the discovery of evidence related to a court proceeding or introduced in evidence in a court proceeding." Alaska Statutes § 08.95.900(a) (4) (2004)
Arizona	Arizona Revised Statutes Annotated § 32-3283 (1996). Privilege does not apply in some investigations, when the professional has a duty to communicate a danger to a potential victim and when reporting is required by law	
Arkansas		Arkansas Code Annotated §§ 17-103-107 (2012). Exceptions include client consent, when the client communicates the contemplation of a crime or harmful act, when the client is the victim of a crime and the social worker is required to testify, and when the client waives the privilege

(continued)

Table 2.3 (continued)

State	Provision relating to mental health professionals	Provision relating to social workers specifically
California		California Evidence Code § 1014 (2013) applies to psychotherapists. California Evidence Code § 1010(c) includes clinical social workers in the definition of psychotherapist when "engaged in applied psychotherapy of a nonmedical nature"
Colorado	Colorado Revised Statutes § 12-43-218 (2009) applies to licensee, which includes social workers. Exceptions include specified investigations, lawsuits against the licensee, and a review of licensee services	
Connecticut		Connecticut General Statutes Annotated § 52-146q (2012). Exceptions include "substantial risk of imminent physical injury" to the client or others, disclosures mandated by statute, and court-ordered examinations. Civil proceedings, in which the client's mental status is an element of the claim or defense, and communications to other individuals engaged in the client's diagnosis or treatment
Delaware		24 Delaware Code § 3913 (2017). Exceptions include client written consent, client planning of a crime or violent act, known or suspected child abuse or neglect, and client initiation of charges against the social worker
District of Columbia	D.C. Code § 14-307 (2016). Statute encompasses mental health professionals. Exceptions include disclosure in the context of specified legal proceedings where "disclosure is required in the public interest," criminal trials in which the mental competency or sanity of the client is in issue, proceedings relating to the mental competence of a child in the Family Division of Superior Court, and various other judicial proceedings	
Florida	Florida Statutes Annotated § 90-503 (2014). Social worker is included in definition of psychotherapist. Exceptions include proceedings to compel client hospitalization, court-ordered examination, and proceedings in which the client is relying on his or her condition as an element of the claim or defense	

Disclosure of Confidential Communications 29

Georgia		Georgia Code Annotated § 24-9-21 (7) (2010)
Hawaii		Hawaii Revised Statutes § 467E-15 (2002)
Idaho		Idaho Code § 54-3213 (2005). Exceptions include client or authorized representative consent; client contemplation of the commission of a harmful act or crime, when the client is a minor who is the victim of a crime; client waiver of the privilege in connection with a charge against the social worker; and as required by an evaluation committee
Indiana		Indiana Code Annotated § 25-23.6-6-1 (2014). Exceptions include client contemplation of a crime or serious harmful act, in a criminal proceeding if the disclosure relates to the homicide; in proceedings to determine mental competency, if the client is an unemancipated minor or incompetent adult and was a victim of a crime or abuse; in malpractice actions against the social worker and with client consent
Iowa	Iowa Code Annotated § 622.10 (2011). Statute refers to "mental health professionals"	
Kansas		Kansas Statutes Annotated § 65-6315 (2000). Exceptions include client consent, when client is under 18 years of age and was the victim of a crime, client waiver, and court hearings relating to adult abuse, adoption, child abuse or neglect, "or other matters pertaining to the welfare of children" including consultation with other professionals on behalf of the client
Kentucky		Kentucky Rule of Evidence, Rule 507. Exceptions include client hospitalization for mental illness, court-ordered examination, and when client's mental condition is an element of client's claim or defense
Louisiana		Louisiana Code of Evidence Annotated, art. 510 (2014). Statute refers to psychotherapists, which explicitly include licensed social workers. Exceptions include specified administrative and judicial proceedings; proceedings relating to the custody or visitation of a child; client contemplation of a crime or fraud; court-ordered examination; peer review of provider; malpractice action against provider; proceedings related to abuse of a child, elder, disabled, or incompetent person; actions for damages against the client when communication relates to level of blood alcohol or presence of drugs

(continued)

Table 2.3 (continued)

State	Provision relating to mental health professionals	Provision relating to social workers specifically
Maine		32 Maine Revised Statutes Annotated § 7005 (1985). Exception for actions in which client's mental condition is in issue and "a court in the exercise of sound discretion deems the disclosure necessary to the proper administration of justice, no information communicated to, or otherwise learned by, that licensed person in connection with the provision of social work services may be privileged and disclosure may be required"
Maryland		Maryland Code of Courts and Judicial Procedure § 9-121 (2016). Exceptions include client hospitalization for mental illness, client waiver, client consent, nondelinquent juvenile proceedings, specified guardianship and adoption proceedings, and criminal and delinquency proceedings related to child abuse or neglect
Massachusetts		Massachusetts General Law C.112-135A; 258 Code of Massachusetts Regulations § 22.00 (2017); Massachusetts Rule of Evidence 702. See *Commonwealth v. Pelosi*, 441 Mass. 257, 261 n.6, 805 N.E.2d 1, 5 n.6 (2004). The privilege is not self-executing. See *Commonwealth v. Oliveira*, 438 Mass. 325, 331, 780 N.E.2d 453, 458 (2002). Disclosure is permitted with client consent under specified conditions, when necessary to prevent harm to the client or to prevent the client from harming others; to comply with statutory abuse reporting obligations, in connection with elderly and disabled persons protective service investigations and specified child custody or protection proceedings, and to collect payment for services rendered and under specified conditions to third-party payers. Parents may access the records of their minor children under specified conditions. See also Massachusetts Guide to Evidence § 507 (2017)
Michigan	Michigan Comp. Laws § 333.18513 (2004)	
Minnesota		Minnesota Statutes Annotated § 595.02(g) (2016). Exceptions include maltreatment of minors and vulnerable adults

Disclosure of Confidential Communications

Mississippi		Mississippi Code Annotated § 73-53-29 (2016). Exceptions include client contemplation of crime or harmful act, client is a minor who is a victim of a crime, client waiver, specified proceedings relating to child welfare, collaboration with professionals on behalf of the client
Missouri	Missouri Revised Statutes § 337.636 (2013). Exceptions include client consent, client is under the age of 18 and is a victim of a crime, client waiver, specified proceedings relating to child welfare, and collaboration with professionals on behalf of the client	
Montana		Montana Code Annotated § 37-22-401 (2015). Exceptions include client consent, client contemplation of a crime or imminent threat of harm to client or others, client actions against the social worker, client waiver, and as required by law
Nebraska	Nebraska Revised Statutes § 38-2136 (2014). Exceptions include client consent, client waiver, duty to warn, client waiver for conjoint family therapy	
Nevada		Nevada Revised Statutes §§ 49.251-49.252 (1987). Exceptions include client contemplation of crime or fraud, specified proceedings involving the welfare of a minor, actions against the social worker for breach of duty, communications to others involved in the client's diagnosis or treatment, and as otherwise required by law
New Hampshire	New Hampshire Revised Statutes Annotated § 330-A:19 (2014). Statute encompasses licensed "mental health counselors," which may include social workers meeting specified criteria	
New Jersey		New Jersey Statutes Annotated § 45:15BB-13 (2013). Exceptions include as required by law, when failure to disclose presents "a clear and present danger to the health or safety of an individual," when social worker is a party or defendant in action relating to the provision of social work services, in criminal proceedings meeting specified criteria, and client waiver

(continued)

Table 2.3 (continued)

State	Provision relating to mental health professionals	Provision relating to social workers specifically
New Mexico		New Mexico Statutes Annotated § 61-31-24 (2006) repealed effective July 1, 2022. Exceptions include client consent, client contemplation of crime or harmful act, client under the age of 16 or a mentally fragile adult who has been the victim of a crime, client waiver, and specified proceedings relating to child welfare
New York		New York Civil Practice Law & Rules § 4508 (2012). Exceptions include client consent, client contemplation of a crime or harmful act, client is under the age of 16 and has been the victim of a crime, and client waiver
North Carolina		North Carolina General Statutes § 8-53.7 (2005).
North Dakota	Statute relating to privilege <u>does not apply</u> to social workers. North Dakota Rules of Evidence, Rule 503*	North Dakota Century Code 75.5-02-06.1-01-7 provides that social workers "shall protect the confidentiality of all information obtained in the course of professional service, except for compelling professional reasons." This does not apply to situations involving "serious, foreseeable, and imminent harm to a client or other identifiable person or when the laws or regulations require disclosure without a client's consent." Disclosure is required in situations involving mandated reporting of abuse of child or vulnerable adult (Century Code 50-25.2-03, 2013)
Ohio		Ohio Revised Code Annotated § 2317.02(G) (2017). Exceptions include client consent, client communications indicating a "clear and present danger" to the client or others, consent of deceased client's spouse or legal representative, court decision following *in camera* viewing (meaning for the court's viewing only), and court-ordered assessment or treatment
Oklahoma		59 Oklahoma Statutes Annotated § 1261.6 (2014). Exceptions include client consent, when communication relates to criminal acts or law violations, client waiver, specified matters and proceedings relating to child welfare, and in situations in which a child under the age of 18 reports that he or she is a victim of a crime. (See also *Penninger v. Oklahoma*, 1991)

Oregon	Oregon Revised Statutes § 40.250 (2015). Exceptions include consent of client or legally authorized representative; communication of clear intent to commit a crime that is reasonably expected to lead to injury of another; communication revealing that a minor was the victim of a crime, abuse, or neglect; specified proceedings involving a social worker who is a public employee
Pennsylvania	42 Pennsylvania Consolidated Statutes Annotated § 5945.1 (2014) establishes a privilege for sexual assault counselors, including social workers, who counsel victims of sexual assault at a rape crisis center. Individuals must have been trained for ≥40 hours under the supervision of a director of a rape crisis center. The privilege overrides the constitutional rights of a criminal defendant (*V.B.T. v. Family Services of Western Pennsylvania* (1998, 1999))
Rhode Island	Rhode Island General Laws § 5-39.1-4 (2016). Exceptions include client or legal representative's consent, clear and present danger to the safety of the client or another individual, and proceedings involving child abuse related to a minor client, in an action by the client against the social worker, in specified proceedings related to adoptive and foster placements, and in consulting with superiors on behalf of the client
South Carolina	South Carolina Code § 19-11-95 (1989). Privilege pertains to "a person licensed under the provisions of any of the following and who enters into a relationship with a patient to provide diagnosis, counseling, or treatment of a mental illness or emotional condition." Permissive disclosures include with client consent, when permitted by law, in order to prevent client's intended harm to self or crime and in order to collect owed fee or defend against client charge. Mandated disclosures include when required by law or court order and pursuant to subpoena and other specified proceedings of a licensing or disciplinary board

(continued)

Table 2.3 (continued)

State	Provision relating to mental health professionals	Provision relating to social workers specifically
South Dakota		South Dakota Codified Laws § 36-26-30 (1975). Exceptions include consent of client or legal representative; client contemplation of crime or harmful act, when client is a minor and appears to have been the victim of a crime; and client waiver
Tennessee		Tennessee Code Annotated § 63-23-107 (2003). Exceptions include mandated reporting of child abuse, judicial proceedings to commit a person with mental illness, and court-ordered examination
Texas	Texas Rule of Civil Evidence, Rule 510 (2010). Exceptions include written waiver by client or legal representative, to substantiate and collect on claim for services, court-ordered examination, when client relies on mental condition as element of claim or defense, and proceedings related to abuse or neglect of an institutional resident	
Utah	Utah Code Annotated § 58-6-114 (2011)	
Vermont	Vermont Rules of Evidence, Rule 503 (1991). Exceptions include communications to or from mental health professional while attending the client, court-ordered examination, client use of mental health condition as element of claim or defense, when client is under the age of 16 and has been the victim of a crime, mandated statutory reports, and under specified conditions relating to risk of harm to a child	
Virginia		Virginia Code § 8.01-400.2 (2005). Privilege does not apply when the physical or mental condition of the client is in issue, when court deems disclosure necessary to the proper administration of justice, and in matters related to child abuse and neglect
Washington		Washington Revised Code Annotated § 18.19.180 (2001). Exceptions include consent of client or legal representative, when client is a minor and has been the victim of a crime, client waiver, and in response to specified subpoenas

West Virginia	West Virginia Code § 30-30-24 (2016). Exceptions include when conferring or reporting with professional colleagues, consent of client or legal representative, client waiver, and client intent to commit a crime or harmful act, and disclosure is needed to protect an individual from "a clear, imminent risk of serious mental or physical harm or injury," or to prevent a serious threat to public safety, when the client is a minor and has been the victim of a crime, and in specified proceedings relating to child welfare
Wisconsin	Wisconsin Statutes Annotated § 905.04(1)(g), (4) (2016). Exceptions include proceedings for commitment, guardianship, protective services, protective placement, or control, care, or treatment of a sexually violent person; guardianship proceedings; court-ordered examination; when the client's condition is an element of a claim or defense; homicide trials; situations involving child abuse or neglect or abuse of an unborn child; tests for intoxication; paternity proceedings; and provision of services to the court in juvenile matters
Wyoming	Wyoming Statutes Annotated § 33-38-113 (2015). Exceptions include situations involving known or suspected abuse or neglect of children, elderly, disabled, or incompetent individuals; validity of a client or former client's will to defend against malpractice; disclosures involving the client's "immediate threat of physical violence against a readily identifiable victim"; when client's condition is an element of specified proceedings relating to child custody or visitation; in civil commitment proceedings; court-ordered examination; and in conjunction with specified hearings and investigations

*State statute specifically excludes social workers from provision relating to privilege *(N.D. v. Copeland,* 1989)

Working with Minor Clients

Understanding and conveying the extent of confidentiality to be provided may be particularly challenging when working with minor clients (Hendrix, 1991; Lawrence & Robinson Kurpius, 2000). Four possibilities have been identified in the literature: (1) an assurance of complete confidentiality of information from disclosure to and access by the minor's parents; (2) limited confidentiality, whereby the minor client is required to waive prospectively his or her right to know what will be revealed to his or her parent or guardian; (3) informed forced consent, so that the minor client is informed in advance that information will be conveyed to his or her parent or guardian, but the minor has no control over the substance of that disclosure; and (4) absence of any guarantee of confidentiality (Lawrence & Robinson Kurpius, 2000). Each of these scenarios is fraught with difficulty. Complete confidentiality may enhance the likelihood that the minor will confide in the social worker but may also lead to potential conflict with the parents/guardians and their termination of services to the child. Reliance on any of the remaining three options may lead to the minor's withholding of critical information from the social worker and/or or the client's active or passive refusal to participate in treatment.

The disclosure of confidential client information may be ethically and legally justifiable with the client's consent and when it is legally mandated, such as in the context of an obligation to warn, the mandated reporting of abuse or neglect, and the issuance of a subpoena. Each of these circumstances is discussed in greater detail below.

Client Consent

Confidential information regarding the client may be released with the consent of the client. Clients are to be provided with reasonable access to their records, as well as assistance in interpreting the information that is contained in the records (National Association of Social Workers, 2008, Standard 1.08(a)). However, the social worker must ensure that such access does not result in the release of confidential information about other individuals. Client consent is ethically required for the use of their identifying information for teaching or training purposes and when discussing client circumstances with consultants (National Association of Social Workers, 2008, Standard 1.07(p), (q)).

It is suggested that a written release from the client for the disclosure of information include the following, at a minimum:

- Name of the client
- Date of the release
- Period of time during which the release is valid
- Person(s) to whom the information is to be disclosed
- Period of time to which the information to be released pertains

- Scope of the information for which consent to release is being provided
- Purpose for which information is to be released
- Client's printed name
- Client's signature
- Date of client's signature

In some jurisdictions, the requisite elements for a valid release of information may be set by law or regulation.

Duty to Warn/Protect

In many, but not all, jurisdictions, a social worker may have an affirmative "duty to warn" third parties of the possibility of harm by their client; this has also been referred to as a duty to protect. In such situations, the social worker may disclose confidential information to the extent necessary to protect the client and/or other members of society.

The duty arises as the result of a line of court cases that began in 1976 with the now-famous case of *Tarasoff v. Regents of the University of California*. The case involved a lawsuit by the Tarasoff family against the University of California and a psychologist at the Berkeley campus of the university for the death of their daughter Tatiana. Tatiana had refused the advances of another graduate student at Berkeley. The would-be suitor had revealed his intent to kill Tatiana during the course of counseling sessions with a psychologist at the school's counseling services. The psychologist and several colleagues sought to have this student involuntarily hospitalized for observation purposes, but he was released after a brief observation period, during which it was concluded that he was rational. He subsequently shot and killed Tatiana.

The majority of the court rejected the psychologist's claim that he could not have advised either the family or Tatiana of the threat because to do so would have breached the traditionally protected relationship between the therapist and the patient. Instead, the court held that when a patient "presents a serious danger … to another [person], [the therapist] incurs an obligation to use reasonable care to protect the intended victim against such danger." That obligation could be satisfied by warning the intended victim of the potential danger, by notifying authorities, or by taking "whatever other steps are reasonably necessary under the circumstances" (*Tarasoff v. Regents of the University of California*, 1976, p. 340). The court specifically noted that the therapist-patient privilege was not absolute:

> We recognize the public interest in supporting effective treatment of mental illness and in protecting the rights of patients to privacy and the consequent public importance of safeguarding the confidential character of psychotherapeutic communication. Against this interest, however, we must weigh the public interest in safety from violent assault …. We conclude that the public policy favoring protection of the confidential character of patient-psychotherapist communications must yield to the extent to which disclosure is essential to avert danger to others. The protective privilege ends where the public peril begins. (*Tarasoff v. Regents of the University of California*, 1976, p. 346)

Some later cases have followed the reasoning of the *Tarasoff* court. A New Jersey court ruled in *McIntosh v. Milano* (1979) that the doctor-patient privilege protecting confidentiality is not absolute but is limited by the public interest of the patient. In reaching this conclusion, the court relied on the 1953 case of *Earle v. Kuklo*, in which the court had stated that "a physician has a duty to warn third persons against possible exposure to contagious or infectious diseases." A Michigan appeals court held in *Davis v. Lhim* (1983) that a therapist has an obligation to use reasonable care whenever there is a person who is foreseeably endangered by his or her patient. The danger would be deemed to be foreseeable if the therapist knew or should have known, based on a professional standard of care, of the potential harm. This decision, however, was later reversed in *Canon v. Thumundo* (1988), also a Michigan case. In that case, the Michigan Supreme Court held that psychiatrist's decision relating to the patient's involuntary hospitalization fell within a scope of immunity from tort liability. More recently, a California court held that a duty to warn may be triggered by the communication of an immediate family member to the therapist, even in the absence of a direct threat by the client (*Ewing v. Goldstein*, 2004; *Ewing v. Northridge Hospital Medical Center*, 2004).

Courts are divided, however, on whether the patient/client must make threats about a specific, intended victim to trigger the duty to warn. The court in *Thompson v. County of Alameda* (1980) found no duty to warn in the absence of an identifiable victim. Other courts have found similarly (*Brady v. Hopper*, 1983, 1984). Another court, though, held that the duty to warn exists even in the absence of specific threats concerning specific individuals, if the patient's previous history suggests that he or she would be likely to direct violence against a person (*Jablonski v. United States* 1983).

Subsequent to *Tarasoff*, many jurisdictions promulgated legislation in an effort to clarify and specify the duty owed by health-care professionals to third parties in similar circumstances. As of 2004, 23 states had implemented such legislation, although the terms of the statutes differ across states (Kachigan & Felthous, 2004). As an example, a duty to warn no longer exists in California, and there is now only a duty to protect due to statutory revisions subsequent to these judicial decisions. (See Taubman, 2012; Weinstock, Bonnici, Seroussi, & Leong, 2014 for additional analysis.) One scholar has suggested that, despite the differences across state statutes relating to the duty to warn/protect, four conditions must exist to justify the disclosure of confidential client information:

1. Evidence exists that the client presents a threat to him- or herself or to another individual.
2. The violence must be foreseeable.
3. The violence must be impending.
4. There is an identifiable potential victim of the violence (Reamer, 1998).

Some jurisdictions still do not statutorily mandate a duty to protect third parties. As an example, the Court of Appeal in Florida has interpreted that state's statute as permissive, allowing disclosure of confidential information to only the potential victim, a family member, or appropriate authorities and only where there exists a "clear and immediate probability of physical harm to the patient or client, to other individuals, or to society ...." (Florida Annotated Statutes § 491.0147, 1991; *Green v. Ross*, 1997). Accordingly, the court held that a mental health professional does not have an affirmative duty to warn.

Despite judicial and legislative efforts to clarify and specify the obligations owed by mental health professionals to third parties, the social worker's obligation to warn or protect may nevertheless be unclear in some situations. As an example, the existence of a duty to warn/protect a third party from the possibility of becoming infected with HIV as the result of unprotected intercourse with an HIV-infected client likely depends on the wording of the relevant legislation, the holdings of previous court decisions, the immediacy of the intended act, the likelihood of infection, and the identifiability of the client's sexual partner, as well as other factors (Reamer, 1991). Some states have addressed such situations through the promulgation of specific HIV-focused statutes, which specify whether such disclosures are permissive or mandated, the circumstances under which such disclosures to third parties may occur, the persons authorized to communicate such disclosures of confidential client information, and the potential (non)liability of the provider.

It has been suggested that the best practice for the social worker seeking to determine whether a duty to warn or protect exists is to conduct a careful and thorough assessment of the client, to implement appropriate interventions on a timely basis, and to document all circumstances, information, decisions, and actions in the client record (Kopels & Kagle, 1993). The intake assessment should include an assessment of the client's dangerousness; a more complete assessment is warranted if it appears from the client's responses to initial questioning that he or she has communicated a threat or appears to have violent ideas or behaviors. Interventions may include the intensification of services, the relinquishment of any weapons to which the client may have access, and/or the issuance of warnings to intended victims and/or appropriate authorities.

Reporting Abuse and Neglect

All states have promulgated laws requiring licensed social workers to report suspected or known cases of child abuse or neglect. In doing so, states have made clear that the welfare of the children supersedes the privacy and confidentiality interests that others may have. Accordingly, there generally is no privilege related to communications involving child abuse or neglect. Many states have also implemented legislation that requires social workers to report the abuse or neglect of individuals who are elderly, mentally ill, physically ill or disabled, or dependent (Stiegel & Klem, 2006). (Additional legal issues relating to abuse and neglect are addressed in Chap. 11.)

Responding to Subpoenas

A subpoena "is a mandate that requires documents (*duces tecum*) or testimony be provided at a specific time and location" (Felton & Polowy, 2015b). A subpoena can be issued by a judge, a clerk of the court, an administrative agency that has subpoena power, a Congress, or an attorney and may be served (delivered) to a social worker in person or through the mail. A subpoena is most likely to be issued in situations involving child custody or visitation, termination of parental rights, divorce, employment discrimination, wrongful termination, disability claims, personal injury claims, social worker malpractice, and criminal prosecution. Although a subpoena should not be ignored, neither should the social worker assume that he or she must immediately comply with it.

Social workers are ethically obligated to protect client confidentiality to the extent permitted by law, even in the context of legal proceedings. The Code of Ethics provides:

> Social workers should protect the confidentiality of clients during legal proceedings to the extent permitted by law. When a court of law or other legally authorized body orders social workers to disclose confidential or privileged information without a client's consent and such disclosure could cause harm to the client, social workers should request that the court withdraw the order or limit the order as narrowly as possible or maintain the records under seal, unavailable for public inspection. (National Association of Social Workers, 2008, Standard 1.07(j))

Accordingly, social workers are obligated to claim a privilege on behalf of the client in the absence of client consent or a legally recognized exception.

Several courses of action are possible in the event that a social worker receives a subpoena. First, the social worker should consult with his or her client regarding the releases of the requested information. If the client consents to its release, there is no legal or ethical issue. The client's agreement to its release should be carefully documented. The social worker will also want to notify his or her liability insurance company, his or her own attorney, and the client's attorney, if the client has an attorney and if he or she provides consent to do so.

In situations in which the subpoena was not accompanied by a court order signed by a judge, the social worker can advise the attorney requesting the information that the information cannot be released in the absence of a court order or the client's consent. This communication should be done in writing and the social worker should retain a copy. However, in all cases, the requested information should not be released unless the social worker has obtained the client's written consent or has received a court order signed by a judge for the release of the information or testimony.

Alternatively, the social worker can confer with the client to ask if the client's attorney will be filing a motion to quash the subpoena. A motion to quash is a request made in court to a judge to either nullify the subpoena or modify it so that the information sought is more limited in scope. If the client does not have an attorney or the client's attorney does not file a motion to quash but the client does not consent to the release of the information, the social worker may wish to consult with his or her own attorney regarding the advisability of seeking a motion to quash the subpoena. In some situations, the liability insurance carrier for the social worker may cover the cost of the social worker's legal services to do so.

Depending on the circumstances involved in a specific case, a judge may be unwilling to grant a motion to quash a subpoena in its entirety but may be willing to grant it in part and deny it in part. *Nelson v. Green* (2014) involved a lawsuit by the child's father against a child's mother and a county department of social services alleging their intentional infliction of emotional distress based on his contention that they had coerced his daughter to falsely accuse him of child abuse. In reviewing the scope of the subpoena, the court found that some of the information requested was protected by privilege but that some was not. Accordingly, the court granted the motion to quash in part and denied it in part and granted the plaintiff's motion to compel the production of documents in part and denied it in part.

A judge may in some situations find that a motion to seal the records is appropriate but a motion to quash is not. As an example, the case of *Doe v. Maryland Board of Social Workers* (2004) involved a complaint to a Board of Social Work Examiners alleging that a social worker had failed to report a client's sexual abuse of a child. The Board investigated the complaint and issued a subpoena requiring the social worker to deliver the client's files. The client filed a motion to quash the subpoena and also moved to have the record sealed. The trial court granted the motion to seal the records but denied the motion to quash the subpoena. In reviewing the trial court's decision, the appeals court found that the client did not have a right to have the subpoena quashed because the records were not privileged and further found that the state's interest in the limited disclosure of mental health records outweighed the client's constitutional right to privacy. It should be noted that although social workers cannot be held liable for what they say in court or the information they produce in response to a subpoena, they may be found liable for failing to advise the client of the possibility of disclosure (Bernstein, 1977).

References

Bernstein, B. E. (1977). Privileged communications to the social worker. *Social Work, 22*(4), 264–268.

Collingridge, M., Miller, S., & Bowles, W. (2001). Privacy and confidentiality in social work. *Australian Social Work, 54*(2), 3–13.

Dunn, R. T., Rose, A. D., & Wieland, L. (2013). Authorization requirements for the disclosure of protected health information (2013 update). American Health information Management Association. http://library.ahima.org/doc?oid=107284#.WZmlOsaQxEY. Accessed 17 August 2017.

Felton, E. M., & Polowy, C. I. (2015a). Legal considerations when a client dies by suicide. http://naswcanews.org/legal-considerations-when-a-client-dies-by-suicide/. Accessed 17 August 2017.

Felton, E. M., & Polowy, C. I. (2015b). Quick reference guide for responding to a subpoena. http://naswcanews.org/quick-reference-guide-for-responding-to-a-subpoena/. Accessed 17 August 2017.

Hendrix, D. H. (1991). Ethics and intrafamily confidentiality in counseling with children. *Journal of Mental Health Counseling, 13*, 323–358.

Herlihy, B., & Sheeley, V. L. (1987). Privileged communication in selected helping professions: A comparison among statutes. *Journal of Counseling and Development, 65*, 479–483.

Kachigan, C., & Felthous, A. R. (2004). Court responses to Tarasoff statutes. *Journal of the American Academy of Psychiatry & Law, 32*, 263–273.

Kopels, S., & Kagle, J. D. (1993). Do social workers have a duty to warn? *Social Service Review, 67*(1), 101–126.

Kutchins, H. (1991). The fiduciary relationship: The legal basis for social workers' responsibilities to clients. *Social Work, 36*(2), 106–113.

Lawrence, G., & Robinson Kurpius, S. E. (2000). Legal and ethical issues involved when counseling minors in nonschool settings. *Journal of Counseling & Development, 78*, 130–136.

Millstein, K. (2000). Confidentiality in direct social-work practice: Inevitable challenges and ethical dilemmas. *Families in Society: The Journal of Contemporary Human Services, 81*(3), 270–282.

Morgan, S., Polowy, C. I., & Khan, A. (2010). Privacy protections for deceased clients' records. http://c.ymcdn.com/sites/www.naswin.org/resource/resmgr/imported/Privacy%20Protections%20for%20Deceased%20Clients.pdf. Accessed 17 August 2017.

National Association of Social Workers. (2008). *Code of ethics*. https://www.socialworkers.org/pubs/code/code.asp. Accessed 11 February 2016.

Reamer, F. (1991). AIDS, social work, and the "duty to protect". *Social Work, 36*(1), 56–60.

Reamer, F. (1998). *Ethical standards in social work: A critical review of the NASW code of ethics*. Washington, DC: NASW Press.

Reamer, F. G. (2005). Ethical and legal standards in social work: Consistency and conflict. *Families in Society: The Journal of Contemporary Social Services, 86*(2), 163–169.

Stiegel, L., & Klem, E. (2006). Citations to adult protective services (APS), institutional abuse and long term care ombudsman program (LTCOP) laws. American Bar Association Commission on Law and Aging. https://www.americanbar.org/content/dam/aba/administrative/law_aging/APS_IA_LTCOP_Citations_Chart.authcheckdam.pdf. Retrieved 18 August 2017.

Substance Abuse and Mental Health Services Administration, Center for Substance Abuse Treatment. (2004). The confidentiality of alcohol and drug use patient records regulation and the HIPAA privacy rule: Implications for alcohol and substance abuse programs. Washington, DC: Author. https://www.samhsa.gov/sites/default/files/part2-hipaa-comparison2004.pdf. Accessed 22 August 2017.

Taubman, S. (2012). Dangerousness to self and others in social work practice. Presented at the University of California School of Social Welfare Field Preparation Panel. http://socialwelfare.berkeley.edu/sites/default/files/docs/Handouts__Dangerousness_to_Self_and_Others_in_Social_Work_Practice.pdf. Accessed 18 August 2017.

United States Department of Health and Human Services, Office for Civil Rights. (2013). Summary of the HIPAA privacy rule. https://www.hhs.gov/hipaa/for-professionals/privacy/laws-regulations/index.html. Accessed 23 March 2017.

United States Department of Health and Human Services, Office for Civil Rights. (2017). HIPAA privacy rule and sharing information related to mental health. https://www.hhs.gov/hipaa/for-professionals/special-topics/mental-health/index.html. Accessed 20 August 2017.

Ward, K. (2002). Confidentiality in substance abuse counseling. *Journal of Social Work Practice in the Addictions, 2*(2), 39–52.

Watkins, S. A., & Watkins, J. C., Jr. (1983). Malpractice in clinical social work: A perspective on civil liability in the 1980s. *Behavioral Sciences & the Law, 1*(1), 55–69.

Wertheimer, M. (2016). Remember to keep psychotherapy notes separate from patient's medical record. *Psychiatric News*, October 3. https://psychnews.psychiatryonline.org/doi/full/10.1176/appi.pn.2016.10a19. Accessed 01 May 2018.

Weinstock, R., Bonnici, D., Seroussi, A., & Leong, G. S. (2014). No duty to warn in California: Now unambiguously solely a duty to protect. *Journal of the American Academy of Psychiatry and the Law, 42*(1), 101–108.

Legal References

Cases

Alfred v. Alaska, 554 P.2d 411 (1976).
Brady v. Hopper, 570 F. Supp. 1333 (D. Colo. 1983), *affirmed*, 751 F.2d 329 (10th Cir. 1984).
Commonwealth v. Oliveira, 438 Mass. 325, 780 N.E.2d 453 (2002).
Commonwealth v. Pelosi, 441 Mass. 257, 805 N.E.2d 1 (2004).
Davis v. Lhim, 124 Mich. App. 291 (1983), *affirmed on remand,* 147 Mich. App. 8 (1985), *reversed* on grounds of government immunity in *Canon v. Thumudo*, 430 Mich. 326 (1988).
Doe v. Maryland Board of Social Workers, 840 A.2d 744 (Md. 2004), *cert. granted*, Doe v. Social Workers, 849 A.2d 473 (2004), *aff'd,* Doe v. Maryland Board of Social Work Examiners, 2004 Md. LEXIS 780 (Md., Dec. 9, 2004).
Earle v. Kuklo, 26 N.J. Super. 471 (App. Div. 1953).
Ewing v. Goldstein, 120 Cal. App. 4th 807 (2004).
Ewing v. Northridge Hospital Medical Center, 120 Cal. App. 4th 1289 (2004).
Green v. Ross, 691 So. 2d 542 (Fla. Ct. Appeal 1997).
Jablonski v. United States, 712 F.2d 391 (9th Cir. 1983).
Jaffee v. Redmond, 518 U.S. 1 (1996).
N.D. v. Copeland, 448 N.W.2d 611 (1989).
Nelson v. Green, 2014 U.S. Dist. LEXIS 4432 (W.D. Va., Jan. 14, 2014), 2014 US. Dist. LEXIS 83779 (June 12, 2014).
Penninger v. Oklahoma, 811 P.2d 609 (Okla. Crim. App. 1991).
People v. Newman. (1973). 298 N.E.2d 651 (App. Div.).
Tarasoff v. Regents of the University of California, 17 Cal. 3d 425 (1976).
Thompson v. County of Alameda., 27 Cal. 3d 741 (1980).
V.B.T. v. Family Services of Western Pennsylvania, 705 A.2d 1325 (Pa. Super. 1998), *appeal granted,* 727 A.2d 132 (Pa. 1998), *affirmed,* 728 A.2d 953 (Pa. 1999).

Statutes

24 Delaware Code § 3913 (2017).
32 Maine Revised Statutes Annotated § 7005 (1985).
59 Oklahoma Statutes Annotated § 1261.6 (2014).
258 Code of Massachusetts Regulations § 22.00 (2017).
Alabama Rule of Evidence 503A.
Alaska Statutes § 08.95.900(a) (2004).
Arizona Revised Statutes Annotated § 32-3283 (1996).
Arkansas Code Annotated §§ 17-103-107 (2012).
California Evidence Code §§ 1010(c), 1014 (2013).
Colorado Revised Statutes § 12-43-218 (2009).
Confidentiality of Alcohol and Drug Abuse Patient Records Act, 42 U.S.C. § 290 dd-2
Connecticut General Statutes Annotated § 52-146q (2012).
D.C. Code § 14-307 (2016).
Florida Statutes Annotated § 90-503 (2014).
Florida Annotated Statues § 491.0147 (1991).
Georgia Code Annotated § 24-9-21 (7) (2010).
Hawaii Revised Statutes § 467E-15 (2002).
Health Insurance Portability and Accountability Act, Pub. L. 104-191 (1996).

Idaho Code § 54-3213 (2005).
Indiana Code Annotated § 25-23.6-6-1 (2014).
Iowa Code Annotated § 622.10 (2011).
Kansas Statutes Annotated § 65-6315 (2000).
Kentucky Rule of Evidence, Rule 507 (1996).
Louisiana Code of Evidence Annotated, art. 510 (2014).
Maryland Code of Courts and Judicial Procedure § 9-121 (2016).
Massachusetts General Law C.112-135A.
Massachusetts Guide to Evidence § 507 (2017). http://www.mass.gov/courts/case-legal-res/guidelines/mass-guide-to-evidence/article-v-privileges-and-disqualification.html#507. Accessed 19 August 2017.
Massachusetts Rule of Evidence 702
Michigan Comp. Laws § 333.18513 (2004).
Minnesota Statutes Annotated § 595.02(g) (2016).
Mississippi Code Annotated § 73-53-29 (2016).
Missouri Revised Statutes § 337.636 (2013).
Montana Code Annotated § 37-22-401 (2015).
Nebraska Revised Statutes § 38-2136 (2014).
Nevada Revised Statutes §§ 49.251-49.252 (1987).
New Hampshire Revised Statutes Annotated § 330-A:19 (2014).
New Jersey Statutes Annotated § 45:15BB-13 (2013).
New Mexico Statutes Annotated § 61-31-24 (2006), repealed effective July 1, 2022.
New York Civil Practice Law & Rules § 4508 (2012).
North Carolina General Statutes § 8-53.7 (2005).
North Dakota Century Code 50-25.2-03, 75.5-02-06.1-01-7 (2013).
North Dakota Rules of Evidence, Rule 503.
Ohio Revised Code Annotated § 2317.02(G) (2017).
Oregon Revised Statutes § 40.250 (2015).
42 Pennsylvania Consolidated Statutes Annotated § 5945.1 (2014).
Rhode Island General Laws § 5-39.1-4 (2016).
South Carolina Code § 19-11-95 (1989).
South Dakota Codified Laws § 36-26-30 (1975).
Tennessee Code Annotated § 63-23-107 (2003).
Texas Rule of Civil Evidence, Rule 510 (2010).
Utah Code Annotated § 58-6-114 (2011).
Vermont Rules of Evidence, Rule 503 (1991).
Virginia Code § 8.01-400.2 (2005).
Washington Revised Code Annotated § 18.19.180 (2001).
West Virginia Code § 30-30-24 (2016).
Wisconsin Statutes Annotated § 905.04(1)(g), (4) (2016).
Wyoming Statutes Annotated § 33-38-113 (2015).

Regulations

42 Code of Federal Regulations Part 2 (2017a).
42 Code of Federal Regulations §§ 2.11, 2.13(a) (2017b).
45 Code of Federal Regulations §§ 164.502(a), 164.508(a)(2) (2013).

Chapter 3
Licensing Issues

Licensure and Licensing Boards: Purpose and Scope

Licensure is intended to ensure that individuals do not engage in the practice of social work except under specified conditions, including satisfaction of particular educational requirements and a period of practice under the supervision of a more experienced provider, who is frequently a licensed social worker (Hardcastle, 1977). It is believed that this regulation of social practice will protect members of the public from the errors and unethical conduct that could occur in the context of social service provision (Donaldson, Hill, Ferguson, Fogel, & Erickson, 2014; Hardcastle, 1977), protect both individual practitioners and the social work profession (Cavazos, 2001), and provide a mechanism to hold accountable those who violate delineated standards (Donaldson et al., 2014). However, questions have been raised as to whether licensure is sufficient to accomplish these purposes in view of the "grandparenting" in state licensure of nondegreed social workers (Cohen & Deri, 1992), as well as the absence of education or training requirements in specified areas (e.g., Quinn & Straussner, 2010). Accordingly, various states, either through statute or as a mandate by a social work board, have instituted specific continuing education requirements as a prerequisite to license renewal, e.g., diversity or cultural competence, professional ethics, and practice with specifically delineated populations. In some states, legislatures and/or social work boards have developed certifications in specific areas of practice that extend beyond the requirements for licensure (Birmingham, Berry, & Bussey, 1996).

State laws governing social workers and the practice of social work vary across states. In general, these laws define what is meant by social work, delineate who may use the title of social worker, provide for the establishment of the examination board, set forth education requirements, and outline disciplinary processes (Birmingham et al., 1996; Dyeson, 2004). The majority of states have multiple tiers of licensing, e.g., those with a bachelor's degree or master's degree in social work

(Donaldson et al., 2014; Dyeson, 2004). As an example of one approach, Ohio law defines the practice of social work as the:

> application of social work theory and specialized knowledge of human development and behavior and social, economic, and cultural systems in directly assisting individuals, families, and groups in a clinical setting to improve or restore their capacity for social functioning, including counseling, the use of psychosocial interventions, and the use of social psychotherapy, which includes the diagnosis and treatment of mental and emotional disorders (Ohio Revised Code § 4757.01(C), 2014a).[1]

The law further provides that:

> No person shall use the title 'social worker,' 'independent social worker,' 'social work assistant,' or any other title or description incorporating the words 'social worker' or any initials used to identify persons acting in those capacities unless the person is currently authorized by licensure or registration under this chapter to act in the capacity indicated by the title or initials. (Ohio Revised Code § 4757.02(B)(2), 2014b)

The law also creates a combined counselor, social worker, and marriage and family therapist board (Ohio Revised Code § 4757.03(A), 2014c). The board's membership includes representatives of each of these occupations, including social workers:

> Two members shall be individuals licensed under this chapter as independent social workers. Two members shall be individuals licensed under this chapter as social workers, at least one of whom must hold a bachelor's or master's degree in social work from an accredited educational institution recognized by the board. At all times, the social worker membership shall include one educator who holds a teaching position in a baccalaureate or master's degree social work program at an accredited educational institution recognized by the board (Ohio Revised Code § 4757.03(A)(3), 2014c).

Licensing Boards and Disciplinary Proceedings

Bases for Disciplinary Action

As noted, licensing boards are empowered by state law to determine whether the conduct of a social worker has violated the ethical standard set forth in the state law for the practice of social work and to determine the appropriate response to that violation. Ohio law, for example, provides in pertinent part:

---

[1] Compare Ohio's definition of social work to that adopted by Wyoming:

> "Practice of social work" means applying social work theory and methods to the diagnosis, treatment and prevention of psychosocial dysfunction, disability or impairment, including emotional and mental disorders. It is based on knowledge of one (1) or more theories of human development within a psychosocial context. The perspective of person-in-situation is central to professional social work ptactice. Professional clinical social work includes but is not limited to interpersonal interactions, intrapsychic dynamics, and life support and management issues. Professional clinical social work services consist of assessment, diagnosis, treatment, including psychotherapy and counseling, client-centered advocacy, consultation and evaluation with individuals, families, groups, communities and organizations (Wyoming Statutes Annotated § 33-38-102(a)(v), 2005).

The board shall establish a code of ethical practice for persons licensed under this chapter as independent social workers or social workers, persons registered under this chapter as social work assistants, and persons licensed as independent marriage and family therapists or marriage and family therapists ... The codes of ethical practice shall define unprofessional conduct, which shall include engaging in a dual relationship with a client or former client, committing an act of sexual abuse, misconduct, or exploitation of a client or former client, and, except as permitted by law, violating client confidentiality. The codes of ethical practice may be based on any codes of ethical practice developed by national organizations representing the interests of those involved in professional counseling, social work, or marriage and family therapy. The board may establish standards in its codes of ethical practice that are more stringent than those established by national organizations (Ohio Revised Code § 4757.11, 2014).

Public records relating to disciplinary actions against social workers across several states (Alabama, California, Maryland, Michigan, New Jersey, New York, Ohio, Oregon, Pennsylvania, and Wyoming) during the past 10 years suggest that a wide range of offenses have led to disciplinary action by the respective state boards. Specific grounds include:

- Failure to maintain professional boundaries by engaging in sexual conduct with a client
- Failure to maintain professional boundaries by exploiting a position of trust with a client
- Engaging in conduct that discredits the social work profession
- Failure to be responsible to setting and maintaining professional boundaries
- Unethical conduct
- False, misleading, deceptive, or fraudulent claims about services and professional credentials and qualifications
- Using alcohol or drugs at work
- Dual relationship
- Failure to respond to and provide information to a patient regarding a request for patient records
- Failure to keep accurate client records
- Failure to include in therapy records the nature of the client's presenting problem, a psychosocial history, a treatment plan, and a consent for treatment
- Inappropriate treatment with a client
- Practicing outside the scope of licensure and without appropriate supervision
- Failure to submit a written report to the board regarding an arrest and conviction
- Failure to cooperate with a board investigation
- Conviction for Medicaid fraud
- Failure to report an arrest to the board in a timely manner
- Making threatening and harassing comments to a former employer
- Making suggestive, lewd, lascivious, or improper remarks or advances to a client or coworker
- Knowingly offering to provide professional services to individuals concurrently receiving services from another mental health services provider, without the provider's knowledge
- Practicing as a social worker with an expired license

- Failing to take proper precautions to prevent clients from physical/emotional harm by facility staff
- Failing to adhere to reporting standards for suspected abuse or neglect of clients
- Providing services while impaired
- Failure to provide a written description of services, schedules, fees
- Failure to obtain the appropriate consent to treatment from the parents of a minor child
- Failure to retain and dispose of confidential client records
- Failure to maintain accurate records to include dates of service, types of services, progress or case notes, billing information
- Charging clients for services not rendered
- Failure to ensure that the client or a legally authorized person representing the client signed a consent form for services
- Failure to properly secure confidential client files in office
- Failure to submit to a mental examination ordered by a professional standards committee
- Misdemeanor and felony convictions (resisting arrest, aggravated harassment, criminal possession of a controlled substance, driving while intoxicated, offering a false instrument for filing, failure to register as a sex offender, attempted sexual intercourse under pretext of medical treatment, health-care fraud)
- Felony charges (not yet convicted) (sexually groping a teenager, child abuse, falsifying public records)

(Alabama State Board of Social Work Examiners, 2017; Consent Agreement between Shelley J. Ahleman and State of Ohio Counselor, Social Worker, Marriage and Family Therapist Board, 2008; Consent Agreement between Michael Wilson and State of Ohio Counselor, Social Worker, Marriage and Family Therapist Board, 2015; *Fiore v. Bureau of Professional and Occupational Affairs, State Board of Social Workers, Marriage and Family Therapists, and Professional Counselors,* 2011; Lawlor, 2016a, b; Lawlor & Byrne, 2016; *Matter of Bass,* 2017; *Matter of Currie,* 2011; *Matter of James,* 2001; *Matter of Licensure of Penny v. State of Wyoming,* 2005; *Matter of Nedoba,* 2013; *Matter of Tartakoff v. New York State Education Department,* 2015; Michigan Department of Community Health, 2006a, b; Department of Licensing and Regulatory Affairs, 2013; Office of the Professions, New York State Education Department, 2014; Oregon State Board of Licensed Social Workers, 2016; Parsons, 2014; Ohio Administrative Code § 4757-5-01(C), 2017; Consent Agreement between Wilson and State of Ohio Counselor, Social Worker, Marriage and Family Therapist Board, 2015; Texas Department of State Health Services, Texas State Board of Social Work Examiners, 2017; Therolf, 2016a, b).

Social workers with supervisory responsibilities may face both disciplinary procedures in connection with their licensure and legal liability for the actions of those who they supervise (Zakutansky & Sirles, 1993). (The legal doctrine of *respondeat superior*, referring to the liability of the supervisor for the actions of those under his or her direction or supervision, in addition to the liability of the supervisee, is discussed in Chap. 4, which focuses on liability.) As an example, several social workers in California, as well as their supervisor, were charged with child abuse following the torture and death of a child (Therolf, 2016a, b). As of the time of this writing, the license of at least one of the individuals had been suspended, as was the supervisor's.

Gatekeeping and Licensure

Both the need to protect the public and the potential for supervisor accountability for the actions of a supervisee call for consideration of the extent to which licensed social workers with training and/or supervisory responsibilities should fulfill a gatekeeping function with respect to the entry of individuals into the field of social work (Cole, 1991; Cole & Lewis, 1993; Strom-Gottfried, 2000; Zakutansky & Sirles, 1993. Cf. Stromwall, 2002). This gatekeeping function is often reflected in state law mandating the reporting to the licensing board of those colleagues who may be harming their clients or who are in violation of the ethical standards of conduct. This is exemplified by the provision in Ohio law that states:

> Mandatory reporting: All licensees, registrants, supervisors and trainees have a responsibility to report any alleged violations of this act or rules adopted under it to the counselor, social worker, and marriage and family therapist board. Also, if they have knowledge or reason to suspect that a licensed colleague or other licensee is acting in an unethical way or is incompetent or impaired they shall report that practitioner to the board. All mandatory reporting shall be in writing and bear the name and license number or registration of the reporter. When client confidentiality limits the licensee's ability to provide details the licensee is still mandated to report the allegations against another licensee without breaching client confidentiality (Ohio Administrative Code § 4757-5-10(A), 2014).

This obligation is also reflected in the NASW Code of Ethics:

> 2.09 Impairment of Colleagues
>
> (a) Social workers who have direct knowledge of a social work colleague's impairment that is due to personal problems, psychosocial distress, substance abuse, or mental health difficulties and that interferes with practice effectiveness should consult with that colleague when feasible and assist the colleague in taking remedial action.
> (b) Social workers who believe that a social work colleague's impairment interferes with practice effectiveness and that the colleague has not taken adequate steps to address the impairment should take action through appropriate channels established by employers, agencies, NASW, licensing and regulatory bodies, and other professional organizations.
>
> 2.10 Incompetence of Colleagues
>
> (a) Social workers who have direct knowledge of a social work colleague's incompetence should consult with that colleague when feasible and assist the colleague in taking remedial action.
> (b) Social workers who believe that a social work colleague is incompetent and has not taken adequate steps to address the incompetence should take action through appropriate channels established by employers, agencies, NASW, licensing and regulatory bodies, and other professional organizations.

2.11 Unethical Conduct of Colleagues

(a) Social workers should take adequate measures to discourage, prevent, expose, and correct the unethical conduct of colleagues.
(b) Social workers should be knowledgeable about established policies and procedures for handling concerns about colleagues' unethical behavior. Social workers should be familiar with national, state, and local procedures for handling ethics complaints. These include policies and procedures created by NASW, licensing and regulatory bodies, employers, agencies, and other professional organizations.
(c) Social workers who believe that a colleague has acted unethically should seek resolution by discussing their concerns with the colleague when feasible and when such discussion is likely to be productive.
(d) When necessary, social workers who believe that a colleague has acted unethically should take action through appropriate formal channels (such as contacting a state licensing board or regulatory body, an NASW committee on inquiry, or other professional ethics committees).
(e) Social workers should defend and assist colleagues who are unjustly charged with unethical conduct (National Association of Social Workers, 1996, rev. 2008).

These mandates raise significant ethical and legal issues for social workers employed in academic settings and those who assume the role of field instructor or field liaison for social work students. By the very nature of their role, students are learning and function at varying points along a continuum of knowledge, professional responsibility, and professional identity. Consequently, it may be difficult for those who have assumed supervisory responsibility to determine whether a trainee's seemingly unprofessional attitudes and/or behaviors are attributable to a lack of knowledge and/or experience and may be remediable, or whether they reflect a level of incompetence or unethical conduct that signifies either an inability to attain even the minimally acceptable standard of professional functioning or diminished professional functioning that may not be amenable to remediation efforts (Forrest, Elman, Gizara, & Vacha-Haase, 1999; Hahn & Molnar, 1991). Yet, such assessments are critical if social workers are to fulfill their ethical and legal responsibilities associated with their gatekeeping function and licensure.

Lamb and colleagues (1987) have suggested that it may be helpful to distinguish between a training problem and an impairment. Impairment during training is said to exist when there is:

an interference in professional functioning that is reflected in one or more of the following ways: (a) an inability and/or unwillingness to acquire and integrate professional standards into one's repertoire of professional behavior; (b) an inability to acquire professional skills to reach an adequate level of competency; (c) an inability to control personal stress, psychological dysfunction and/or emotional reactions that interfere with professional functioning (Lamb. Presser, Pfost, Baum, Jackson, and Jarvis, 1987, p. 598).

In their view, a problem constitutes impairment if:

(a) the intern does not acknowledge, understand, or address the problem when it is identified; (b) the problem is not merely a reflection of the skill deficit that can be rectified by academic or didactic training; (c) the quality of services delivered by the intern is consistently negatively affected; (d) the problem is not restricted to one area of professional functioning; (e) a disproportionate amount of attention by training personnel is required and/or (f) the intern's behavior does not change as a function of feedback, remediation efforts, and/or time (Lamb. Presser, Pfost, Baum, Jackson, and Jarvis, 1987, p. 599).

Social work educators, field instructors, and field liaisons may find it helpful to consider trainee development in the following domains in the context of their evaluations of trainee competence and progress: academic skills, assessment skills, clinical judgment, clinical skills, ethics, interpersonal skills, intrapersonal skills, response to supervision, and theoretical skills (cf. Forrest et al., 1999). Potential remediation strategies include counseling the trainee to leave the field of social work, assigning additional coursework, requiring and providing increased supervision, requiring the trainee to take a leave of absence, requiring the trainee to leave the program, recommending or requiring that the trainee obtain personal therapy, requiring the trainee to repeat the practicum, having the trainee participate in a growth group, and/or requiring tutoring (Forrest et al., 1999).

Clearly, the approach must necessarily relate to the underlying cause of the perceived deficiency. It is critical that, prior to initiating any remediation, an assessment be made regarding the nature of the deficiency and impairment, whether it is remediable, and the congruence between the perceived deficiency or impairment, the program goals, the remediation strategy, and the expected outcome of the remediation. It has been suggested that a remediation plan should:

> (a) identify and describe deficiencies that are directly tied to the program's evaluation criteria, (b) identify specific goals and changes that need to be made by the trainee, (c) identify possible methods for meeting these goals, (d) establish criteria for judging whether remediation has been successful, and (e) determine a timeline for evaluation (Forrest et al., 1999, p. 650).

Disciplinary Proceedings

The disciplinary process is generally initiated by the filing of a complaint with the appropriate licensing body within the state in which the social worker is licensed. The complaint may be filed by a colleague, a client, a supervisor, a field instructor, or a field liaison. In some cases, an individual may be practicing social work without having the necessary license, e.g., the application was denied or the individual failed to renew it, or the person may be holding themselves out as a social worker without actually having had the requisite education, training, and licensure. In such cases, the complaint would be filed in the state in which the individual is carrying out the social work activities.

Many boards have a committee that is charged with the responsibility of investigating all complaints (Association of Social Work Boards, 2011). The committee will determine whether there is sufficient basis to move forward with the complaint. The committee may hold an informal closed meeting with the social worker against whom the complaint was lodged in an effort to reach a resolution and agreement. Agreements that are concluded and confirmed become part of the public record.

If no agreement is reached in a more informal meeting or if there is no informal meeting, and the investigation committee has concluded that there is sufficient basis to move forward on the complaint, the process will proceed to a formal hearing.

State statute generally sets a period of time during which this must occur, e.g., within 30 days. The social worker will be afforded due process rights during the hearing, e.g., he or she may be represented by counsel, may call witnesses, and produce evidence on his or her behalf. In cases in which the board determines that there is a risk to the safety or welfare of the public, it may summarily suspend the individual's license even prior to a formal hearing (Association of Social Work Boards, 2011; Therolf, 2016a).

Disciplinary actions of various boards have included cease and desist orders, denials of an initial application for a license, reprimands, fines, license suspensions, denials of license renewal, probation, permanent license revocations, and mandated supervision for a specified period of time (Alabama State Board of Social Work Examiners, 2017; Consent Agreement between Shelley J. Ahleman and State of Ohio Counselor, Social Worker, Marriage and Family Therapist Board, 2008; Consent Agreement between Michael Wilson and State of Ohio Counselor, Social Worker, Marriage and Family Therapist Board, 2015; Lawlor, 2016a, b; *Matter of Bass*, 2017; *Matter of Currie*, 2011; *Matter of James*, 2001; Matter of King, 2011; *Matter of Nedoba*, 2013; *Matter of Tartakoff v. New York State Education Department*, 2015; Michigan Department of Community Health, 2006a, b; Michigan Department of Licensing and Regulatory Affairs, 2013; Office of the Professions, New York State Education Department, 2014; Oregon State Board of Licensed Social Workers, 2016; Parsons, 2014; Ohio Administrative Code § 4757-5-01(C), 2017; Consent Agreement between Wilson and State of Ohio Counselor, Social Worker, Marriage and Family Therapist Board, 2015; Texas Department of State Health Services, Texas State Board of Social Work Examiners, 2017; Therolf, 2016a, b). A cease and desist order may be instituted against an individual who is practicing social work without a license. Suspension refers to a withdrawal by the social work board of an individual's right to practice social work for a specified period of time (Association of Social Work Boards, 2011). A decision to place a social worker's license on probation means that the individual may continue to practice social work but only under specified conditions for a predetermined period of time. Violation of these conditions may subject the individual to additional disciplinary proceedings. As an example, a social worker whose performance has been found to be impaired due to substance use may be allowed to continue to practice with the condition that he or she participate in substance abuse treatment and file periodic reports with the board. A failure to comply with these conditions could potentially lead to license suspension or revocation. Revocation terminates the right of the individual to engage in the practice of social work.

It is important to note that board action may be in addition to any civil lawsuit or criminal proceeding that may be brought against the social worker and/or his or her employing agency or practice. Sexual relations with a client, for example, may not only constitute the basis for a complaint before the social work board but may also provide the basis for a lawsuit against the social worker and possibly his or her supervisor and/or employer, depending upon the specific circumstances (Reamer, 2015). As an example, sexual impropriety with clients represented one of the two largest claim categories against social workers processed through the NASW Insurance Trust during the period from 1969 through 1990 (Reamer, 1995), comprised almost one-third of a random sample of 300 NASW-adjudicated cases during the period from 1982 through 1992 (National Association of Social Workers, 1995), and accounted for almost three-quarters of the 147 ethics complaints to the NASW that resulted in a finding of some form of boundary violation during an 11-year period (Strom-Gottfried, 1999).

References

Alabama State Board of Social Work Examiners. (2017). Disciplinary actions. http://socialwork.alabama.gov/discipline.aspx. Accessed 26 March 2017.
Association of Social Work Boards. (2011). Guidebook for social work disciplinary actions. https://www.aswb.org/wp-content/uploads/2013/10/ASWBDisciplinaryGuidebook.pdf. Accessed 07 April 2017.
Birmingham, J., Berry, M., & Bussey, M. (1996). Certification for child protective services staff members: The Texas initiative. *Child Welfare, 75*(6), 727–740.
Cavazos, A. (2001). Baccalaureate social work licensure: Its effects on salary and use of job titles. *Journal of Baccalaureate Social Work, 6*(2), 69–80.
Cohen, M. B., & Deri, R. (1992). The dilemma of "grandparenting" in state licensure: Confronting the training needs of nondegreed workers. *Social Work, 37*(2), 155–158.
Cole, B. S. (1991). Legal issues related to social work program admissions. *Journal of Social Work Education, 27*(1), 18–24.
Cole, B. S., & Lewis, R. G. (1993). Gatekeeping through termination of unsuitable social work students: Legal issues and guidelines. *Journal of Social Work Education, 29*(2), 150–159.
Donaldson, L. P., Hill, K., Ferguson, S., Fogel, S., & Erickson, C. (2014). Contemporary social work licensure: Implications for macro social work practice and education. *Social Work, 59*(1), 52–61.
Dyeson, T. B. (2004). Social work licensure: A brief history. *Home Health Care Management & Practice, 16*(5), 408–411.
Forrest, L., Elman, N., Gizara, S., & Vacha-Haase, T. (1999). Trainee impairment: A review of identification, remediation, dismissal, and legal issues. *The Counseling Psychologist, 27*(5), 627–686.
Hahn, W. K., & Molnar, S. (1991). Intern evaluation in university counseling centers: Process, problems, and recommendations. *The Counseling Psychologist, 19*, 414–430.
Hardcastle, D. A. (1977). Public regulation of social work. *Social Work, 22*(1), 14–20.
Lawlor, J. (2016a). Portland socialworker accused of sexwith a patient to suspend his practice. *Press Herald*, July 18. https://www.pressherald.com/2016/07/18/licensing-board-reaches-approves-consent-agreement-with-portland-social-worker/. Accessed 01 May 2018.
Lawlor, J. (2016b). Social worker pleads not guilty to accusation of having sex with a client. *Press Herald*, September 7. https://www.pressherald.com/2016/09/07/social-worker-pleads-not-guilty-to-accusations-of-havin-gsex-with-a-client/. Accessed 01 May 2018.
Lawlor, J., & Byrne, M. (2016, July 12). Portland social worker practiced for months after complaint of sexual relations with client. *Portland Press Herald*. http://www.pressherald.com2016/07/12/portland-social-worker-practiced-fr-months-after-complaint-of-sexual-relations-with-client/. Accessed 26 March 2017.
Michigan Department of Community Health. (2006a). Cutlerville social worker has license summarily suspended, October 3. http://www.michigan.gov/mdhhs/0,5885,7-339-73970_71692_8347-152753--,00.html. Accessed 26 March 2017.

Michigan Department of Community Health. (2006b). Social worker's license summarily suspended, November 6. http://www.michigan.gov/som/0,4669,7-192-26847-155656--,00.html. Accessed 26 March 2017.

Michigan Department of Licensing and Regulatory Affairs. (2013). Romulus social worker summarily suspended, September 12. http://www.michigan.gov/lara/0,4601,7-154-10573_11472-312324--,00.html. Accessed 26 March 2017.

National Association of Social Workers. (1995). Study cites most-reported ethics breaches. *NASW News, 40*(4), 4.

National Association of Social Workers. (1996, 2008). Code of ethics. http://www.socialworkers.org/pubs/Code/code.asp. Accessed 07 April 2017.

New York State Education Department, Office of the Professions. (2014). Summaries of Regents actions on professional misconduct and discipline, January. http://www.op.nysed.gov/opd/January2014.htm. Accessed 26 March 2017.

Oregon State Board of Licensed Social Workers. (2016). Disciplinary action report, August 2. http://www.oregon.gov/blsw/Documents/OREGON%20BLSW%20DISCIPLINARY%20ACTION%20REPORT%20%20UPDATED%2008.02.2016.pdf. Accessed 17 April 2017.

Parsons, R. (2014, 29 October). Merced social worker charged with child molestation. *Merced Sun-Star.* http://www.mercedsunstar.com/news/local/crime/article3464137.html. Accessed 26 March 2017.

Quinn, G., & Straussner, S. L. A. (2010). Licensure and continuing education requirements for substance abuse training in social work. *Journal of Social Work Practice in the Addictions, 10*(4), 433–437.

Reamer, F. G. (1995). Malpractice claims against social workers: First facts. *Social Work, 40*(5), 595–601.

Reamer, F. G. (2015). Ethical misconduct and negligence in social work. *Social Work Today, 15*(5), 20. http://www.socialworktoday.com/archive/090915p20.shtml. Accessed 26 March 2017.

Strom-Gottfried, K. (1999). Professional boundaries: An analysis of violations by social workers. *Families in Society: The Journal of Contemporary Human Services, 80*(5), 439–449.

Strom-Gottfried, K. (2000). Ethical vulnerability in social work education. *Journal of Social Work Education, 36*(2), 241–252.

Stromwall, L. K. (2002). Is social work's door open to people recovering from psychiatric disabilities? *Social Work, 47*(1), 75–83.

Texas Department of State Health Services, Texas State Board of Social Worker Examiners Enforcement Actions. (2017, January 24). Final disciplinary actions—License denial, surrender, revocation. http://www.dshs.texas.gov/socialwork/sw_cmp.shtm. Accessed 26 March 2017.

Therolf, G. (2016a, June 2). Ruling suspends the social worker license for a man charged in an 8-year-old boy's death. *Los Angeles Times.* http://latimes.com/local/lanow/ls-me-ln-social-worker-criminal-charges-20160602-snap-story.html. Accessed 26 March 2017.

Therolf, G. (2016b, April 7). Social workers charged with child abuse in case involving torture and killing of Gabriel Fernandez, 8. *Los Angeles Times.* http://latimes.com/local/lanow/ls-me-ln-social-workers-charged-gabriel-fernandez-torture-20160407-story-html. Accessed 26 March 2017.

Zakutansky, T. J., & Sirles, E. A. (1993). Ethical and legal issues in field education: Shared responsibility and risk. *Journal of Social Work Education, 29*(3), 338–347.

Legal References

Cases

Fiore v. Bureau of Professional and Occupational Affairs, State Board of Social Workers, Marriage and Family Therapists and Professional Counselors, No. 641 C.D., Unpub. LEXIS 460 (Pa. 2011), *appeal denied*, Commonwealth v. Fiore, LEXIS 978 (Pa. 2012).
Matter of Licensure of Penny v. State of Wyoming, 120 P.3d 152 (Wyo. S. Ct. 2005).
Matter of Tartakoff v. New York State Education Department, NY Slip Op. 06276 (Appellate Div., 3d Dept. 2015).

Administrative Actions

Consent agreement between Michael Wilson and the State of Ohio Counselor, Social Worker, Marriage and Family Therapist Board, 2015. Counselor, Social Worker, & Marriage and Family Therapist Board. http://cswmft.ohio.gov/Investigations/DisciplinedLicensees.aspx. Accessed 26 March 2017.
Matter of Ahleman, (Counselor, Social Worker, & Marriage and Family Therapist Board, Ohio, 2008). http://cswmft.ohio.gov/Investigations/DisciplinedLicensees.gov. Accessed 26 March 2017.
Matter of Bass (Counselor, Social Worker, & Marriage and Family Therapist Board, Ohio, 2017). http://cswmft.ohio.gov/Investigations/DisciplinedLicensees.gov. Accessed 26 March 2017.
Matter of Currie, Case No. 10-1535 (Maryland State Bd. of Social Work Examiners 2011). Dhmh.maryland.gov/bswe/Documents/Orders/Currie-1535.pdf. Accessed 16 April 2017.
Matter of James, Final Order of Discipline (State of New Jersey, Department of Law & Public Safety, Division of Consumer Affairs, Board of Social Work Examiners 2001). http://njpublicsafety.com/ca/action/20011017_44SC01297700.pdf. Accessed 27 March 2017.
Matter of King, Recommendation of Administrative Law Judge, Case No. 10-1762C-06. (Alabama State Board of Social Work Examiners 2011). http://socialwork.alabama.gov/discipline.aspx. Accessed 26 March 2017.
Matter of Nedoba, Findings of Fact, Conclusions of Law, Decision and Order, DIA No. 12SW008 (Iowa Board of Social Work 2013). http://www.idph.state.ia.us/IDPHChannels-Service/file.ashx?file=B5221FE3-D8F1-4A02. Accessed 27 March 2017.

Statutes

Ohio Administrative Code § 4757-5-01(C) (2017).
Ohio Administrative Code § 4757-5-10(A) (2014).
Ohio Revised Code § 4757.01(C) (2014a).
Ohio Revised Code § 4757.02(B)(2) (2014b).
Ohio Revised Code § 4757.03(A)(3) (2014c).
Wyoming Statutes Annotated § 33-38-102(a)(v) (LexisNexis 2005).

Chapter 4
Liability Issues for Social Workers in the Clinical Context: An Overview

Social Work and Legal Liability

Various writers have been suggesting for decades that while social workers were, at one time, rarely sued civilly or prosecuted criminally for their actions or inactions, such claims are now more likely and are increasing in frequency (Bernstein, 1978; Berliner, 1989; Green & Cox, 1978; Kirk & Hutchins, 1988; Pollack & Marsh, 2004; Reamer, 1989, 1995, 2015; Watkins & Watkins, 1983). One writer observed in 1985:

> Social worker liability is a relatively new phenomenon. As recently as ten years ago, there were almost no lawsuits, let alone successful ones, against social workers. Since then, though, a number of changes, some in the law and some in the social work profession, have combined to increase the likelihood of lawsuits generally. (Besharov, 1985, p. 13)

An early study by Reamer (1995) using data from the NASW malpractice insurance program found that only one claim was filed in 1970, but 40 claims were filed in 1980 and, between 1969 and 1990, a total of 634 liability claims were filed, for an average of just over 30 claims per year during this period. Reamer found that claims tended to fall into two broad categories: misfeasance or malfeasance, that is, the improper performance by the social worker of his or her responsibilities (errors of commission) or their performance in a manner that was inconsistent with the requisite standard of care and nonfeasance, i.e., the social worker's failure to perform a duty that he or she would be expected to perform (errors of omission). Malfeasance claims included allegations such as sexual impropriety, breaches of confidentiality or privacy, breach of contract, and wrongful removal of a child from his or her home. Nonfeasance claims included complaints relating to failure to prevent a client's suicide, failure to diagnose properly, and failure to protect third parties from harm. Allegations of incorrect treatment and sexual impropriety accounted for almost 40% of the total number of claims (Reamer, 1995).

Potential liability can arise in a wide range of other situations that are classifiable as either malfeasance or nonfeasance. These include providing treatment without first obtaining client informed consent, defamation, abandonment, inadequate treatment, assault and battery, failure to refer the client to a specialist when necessary, failure to provide treatment, and failure to warn the client of the risk of bodily injury (Green & Cox, 1978; Reamer, 1995).

The same action or inaction may potentially give rise to either civil or criminal liability or both civil and criminal liabilities. Civil liability involves a lawsuit by a private person or entity against an individual or entity. The remedy sought in such situations is frequently a monetary payment and/or a change in procedures or policies. Criminal liability involves a decision by a government prosecutor, such as a district attorney at a local level or a US attorney at a federal level, to charge an individual or entity with a crime. If convicted of the alleged criminal offense, the offender may be required to serve time in prison or be placed on probation and/or pay a sum of money. It should be noted that a particular situation may also have implications for the social worker's ability to maintain his or her license, depending upon the nature of the social worker's action or inaction and the governing laws and regulations of a particular state, as discussed in the previous chapter in this text.

Professional Malpractice

Defining Malpractice

Malpractice is one form of negligence, that is, conduct that has fallen short of a specified standard. A successful claim for negligence must demonstrate four elements: (1) that the social worker owed a legal duty to the client; (2) that the social worker breached that duty, through either his or her action or inaction; (3) that the client suffered some harm or injury; and (4) that the social worker's omission or commission was the direct and proximate cause of the harm or injury that was suffered by the client (*Grzan v. Charter Hospital of Northwest Indiana*, 1998), meaning that the harm was caused in fact by the omission or commission and that there is a reasonable connection between the (in)action and the resulting harm (Kionka, 1999). In order to demonstrate that a claim falls within the framework of malpractice, and not ordinary negligence, the plaintiff will also have to demonstrate that (1) the claim relates to an action or inaction that arose during the course of a professional relationship and (2) the claim raises questions of judgment that are beyond that of ordinary knowledge and experience (Cf. *Bryant v. Oakpointe Villa Nursing Centre*, 2004; *Grzan v. Charter Hospital of Northwest Indiana*, 1998). For example, a client might claim that the social worker owed him the duty to inform him of the risks and benefits of a particular modality of treatment; the social worker breached that duty by failing to advise him of the risks associated with a particular form of therapy; the client suffered a deterioration in his emotional and mental state; and the social worker's failure to inform him of the risks associated with that particular modality and to obtain actual informed consent was the direct and proximate cause of his deterioration.

The satisfaction by the plaintiff—the individual seeking the remedy—of each of these elements will be a question for the judge or jury to decide. The social worker's actions or inactions will be judged against the standard of care demanded of social workers in such circumstances. Although the specifics of the standard of care may vary across legal jurisdictions, cases involving medical malpractice suggest that the standard of care is that which "an ordinarily prudent person would use under the circumstances for the discharge of the duty ..." (*St. John v. Pope,* 1995, p. 422). Accordingly, the standard to assess the existence of malpractice would be that which an ordinarily prudent social worker would use under the circumstances to discharge his or her duty in that situation. An Indiana case involving social worker malpractice suggested that the social worker's actions be examined as to whether the social worker had exercised "the degree of care, skill, and proficiency" that a "reasonably careful, skillful, and prudent" social worker would utilize under similar circumstances (*Grzan v. Charter Hospital of Northwest Indiana,* 1998, p. 790).

Treatment Selection and the Standard of Care

In some situations, a social worker might use a more "radical" form of treatment. The forms of treatment that might be deemed "radical" likely vary by time and place. Regardless of what the specific form may be, it is imperative that the social worker explain all associated risks and benefits to the client and advise the client of possible alternative treatments in obtaining client consent prior to initiating the treatment. One scholar explained:

> The method of treatment does not have to be one thought to be best by the majority. It is enough that it is accepted by a respected minority. But still, departure from standard practice must be justified. (Tarshis, 1972, p. 85)

It is theoretically possible that the increasing emphasis by third-party payers on the use of evidence-based therapies may lead to increased questioning about the use of therapeutic modalities that are not considered to be evidence-based. It is important, therefore, to understand what is meant by an evidence-based treatment.

In psychology, evidence-based practice refers to "the integration of the best available research with clinical expertise in the context of patient characteristics, culture, and preferences" (APA Presidential Task Force on Evidence-Based Practice, 2006, p. 273). The definition closely resembles the definition of evidence-based practice in the field of medicine: "the integration of best research evidence with clinical expertise and patient values" (Institute of Medicine, 2001, p. 147). In social work, it has been:

> thought of as a process undertaken by professionals wherein the scientific status of potential interventions is investigated and a thorough explication of the results is shared with clients, so that practitioner and client together can select the most appropriate steps for addressing a specific problem. (Edmond, Megivern, Williams, Richman, & Howard, 2006, p. 377)

Evidence-based practice has been proffered as an alternative to the provision of services based solely on a practitioner's own expertise or experience (Gambrill, 2003; Gibbs & Gambrill, 2002). The evidence that is used to evaluate any treatment for a specific disorder is assessed with respect to its efficacy—the strength of the causal relationship between the treatment/intervention and the specific disorder—and the clinical utility of the intervention: the generalizability, feasibility, costs, and benefits of the specific intervention (APA Presidential Task Force on Evidence-Based Practice, 2006).

The concept of evidence-based practice is related to, but broader than, the concept of empirically supported treatment. First, evidence-based practice considers numerous clinical functions, such as assessment, intervention, and others, whereas the concept of empirically supported treatments focuses on psychological interventions that have been examined in controlled trials and have been found to be effective. Second, evidence-based practice looks at existing research to determine what can be used to obtain the best outcome for a particular patient. That body of research includes the results obtained through clinical observation, qualitative research, systematic case studies, single-case experimental designs, public health research, ethnographic research, process-outcome studies, intervention studies, randomized clinical trials, and meta-analyses. The strength and limitations of the evidence obtained from each of these types of evidence must be evaluated to reach a conclusion. The concept of empirically supported treatments asks whether a specific intervention is effective for a particular diagnosis under specific circumstances (APA Presidential Task Force on Evidence-Based Practice, 2006).

The evaluation of the strength of the available evidence for a particular modality for use with a specific diagnosis may vary across panels of professionals (Feinstein & Horwitz, 1997). Additionally, the evaluation of the research evidence does not consider the priorities and preferences of the individual client, the feasibility of using the particular intervention with a specific individual, or the responsiveness of the client to an intervention over time (APA Presidential Task Force on Evidence-Based Practice, 2006; Feinstein & Horwitz, 1997).

The Australian Psychological Society's (2010) literature review of evidence-based psychological interventions in the treatment of mental disorders provides an example of how evidence-based practice might be used. The literature review evaluates the evidence supporting the use of a particular intervention for specific diagnoses. The source of the research evidence is rated on a scale from I, signifying the systematic review of randomized clinical trials, considered the most reliable form of evidence, to IV, referring to a case series, the least stringent approach to research. The literature review concluded that the use of cognitive behavior therapy for a diagnosis of depression is supported by Level I evidence, whereas there is insufficient evidence available to support the use of narrative therapy for dissociative disorders (Australian Psychological Society, 2010). This lack of adequate evidence does not mean, however, that narrative therapy is either ineffective or contraindicated for the treatment of dissociative disorders; it merely means that this modality has not been subjected to rigorous empirical testing for this disorder. It cannot be assumed to be either effective or ineffective. Clearly, a large "gray zone" exists with respect to some modalities and their use with a variety of disorders (Naylor, 1995).

Whether a specific evidence-based practice is appropriate for a particular client requires the exercise of clinical judgment and an examination of the associated ethical issues (Stalker, 2003; Taylor & White, 2001). This evaluation may be even more rigorous when contemplating the use of a therapeutic intervention for which there is relatively little empirical evidence or only "lower" level empirical evidence available to establish its efficacy.

As an example, there is relatively strong research evidence supporting the use of cognitive behavior therapy for the treatment of depression in adult clients (Australian Psychological Society, 2010). However, this conclusion is based on the "average" client that participated in the studies that constitute the basis of that conclusion (cf. Feinstein & Horwitz, 1997). Whether a therapist should use that modality with a particular client is going to depend—or should depend—not only on an understanding of the benefits of that intervention but also the underlying assumptions and the limitations of the intervention, the client's preferences, whether that intervention has been utilized previously with the client, and, if it has been, whether its use was successful or counterproductive. The therapist must monitor the client's progress during the course of treatment with this intervention and, if inadequate improvement is forthcoming, adapt the treatment, seek supervision, and/or refer the client for other services or to another therapist. Utilization of cognitive behavior therapy presupposes that a client has the cognitive capacity to engage, is developmentally capable, and has a mental health presentation which is accepting of cognitive approaches and that the therapist is cognizant of new implications in neuropsychotherapy for "talking therapies."

As an example of a therapy that might ultimately lead to a claim of malpractice, consider the use of conversion therapy with a client who self-identifies as homosexual or gay. Perhaps the social worker believes that the client's anxiety and depression result not from his family's refusal to accept his sexual orientation but from his sexual orientation itself. If the social worker were to initiate a course of conversion therapy to alter the client's sexual orientation to one of heterosexuality, he or she would be obligated to advise the client that there have been no scientifically rigorous studies to date that have established the efficacy of the intervention and that various professional associations of mental health providers have decried the intervention because it rests on the presumption that homosexuality is a developmental arrest, a severe form of psychopathology, or a combination of both (American Psychiatric Association, 2000; American Psychological Association, n.d.), in essence, that homosexuality is deviant. It would also be important to explore with the client the potential beneficial effects of conversion therapy; whether the anticipated beneficial effects of conversion therapy can be achieved by other means; the potential adverse effects of such an intervention, such as poor self-esteem, depression, social withdrawal, sexual dysfunction, de-masculinization, and celibacy (Haldeman, 2001); and whether the therapist is the appropriate provider to furnish this intervention. Whether the client should be provided with a listing of available resources related to conversion therapy raises serious ethical issues, since conversion therapy itself may be unethical in many or most situations.

Internet-Based Services and Malpractice

Traditionally, diagnostic assessments, counseling, and therapy have been provided by social workers in a face-to-face relationship with clients (McCarty & Clancy, 2002). The supervision or consultation process has also customarily occurred in a face-to-face relationship between the supervising mental health-care provider and the supervisee. As technology has developed and professionals' comfort level with it has increased, technological means, such as telephone and fax, have been utilized to augment this relationship (VandenBos & Williams, 2000).

These delivery methods have now been expanded to include a broad range of technological mechanisms that utilize the Internet for information-gathering regarding mental health issues, for participation in self-help groups in chat rooms and via videoteleconferencing, for the exchange of information via e-mail, to complete computer-based diagnostic assessments, for e-therapy, and for cybertherapy (Banach & Barnat, 2000; Manhal-Baugus, 2001; Reamer, 2013).[1] Mental health-care providers, including social workers, utilize various forms of electronic media to communicate with their colleagues for the purpose of seeking advice regarding a particular situation, a particular client, or as part of an ongoing supervisory-consultative relationship. In addition, electronic media are often used to communicate with social workers' students, supervisees, and members of the public who may or may not be considered clients, depending upon the particular circumstances of the communications (Banach & Barnat, 2000; McCarty & Clancy, 2002; Parkinson & Loue, 2015)[2] In all likelihood, this reliance on the Internet for the provision and receipt of mental health services is likely to increase in the future in view of the widespread use of the Internet itself. It has been estimated that 34.3% of individuals worldwide and 77% of adult Americans now utilize electronic mechanisms for communication (Internet World Stats, 2013; Pew Research Center, 2014).

---

[1] E-therapy has been defined as:

> the process of interacting with a therapist online in ongoing conversations over time when the client and counselor are in separate or remote locations and utilize electronic means to communicate with each other .... a licensed mental health care professional providing mental health services via e-mail, video conferencing, virtual reality technology, chat technology or any combination of these. It does not include self-help methods such as public bulletin boards or private listservs. E-therapy is not psychotherapy or psychological counseling per se since it does to [sic] presume to diagnose or treat mental or medical disorders. (Manhal-Baugus, 2001, pp. 551, 552)

Services offered in this context are said to include advice, i.e., the provision of concrete, specific information in response to an individual's well-defined issue, and e-therapy, which involves the formation of a relationship with a trained counselor (Manhal-Baugus, 2001). Cybertherapy encompasses the provision of individual or group counseling services through the use of avatars (digitally generated graphic images) in a virtual therapy room (Reamer, 2013).

[2] For a detailed discussion of the ethical issues associated with the use of cybersupervision, see Parkinson and Loue (2015).

The use of the Internet for the provision of social work-related services, such as counseling and psychoeducation, offers numerous advantages. Clients can access services more easily, a particular advantage for those who reside in geographic areas with few practicing social workers. The Internet also provides a mechanism for clients to overcome other barriers in their efforts to obtain services, e.g., limited transportation, physical disability limiting access, agoraphobia, caregiving responsibilities, and schedules that demand frequent travel and preclude regular face-to-face meetings (Childress, 1998; Lebow, 1998). It has also been suggested that, because some forms of Internet-based communication do not reveal the participants' age, sex, sexual orientation, and physical characteristics, this modality equalizes to a greater degree the power relationship that exists between the provider and the client (Giffords, 1998).

However, reliance on Internet-mediated communications alone for the provision of social work services, such as diagnosis, assessment, counseling, and therapy, also creates malpractice risk. Interactive text-based communications, such as e-mail, are devoid of the nonverbal cues that might give a social worker pause to consider that something might be amiss or awry with a client (Childress, 2000). It may be more difficult for the social worker providing client services solely online to assess the benefit of such services and the need to refer the client elsewhere, raising the issue of inadequate or improper treatment. It may also be more difficult to determine whether a client is experiencing a crisis that would demand an immediate intervention and how that intervention might be effectuated and by whom. This may be a particular difficulty if the social worker is practicing online across various geographic localities. In addition, the social worker contemplating the provision of online services must evaluate whether practice with this modality is within or beyond their scope of practice; the provision of Internet-based services demands a level of competence with not only the content of the approach but the mechanics of the approach as well, which are adequate to address the needs of the clients who engage the service.

The ethical standards adopted by both the National Association of Social Workers and the Association of Social Work Boards (2005) reflect this requirement. Standard 3 provides, "Social workers shall select and develop appropriate online methods, skills, and techniques that are attuned to their clients' cultural, bicultural, or marginalized experiences" (National Association of Social Workers and Association of Social Work Boards, 2005). Standard 4 specifies that social workers:

> [s]hall select and develop appropriate online methods, skills, and techniques that are attuned to their clients' cultural, bicultural, or marginalized experiences in their environments. in their environments. (National Association of Social Workers and Association of Social Work Boards, 2005)

Supervisory Liability

Supervisors may be potentially liable for the actions and inactions of those they supervise under the doctrine of *respondeat superior* (*Currier v. Doran,* 2001). The potential for such liability could arise in situations in which the supervisor fails to adequately supervise his or her supervisee(s) and the supervisee inappropriately divulges confidential client information, fails to conduct an adequate assessment, fails to diagnose or misdiagnoses a client's condition, implements a deficient treatment plan, fails to refer the client to a specialist when warranted, fails to adequately document the client's record, fails to warn third parties of a threat of harm, engages in inappropriate physical or sexual contact with a client, or maintains a dual relationship with the client. A court may find that a supervisor-supervisee relationship exists in situations in which the supervisee is under the direct supervision of the supervisor, such as in the case of a regularly employed social worker who reports to a clinical supervisor; in situations in which the supervising social worker delegates responsibility to an unlicensed assistant, such as a student intern working under a social work supervisor in states that do not require students fulfilling their field work requirement to hold a license as a student intern; and in situations in which the supervisor relies on an employee that is not usually under his or her supervision. In some situations, an agency may be found liable for the negligent acts of those serving not as supervisees but as independent contractors (*Vonner v. State of Louisiana,* 1973).

Liability exposure may be elevated for social work supervisors who provide distance supervision via the Internet. Admittedly, such distance supervision, also known as cybersupervision (Parkinson & Loue, 2015), may be critical for some supervisees. Social workers who are practicing in geographic areas that are relatively isolated or in which there are no other providers trained in a specific therapeutic modality may need to look far afield to identify a colleague who can provide competent supervision (cf. Schank, 1998). The Internet may facilitate the receipt of supervision from a provider with greater familiarity with the client's culture or an understanding of the client's primary language than would otherwise be obtainable and that may be critical to the provision of competent care (cf. Kanz, 2001).

E-mail, chat rooms, and instant messaging, unlike televideoconferencing, do not require face-to-face contact between the supervisor and the supervisee. These mechanisms may, therefore, provide the supervisor, supervisee, or both with a sense of psychological safety (cf. Zuboff, 1988). It has been suggested that "reading and writing through e-mail may involve a unique personal mechanism that facilitates self-disclosure, ventilation, and externalization of problems and conflicts and that promotes self-awareness" (Barak, 1999, p. 237). Additional benefits attributed to the use of e-mail include the individual's disinhibition (Joinson, 1998), thereby facilitating greater disclosure of personal feelings and issues (Stebnicki & Glover, 2001), an increase in supervisee reflectivity (Clingerman & Bernard, 2004), and an increased sense of support among supervisees (Stebnicki & Glover, 2001).

Notwithstanding these apparent benefits, this approach may heighten the supervisor's potential liability. He or she must rely on the representations of the supervisee to assess the appropriateness of the diagnostic assessment, treatment approach, and/or client termination. It must be taken by the supervisor on trust that any records transmitted electronically for their review represent all of the records and that nothing has been omitted. Cues that would potentially be available to a supervisor physically present in the same physical location as the supervisee that might suggest that something is amiss (or not) in the supervisee-client relationship are not available to the distance supervisor. Ultimately, whether a supervisor or employer may ultimately be found liable for negligent supervision will often turn on whether he or she knew or should have known of the supervisee's misconduct or whether he or she was deliberately indifferent to or tacitly approved of practice that led to the client's harm (*Grzan v. Charter Hospital of Northwest Indiana,* 1998; *M.R. v Cox,* 1994).

A summary of common grounds of social worker liability, together with legal references, is presented in Table 4.1 below. Each type of claim is explained in additional detail in the sections that follow.

Unintentional and Intentional Torts

Many legal actions against social workers fall under the broad umbrella of "tort." A tort has been defined as:

> a civil wrong, wherein one person's conduct causes a compensable injury to the person, property, or recognized interest of another, in violation of a duty imposed by law. (Kionka, 1999, p. 4)

These actions are predicated on the belief that individuals who have suffered a loss as the result of another's (in)actions should be compensated for the harm that was brought about; that fairness demands that the cost of the loss be imposed on those that caused it, if identifiable; and that by holding individuals accountable for wrongdoing, individuals will modify their behavior accordingly (Kionka, 1999). In some instances, the commission of a tort may be unintentional, while in others, the wrongdoer may have intended to either engage in the behavior that caused the harm or to bring about the harmful result.

Breach of Confidentiality/Privacy

Violations of client confidentiality and privacy by the social worker may occur either intentionally or unintentionally. A social worker may publicly disclose private facts about a client, such as by carrying on a conversation with a colleague about a client in the building elevator, not realizing that he or she has communicated

Table 4.1 Summary of common grounds for social worker civil liability[a]

Nature of claim	Definition	Reference/example
Assault and battery	Assault: "intentionally putting another person in reasonable apprehension of an imminent harmful or offensive contact" (Legal Information Institute, n.d.) Battery: the intentional causation of a harmful or offensive contact with another person without that person's consent	Ringstad (2005)
Breach of confidentiality	The disclosure of confidential information not in the public domain by an individual with a duty to keep the information confidential without the consent of and to the detriment of the confider of the information	*MacDonald v. Clinger*, 446 N.Y.S.2d 801 (Sup. Ct. 1982)
Breach of contract	Requires, in general, the existence of a valid contract, a breach of the duty imposed by the contract, and damages	*Martino v. Family Services Agency of Adams County*, 445 N.E.2d 6 (Ill. Ct. App. 1982).
Defamation	Communication of a false statement that harms an individual, group, corporation, or business. When the statement is made in writing, the alleged wrong is slander; when the communication is made orally, the alleged wrong is libel	
Duty/failure to warn	Duty to warn a third party arises where a client makes an identifiable threat to a specific individual and disclosure of that information is necessary to prevent the threatened harm and supersedes therapist obligation to maintain confidentiality in such circumstances	*Tarasoff v. Regents of the University of California*, 17 Cal. 3d 425 (1976). Application varies across states due to statute and/or court interpretation
Negligent infliction of emotional distress	The defendant acted negligently in such a way as to cause some kind of physical contact OR the plaintiff was in the zone of danger of the defendant's actions OR it was reasonably foreseeable that the negligent act would cause harm AND the emotional harm was so severe that it caused physical symptoms. The specific requirements for negligent infliction of emotional distress vary across states	
Negligent supervision	Based on legal doctrine of *respondeat superior*, through which the supervisor is responsible for the actions or inactions of those who he or she supervises in the course of their employment	*Tylena M. v. Heartshare Children's Services*, 390 F. Supp. 22d 296 (S.D.N.Y. 2005)

[a]The specific elements required to establish a successful claim for each named action vary across states due to differences in state statutes and judicial decisions

information sufficient for bystanders to identify the person who is the subject of the conversation. Social workers providing services to individuals within a family and to the family as a whole may inadvertently or intentionally disclose information to one family member that was communicated confidentially to him or her by another family member (e.g., *Martino v. Family Service Agency of Adams County,* 1981). The provision by a social worker of his or her clinical notes without client consent in response to a subpoena, under the mistaken belief that it is equivalent to a court order, may result in those notes being used against a client in a divorce or custody proceeding. Written and computer records may be accessed if they have been misplaced and cannot be found (*Penny v. State of Wyoming,* 2005) or they have not been appropriately safeguarded with locked cabinets or passworded computers and strict limitations on others' access to the records.

The provision of services electronically, regardless of the specific modality utilized, presents unique challenges in safeguarding client confidentiality and privacy. Text messages and e-mails can be hacked or inadvertently misdirected to the wrong individual. Digitized recordings retained as part of a client's electronic health record can be surreptitiously intercepted as they are being made and/or later accessed and re-recorded or disseminated to others.

As an example of conduct that might lead one to believe that a breach of confidentiality was not only careless but may have been intentional, consider a situation in which a social worker fails to maintain his or her written client records in a locked cabinet in a locked office; does not password his or her computer; does not use encryption software for electronic transmissions; does not close the door to the office when discussing clients' status with other employees and/or discusses clients' status in public spaces; does not place any advisory about confidentiality in his or her e-mails to clients; and has never advised his or her clients of the risks associated with the use of Internet communications for counseling services.

Fraud

Allegations of fraud may be raised in various contexts, such as in providing services and in seeking reimbursement for services. The establishment of fraud would require a showing that the social worker withheld or misrepresented information that he or he was under a duty to disclose; that the withheld or misrepresented information was material to the issue at hand; that the social worker knew the information to be false or had conscious disregard for its truth or falsity; that the information was conveyed with the intention that the other party would rely on it; and that the party receiving the information did, in fact, rely upon it to their detriment (*Burr v. Board of County Commissioners,* 1986).

The legal case of *Burr v. Board of County Commissioners* illustrates the circumstances under which a social worker might be found liable for fraud. This case involved the adoption of an infant by the Burr family, through the county adoption agency. The social worker represented to the family that the infant had been born to a teenage mother who had been unable to care for the 17-month-old infant and that he was a healthy baby. Following the adoption, the child developed numerous physical and mental health problems and was ultimately diagnosed with Huntington's disease, a genetic disorder that leads to the destruction of the central nervous system. His adoptive parents obtained a court order to unseal the child's records and learned, as a result, that he had actually been born in a state mental hospital during his 30-year old mother's hospitalization there. The Burrs prevailed in their lawsuit that alleged wrongful adoption and were awarded funds to cover the child's medical expenses.

Misdiagnosis may be due to negligence and constitute malpractice. Alternatively, misdiagnosis may be a deliberate effort by the provider to underdiagnose a client's condition to reduce the possibility that the client will later experience stigmatization as a result of the diagnosis or, conversely, an effort to overdiagnose the client in order to receive a greater reimbursement from a third-party payer and/or to assist the client in obtaining any third-party reimbursement (Kirk & Hutchins, 1988). In either case, the action reflects knowledge of the falsity of the information provided and an intent to mislead the recipient of the information. While the misdiagnosis is potentially helpful to the client in obtaining coverage or reducing the likelihood of stigmatization, reliance on the misrepresentation is damaging to the third-party payer in that it increases its liability for the services rendered beyond what had been agreed to as part of the health insurance contract.

Breach of Contract

A successful action for breach of contract requires that the plaintiff demonstrate that a valid contract existed, that the contract established a particular duty, that the defendant breached a duty that existed under the contract, and that the plaintiff was harmed. It appears that relatively few lawsuits against social workers for breach of contract have been successful. As an example, a Georgia court concluded that an agency had not breached a contract where it was claimed that the agency had promised the plaintiffs that they would not experience entanglements in the adoption process (*Moore v. Department of Human Resources,* 1996). However, a breach may be found in situations in which there is an implicit promise of confidentiality and the social worker reveals confidential information without client authorization (*Martino v. Family Service Agency of Adams County,* 1982).

Federal Claims: Violations of Civil Rights and Constitutional Claims

Section 1983 of title 42 of the US Code allows an aggrieved individual to being a legal action against any "person who, under color of any statute, ordinance, regulation, custom, or usage, of any State ... subjects, or causes to be subjected, any ... person within the jurisdiction thereof to the deprivation of any rights, privileges, or immunities secured by the Constitution and laws" (42 US.C. § 1983, 2015). Accordingly, to be successful on this basis, the plaintiff must prove that (1) the person performing the action did so under color of law, and (2) the action resulted in the deprivation of a federal right, e.g., violation of a constitutionally guaranteed right or violation of rights secured by a federal statute, such as the Americans with Disabilities Act (42 U.S.C.A. § 12102, 2002).

A social worker may be found to be a state actor if he or she is employed by a state government agency and is responsible for carrying out a public function and is paid with public funds. The case of *Schaefer v. Wilcock* (1987) involved a social worker in private practice who conducted psychological assessments of applicants for state trooper positions for the state of Utah. Because of her role for the state of Utah, she could be considered to be a state actor for the purposes of a section 1983 action. Lawsuits have been maintained for violations of constitutional or other federal rights in situations involving the Fourteenth Amendment due process right of children in foster care to be protected from harm (*Marisol v. Giuliani*, 1996; *Phelan v. Torres*, 2005); the due process right of parent to a prompt hearing following the removal of a child (*B.S. v. Somerset County*, 2013); the due process right of parents not to be subjected to criminal charges based on government-fabricated evidence (*Haldeman v. Golden*, 2008); and the deprivation of equal protection based on sexual orientation (*Zavatsky v. Anderson*, 2001).

The situations in which a public employer may be found liable under section 1983 for the actions of its social worker employee are extremely limited. As one court explained:

> Supervisory responsibility may be assigned under section 1983 when citizens 'face a pervasive and unreasonable risk of harm from some specified source and the supervisor's corrective inaction amounts to deliberate indifference or tacit authorization of the offensive practices' ... To succeed, a plaintiff must show 1) 'actual or constructive knowledge of a risk of constitutional injury;' 2) 'deliberate indifference to that risk;' and 3) 'an "affirmative causal link" between the supervisor's inaction and the particular constitutional injury suffered by the plaintiff.' (*Loughlin et al. v. Vance County Department of Social Services*, 2015. See also *Phelan v. Torres*, 2005)

The plaintiffs must establish the existence of an official policy or custom that is attributable to the municipality and that is the proximate cause of the deprivation of their rights. Neither the employment of the wrongdoer alone nor the occurrence of a single incident is sufficient to establish liability of the municipality (*Loughlin v. Vance County Department of Social Services*, 2015).

The Legal Process Simplified

Civil Lawsuits

A lawsuit against a social worker and/or his or her agency or practice firm is commenced by the filing of a complaint in court. Malpractice claims are almost uniformly filed in state court. Claims that involve solely federal law, such as a claim that is based on a violation of a federal constitutional right, may be filed in either state or federal court.

In all cases, the client must specify in his or her complaint the relevant facts and state a cause of action, that is, the legal basis for the lawsuit, as well as the remedy being sought. The complaint must be filed within the period of time specified by the relevant state law for the filing of such actions, which is often several years after the client knew or should have known of the alleged harm. This period of time, known as the statute of limitations, varies depending upon the state and the basis of the claim, e.g., whether it is for breach of contract or for malpractice. In most cases, the plaintiff will be precluded from filing the complaint after the specified period of time. The social worker and/or his or her agency or practice group will then have an opportunity to file an answer, in which the facts and allegations set forth by the plaintiff may be admitted or denied.

There is a period of discovery prior to settlement efforts or proceeding to trial. Various mechanisms can be employed during this period of time to gather information from the adversarial party. Table 4.2 provides a summary of the most common discovery mechanisms that might be used in a civil lawsuit against a social worker. In situations in which the parties are unable to agree on a settlement and the case proceeds to trial, all of the information obtained during the period of discovery can be used at trial.

It is important that social workers understand the difference between a court order and a subpoena. A court clerk or an attorney may issue a subpoena to demand that the social worker release information. In some situations, the social worker's disclosure of

Table 4.2 Summary of discovery mechanisms

Mechanism	Definition
Deposition	Questioning of the plaintiff, defendant, or other individual by the attorney for the opposing side. This is done under oath and the procedure is recorded. The resulting record may be used later in court in an effort to demonstrate inconsistencies in the individual's account of what happened or to discredit him or her in some other way. Expert witnesses to be called by one party in the lawsuit may be deposed by the attorney for the opposite side in an effort to determine whether their testimony can later be challenged on some basis at the time of trial
Interrogatories	Written questions directed to the plaintiff by the defendant's attorney and to the defendant by the plaintiff's attorney, to be answered in writing. Unlike depositions, interrogatories can be asked of only the parties to the lawsuit, i.e., the plaintiff(s) and the defendant(s)
Request for production of documents	Each party (plaintiff and defendant) to the litigation can seek production of relevant documents that it believes are being held by the other party. Examples include billing statements, clinical notes, calendars, records of phone calls made, and medical and hospital records

information in response to such a subpoena may itself constitute a breach of confidentiality. For example, a client may not be bringing an action against the social worker but may be seeking a divorce. The opposing spouse wishes to access the client's social work records in order to garner evidence supporting his or her request for sole custody of the children. In such a situation, the release of the information in response to the subpoena would likely constitute a breach of confidentiality. The better course of action would be for the social worker to contact the client so that the client has an opportunity to object to the disclosure and the social worker should seek a protective order from the court (cf. United States Department of Health and Human Services, n.d.). Even if a court issues an order requiring the disclosure of information, the social worker should request—generally through a lawyer that the social worker hires—that the court reconsider the order and limit the scope of the order or, alternatively, that the judge first view the records prior to requiring their release to ensure their relevance.

In a malpractice action, the plaintiff must provide evidence to support each of the elements of negligence and malpractice. He or she bears the burden of proof to demonstrate by a preponderance of the evidence that the social worker failed to adhere to the relevant standard of care. In general, in situations in which a client is suing a social worker for malpractice, the social worker may disclose the records as part of his or her defense against the lawsuit, e.g., if the client is claiming that the social worker caused harm due to an omission, the records may be introduced to establish that there was no such claimed omission.

Criminal Prosecution

As previously indicated, in some cases, the (in)action being complained of by the client as the basis for malpractice may also serve as the basis for an effort to bring a criminal case against the social worker. As an example, a child might sue a social worker through a court appointed guardian for malpractice premised on the social worker's alleged physical or sexual abuse of the child and the district attorney might seek to prosecute the social worker criminally for the abuse. A social worker who deliberately misdiagnoses a client's condition in order to receive greater reimbursement from the insurance company might be sued by the client for malpractice and could also face criminal charges for insurance fraud (See Kirk & Hutchins, 1988).

Social workers have been convicted for such crimes as sexual abuse of a minor (Di Marzo, 2015; Gomez, 2016), theft of public funds (United States Department of Justice, 2014), and felony Medicaid fraud (Cunningham, 2005). At the time of this writing, news reports indicate that social workers are facing criminal charges for such crimes as involuntary manslaughter, child abuse, and falsification of public records (Allen, 2016; Etehad & Winton, 2017). The charges of child abuse and manslaughter have resulted from their alleged gross negligence in the torture and deaths of children on their caseloads.

It is beyond the scope of this text to review all such cases and the underlying law that may support such charges, as the requisite elements required to establish the commission of these crimes varies across states. Because these are criminal charges, the government is held to a standard of proof far greater than what is required, for example, for a plaintiff to prevail in a malpractice action; the government must present sufficient evidence to convince the jury or judge that the defendant social is guilty beyond a reasonable doubt.

Strategies to Manage Risk and Reduce Potential Liability

Risk is both complex and multifaceted (Stalker, 2003), involving individuals, groups, and systems. Risk management is effectuated through "processes devised by organizations to minimize negative outcomes which can arise in the delivery of … services" (Gurney, 2000, p. 300), requiring a focus on seven key questions:

- The extent to which focus should be placed on the proactive anticipation and avoidance of specific risks versus the development of general resilience to unexpected crises
- The extent to which the focus should be on blame or on the creation of a culture supportive of learning
- The extent to which risk should be assessed by quantitative or qualitative approaches
- The extent to which application of an orthodox engineering approach is appropriate to the design of a complex socio-technical system
- The costs associated with reducing risk and the nature of those costs, as weighed against other competing goals and risks
- The extent to which others, in terms of both group size and composition, should participate in decisionmaking processes
- Whether the appropriate target should be framed in terms of outcomes, processes, or both (Hood, Jones, Pidgeon, Turner, & Gibson, 1992)

It has been suggested that the current focus on the use of evidence-based practices is an attempt to manage risk by preventing practitioners from:

> making bad decisions based on gut feelings or common sense rather than objective, dispassionate ones based on careful appraisal of the evidence and recourse to broader, research-based generalizations about problems and effective solutions. In effect, this present a simple dichotomy between head and heart, with head very definitely privileged at best.... (Taylor & White, 2001, p. 40)

Indeed, although research can help social workers analyze the risks of a particular situation and identify the potential harms, in many situations, the social worker must ultimately decide which facts are relevant to the situation and how to interpret and apply them to issues that may be raised. In short, they must often use their best judgment to minimize potential harm and risk and be prepared to justify their decision and actions at a later date if called into question (Taylor & White, 2001).

Table 4.3 summarizes the broad range mechanisms that have been suggested as mechanisms that can be implemented in order to reduce risks to clients and the risk of liability for the social work practitioner.

Adequate documentation is critical to reduce potential risks to clients and the risk of individual and agency/practice liability for the social worker. Documentation

Table 4.3 Summary of suggested risk management strategies

Domain of risk	Risk management strategy	References
Malpractice	• Carefully documented files, e.g., notes regarding all phone calls, messages, and sessions, avoiding too much or too little detail • Clearly documented advisories to the client regarding expectations of what is expected • Avoidance of representations relating to guaranteed specific outcomes • Arranging for adequate coverage if unavailable • Obtaining appropriate supervision or consultation • Avoidance of practice outside of one's areas of training and experience • Awareness of and sensitivity to regional and cultural variations that may be relevant to diagnosis and treatment approach • Verification of state licensing, e.g., if providing services electronically across state or national borders • Development and implementation of systems to ensure appropriate turnaround time for messages, backups for electronically maintained records, forwarding of messages, coverage when away • Assessment of client safety and development with client of safety plan, e.g., if client is in a physically threatening situation • Increased knowledge of legal duties, liability law, negligence, and malpractice through ongoing continuing education efforts • Establishment of office procedures and periodic review of adequacy of office forms and procedures • Development and implementation of suicide prevention protocols • Regular review of cases with supervisees and supervision practices	Banach and Barnat (2000); McCarty and Clancy (2002); Reamer (1989, 1995, 2005, 2013). Cf. Kopels and Gustavsson (1996); Madden (2000)
Informed consent	• Verification of client identity • Specification of what can be assessed without a comprehensive medical evaluation • Provision to client of complete information relating to risks and benefits associated with suggested approach, as well as treatment alternatives	Banach and Barnat (2000); Reamer (2000, 2005)
Confidentiality and privacy	• Encryption technology for electronic transmissions, e.g., e-mails • Scramblers for teleconferencing • Use of a virtual private network (VPN) for electronic transmissions • Passworded computers • Screen savers • Avoidance of disclosures of identifying information whenever possible • Locked file cabinets • Locked office doors when not in use • Closed office doors when in conference or discussion with or about a client	Banach and Barnat (2000); McCarty and Clancy (2002); Reamer (2000, 2005, 2013)

is needed in six specific domains: assessment and planning; service delivery; continuity and continuation of services; evaluation of services; and relationships demanding accountability, e.g., third-party payers, clients, the legal system, and peer review bodies (Reamer, 2003). There is an adage in law that if something is not in writing, it didn't happen and doesn't exist.

Social workers must be cognizant of the content of their documentation, the language and terminology used, the credibility of their statements and the documentation itself, and who may have access to the documentation (Reamer, 2005). Documentation relating to the provision of clinical services should include a social history of the client; assessments conducted; treatment plans developed; client contacts; consultations with other professionals; decisions made and the basis for such decisions; referrals made; appointments that were kept, canceled, or rescheduled; any psychiatric, psychological, or medical evaluations; fees charged and payments made; arrangements for the termination of services; and the final assessment (Reamer, 2005). Supervision sessions that relate to a specific client should also be documented in the client file. As one attorney has noted, "Inadequate notes leave the clinician at the mercy of a plaintiff's attorney, especially when he is asked years later to recall an event that is poorly documented, if at all" (Gould, 1998, p. 345).

However, social workers should be especially careful in their decisionmaking regarding the content and the language to be used in documenting their services to families and couples (Reamer, 2005). There is always a possibility that one party in the family or couple will later bring a legal action against the other, e.g., in a divorce or custody proceeding, and the social worker will be required by the court to provide a copy of his or her records. Inappropriate word choice or over- or underdocumentation may lead to adverse consequences for one of the parties and an ensuing legal action against the social worker. Untrue or exaggerated written statements relating to one of the parties, e.g., a deliberate overdiagnosis in order to obtain third-party reimbursement for services, may lead to a claim of slander. Such a claim could be successful if the client-plaintiff were able to demonstrate that the social worker knew or should have known that the statement contained in the documentation was untrue and the client was harmed as a result.

Notes should be recorded as soon after a session or event as possible. First, the social worker's memory may fade, even after a relatively short period of time due to the constant influx of information. Events or exchanges relevant to one client may become confused with another client and key details may be inadvertently omitted. Additionally, the timing of the notetaking has legal significance; notes taken contemporaneously with an event are considered to be more trustworthy than notes recorded at a later time (Barsky & Gould, 2002).

Reamer (2000) has suggested that practitioners conduct periodic ethics audits as a risk management strategy. In conducting the audit, each item can be assigned to one of four risk categories: no risk, in that current practices are acceptable and no changes are required; minimal risk, indicating that current practices are adequate and would require only minor revisions; moderate risk, suggesting that current practices are problematic and require attention; or high risk, indicating the existence of serious deficiencies and the need for significant revisions. Table 4.4 provides a listing of suggested domains and topics of focus.

Table 4.4 Domains and topics for ethics audit

Domain	Topics
Client rights	Practitioner/agency policies and procedures relating to confidentiality, privacy, and disclosure of information Policy and procedures related to access to and copies of records Rights regarding refusal of services Policies and procedures relating to termination of services Grievance processes
Informed consent	Procedures utilized to obtain informed consent, e.g., from whom, by whom, under what circumstances Documentation of informed consent Risks and benefits associated with treatment approach Alternative treatments Fees and schedules of payments
Confidentiality and privacy	Policies and procedures regarding release of information, e.g., under what conditions and by whom, necessity of release from client Procedures for obtaining and content of confidentiality agreements from all employees and consultants Policies and procedures for safeguarding written, oral, and electronic information Forms to be utilized for confidentiality agreements, releases of information, and transmittal of information
Service delivery	Policies regarding and procedures for assessing congruence between scope of practitioner's training and experience and higher scope of practice Policies and procedures regarding decisionmaking with respect to consultation and referral Policies and procedures for assessing client outcomes
Boundary issues	Policies relating to dual relationships with clients, ex-clients, and significant persons in clients' and ex-clients' lives Procedures to assess and address violations of boundary policies
Documentation	Policies relating to and procedures for the assessment of currency and adequacy of practitioners' documentation of assessments, treatment pan, goals, activities, progress, termination Policies relating to and procedures to ensure congruence between requirements of third-party payers, per review groups, and others and adequacy of documentation Procedures to address deficiencies in provider documentation
Supervision	Policies and procedures relating to assignment of supervisees, frequency of supervision sessions, documentation of supervision sessions, review of supervisee performance and progress, interventions with supervisees, and correction strategies to prevent potential harms
Licensing and training	Policies relating to provider licensure and licensure renewal Mechanisms for verification of provider licensing and maintenance of valid license Mechanisms for assuring adequate ongoing continuing educations Mechanisms for ongoing training relating to ethical and legal issues relevant to the practice Policies and procedures related to failure to engage in required continuing education and maintenance of licensure

(continued)

Table 4.4 (continued)

Domain	Topics
Consultation	Policies relating to when consultations are to be requested
	Procedures relating to identification of appropriate consultation, determination of fees
Referral	Policies relating to when referrals are to be made
	Procedures relating to identification of appropriate referrals, who can make them and how they are to be made
Termination/discharge	Policies and procedures for termination of client services, notification to client

Adapted from Hopewell, 2015; Reamer, 2000

References

Allen, R. (2016, November 14). 2 social workers charged with manslaughter in Detroit toddler's death. *Detroit Free Press*. http://www.freep.com/story/news/local/michigan/detroit/2016/11/14/social-workers-charged-toddler-death/93796132/. Accessed 16 April 2017.

American Psychiatric Association. (2000). *Diagnostic and statistical manual, text revision, fourth edition (DSM-IV-TR)*. Washington, DC: Author.

American Psychological Association. (n.d.). Resolution on appropriate affirmative responses to sexual orientation distress and change efforts. http://www.apa.org/about/policy/sexual-orientation.aspx. Accessed 24 January 2013.

APA Presidential Task Force on Evidence-Based Practice. (2006). Evidence-based practice in psychology. *American Psychologist, 61*(4), 271–285.

Australian Psychological Society. (2010). *Evidence-based psychological interventions in the treatment of mental disorders: A literature review* (3rd ed.). Melbourne: Australian Psychological Society Limited. https://www.psychology.org.au/Assets/Files/Evidence-Based-Psychological-Interventions.pdf. Accessed 09 September 2014.

Banach, M., & Barnat, F. P. (2000). Liability and the internet: Risks and recommendations for social work practice. *Journal of Technology in Human Services, 17*(2-3), 153–171.

Barak, A. (1999). Psychological applications on the internet: A discipline on the threshold of a new millennium. *Applied & Preventive Psychology, 8*(4), 231–245.

Barsky, A., & Gould, J. (2002). *Clinicians in court: A guide to subpoenas, depositions, testifying, and everything else you need to know*. New York: Guilford Press.

Berliner, A. K. (1989). Misconduct in social work practice. *Social Work, 34*(1), 69–72.

Bernstein, B. E. (1978). Malpractice: An ogre on the horizon. *Social Work, 23*(2), 106–112.

Besharov, D. J. (1985). *The vulnerable social worker: Liability for serving children and families*. Silver Spring, MD: National Association of Social Workers.

Childress, C. (1998). Potential risks and benefits of online psychotherapeutic interventions. International Society for Mental Health Online. http://www.ismho.org/issues/9801.htm. Cited in M. Banach, & F.P. Barnat. (2000). Liability and the internet: Risks and recommendations for social work practice. *Journal of Technology in Human Services, 17*(2–3), 153-171.

Childress, C. (2000). Ethical issues in providing online psychotherapeutic services. *Journal of Medical Internet Research, 2*(1), e5. http://www.jmir.org/2000/1/e5/?utm_source=TrendMD&utm_medium=cpc&utm_campaign=JMIR_TrendMD_0. Accessed 04 April 2017.

Clingerman, T. L., & Bernard, J. M. (2004). An investigation of the use of e-mail as a supplemental modality for clinical supervision. *Counselor Education & Supervision, 44*, 82–95.

References

Cunningham, E. (2005, July 1). Social worker convicted of fraud. *Frederick News-Post.* https://www.fredericknewspost.com/archives/social-worker-convicted-of-fraud/article_d799c0c8-6d3d-5658-8041-2598b6af3aa6.html. Accessed 17 April 2017.

Di Marzo, M. (2015, May 21). Clinical social worker convicted of sexual abuse of a minor. *NBC Washington.* http://www.nbcwashington.com/news/local/Clinical-Social-Worker-Convicted-of-Sexual-Abuse-of-a-Minor-304661441.html. Accessed 16 April 2017.

Edmond, T., Megivern, D., Williams, C., Rochman, E., & Howard, M. (2006). Integrating evidence-based practice and social work field education. *Journal of Social Work Education, 42*(2), 377–396.

Etehad, M., & Winton, R. (2017, March 20). 4 L.A. County social workers to face trial in horrific death of 8-year old boy. *Los Angeles Times.* http://www.latimes.com/local/lanow/la-me-ln-social-worker-charges-20170320-story.html. Accessed 16 April 2017.

Feinstein, A. R., & Horwitz, R. I. (1997). Problems in the "evidence" of "evidence-based medicine". *American Journal of Medicine, 103*, 529–535.

Gambrill, E. D. (2003). Evidence-based practice: Sea change or the emperor's new clothes? *Journal of Social Work Education, 39*, 3–23.

Gibbs, L., & Gambrill, E. D. (2002). Evidence-based practice: Counterarguments to objections. *Research on Social Work Practice, 12*, 452–476.

Giffords, E. D. (1998). Social work on the Internet: An introduction. *Social Work, 43*, 243–251.

Gomez, M. (2016, April 12). Former San Mateo County social worker sentenced for sex with minors. *Mercury News.* http://www.mercurynews.com/2016/04/12/former-san-mateo-county-social-worker-sentenced-for-sex-with-minors/. Accessed 16 April 2017.

Gould, D. (1998). Listen to your lawyer. In L. Lifson & R. Simon (Eds.), *The mental health practitioner and the law: A comprehensive handbook* (pp. 344—356). Cambridge, MA: Harvard University Press.

Green, R. K., & Cox, G. (1978). Social work and malpractice: A converging course. *Social Work, 23*(2), 100–105.

Gurney, A. (2000). Risk management. In M. Davies (Ed.), *The Blackwell encyclopedia of social work*. Oxford: Blackwell.

Haldeman, D. C. (2001). Therapeutic antidotes: Helping gay and bisexual men recover from conversion therapies. *Journal of Gay and Lesbian Psychotherapy, 5*(3/4), 117–130.

Hood, C. C., Jones, D. K. C., Pidgeon, N. F., Turner, B. A., & Gibson, R. (1992). Risk management. In *Risk: Analysis, perception and management: Report of a Royal Society study group.* London: Royal Society.

Hopewell. (2015). *Hopewell manual of personnel policies and procedures.* Mesopotamia, OH: Author.

Institute of Medicine. (2001). *Crossing the quality chasm: A new health system for the 21st century.* Washington, DC: National Academies Press.

Internet World Stats. (2013). World internet usage and population statistics, June 30, 2012. http://www.internetworldstats.com/stats.htm. Accessed 11 May 2014.

Joinson, A. (1998). Causes and implications of disinhibited behavior on the internet. In J. Gackenbach (Ed.), *Psychology and the internet: Intrapersonal, interpersonal and transpersonal implications* (pp. 43–60). San Diego, CA: Academic Press.

Kanz, J. E. (2001). Clinical-supervision.com: Issues in the provision of online supervision. *Professional Psychology: Research and Practice, 32*(4), 415–420.

Kionka, F. J. (1999). *Torts in a nutshell* (3rd ed.). St. Paul, MN: West Group.

Kirk, S. A., & Hutchins, H. (1988). Deliberate misdiagnosis in mental health practice. *Social Service Review, 62*(2), 225–237.

Kopels, S., & Gustavsson, N. S. (1996). Infusing legal issues into the social work curriculum. *Journal of Social Work Education, 32*(1), 115–125.

Lebow, J. (1998). Not just talk, maybe some risk: The therapeutic potentials and pitfalls of computer-mediated conversation. *Journal of Marriage and Family Therapy, 24*(2), 203–206.

Legal Information Institute. (n.d.). Assault. https://www.law.cornell.edu/wex/assault. Accessed 16 April 2017.

Madden, R. G. (2000). Legal content in social work education. *Journal of Teaching in Social Work, 20*(1–2), 3–17.

Manhal-Baugus, M. (2001). E-therapy: Practical, ethical, and legal issues. *Cyberpsychology & Behavior, 4*(5), 551–563.

McCarty, D., & Clancy, C. (2002). Telehealth: Implications for social work practice. *Social Work, 47*(2), 153–161.

National Association of Social Workers, & Association of Social Work Boards. (2005). *NASW & ASWB standards for technology & social work practice.* Washington, DC, National Association of Social Workers.: https://www.socialworkers.org/practice/standards/NASWTechnologyStandards.pdf. Accessed 03 April 2017.

Naylor, C. D. (1995). Grey zones of clinical practice: Some limits to evidence-based medicine. *The Lancet, 345*, 840–842.

Parkinson, J., & Loue, S. (2015). Ethical issues in sandplay cyber-supervision. In S. Loue (Ed.), *Ethical issues in sandplay therapy practice and research* (pp. 11–22). New York: Springer Science+Business.

Pew Research Center. (2014). Pew Research Internet Project: Internet user demographics. http://www.pewinternet.org/data-trend/internet-use/latest-stats/. Accessed 11 May 2014.

Pollack, D., & Marsh, J. (2004). Social work misconduct may lead to liability. *Social Work, 49*(4), 609–612.

Reamer, F. G. (1989). Liability issues in social work supervision. *Social Work, 34*(5), 445–448.

Reamer, F. G. (1995). Malpractice claims against social workers: First facts. *Social Work, 40*(5), 595–601.

Reamer, F. G. (2000). The social work ethics audit: A risk-management strategy. *Social Work, 45*(4), 355–366.

Reamer, F. G. (2003). *Social work malpractice and liability: Strategies for prevention* (2nd ed.). New York: Columbia University Press.

Reamer, F. G. (2005). Documentation in social work: Evolving ethical and risk-management standards. *Social Work, 50*(4), 325–334.

Reamer, F. G. (2013). Social work in a digital age: Ethical and risk management challenges. *Social Work, 58*(2), 163–172.

Reamer, F. G. (2015). Ethical misconduct and negligence in social work. *Social Work Today, 15*(5), 20. http://www.socialworktoday.com/archive/090915p20.shtml. Accessed 26 March 2017.

Ringstad, R. (2005). Conflict in the workplace: Social workers as victims and perpetrators. *Social Work, 50*(4), 305–313.

Schank, J. A. (1998). Ethical issues in rural counseling practice. *Canadian Journal of Counselling, 32*, 270–283.

Stalker, K. (2003). Managing risk and uncertainty in social work. *Journal of Social Work, 3*(2), 211–233.

Stebnicki, M. A., & Glover, N. M. (2001). E-supervision as a complementary approach to traditional face-to-face clinical supervision in rehabilitation counseling: Problems and solutions. *Rehabilitation Education, 15*, 283–293.

Tarshis, C. B. (1972). Liability for psychotherapy. *University of Toronto Faculty Law Review, 30*, 75–96.

Taylor, C., & White, S. (2001). Knowledge, truth and reflexivity: The problem of judgment in social work. *Journal of Social Work, 1*(1), 37–59.

United States Department of Health and Human Services. (n.d.). Court orders and subpoenas. https://www.hhs.gov/hipaa/for-individuals/court-orders-subpoenas/index.html. Accessed 04 May 2017.

United States Department of Justice, U.S. Attorney's Office, District of Nebraska. (2014, July 9). Former social worker convicted of theft of public money. https://www.justice.gov/usao-ne/pr/former-social-worker-convicted-theft-public-money. Accessed 17 April 2017.

VandenBos, G. R., & Williams, S. (2000). The Internet versus the telephone: What is telehealth anyway? *Professional Psychology: Research and Practice, 31*, 490–492.

Watkins, S. A., & Watkins, J. C., Jr. (1983). Malpractice in clinical social work: A perspective on civil liability in the 1980s. *Behavioral Sciences & the Law, 1*(1), 55–69.

Zuboff, S. (1988). *In the age of the smart machine: The future of work and power.* New York: Basic Books.

Legal References

Cases

Bryant v. Oakpointe Villa Nursing Centre, 684 N.W.2d 864 (2004).
B.S. v. Somerset County, 704 F.3d 250 (3d Cir. 2013).
Burr v. Board of County Commissioners, 491 N.E.2d 1101 (Ohio 1986).
Currier v. Doran, 242 F.3d 905 (10th Cir. 2001), *cert. denied*, 112 S.Ct. 543 (2001).
Grzan v. Charter Hospital of Northwest Indiana et al., 702 N.E.2d 786 (Ind. Ct. Appeals 1998).
Haldeman v Golden, 2008 U.S. Dist. LEXIS 31157, *summary judgment granted in part, reversed in part*, Haldeman v. Golden, 2008 U.S. Dist. 32310 (D. Haw. Apr. 15, 2008), *reversed and remanded*, Haldeman v Golden, 2009 U.S. App. LEXIS 25610 (9th Cir. Haw., Nov. 23, 2009).
Loughlin et al. v. Vance County Department of Social Services et al., 2015 U.S. Dist. LEXIS 121680 (No. 5:14-CV-219-FL).
MacDonald v. Clinger, 446 N.Y.S.2d 801 (Sup. Ct. 1982).
Martino v. Family Service Agency of Adams County, 445 N.E.2d 6 (Ill. App. Ct. 1982).
Moore v. Department of Human Resources, 469 S.E.2d 511 (Ga. Ct. App. 1996).
M.R. v. Cox, 881 P.2d 108 (Ok. App. 1st Div. 1994), *cert. denied*, 514 U.S. 1019 (1995).
Penny v. State of Wyoming, 120 P.3d 152 (Wyo. S.Ct. 2005).
Phelan v. Torres, 2005 U.S. Dist. LEXIS 43228 (E.D.N.Y. 2005), *motion denied*, Pehlan v. Torres, 2010 U.S. Dist. LEXIS 33450 (E.D.N.Y. Mar. 31, 2010).
Schaefer v. Wilcock, 676 F Supp. 1092 (D. Utah 1987).
St. John v. Pope, 901 S.W.2d 420 (Tex. 1995).
Tarasoff v. Regents of the University of California, 17 Cal. 3d 425 (1976).
Tylena M. v. Heartshare Children's Services, 390 F. Supp. 22d 296 (S.D.N.Y. 2005).
Vonner v. State of Louisiana, 273 So. 2d 252 (La. S.Ct. 1973).
Zavatsky v. Anderson, 130 F Supp. 2d 349 (D. Conn. 2001).

Statutes

82 US.C. § 1983 (2015)
Americans with Disabilities Act, 42 U.S.C.A. § 12102 (West 2002)

Chapter 5
Legal Issues in Social Work Research

Introduction

Social workers engaged in social work research frequently focus their efforts on evaluating program effectiveness, the impact of particular social policies, and/or the causes of problems such as poverty, homelessness, and substance use (National Association of Social Workers, 2002). The findings of such research often provide the basis for advocacy efforts on behalf of clients and communities (Maschi & Youdin, 2012). It is important to have an understanding of not only the methodological challenges of research but also the legal obligations associated with the conduct of research, much of which often involves reliance on human participants. As examples of research involving human participants, social workers have led studies related to issues as diverse as child care (Groza, Bunkers, & Gamer, 2011), partner violence (Messing, Amanor-Boadu, Cavanaugh. Glass, & Campbell, 2013), resilience (Fraser, Galinsky, & Richman, 1999), discrimination (Gattis & Larson, 2017), women's adjustment to prison (Fedock, 2017), and the underlying causes of HIV risk (Loue, 2011).

Legal and Ethical Obligations to Participants

It may come as a surprise to some readers to learn that many legal obligations involving responsibilities to human research participants that are often associated with biomedical research are arguably relevant to social work research. Additionally, several court decisions relating to claims for injuries arising out of research could serve as a basis for arguments that social workers conducting research with human participants are obligated to adhere to the norms of international law that pertain to research (*Abdullahi v. Pfizer*, 2009). These laws and norms are embodied in the Nuremberg Code (1946), the Helsinki Declaration (World Medical Association,

Table 5.1 Provisions of the Nuremberg Code

Voluntary consent is essential
The experiment must yield fruitful results for the good of society
The experiment should be based on the results of animal experimentation and a knowledge of the natural history of the disease under study to justify performance of the study
The experiment should be conducted to avoid all unnecessary physical and mental suffering and injury
In general, no experiment should be conducted where there is a priori reason to believe that death or disabling injury will occur
Proper precautions must be taken to provide adequate facilities to protect the participant against the risk of injury, disability, or death
The experiment may be conducted by only scientifically qualified persons
The participant may end the experiment
The researcher must be prepared to end the experiment at any time

2013), and the International Covenant on Civil and Political Rights (1966)[1]; each of these three international documents expressly requires the informed consent of an individual as a prerequisite to his or her participation in research. This requirement is reflected in US federal regulations governing the conduct of human subject research (45 Code of Federal Regulations Part 46, 2009). Depending upon the state in which US-based research is undertaken and the focus of the particular research, social work research may also fall within the scope of state laws and/or regulations. Table 5.1 sets forth the requirements of the Nuremberg Code.

The provisions of the Nuremberg Code give rise to three basic principles that are deemed to be foundational to the conduct of research involving human beings: respect for persons, beneficence, and justice. *Respect for persons* encompasses the concept of autonomy and serves as the basis for the requirement that research with human beings can be conducted only with the informed consent of the individual. How we understand autonomy depends upon our notion of personhood. In the US context, this is often interpreted as reference to individual rights, self-determination, and privacy (De Craemer, 1983). *Beneficence* refers to the researcher's obligation to maximize good to the research participants. This principle is sometime parsed into two, the second being *nonmaleficence* or the obligation to minimize harm to the research participants. *Justice*, frequently interpreted as distributive justice, is predicated on the researcher's responsibility to equitably distribute the benefits and burdens of research across groups.

---

[1] The Nuremberg Code was promulgated in 1947 by a military tribunal as part of its final judgment against 15 Nazi physicians who were found guilty of war crimes and crimes against humanity due to their conduct of medical experiments on individuals without their consent (Annas, 1992). The International Covenant on Civil and Political Rights, which is legally binding on more than 160 nations that have ratified it, guarantees the right to individuals to be free from nonconsensual medical experimentation by any entity.

Respect for Persons

The principle of respect for persons encompasses both the concept of autonomy and the requirement that special protections in research be provided for vulnerable persons. This principle suggests that (1) individuals and groups may be different in ways that are relevant to their world view and their response to any variety of situations; (2) the researcher must respect these differences and fashion their research protocols in a way that is sensitive to these varying understandings, while still ensuring that fundamental principles of informed consent are observed; and (3) the researcher is responsible for ensuring that individuals with impaired or diminished autonomy who are participating in the research are protected from harm or abuse.

It has been suggested that a person can act autonomously only if he or she "acts (1) intentionally, (2) with understanding, and (3) without controlling influences" (Faden & Beauchamp, 1986, p. 238). In order to act with understanding, the individual must have the capacity to do so and must have the information necessary for understanding. Influences exist along a continuum, ranging from controlling to noncontrolling; beyond a certain point on that continuum, the degree of control becomes so great that a decision cannot be said to be voluntary.

Capacity refers to the ability of an individual to evidence a choice, the ability to understand relevant information, the ability to appreciate a situation and its consequences, and the ability to manipulate information rationally. This is different from competence, which is a legal determination relating to an individual's ability to care for him- or herself and/or his or her financial affairs.

There is a presumption at the beginning of all research studies that a prospective adult participant has the capacity to consent unless there is reason to believe either that he or she does not have capacity or that the capacity to consent may be limited in some way. (Children are by law presumed to lack adequate capacity to consent, although the age at which childhood ends and adulthood begins may differ across states in the United States and across countries.) Decisionmaking ability in the context of participation in research requires that the individual be able to understand basic study information, including the procedures to be performed, the risks associated with participation, the potential benefits he or she may gain from participation, alternatives to study participation, the difference between research interventions and established therapy, and the individual's ability to refuse to participate without suffering a penalty (Dresser, 2001).

Vulnerable participants are often thought to be individuals with "insufficient power, prowess, intelligence, resources, strength or other needed attributes to protect their own interests through negotiations for informed consent" (Levine, 1988). Vulnerability and capacity may be interrelated, as in the case of research participants who have illnesses that affect capacity, e.g., more advanced Alzheimer's disease and active psychosis. The capacity to provide informed consent may be understood as fluctuating (National Bioethics Advisory Commission, 1998), e.g., when a participant is experiencing delusions due to mental illness.

Although the concept of vulnerability has traditionally been applied to encompass members of specific groups, such as children, prisoners, and pregnant women, it is now recognized that that vulnerability is inherent in situations, not people (Kipnis, 2001); e.g., a pregnant woman may be vulnerable in some physical or biomedical procedures but is likely not vulnerable in survey research about social services that would benefit her community. Further, although often treated as a binary classification (one is either vulnerable or not), it is open to debate whether vulnerability is better conceptualized as a spectrum of attributes with greater and lesser vulnerability. Vulnerability has also been conceived of as existing in layers, whereby characteristics possessed by an individual can cumulatively add layers of vulnerability, e.g., poverty, race, and illiteracy may combine in a particular research context to compound the vulnerability of an individual beyond that which would result from the existence of only one such characteristic (Luna, 2009).

Relying on the definition of vulnerability above, it appears that many of the populations with which social workers work and who might be involved as participants in social work research may have attributes that, depending upon the nature of the research and the context in which it is conducted, would render them vulnerable or potentially vulnerable. This may include students; elderly persons; residents of nursing homes; hospitalized patients; people receiving welfare benefits or social assistance and other poor people and the unemployed; some ethnic, racial, and religious minority groups; homeless persons; nomads; refugees or displaced persons; prisoners; patients with incurable diseases; individuals who are politically powerless; members of relatively isolated communities; and individuals with serious, potentially disabling or life-threatening diseases.

Accordingly, researchers assessing the potential vulnerability of their research participants and how best to reduce their vulnerability must understand the nature of vulnerability; they cannot simply depend on existing guidelines. Indeed, they must understand the social, historical, and other contextual realities in which the research participants are living in order to understand whether and the degree to which they may be vulnerable in the proposed research (Kipnis, 2003; Levine et al., 2004).

Although traditionally researchers' responsibilities have devolved only to the individual research participant and to his or her community or group in assessing vulnerability, e.g., persons with mental illness, it is suggested here that researchers must be cognizant of the context in which individual participants live and function and, in some circumstances, must consider the potential vulnerability of individuals who are linked to the participant and who may be impacted by an individual's decision to participate in a particular research study. For example, some faith communities continue to believe that mental illness is a punishment from God or a moral failing. Family members connected with a participant, as well as the individual him- or herself, might face ostracism from their faith community where it becomes known that the community member was participating in a study related to mental illness.

Understanding and Information To act with understanding also suggests that the prospective research participant has been provided with adequate information regarding the nature of the research and its potential implications and consequences to enable him or her to make an informed choice regarding participation. Many of these elements are also included in US federal regulations that govern all research conducted in institutions that receive federal funding, e.g., hospitals and institutions that receive Medicare or Medicaid payments and universities that receive federal research grants.

Ethical guidelines relating to the conduct of social work research reflect the norms embodied by these international documents and federal regulations. Social workers are ethically obligated to ensure that participants in their research are adequately informed and protected. The *Code of Ethics* of the National Association of Social Workers (2008) advises that:

> Social workers engaged in evaluation or research should obtain voluntary and written informed consent from participants, when appropriate, without any implied or actual deprivation or penalty for refusal to participate; without undue inducement to participate; and with due regard for participants' well-being, privacy, and dignity. Informed consent should include information about the nature, extent, and duration of the participation requested and disclosure of the risks and benefits of participation in the research.
> (f) When evaluation or research participants are incapable of giving informed consent, social workers should provide an appropriate explanation to the participants, obtain the participants' assent to the extent they are able, and obtain written consent from an appropriate proxy.
> (g) Social workers should never design or conduct evaluation or research that does not use consent procedures, such as certain forms of naturalistic observation and archival research, unless rigorous and responsible review of the research has found it to be justified because of its prospective scientific, educational, or applied value and unless equally effective alternative procedures that do not involve waiver of consent are not feasible.
> (h) Social workers should inform participants of their right to withdraw from evaluation and research at any time without penalty.
> (i) Social workers should take appropriate steps to ensure that participants in evaluation and research have access to appropriate supportive services.
> (j) Social workers engaged in evaluation or research should protect participants from unwarranted physical or mental distress, harm, danger, or deprivation. (National Association of Social Workers, 2008, par. 5.02(3)-(j))

It is possible that even after providing an individual with all of the information that can possibly be provided, the person misunderstands the purpose of the study due to a misbelief about the underlying purpose of inviting his or her participation. Suppose, for example, that the social worker wishes to evaluate the efficacy of a particular behavioral intervention to address depression associated with chronic illness. He or she proposes to randomize the agency's clients into two groups, one of which will receive the usual care for depression management and the other of which will receive the usual care plus the intervention, which includes spiritual exercises. A client may erroneously believe that the social worker truly does know what will work best for the client and is offering this opportunity because it will be of clinical benefit to the client. This misbelief, known as the therapeutic misconception (Appelbaum, Roth, Lidz, & Bensen, 1987; Grisso & Appelbaum, 1998), may be difficult to detect when discussing research participation with an ongoing client.

The Nuremberg Code suggests that there must be a balance of the risks and benefits to the prospective research participants that are involved in any specific research undertaken and that provisions be made to reduce the likelihood of or impact of the potential risks. In the context of social work research, these provisions might focus on access to supportive services and protecting participants from unwarranted distress. In almost every research situation involving human participants, there exists a potential risk that confidentiality may be inadvertently breached.

Voluntariness What constitutes a "controlling influence" varies across cultures. As an example, many Americans conceive of themselves as independent agents free to make decisions without consideration of or reference to either the opinions of others or the potential impact of their decisions on others. In contrast, individual identity in other cultures may rest on the idea of an "enlarged self"; individuals in these cultures see themselves not as autonomous agents but as the aggregation and integration of various roles and relationships, each with corresponding responsibilities. Individuals who are fiercely wed to the Western ideal of individualism may perceive reference to and consideration of others' viewpoints to be a "controlling influence." Nevertheless, where this consultation by a prospective research participant with others is voluntary, it is entirely consistent with the principle of respect for persons.

These issues may have particular relevance in the context of conducting cross-cultural research. Consider the following example. A client who is to receive counseling services from a social worker at an agency signs an informed consent form for treatment. Maybe the form includes a paragraph specifying that, after an appropriate passage of time, the social worker may present the client's case at a conference or in a journal article. Or, maybe the social worker provides the client with a separate release form allowing him or her to use the client's case in this way. A client who strongly identifies as a member of a specific, relatively insulated religious community with responsibilities to that community may be reluctant to agree without first considering the potential implications of their agreement on others within his or her community. The client may feel, for example, that public attention to their situation, even when their identity is masked, may somehow bring shame to their family or community or indicate disloyalty. Such considerations may be even more likely if the focus of the study is potentially socially stigmatizing, such as mental illness.

There is also the issue of the power differential that exists between the social worker-researcher and the client. As one scholar has noted:

> The process of conducting research tends to reinforce the power imbalances of society. Researchers usually turn their gaze downward in the social power hierarchy, studying people who are poorer, less educated, more discriminated against, and in a variety of ways less socially powerful than themselves. (Aronson Fontes, 1998, p. 54)

In some cases a researcher has no relationship with the individual research participant, such as when the researcher sends out a survey to everyone living in a specific neighborhood to determine how the level of violence in their neighborhood is affecting their emotional health. In these situations, the power differential may not be an issue because the potential participant can easily ignore the mailed survey.

This is not, however, the case if a social worker wishes to conduct research using his or her own clients as the research cases or participants. An individual who is obtaining services might feel that the social worker will not provide the same quality of care, will not listen as well, or will terminate services prematurely if the client does not agree to be part of a study. Even if the client is no longer receiving services from the social worker, e.g., case management or counseling, he or she might fear that a refusal to participate in the research would lead to a refusal by the social worker to provide future services if the client wished to have them.

Monetary payments are frequently offered to individuals who consent to participate in research. Such payments may be provided to enhance the likelihood that an adequate number of participants will be recruited for a particular study; to overcome "opportunity costs" and increase the recruitment of individuals from underrepresented groups; to reimburse individuals for the costs associated with their participation, e.g., lost wages, transportation, and child care expenses; and/or to provide participants with fair compensation for their contribution of their time and any associated inconvenience (Grady, 2005).

Concerns have been raised, however, with respect to the potential impact that such payments may have on the voluntariness of participants' consent (Denny & Grady, 2007; Grady, 2001; Largent, Grady, Miller, & Wertheimer, 2012). These concerns have been especially pronounced with regard to the payment of participants who are economically disadvantaged due to possibly lower educational levels that may impede their comprehension and their vulnerability to exploitation due to their low economic status (Denny & Grady, 2007). It has been suggested that payment may be coercive, may represent an undue inducement by reducing an individual's willingness to evaluate the risks and benefits associated with research participation or reduce the level of voluntariness of their decision, and may lead to a disproportionate burden on economically disadvantaged individuals, who may choose to participate because it represents their sole access to resources (Grady, 2005). Although these issues have been raised primarily in the context of clinical research, they are also relevant to the types of studies that might be conducted in social work research, e.g., behavioral intervention trials, studies relating to individuals' identity or family relationships.

Scholars appear to agree that payments to research participants are generally not coercive because coercion involves a threat of harm, which is absent from such interactions (Beauchamp & Childress, 1994; Largent et al., 2012). Additionally, it has been thought, as well, that modest payments to research participants to compensate them for their contribution minimize the likelihood that payment would constitute an undue inducement, whereas the payment of large sums of money increases the likelihood that the payment may be irresistible to potential participants and cause them to disregard the risks associated with a study and to feel that they have no choice but to participate (Faden & Beauchamp, 1986).

Various strategies can and should be utilized in an effort to maximize the likelihood that the research participant-client understands the nature of the research and that he or she may or may not derive any benefit from participation. In addition to the risks and benefits, participants must also understand three particular aspects in order to understand that a study involves research:

- That they will be contributing to the development of generalizable knowledge that will be used to help others in the future (research contribution).
- That the investigators will rely on the participants to gather this generalizable knowledge (research relationship).
- The extent to which what the participants do and what happens to them will be altered because of their participation in the particular research (Wendler & Grady, 2008).

Various strategies have been utilized in an effort to enhance the communication of these elements. These have included attuning the literacy level of the informed consent document to the prospective participant's reading level; using language and terms in both the written informed consent form and in discussions about the study that are easily understandable by non-researchers and nonprofessionals; formatting the informed consent form and process to facilitate understanding, e.g., using multiple columns of text rather than writing across the page and using a video to explain the study; asking the prospective participant questions about the study and what will be expected of him or her to assess their level of understanding; providing a stipend in an amount and/or form that is congruent with what is expected of the participant; and allowing the prospective participant time to confer with others regarding participation, if desired, prior to deciding whether or not to participate in the research (Flory & Emanuel, 2004).

Beneficence and Nonmaleficence

As indicated previously, this dual principle states that the benefits of the research are to be maximized and the harms are to be minimized. This principle gives rise to the requirements that the potential risks of the research be outweighed by the potential benefits, that the research design be sound, that the researcher be competent to conduct the proposed research, and that the welfare of the research participants be protected. There exists the possibility, however, that the principle might be unintentionally violated in the context of conducting social work research related to a specific community where the social worker-researcher's knowledge of the dynamics within participants' communities is inadequate, inadvertently resulting in an inability to assess accurately the potential benefits and risks to potential participants.

Justice

Justice refers to the obligation of the researcher to assist in the fair allocation of resources and burdens. Rawls conceived of differences between individuals in terms of the resources and benefits available to them—"the difference principle"—as

> an agreement to regard the distribution of natural talents as in some respects a common asset and to share in the greater social and economic benefits made possible by the complementarities of the distribution, Those who have been favored by nature, whoever they are, may gain from their good fortune only on terms that improve the situation of those who have lost out. (Rawls, 1999, p. 87)

Accordingly, justice has not been effectuated unless:

> All social values—liberty and opportunity, income and wealth, and the social bases of self-respect—are to be distributed equally unless an unequal distribution of any, or all, of these values is to everyone's advantage. (Rawls, 1999, p. 54)

The *Belmont Report* (National Commission for the Protection of Human Subjects of Biomedical and Behavioral Research, 1979, pp. 7–8) noted

> Justice is relevant to the selection of subjects of research at two levels: the social and the individual. Individual justice in the selection of subjects would require that researchers ... not offer potentially beneficial research only to some patients who are in their favor.
>
> Injustice may appear in the selection of subjects, even if individual subjects are selected fairly by investigators and treated fairly in the course of research. This injustice arises from social, racial, sexual, and cultural biases institutionalized in society ....
>
> Although individual institutions or investigators may not be able to resolve a problem that is pervasive in their social setting, they can consider distributive justice in selecting research subjects.

These observations suggest that the social worker conducting research must consider prior to initiating a study whether the individuals who are to be burdened by their participation will also benefit from the study findings. As an example, if individuals participate in a study to evaluate the effectiveness of a behavioral intervention, will they have access to that intervention following the conclusion of the study?

Legal Issues Associated with Data

Discussions related to legal issues and obligations associated with data often focus on confidentiality protections, limitations on confidentiality, and data ownership and sharing. (The concept of confidentiality is to be distinguished from privacy, which refers specifically to the person, rather than the data.)

Confidentiality and Its Limits

Legal Obligations In general, social workers who conduct research are legally required to maintain the confidentiality of the data that they collect from research participants.

Depending upon the nature and the source of the data collected, the obligation to maintain confidentiality may also derive from the federal Health Insurance Portability and Accountability Act of 1996, known as HIPAA, and related regulations. This federal law is discussed more fully in Chap. 1. Briefly, every health-care provider, who transmits health information in connection with certain transactions, is covered by the law. Even if a social worker is acting in his or her capacity as a researcher, if he or she receives or sends health-related information electronically, that communication is likely to fall within the parameters of the law. As an example, a social worker conducting research relating to mental health outcomes may wish to obtain copies of the participants' clinical records to compare provider observations with the participants' subjective opinions about their mental health status. Or, a social worker may assess participants' mental health status to verify eligibility to participate in a study involving mentally ill persons. One or more participants ask the social worker-researcher to transmit copies of their assessment to their health-care providers. Using electronic technology alone, such as e-mail, will not bring the transmission under HIPAA; "the transmission must be in connection with a standard transaction" (United States Department of Health and Human Services, n.d.). It could be argued, however, that the request for or release of such information constitutes a standard transaction.

The HIPAA privacy rule covers "protected health information," which encompasses information about an individual's past, present, or future physical or mental health condition and identifies the individual or provides such information that there is a reasonable basis to believe that the individual could be identified (45 C.F.R. § 160.103, 2013). If the individual providing the information is considered to be a covered entity under the law, such as a physician's office providing a previous mental health assessment, that entity must obtain the individual's written consent to use or disclose the private health information if that disclosure is not for payment, treatment, or health-care operations or otherwise permitted or protected by the privacy rule (45 C.F.R. § 164.508, 2013). The provisions of HIPAA's privacy rule are quite complex, and social workers conducting research relating to individuals' health status are urged to consult its provisions to ensure that they are in compliance.

Logistical and technological issues associated with the use of electronic media to conduct research may heighten concerns about confidentiality and present additional challenges. Electronic media used in research may include e-mail, chat rooms and instant messaging, videoconferencing programs, and videoteleconferencing systems. Mechanisms such as e-mail are asynchronous in that, while they allow the instant delivery of a message, the response to such messages may be time-delayed at the discretion of the recipient. In contrast, mechanisms such as chat rooms and instant messaging are synchronous, permitting users to respond to each other in real time. Videoteleconferencing, such as through Skype or ooVoo, can allow the researcher and the research participant(s) to meet in real time (cf. Neukrug, 1991; Smith, Mead, & Kinella, 1998). Documents to be viewed as part of the interview or research process can be transmitted via e-mail attachment or by sharing a file in Dropbox, Google Groups, or the iCloud.

Numerous strategies can be utilized in an effort to reduce risks associated with electronic transmissions. These include the use of complex passwords for computers, iPads, and cell phones; screen savers to prevent others from seeing computer screens while they are in use; establishment of a virtual private network (VPN) to further safeguard communications from being accessed over public networks; and encryption software.

There is a corollary ethical requirement to maintain the confidentiality of the data. The *Code of Ethics* of the National Association of Social Workers provides:

> Social workers should respect clients' right to privacy. Social workers should not solicit private information from clients unless it is essential to providing services or conducting social work evaluation or research. Once private information is shared, standards of confidentiality apply. (National Association of Social Workers, 2008, standard 1.07)

Legal Limitations on Confidentiality in Research The social worker-researcher's ability to assure confidentiality may also be limited due to a duty to warn, state-imposed reporting requirements, and legal attempts to access the data. Although these issues may arise during any research, they may be especially likely to arise in studies conducted over an extended period of time as the social worker-researcher acquires an increasing amount of information related to each participant and as the participant engages in more relevant activities that are the focus of the investigation, e.g., participant responses to stress or violence, illicit substance use, and sex work.

A "duty to warn" may exist as the result of a line of court cases that began in 1976 with the now famous case of *Tarasoff v. Regents of the University of California*. The case involved a lawsuit by the Tarasoff family against the University of California and a psychologist at the Berkeley campus of the university for the death of their daughter Tatiana. Tatiana had refused the advances of another graduate student at Berkeley. The would-be suitor had revealed his intent to kill Tatiana during the course of counseling sessions with a psychologist at the school's counseling services. The psychologist and several colleagues sought to have this student involuntarily hospitalized for observation purposes, but he was released after a brief observation period, during which it was concluded that he was rational. He subsequently shot and killed Tatiana.

The majority of the court rejected the psychologist's claim that he could not have advised either the family or Tatiana of the threat because to do so would have breached the traditionally protected relationship between the therapist and the patient. Instead, the court held that when a patient "presents a serious danger … to another [person], [the therapist] incurs an obligation to use reasonable care to protect the intended victim against such danger." That obligation could be satisfied by warning the intended victim of the potential danger, by notifying authorities, or by taking "whatever other steps are reasonably necessary under the circumstances" (*Tarasoff v. Regents of the University of California*, 1976, p. 340). The court specifically noted that the therapist-patient privilege was not absolute:

> We recognize the public interest in supporting effective treatment of mental illness and in protecting the rights of patients to privacy and the consequent public importance of safeguarding the confidential character of psychotherapeutic communication. Against this interest, however, we must weigh the public interest in safety from violent assault .... We conclude that the public policy favoring protection of the confidential character of patient-psychotherapist communications must yield to the extent to which disclosure is essential to avert danger to others. The protective privilege ends where the public peril begins. (*Tarasoff v. Regents of the University of California*, 1976, p. 346)

Some later cases have followed the reasoning of the *Tarasoff* court. A New Jersey court ruled in *McIntosh v. Milano* (1979) that the doctor-patient privilege protecting confidentiality is not absolute but is limited by the public interest of the patient. In reaching this conclusion, the court relied on the 1953 case of *Earle v. Kuklo*, in which the court had stated that "a physician has a duty to warn third persons against possible exposure to contagious or infectious diseases." A Michigan appeals court held in *Davis v. Lhim* (1983) that a therapist has an obligation to use reasonable care whenever there is a person who is foreseeably endangered by his or her patient. The danger would be deemed to be foreseeable if the therapist knew or should have known, based on a professional standard of care, of the potential harm. More recently, a California court held that a duty to warn may be triggered by the communication of an immediate family member to the therapist, even in the absence of a direct threat by the client (*Ewing v. Goldstein*, 2004; *Ewing v. Northridge Hospital Medical Center*, 2004). (It should be noted, however, that a duty to warn no longer exists in California and there is now only a duty to protect due to statutory revisions subsequent to these judicial decisions. See Weinstock, Bonnici, Seroussi, & Leong, 2014, for additional analysis.)

Courts are divided, however, on whether the patient/client must make threats about a specific, intended victim to trigger the duty to warn. The court in *Thompson v. County of Alameda* (1980) found no duty to warn in the absence of an identifiable victim. Another court, though, held that the duty to warn exists even in the absence of specific threats concerning specific individuals, if the patient's previous history suggests that he or she would be likely to direct violence against a person (*Jablonski v. United States*, 1983).

Depending on the particular state, however, researchers may also be required to report instances of child sexual abuse, child abuse or neglect, elder abuse, or intimate partner violence that may be committed by or perpetrated on a research participant. Whether such an obligation exists often depends on the age and state of residence of the victim, the state's definition of the offense, the recency of the event, and the status of the reporter, that is, whether a researcher who holds a social work license under that state's laws is a mandated reporter, even when acting in the role of a researcher rather than as a provider of social work services.

Confidentiality may also be limited due to a subpoena. A subpoena is an order from a court or administrative body to compel the appearance of a witness or the production of specified document or records. This discussion focuses on subpoenas issued to compel the production of records or documents associated with the research.

A subpoena can be issued by a court or administrative body at the state or federal level. The information sought may be believed to be important to the conduct of an investigation, a criminal prosecution, or a civil lawsuit. The issuance of subpoenas against researchers had become increasingly common (Auriti, 2013), and they have been used as a mechanism to obtain data relating to identifiable research participants (e.g., Hayes, 2011). (See Chap. 4 for additional discussion relating to the difference between a court order and a subpoena and the obligations with respect to each.)

Certificates of confidentiality, available in some circumstances in the United States for research conducted within the United States, may potentially limit the extent to which research data may be obtained by subpoena. Certificates of confidentiality are issued by the appropriate institute of the National Institute of Health and other agencies of the US Department of Health and Human Services. It is not necessary, however, that the research for which a certificate is requested be funded by the National Institutes of Health. Authority for their issuance derives from Section 301(d) of the Public Health Service Act, which provides that:

> The Secretary may authorize persons engaged in biomedical, behavioral, clinical, or other research (including research on mental health, including research on the use and effect of alcohol and other psychoactive drugs) to protect the privacy of individuals who are the subject of such research by withholding from all persons not connected with the conduct of such research the names or other identifying characteristics of such individuals. Persons so authorized to protect the privacy of such individuals may not be compelled in any Federal, State, or local civil, criminal, administrative, legislative, or other proceedings to identify such individuals.

Certificates are potentially available for research where the participants may be involved in litigation that relates to the exposure under study, such as sexual transmission of HIV; that collects genetic information; or that collects data pertaining to participants' psychological well-being, their sexual attitudes, preferences, or practices, or their substance use or other illegal activities or behaviors. A certificate of confidentiality is available only for research data collected in the United States; it is not available, for example, if a social worker-researcher in the United States (or elsewhere) is conducting the research outside of the United States. Additional details relating to certificates are available from the various websites sponsored by the Office of Extramural Research of the National Institutes of Health (http://grants.nih.gov/grants/policy/coc/appl_extramural.htm; http://grants.nih.gov/grants/policy/coc/background.htm; http://grants.nih.gov/grants/policy/coc/faqs.htm).

The validity of these certificates was once upheld by a New York court (*People v. Newman*, 1973). However, their validity is subject to question because, in essence, they allow an agency of the federal government to limit the ability of the states to investigate and prosecute possible criminal activity and the ability of the courts and litigants in civil cases to obtain evidence that may be critical.

While a certificate of confidentiality may relieve the social worker-researcher of the legal duty to disclose specific information, it does not relieve him or her of any ethical responsibility to do so. For example, a certificate of confidentiality may relieve the social worker-researcher of the obligation to report to designated authorities that a client-research participant is the current victim of elder abuse. It does not, however, relieve the social worker-researcher of any associated ethical obligation. The client-research participant must be fully informed as part of the informed consent process regarding the extent of confidentiality protection and what the therapist-researcher will report.

The legal and ethical obligations to maintain confidentiality extend even beyond the close of a study. The social worker-researcher is to report the research findings accurately and continue to preserve the confidentiality and privacy of the research participants (National Association of Social Workers, 2008). A variety of strategies can be utilized to protect the identity of the research participants and safeguard the confidentiality of their individual data. These include aggregating the data from multiple individuals, excluding identifying descriptions of individuals, and conflating multiple accounts or scenarios into one representative account or case study (National Association of Social Workers, 2008).

Data Ownership, Storage, and Sharing

Data ownership refers to the legal right to possess the data and to retain the data following completion of a particular study (Clinical Tools, Inc., 2006). Data sharing concerns the dissemination of the data to other researchers, institutions, and the public. "Data" encompasses not only observable details, such as someone's sex, but also the sources of and processes through which those data were collected, such as questionnaires and interviews. Issues related to the ownership and/or sharing of collected data may surface in various contexts, including disputes relating to publication from the collected data; concerns of an individual or community relating to the potential consequences of the data use, sharing, or publication; and the archiving of data for future unspecified research use by unspecified persons. Issues of ownership are often layered and complex, as illustrated by the following example.

Assume that a social worker-researcher conducts interviews with adoptive parents to explore the challenges associated with adoption and parental strategies to address such challenges. The legal concept of copyright refers to ownership of the words in such interviews. The owner of the copyright in the original words is the person who initially uttered them, that is, the interviewee. In contrast, ownership (copyright) of the recording of the interview data rests with the institution in which an investigator is employed, such as a university. The researcher is, in essence, granted "stewardship" over the data and may use the data in a manner that is consistent with the representations and assurances under which the data were collected from the interviewees, e.g., presentation at conferences and publications (Clinical Tools, Inc., 2006). If the investigator, such as the social worker-researcher conducting interviews with adoptive parents, were to change employers, it is likely that the institution would allow him or her to take a copy of the data but also require that a copy of the data be left with the organization.

Although there is generally no requirement that researchers share preliminary data, there may be an obligation to share final data. As an example, recipients of funding from the US National Institutes of Health are generally required to make their final data available to other researchers:

> We believe that data sharing is essential for expedited translation of research results into knowledge, products, and procedures to improve human health. The NIH endorses the sharing of final research data to serve these and other important scientific goals. The NIH expects and supports the timely release and sharing of final research data from NIH supported studies for use by other researchers. (National Institutes of Health, 2003a)

Data hoarding has been said to be "antithetical to the general norms of science emphasizing the principles of openness" (Office of Research Integrity, n.d.). Investigators may choose to hoard data for any number of reasons, including concerns related to confidentiality, security, proprietary or economic interests; the labor and financial costs associated with documenting the data; technical obstacles to sharing the data; the costs to the funders and/or the borrowers; issues related to the provision of materials needed to understand the data or extend the research; and/or personal motivations of the data holder (Sieber, 1989).

The increasing trend toward the globalization of research and the increasing emphasis on cross-disciplinary collaboration to promote better understanding and conserve scarce research resources have fueled interest in the use of data archives as repositories of raw data (Parry & Mauthner, 2004). Most such data archives consist of quantitative data that have been at least partially de-identified or anonymized in an effort to safeguard the confidentiality of individuals whose data have been deposited into the archive, e.g., names, specific residence, and telephone number (Corti, 2000).[2] Researcher utilization of archived quantitative data may require execution of a data use agreement, also known as a data sharing agreement, licensing agreement, and data distribution agreement, that specifies the intended uses of the data and a finite period of time during which the data may be used (National Institutes of Health, 2003b). In some cases, archived quantitative data may be available for public use. One example of such use is the Center for Medicare and Medicaid Services Data at http://hrsonline.isr.umich.edu/rda/userdocs/cmsdua.pdf. Examples of international data archives relevant to social work research include the South African Data Archive (http://sada.nrf.ac.za/), which includes social work data; the Center for International Statistics at the Canadian Council on Social Development (http://www.ccsd.ca/), which includes data on poverty, welfare, and income; and the Australian Social Science Data Archives (http://www.ccsd.ca/), which house data relating to social, political, and economic affairs, as well as data from

---

[2] In some cases, individuals' identities may be deductively disclosed, such as in the case of small geographic areas, specific small populations, and linked databases (National Institutes of Health, 2003b). As an example, a social worker investigating community poverty levels might wish to link information from several databases to better understand not only whether poverty exists but its implications for access to needed services. Although likely not relevant to most social work research, identification of specific individuals is theoretically possible in the context of genetic research that utilizes archived tissue samples, since DNA information is specific to an individual.

opinion polls. Utilization of international data archives often specifies that the investigator makes "responsible use" of the data and refrains from the intentional disclosure of individuals' identity, which would negate the assurances of confidentiality afforded to those whose data are contained in the archive. (See Inter-University Consortium for Political and Social Research, n.d.; South African Data Archive, n.d.).

Investigators may wish to utilize archival data for a number of reasons. They may be interested in conducting supplementary analysis, which permits a more in-depth analysis of a particular aspect of the data compared with what was accomplished through the primary study from which the data were derived (Heaton, 2008). A supra-analysis would involve aims and a focus that go beyond those of the original study. Other purposes could include a reanalysis of the data to confirm and validate the original findings; an amplified analysis, which examines two or more datasets, either to compare them or to combine them; and an assorted reanalysis, which reuses existing qualitative data together with the collection and analysis of primary qualitative data for the same study (Heaton, 2008).

Unique issues are associated with the sharing and archiving of qualitative data. Unlike quantitative data that can often be effectively de-identified, an understanding of qualitative data, such as ethnographies, requires reference to the context in which the data were collected, e.g., details related to the specific community and inclusion of field notes. Removal of identifying data to ensure the anonymity of the study participants would threaten the integrity of the remaining data and potentially render it unusable (Mauthner, Maclean, & McKee, 2000; Parry & Mauthner, 2004), but inclusion of such information could lead to the identification of individual participants and/or their community. The falsification of some data is a strategy to protect the identity and confidentiality of participants but would also raise issues relating to the integrity of the data (Parry, Atkinson, & Delamont, 1997).

In addition, individuals or communities that gave their consent to participate in a qualitative study, such as an ethnography, often do so with the understanding that the data will be utilized for a specific purpose. In some cases, the informed consent process may specify that the researcher will engage in community consultation prior to publication from the collected data. Unless participating individuals and communities have agreed as part of the informed consent process to the later archiving and shared use of qualitative data derived from the study in which they participated, understanding that the primary researchers cannot know how the archived data may later be used or interpreted by others who utilize the archived data, issues could potentially be raised relating to the validity of the informed consent that was obtained and the ownership of the data (Parry & Mauthner, 2004).

Authorship and Publication

Legal and ethical issues extend beyond the conduct of the research and its conclusion to the publication of the research findings. The author of manuscripts originating from the research has an intellectual property interest in that work. The US Copyright Office has explained:

Copyright is a form of protection provided by the laws of the United States (title 17, *U. S. Code*) to the authors of "original works of authorship," including literary, dramatic, musical, artistic, and certain other intellectual works. This protection is available to both published and unpublished works. Section 106 of the 1976 Copyright Act generally gives the owner of copyright the exclusive right to do and to authorize others to do the following:
- reproduce the work in copies or phonorecords
- prepare derivative works based upon the work
- distribute copies or phonorecords of the work to the public by sale or other transfer of ownership, or by rental, lease, or lending
- perform the work publicly, in the case of literary, musical, dramatic, and choreographic works, pantomimes, and motion pictures and other audiovisual works
- display the work publicly, in the case of literary, musical, dramatic, and choreographic works, pantomimes, and pictorial, graphic, or sculptural works, including the individual images of a motion picture or other audiovisual work
- perform the work publicly (in the case of sound recordings) by means of a digital audio transmission. (United States Copyright Office, 2012. See also United States Copyright Office, 2016)

Copyright does not cover name, title, ideas, methods, or systems (United States Copyright Office, 2016).

The intellectual contributions of those who have collaborated on the research and/or the manuscript can be acknowledged in a number of ways. In general, individuals who have made a significant intellectual contribution to the research should be included as co-authors. Others who assisted with the research, such as an assistant for the transcription of recorded interviews or for data entry, can be thanked in an acknowledgment section (Wager & Kleinert, 2010; International Committee of Medical Journal Editors, 2014; National Association of Social Workers, 2008). The researcher should obtain the permission of individuals to be acknowledged in a publication, rather than noting their contribution without their input. An individual may face consequences in his or her community or family as a result of the assistance provided, unbeknownst to the social worker-researcher. As an example, an individual may have served as a gatekeeper to or informant about a particular community. Association of the individual with the particular study could lead to ostracism or marginalization of that individual.

Researchers may be ethically required to maintain the data underlying publication(s) for a specific period of time. The length of time during which data must be retained following the termination of a study is often determined by the specifications of the funding authority, such as a government agency, foundation, or corporation; the policies of the entity for which the investigator works, e.g., university or research enterprise; and the intended uses of the data. Retention of the data permits reanalyses of the data to verify or refute the original findings, the conduct of alternate analyses to refine results, and the conduct of analyses to assess the robustness of the data in light of varying assumptions (Fienberg, Martin, & Straf, 1985).

References

Annas, G. J. (1992). The Nuremberg Code in U.S. courts: Ethics versus expediency. In G. J. Annas & M. A. Grodin (Eds.), *The Nazi doctors and the Nuremberg Code: Human rights in human experimentation* (pp. 201–222). New York: Oxford University Press.

Appelbaum, P., Roth, L., Lidz, C., & Bensen, P. W. W. (1987). False hopes and best data: Consent to research and the therapeutic misconception. *Hastings Center Report, 2*, 20–24.

Aronson Fontes, L. (1998). Ethics in family violence research: Cross-cultural issues. *Family Relations, 47*(1), 53–61.

Auriti, E. (2013). Who can obtain access to research data? Protecting research data against compelled disclosure. *NACUA Notes, 11*(7). Washington, DC: National Association of College and University Attorneys. https://www.calstate.edu/gc/documents/NACUANOTES-WhoCanObtainAccess-to-Research-ProtectingData.pdf. Accessed 19 December 2016.

Beauchamp, T., & Childress, J. (1994). *Principles of biomedical ethics*. New York: Oxford University Press.

Clinical Tools, Inc. (2006). *Guidelines for responsible data management in scientific research*. Office of Research Integrity, United States Department of Health and Human Services. https://ori.hhs.gov/education/products/clinicaltools/data.pdf. Accessed 15 March 2017.

Corti, L. (2000). Progress and problems of preserving and providing access to qualitative data for social research: The international picture of an emerging culture. *Forum: Qualitative Social Research, 1*(3). http://www.qualitative-research.net/index.php/fqs/article/view/1019. Accessed 15 March 2017.

De Craemer, W. (1983). A cross-cultural perspective on personhood. *Milbank Memorial Fund Quarterly: Health and Society, 61*(1), 19–34.

Denny, C. C., & Grady, C. (2007). Clinical research with economically disadvantaged populations. *Journal of Medical Ethics, 33*, 382–385.

Dresser, R. (2001). Advance directives in dementia research: Promoting autonomy and protecting subjects. *IRB: Ethics & Human Research, 23*(1), 1–6.

Faden, R. R., & Beauchamp, T. L. (1986). *A history and theory of informed consent*. Oxford: Oxford University Press.

Fedock, G. L. (2017). Women's psychological adjustment to prison: A review for future social work directions. *Social Work Research, 41*(1), 31–42.

Fienberg, S. E., Martin, M. E., & Straf, M. L. (1985). *Sharing research data*. Washington, DC: National Academy Press.

Flory, J., & Emanuel, E. (2004). Interventions to improve research participants' understanding of informed consent for research: A systematic review. *Journal of the American Medical Association, 292*(13), 1593–1601.

Fraser, M. W., Galinsky, M. J., & Richman, J. M. (1999). Risk, protection, and resilience: Toward a conceptual framework for social work practice. *Social Work Research, 23*(3), 131–143.

Gattis, M. N., & Larson, A. (2017). Perceived microaggressions and mental health in a sample of Black youths experiencing homelessness. *Social Work Research, 41*(1), 7–17.

Grady, C. (2001). Money for research participation: Does it jeopardize informed consent? *American Journal of Bioethics, 1*(2), 40–44.

Grady, C. (2005). Payment of clinical research subjects. *Journal of Clinical Investigation, 115*(7), 1681–1687.

Grisso, T., & Appelbaum, P. (1998). *Assessing competence to consent to treatment: A guide for physicians and other health professionals*. New York: Oxford University Press.

Groza, V. K., Bunkers, K., & Gamer, G. (2011). Ideal components and current characteristics of alternative care options for children outside of parental care. *Monographs of the Society for Research in Child Development, 76*(4), 163–180.

Hayes, C. (2011, September 2). IRA researchers at Boston College file suit against US govt. Irish Central. Available at: http://www.irishcentral.com/news/others-from-boston-college-project-

References

file-separate-suit-to-suppress-ira-interviews-129168208-237409721.html. Accessed 19 June 2014.

Heaton, J. (2008). Secondary analysis of qualitative data: An overview. *Historical Social Research/ Historische Sozialforschung, 33*(3), 33–45.

International Committee of Medical Journal Editors. (2014). Defining the role of authors and contributors. http://www.icmje.org/recommendations/browse/roles-and-responsibilities/defining-the-role-of-authors-and-contributors.html. Accessed 19 June 2014.

Inter-University Consortium for Political and Social Research. (n.d.). https://www.icpsr.umich.edu/icpsrweb/content/datamanagement/confidentiality/index.html. Accessed 15 March 2017.

Kipnis, K. (2001, March). Vulnerability in research subjects: A bioethical taxonomy. In *Ethical and policy issues in research involving human participants. Vol. II: Commissioned papers and staff analysis* (pp. G-1–G-13). Bethesda, MD: National Bioethics Advisory Commission.

Kipnis, K. (2003). Seven vulnerabilities in the pediatric research subject. *Theoretical Medicine, 24*, 107–120.

Largent, E. A., Grady, C., Miller, F. G., & Wertheimer, A. (2012). Money, coercion, and undue inducement: A survey of attitudes about payments to research participants. *IRB, 34*(1), 1–8.

Levine, R. J. (1988). *Ethics and regulation of clinical research*. New Haven, CT: Yale University Press.

Levine, C., Faden, R., Grady, C., Hammerschmidt, D., Eckenwiler, L., Sugarman, J., & Consortium to Examine Clinical Research Ethics. (2004). The limitations of "vulnerability" as a protection for human research participants. *American Journal of Bioethics, 4*(3), 44–49.

Loue, S. (2011). *"My nerves are bad" ("Mis nervios estan malos"): Puerto Rican women managing mental illness and HIV risk*. Nashville, TN: Vanderbilt University Press.

Luna, F. (2009). Elucidating the concept of vulnerability: Layers not labels. *International Journal of Feminist Approaches to Bioethics, 2*(1), 121–139.

Maschi, T., & Youdin, R. (2012). *Social worker as researcher: Integrating research with advocacy*. Boston: Pearson Education.

Mauthner, N. S., Maclean, C., & McKee, L. (2000). "My dad hangs out of helicopter doors and takes pictures of oil platforms": Children's accounts of parental work in the oil and gas industry. *Community, Work, and Family, 3*, 133–162.

Messing, J. T., Amanor-Boadu, Y., Cavanaugh, C. E., Glass, N. E., & Campbell, J. C. (2013). Culturally competent intimate partner violence risk assessment: Adapting the danger assessment for immigrant women. *Social Work Research, 37*(3), 263–275.

National Association of Social Workers. (2002). Social work profession. http://www.socialworkers.org/profession/factsheet.htm. Accessed 14 March 2017.

National Association of Social Workers. (2008). Code of ethics. http://www.socialworkers.org/pubs/code/code.asp. Accessed 7 July 2014.

National Bioethics Advisory Commission. (1998). *Research involving persons with mental disorders that may affect decisionmaking capacity*. Rockville, MD: U.S. Government Printing Office.

National Commission for the Protection of Human Subjects of Biomedical and Behavioral Research. (1979). *The Belmont Report: Ethical principles and guidelines for the protection of human subjects of research*. Washington, DC: United States Department of Health, Education, and Welfare [DHEW Pub. No. OS 78-0012].

National Institutes of Health. (2003a, February 26). Final NIH statement on sharing research data [NOT-OD-03-032]. https://grants.nih.gov/grants/guide/notice-files/NOT-OD-03-032.html. Accessed 15 March 2017.

National Institutes of Health. (2003b, March 5). NIH data sharing policy and implementation guidance. https://grants.nih.gov/grants/policy/data_sharing/data_sharing_guidance.htm#imp. Accessed 15 March 2017.

Neukrug, E. S. (1991). Computer-assisted live supervision in counselor skills training. *Counselor Education and Supervision, 31*, 132–138.

Nuremberg Code. (1946). In K. Lebacqz & R. J. Levine. (1982). Informed consent in human research: Ethical and legal aspects. In W.T. Reich (Ed.). *Encyclopedia of bioethics* (p. 757). New York: The Free Press.

Office of Research Integrity, United States Department of Health and Human Services. (n.d.). Responsible conduct in data management. https://ori.hhs.gov/education/ products/n_illinois_u/ datamanagement/dotopic.html. Accessed 06 May 2017.

Parry, O., Atkinson, P., & Delamont, S. (1997). The structure of PhD research. *Sociology, 31*, 121–129.

Parry, O., & Mauthner, N. S. (2004). Whose data are they anyway? Practical, legal and ethical issues in archiving qualitative research data. *Sociology, 38*(1), 139–152.

Rawls, J. (1999). *A theory of justice* (Rev. ed.). Cambridge, MA: The Belknap Press.

Sieber, J. E. (1989). Sharing scientific data I: New problems for IRBs. *IRB (IRB: A Review of Human Subjects Research), 11*(6), 4–7.

Smith, R. C., Mead, D. E., & Kinsella, J. A. (1998). Direct supervision: Adding computer-assisted feedback and data capture to live supervision. *Journal of Marital and Family Therapy, 24*, 113–125.

South African Data Archive. (n.d.). http://sada.nrf.ac.za/icpsr.html. Accessed 15 March 2017.

United States Copyright Office. (2012). Copyright basics [Circular 1]. Washington, DC: Author. https://www.copyright.gov/circs/circ01.pdf. Accessed 07 May 2017.

United States Copyright Office. (2016). Copyright registration of books, manuscripts, and speeches [FL-109]. https://www.copyright.gov/fls/fl109.pdf. Accessed 06 May 2017.

United States Department of Health and Human Services. (n.d.). Summary of the HIPAA privacy rule. http://www.hhs.gov/hipaa/for-professionals/privacy/laws-regulations/index.html. Accessed 23 March 2017.

Wager, E., & Kleinert, S. (2010, July 22–24). Responsible research publication: International standards for authors. A position statement developed at the Second World Conference in Research Integrity, Singapore. http://publicationethics.org/files/International%20standards_authors_for%20website_11_Nov_2011.pdf. Accessed 19 June 2014.

Weinstock, R., Bonnici, D., Seroussi, A., & Leong, G. S. (2014). No duty to warn in California: Now unambiguously solely a duty to protect. *Journal of the American Academy of Psychiatry and the Law, 42*(1), 101–108.

Wendler, D., & Grady, C. (2008). What should research participants understand to understand they are participants in research? *Bioethics, 22*(4), 203–208.

World Medical Association. (2013). *Helsinki* Declaration—Ethical principles for biomedical research involving human subjects. http://www.wma.net/en/30publications/10policies/b3/index.html. Accessed 14 March 2017.

Legal References

Cases

Abdullahi v. Pfizer, 562 F.3d 163 (2d Cir. 2009).

Davis v. Lhim, 124 Mich. App. 291 (1983), *aff'd on rem* 147 Mich. App. 8 (1985), *rev'd* on grounds of government immunity in *Canon v. Thumudo*, 430 Mich. 326 (1988).

Earle v. Kuklo, 26 N.J. Super. 471 (App. Div. 1953).

Ewing v. Goldstein, 120 Cal. App. 4th 807 (2004).

Ewing v. Northridge Hospital Medical Center, 120 Cal. App. 4th 1289 (2004).

Jablonski v. United States, 712 F.2d 391 (9th Cir. 1983).

McIntosh v. Milano, 168 N.J. Super. 466 (1979).

People v. Newman. (1973). 298 N.E.2d 651 (App. Div.).
Tarasoff v. Regents of the University of California, 17 Cal. 3d 425 (1976).
Thompson v. County of Alameda, 27 Cal. 3d 741 (1980).

Statutes

Health Insurance Portability and Accountability Act of 1996, Pub. L. 104–191.
Public Health Service Act, 42 U.S.C. § 241(d).

U.S. Regulations

68 C.F.R. Part 46 (2009).
45 C.F.R. § 160.103 (2013).
45 C.F.R. § 164.508 (2013).

Other

International Covenant on Civil and Political Rights, December 19, 1966, 999 U.N.T.S. 171.

Chapter 6
The Social Worker and Forensic Social Work

Defining Forensic Social Work

Exactly what constitutes forensic social work has varied across authors, with some viewing it as a relatively narrow subspecialty within social work and others defining it much more broadly. The length of time during which social work has engaged in forensic functions necessarily depends, to a degree, on the definition that one utilizes. Table 6.1 provides a summary of some such definitions.

As these various definitions indicate, forensic social work can be taken to mean any interaction with any component of the legal system, a definition and domain that is quite broad, or forensic social work can be narrowly defined to relate only to situations involving criminality. The field of forensic psychiatry appears to most closely align with the latter narrow definition, whereas forensic epidemiology is conceived of more broadly, encompassing a variety of activities in the legislative, civil, criminal, and advocacy arenas (Loue, 1999, 2009, 2013). This chapter relies a broader definition of forensic epidemiology, which will provide a more in-depth understanding of the many issues that arise at the juncture of law and social work.

Relying on this broader definition, we see that social workers may interact with the legal system through efforts to resolve disputes without litigation, by serving as an expert witness on behalf of a client, as a consultant to an attorney, or as an expert for the court, and by providing data and engaging with legislators, regulators, and/or policymakers in drafting new laws, regulations, or policies, in evaluating programs that connect in some way with the justice system, and in working with communities and their representatives to advocate for a particular position (Butters & Vaughan-Eden, 2011; Galowitz, 1998–1999; Green et al., 2005; Munson, 2011; National Organization of Forensic Social Work, n.d.). Social workers serving as consultants may be involved in evaluating the suitability of various alternative possibilities in the context of custody determinations, the competence of individuals to stand trial, or the success of court-ordered participation in psychotherapy or substance use recovery services (Munson, 2011). Social workers may also work with

Table 6.1 Definitions of forensic social work

Definition	Source
[T]hat area of common concern shared by social workers in probation and parole services, penal departments plus their ancillary services, voluntary agencies in the field of prison aftercare, and services to delinquent youths	Benjamin and Settle (1965, p. 21)
[T]he practice specialty in social work that focuses on the law and educating law professionals about social welfare issues and social workers about the legal aspects of their objectives	Barker (1995, p. 140)
[T]he practice specialty in social work that focuses on the law, legal issues, and litigation, both criminal and civil, including issues in child welfare, custody of children, divorce, juvenile delinquency, nonsupport, relatives' responsibility, welfare rights, mandated treatment, and legal competency. Forensic social work helps social workers in expert witness preparation. It also seeks to educate law professionals about social welfare issues and social workers about the law	Barker (2003, p. 166)
[P]olicies, practices, and social work roles with juvenile and adult offenders and victims of crime	Brownell and Roberts (2002, p. 3)
Forensic social work is a specialty area that is broadly defined as social work activities involving criminal or civil proceedings, criminal offenders, victims of crime, or other systems of justice. Forensic social workers are most often involved with adversarial court proceedings and emotionally charged civil cases that require special attention to ethics … Forensic social work is broadly defined as the application of social work to questions and issues relating to law and legal systems.	Butters and Vaughan-Eden (2011, p. 61)
Practice, which in any manner may be related to legal issues and litigation, both criminal and civil	Green, Thorpe, and Traupmann (2005, p. 1)
It denotes the social case work approach to delinquency and criminality as operationally influenced by the role of legal authority in defining agency function and limits and in giving an authoritative character to the case work situation—its objectives, techniques, and the processes of the case work relationship	Lanzer (1948, p. 24)
[A] subspecialty of social work that applies an integrative approach (i.e., generalist, socialized, and collaborative) to social work practice with diverse populations impacted by legal issues both civil and/or criminal. Forensic social work combines social work and specialized legal and policy skills to target social functioning and socio-legal conditions. The use of the term forensic underscores the infusion of social justice and human rights principles. It also underscores the collaborative nature of effective forensic social work, which includes collaboration with clients, professionals, and other stakeholders within and across formal and informal systems	Maschi and Killian (2011, p. 12)

Definition	Source
Forensic social work is the application of social work to questions and issues relating to law and legal systems. This specialty of our profession goes far beyond clinics and psychiatric hospitals for criminal defendants being evaluated and treated on issues of competency and responsibility. A broader definition includes social work practice which in any way is related to legal issues and litigation, both criminal and civil. Child custody issues, involving separation, divorce, neglect, termination of parental rights, the implications of child and spouse abuse, juvenile and adult justice services, corrections, and mandated treatment all fall under this definition	National Organization of Forensic Social Work, (n.d.)
[I]n the narrowest sense, it is the interaction of social work practice and the legal system.	Robbins, Vaughan-Eden, and Maschi (2015, p. 421)

attorneys as members of public or private law firms to assist clients with applications and proceedings related to Social Security and public health insurance benefits, such as Medicaid and Medicare, and disability-related issues.[1] A number of these domains are explored in greater detail below.

Social Workers and Dispute Resolution

Social workers may participate in efforts to resolve disputes before they escalate into litigation or may be asked by a court to assist with mediation in a particular case in which the judge believes that settlement may be possible. There are various approaches to dispute resolution. Two that are likely to be employed by social workers acting in this capacity are restorative justice and therapeutic jurisprudence. This could occur, for example, in proceedings involving juvenile transgressions against neighbors, landlord-tenant disputes, or child custody issues.

Restorative Justice

According to the Purist model, restorative justice is "a process whereby all the parties with a stake in a particular offence come together to resolve collectively how to deal with the aftermath of the offence and its implications for the future" (Marshall, 1996, p. 37; see also McCold, 2000). The Maximalist model of restorative justice suggests that the process focuses on ensuring that "every action ... is primarily oriented towards doing justice by repairing the harm that has been caused by the crime" (Walgrave, 2000, p. 418; see also Bazemore & Walgrave, 1999). "Complete" restorative justice practice has been depicted as occurring at the intersection of three circles in a Venn diagram; these circles signify "victim reparation," pertaining to the victim; "offender responsibility," relating to the offender; and "communities of care reconciliation," referring to the community, which may comprise the victims' and offenders' family members, friends, neighborhoods, and broader societies (McCold, 2000). Activities occurring outside of the three-circle intersection, such as victim-offender reconciliation efforts or a victim restoration board, have been considered to be mostly restorative or partly restorative, respectively.

Restorative justice is believed to balance the need to hold offenders accountable for their actions with the need to accept and reintegrate them into the community (Braithwaite, 1989; Zehr, 2002). Additionally, this approach addresses the needs of the victims (Clear, 1994; Zehr, 1990), shifts the focus from the offender to include the victims and communities as well (Bazemore & Maloney, 1994), and empowers the victims, the offenders, and the community through a process of negotiation,

---

[1] For one such example, see the website for Hickman & Lowder Co., L.P.A. at http://www.hickman-lowder.com.

mediation, and reparation. The process emphasizes healing the victim and community, the offender's moral and social self, and repairing relationships (Braithwaite, 1998, 2002). Although punishment is frequently a component of restorative justice, its inclusion is not central to the resolution of a situation. In contrast to the unilateral imposition of punishment that occurs within the retributive justice framework, restorative justice "is a collective effort shared between victim, offender, and community," whereby moral meaning "is restored through consensus with the offender" (Wenzel, Okimoto, Feather, & Platow, 2008, pp. 379–380).

Through a process of restorative justice, the aggrieved party may come to understand better the perpetrator's situation and view him, her, or them more compassionately. Importantly, the process also provides an opportunity for the perpetrator(s) to gain an understanding of the impact of their actions on the victim(s). The process is sufficiently broad to encompass negotiation relating to apology and forgiveness, e.g., who is to apologize to whom, under what circumstances, for what, and in what manner. It has been suggested that restorative justice "very neatly bridges the gap between the formality of conventional criminal justice processes and the social work ethos .... [focusing on] uniting rather than dividing people on opposite sides of the law ..." (van Wormer, Roberts, Springer, & Brownell, 2008, p. 335).

Therapeutic Jurisprudence

Therapeutic jurisprudence offers yet another approach. Like restorative justice, the process is sufficiently flexible to permit negotiation of forgiveness and apology. Unlike restorative justice, therapeutic jurisprudence places significant emphasis on the strengths of the parties involved, the negotiation of values, and the maximization of the process' beneficial therapeutic effects, all of which are central to the practice of social work.

Therapeutic jurisprudence has been described as "an interdisciplinary study, which is not a body of knowledge but rather. .. a method by which to analyze, learn about, and act out the law" (Schma, 2003, p. 26). Social science is used to assess the effects of legal rules or practice on individuals' physical and mental health (Slobogan, 1995), with a specific emphasis on the use of psychological knowledge to determine how law and law reform can enhance well-being (Wexler, 1996).

Although concerned with the outcome of a situation, therapeutic jurisprudence approach focuses on the strengths of the various stakeholders, rather than the attribution of blame (Brooks, 1999). Both the negotiation of values and the development of a shared consensus regarding the course of action to be followed are emphasized. The approach may not lead to a shift in concerned parties' values but may bring about changes in their perspective about the weight given to particular values (Kress, 1999).

At its core, therapeutic jurisprudence is concerned with the behavior of legal actors; the extent to which those actors reflect care, trust, and sensitivity with respect to the situation at hand; the maximization of the law's therapeutic effects; and the minimization of anti-therapeutic effects (Brookbanks, 2001). As such, it constitutes a way of viewing the world and working with the law that involves four domains of inquiry: "(1) the role of law in producing psychological dysfunction, (2) therapeutic aspects of the law, (3) therapeutic aspects of the legal system, and (4) therapeutic aspects of judicial and legal roles" (Wexler, 1990, pp. 4–5). "Law" encompasses rules, procedures, and the roles and behaviors of judges, lawyers, and therapists acting in the legal context (Wexler, 2000). Depending on the nature of the conflict, the parties involved, and the circumstances that characterize the larger context, those involved in the conflict resolution process may rely on principles of therapeutic jurisprudence as the basis for formulating a multidisciplinary approach, community collaborative partnerships, multilevel community interventions, and effective family or community interventions (Loue, 2012).

Unlike restorative justice, which looks to and addresses the impact and resolution of past events, therapeutic jurisprudence facilitates a forward-looking perspective. This approach allows those involved to address both the interpersonal and systemic elements implicated in a particular situation, not only to resolve the issue at hand but also to reform or remediate those elements that may portend a recurrence of similar situations with other individuals in the future. As an example, therapeutic jurisprudence may facilitate collaboration between the legal system, the social work system, and a religious community to not only address the harm that may have resulted from religiously motivated parental withholding of their child's medical care but also to reduce the potential future incidence of religiously premised withholding of medical care that may rise to the level of legally defined child neglect or abuse (Loue, 2012).

In the Courtroom: Social Workers as Expert Witnesses

Social workers may be called upon to testify as an expert witness on behalf of their client or by a party in a legal proceeding whose interests are adversarial to those of their client. Either scenario may occur, for example, in the context of a divorce proceeding or custody proceeding, e.g., if one party to the litigation is attempting to demonstrate that he or she was somehow harmed in the relationship, thereby necessitating the divorce, or that he or she merits custody of the children and/or the pet. In other situations, a social worker who is unknown to either party in the litigation may be hired as a consultant by an individual's attorney to help with the preparation of the case (Guin, Noble, & Merrill, 2003) or by the court itself, to provide the court with a more objective assessment of the circumstances relevant to the disposition of the case (e.g., *People v. R.R.*, 2005). Accordingly, it may be helpful to review here the structure and processes used by courts prior to discussing more specifically the circumstances under which a court would allow a social worker to be called as an expert witness.

Court Structure

The state and federal court systems can be thought of as pyramids. At the very base of the pyramid are the lowest courts. At the mid-level of the pyramid sit the courts of first appeal, and at the pinnacle of the pyramid sits the Supreme Court of the state or of the federal court system. Different states, however, name these various levels differently. For instance, the Supreme Court in California is known as the Supreme Court, but in Massachusetts it is known as the Massachusetts Supreme Judicial Court, and in New York it is called the Court of Appeals.

In the state court system, the lowest-level courts are often divided into those that have limited jurisdiction and those that have general jurisdiction. Those with limited jurisdiction often hear cases involving less serious offenses and civil lawsuits that do not involve large sums of money. Courts of general jurisdiction may hear cases involving monetary sums over a specified amount or more serious matters. Courts of general jurisdiction are often divided into special courts due to the volume of cases and the need for specialized expertise. Examples of such specialized courts include juvenile court, family court, and traffic court.

The mid-level courts, or appellate courts, have the power to hear appeals from the decisions of the lower courts. This is known as appellate jurisdiction, as contrasted with original jurisdiction, which is the power to hear a case at its inception. The appellate courts may have original jurisdiction with respect to a limited range of cases. The state Supreme Court may hear appeals from the appellate courts.

The lowest tier on this pyramid in the federal system consists of the federal district courts. These courts hear cases involving crimes that arise under federal statutes, such as making false statements on a federal application. They have jurisdiction over cases in which the citizen of one state is suing a citizen of another state (diversity of citizenship case) if the amount in dispute is greater than a specified minimum. (State courts may also hear cases in which a citizen of one state is suing a citizen of another state. This is known as concurrent jurisdiction. Not infrequently, the party who did not file the original lawsuit may ask to have the case removed to federal court.) The federal district courts may also hear cases arising under the federal constitution and cases arising under federal statutes.

Appeals from the decisions of the federal district courts are made to the federal court of appeal having jurisdiction over the circuit in which the district court sits. Twelve of these circuit courts are for named circuits; one is for cases arising in the District of Columbia, and one is for the Federal Circuit, which has jurisdiction over claims that are exclusively within the domain of federal law and patent and trademark law.

The United States Supreme Court hears appeals from the courts of appeal. However, in most situations, there is no automatic right to appeal to the Supreme Court. Rather, the Supreme Court chooses the cases that it will hear. Request to have an appeal heard is made through a *writ of certiorari*, which is a petition to file an appeal.

The Basics of Court Proceedings

Many situations in which a social worker might be asked to appear are civil matters in which one person is suing either another individual, such as in a divorce, or an entity, e.g., an employee may be suing their employer for sexual harassment and their attorney hires a social worker as a consultant to evaluate and testify about the client's claim for emotional distress. The commencement of a lawsuit in such cases begins with the filing of a complaint by a party to the lawsuit. The complaint must, in general, state the nature of the claim, the facts to support the claim, and the amount in controversy. The defendant will be served with a copy of the complaint, together with a summons. The summons indicates that the defendant must respond to the complaint in some fashion within a specified period of time or the plaintiff will win the lawsuit by default.

The defendant will then answer the complaint and will admit, deny, or plead ignorance to each allegation of the complaint. The defendant may also file a countersuit against the plaintiff or against a third party. The defendant may also ask that the court dismiss the plaintiff's action, claiming that the court has no jurisdiction to entertain the case or that the plaintiff failed to state a cause of action.

Following the initiation of the lawsuit and the answer by the defendant, there will be a period of discovery, during which each party to the action will have the opportunity to gather additional facts to support its case, to identify expert witnesses that the other side may call, and to identify weaknesses in the opposing party's case. Discovery may include depositions, written interrogatories, the production of documents, a request for a mental or physical examination, and a request for admissions. Those that are most relevant to this discussion are depositions, written interrogatories, a request for the production of documents, and a request for admissions.

The trial itself consists of numerous stages:

1. The opening statement of the plaintiff
2. The opening statement of the defendant
3. The presentation of direct evidence by the plaintiff, with cross- examination of each witness by the defendant, redirect by the plaintiff, and re-cross by the defendant
4. The presentation of direct evidence by the defendant, with cross- examination by the plaintiff, redirect by the defendant, and re-cross by the plaintiff
5. Presentation of rebuttal evidence by the plaintiff
6. Presentation of rebuttal evidence by the defendant
7. Plaintiff's argument to the jury
8. Defendant's argument to the jury
9. Plaintiff's closing argument to the jury
10. Defendant's closing argument to the jury
11. Instructions from the judge to the jury
12. Jury deliberation and verdict

The type of remedy that may be available to a plaintiff or plaintiffs in a lawsuit will depend on the basis on which the suit is brought. An individual suing to rectify the unlawful termination of his or her employment due to discrimination may seek reinstatement of his or her employment, monetary damages to compensate for the legal expenditures related to bringing the lawsuit and the loss of income, and/or monetary damages to punish the offending party.

The basic processes in a criminal case are similar, but in a criminal case, it is not another person who is suing. Rather, it is the state or federal government that brings the criminal case on behalf of the interests of the government for its citizens. And, in criminal cases, the case is commenced by the filing of a criminal complaint or an indictment from the grand jury that specifies the charges against the individual. In the context of a criminal case, a social worker may be hired by the defendant's attorney, the state or federal prosecutor, or the court. As an example, the case of *State v. Taylor* (1996) involved the trial of a man indicted and convicted of the first-degree murder of a store clerk committed during the course of an armed robbery. His defense attorneys formed a multidisciplinary mitigation team in an effort to have their client spared the death penalty; that team included two clinical social workers (Guin et al., 2003; *State v. Taylor*, 1996). The social workers were tasked with forming a relationship with the defendant in order to learn the intimate details of the defendant's life, develop an initial social history, and produce objective, reliable information that would help to provide a more holistic perspective about the defendant for jury consideration (Guin et al., 2003).

Before an individual can testify as an expert, he or she must be deemed by the court to be qualified to do so. Additionally, what he or she is to testify to must be deemed by the court to be admissible. As an example, a social worker might be found to be an expert witness on the basis of his or her education and/or experience but would not be permitted to testify about the weather on a particular day because such information would be readily available from existing records. The standards for qualifying as an expert witness often differ between the federal and various state court systems.

Qualifying as an Expert Witness

In the federal courts, an individual must meet the requirements of Rule 702 of the Federal Rules of Evidence in order to qualify as an expert witness. The Rule provides:

> A witness who is qualified as an expert by knowledge, skill, experience, training, or education may testify in the form of an opinion or otherwise if:
> (a) the expert's scientific, technical, or other specialized knowledge will help the trier of fact to understand the evidence or to determine a fact in issue;
> (b) the testimony is based on sufficient facts or data;
> (c) the testimony is the product of reliable principles and methods; and
> (d) the expert has reliably applied the principles and methods to the facts of the case.
> (Federal Rules of Evidence, 2011)

This means that an individual can be qualified to testify as an expert witness on the basis of his or her knowledge OR skill OR experience OR training OR education. Although some courts have interpreted the rule liberally (*Pineda v. Ford Motor Co.*, 2008; Faigman et al., 2011), an expert is still required to have the knowledge of experience in his or her field so that his opinions or inferences would likely aid the trier of fact—either a judge or a jury—in its search for the truth (*U.S. v. Hicks*, 2004).

Each state sets forth in its statutes the requirements for an individual to be qualified as an expert witness, and as indicated previously, the states vary with respect to these requirements. Many states have rules that are similar to those of the federal courts. Table 6.2 provides a brief summary of the various state requirements.

As can be seen from Table 6.2, the language used differs across the states. Many of the states indicate that the witness must have knowledge, skill, experience, training, or education to be qualified as an expert. Pennsylvania's statute requires that the knowledge or skill be beyond that which would be possessed by a layperson.

The party seeking to have an individual qualified as an expert witness must present evidence that is sufficient to demonstrate that the individual has met the statutory requirements to be an expert witness (*Corpus Juris Secundum*, 2012a). In assessing an individual's qualifications to be an expert witness, the judge will review his or her education, licensure, certification, background, training, research studies, publications, presentations, practical experience, and membership in relevant professional associations or societies (*Corpus Juris Secundum*, 2012c). The court makes the ultimate decision with respect to an individual's qualification as an expert (Dore, 2012).

If a party is going to challenge the other party's introduction of an individual as an expert, they will often do so during the process known as voir dire (Dore, 2012). This process, through which the individual's qualifications as an expert are presented and reviewed, may occur only with the judge and the attorneys, prior to the jury hearing the individual's testimony. Some jurisdictions allow this voir dire process in such a way that the court is able to preview the expert's qualifications prior to testimony in front of the jury. During voir dire, the competency, knowledge, and credentials of the expert will be presented and examined (Dore, 2012; Sapir, 2007). The voir dire process is not necessary if there is little doubt that an expert is qualified to testify with respect to a particular issue or if the opposing party does not object to the individual's qualifications (*Corpus Juris Secundum*, 2012b). However, the witness' qualifications may also, under some circumstances, be challenged on appeal. This was the case of the challenge to a social worker's qualifications to serve as an expert witness in a New York court.

The case of *State v. R.R.* (2005) involved two different defendants. The first was a middle-aged man with a history of depression, epilepsy, and head trauma that predated the offense for which he had been convicted. He had been arrested and charged with assault following an altercation in which he stabbed another individual. The second case involved an older man who had been charged with kidnapping in the second degree and endangering the welfare of a child after he took a child from a baby stroller without the permission of the infant's mother. He was found to not be competent to stand trial because of dementia; results of a later medical

Table 6.2 Summary of state requirements for reliance on expert witnesses

Alaska Rule of Evidence 702 (2014)	If scientific, technical, or other specialized knowledge will assist the trier of fact to understand the evidence or to determine a fact in issue, a witness qualified as an expert by knowledge, skill, experience, training, or education, may testify thereto in the form of an opinion or otherwise
Arkansas Rule of Evidence 702 (2016)	If scientific, technical, or other specialized knowledge will assist the trier of fact to understand the evidence or to determine a fact in issue, a witness qualified as an expert by knowledge, skill, experience, training, or education may testify thereto in the form of an opinion or otherwise
California Rule of Evidence 720 (2016)	A person is qualified to testify as an expert if he has special knowledge, skill, experience, training, or education sufficient to qualify him as an expert on the subject to which his testimony relates. Against the objection of a party, such special knowledge, skill, experience, training, or education must be shown before the witness may testify as an expert
Connecticut Code of Evidence 7-2 (2009)	A witness qualified as an expert by knowledge, skill, experience, training, education, or otherwise may testify in the form of an opinion or otherwise concerning scientific, technical, or other specialized knowledge, if the testimony will assist the trier of fact in understanding the evidence or in determining a fact in issue
Delaware Uniform Rule of Evidence 702 (2001)	If scientific, technical, or other specialized knowledge will assist the trier of fact to understand the evidence or to determine a fact in issue, a witness qualified as an expert by knowledge, skill, experience, training, or education may testify thereto in the form of an opinion or otherwise, if (1) the testimony is based upon sufficient facts or data, (2) the testimony is the product of reliable principles and methods, and (3) the witness has applied the principles and methods reliably to the facts of the case
Florida Statutes 90.702 (2013)	If scientific, technical, or other specialized knowledge will assist the trier of fact in understanding the evidence or in determining a fact in issue, a witness qualified as an expert by knowledge, skill, experience, training, or education may testify about it in the form of an opinion or otherwise, if (1) the testimony is based upon sufficient facts or data; (2) the testimony is the product of reliable principles and methods; and (3) the witness has applied the principles and methods reliably to the facts of the case
Hawaii Rule of Evidence 702 (2010)	If scientific, technical, or other specialized knowledge will assist the trier of fact to understand the evidence or to determine a fact in issue, a witness qualified as an expert by knowledge, skill, experience, training, or education may testify thereto in the form of an opinion or otherwise. In determining the issue of assistance to the trier of fact, the court may consider the trustworthiness and validity of the scientific technique or mode of analysis employed by the proffered expert
Idaho Rule of Evidence 702 (1985)	If scientific, technical, or other specialized knowledge will assist the trier of fact to understand the evidence or to determine a fact in issue, a witness qualified as an expert by knowledge, skill, experience, training, or education may testify thereto in the form of an opinion or otherwise

(continued)

Table 6.2 (continued)

Illinois Rule of Evidence 702 (2011)	If scientific, technical, or other specialized knowledge will assist the trier of fact to understand the evidence or to determine a fact in issue, a witness qualified as an expert by knowledge, skill, experience, training, or education may testify thereto in the form of an opinion or otherwise. Where an expert testifies to an opinion based on a new or novel scientific methodology or principle, the proponent of the opinion has the burden of showing the methodology or scientific principle on which the opinion is based is sufficiently established to have gained general acceptance in the particular field in which it belongs
Kentucky Rule of Evidence 702 (2007)	If scientific, technical, or other specialized knowledge will assist the trier of fact to understand the evidence or to determine a fact in issue, a witness qualified as an expert by knowledge, skill, experience, training, or education may testify thereto in the form of an opinion or otherwise, if (1) the testimony is based upon sufficient facts or data; (2) the testimony is the product of reliable principles and methods; and (3) the witness has applied the principles and methods reliably to the facts of the case
Louisiana Rule of Evidence 702 (1989)	If scientific, technical, or other specialized knowledge will assist the trier of fact to understand the evidence or to determine a fact in issue, a witness qualified as an expert by knowledge, skill, experience, training, or education may testify thereto in the form of an opinion or otherwise
Michigan Rule of Evidence 702 (2012)	If the court determines that scientific, technical, or other specialized knowledge will assist the trier of fact to understand the evidence or to determine a fact in issue, a witness qualified as an expert by knowledge, skill, experience, training, or education may testify thereto in the form of an opinion or otherwise if (1) the testimony is based upon sufficient facts or data, (2) the testimony is the product of reliable principles and methods, and (3) the witness has applied the principles and methods reliably to the facts of the case
Minnesota Rule of Evidence 702 (2006)	If scientific, technical, or other specialized knowledge will assist the trier of fact to understand the evidence or to determine a fact in issue, a witness qualified as an expert by knowledge, skill, experience, training, or education may testify thereto in the form of an opinion or otherwise. The opinion must have foundational reliability. In addition, if the opinion or evidence involves novel scientific theory, the proponent must establish that the underlying scientific evidence is generally accepted within the relevant scientific community
Mississippi Rule of Evidence 702 (2003)	If scientific, technical, or other specialized knowledge will assist the trier of fact to understand the evidence or to determine a fact in issue, a witness qualified as an expert by knowledge, skill, experience, training, or education may testify thereto in the form of an opinion or otherwise if (1) the testimony is based upon sufficient facts or data, (2) the testimony is the product of reliable principles and methods, and (3) the witness has applied the principles and methods reliably to the facts of the case
Missouri Revised Statutes 490.065.1 (2017)	In any civil action, if scientific, technical, or other specialized knowledge will assist the trier of fact to understand the evidence or to determine a fact in issue, a witness qualified as an expert by knowledge, skill, experience, training, or education may testify thereto in the form of an opinion or otherwise if (1) the testimony is based upon sufficient facts or data; (2) the testimony is the product of reliable principles and methods; and (3) the witness has applied the principles and methods reliably to the facts of the case

In the Courtroom: Social Workers as Expert Witnesses 115

Montana Code Annotated, Rule of Evidence 702 (2015)	If scientific, technical, or other specialized knowledge will assist the trier of fact to understand the evidence or to determine a fact in issue, a witness qualified as an expert by knowledge, skill, experience, training, or education may testify thereto in the form of an opinion or otherwise
Nebraska Code §27-702, Rule 702 (1975)	If scientific, technical, or other specialized knowledge will assist the trier of fact to understand the evidence or to determine a fact in issue, a witness qualified as an expert by knowledge, skill, experience, training, or education may testify thereto in the form of an opinion or otherwise
Nevada Revised Statutes 50.275 (1971)	If scientific, technical or other specialized knowledge will assist the trier of fact to understand the evidence or to determine a fact in issue, a witness qualified as an expert by special knowledge, skill, experience, training or education may testify to matters within the scope of such knowledge
New Hampshire Rule of Evidence 702 (2011)	If scientific, technical, or other specialized knowledge will assist the trier of fact to understand the evidence or to determine a fact in issue, a witness qualified as an expert by knowledge, skill, experience, training, or education may testify thereto in the form of an opinion or otherwise
North Carolina General Statute 8C-702, Rule 702 (2011)	If scientific, technical or other specialized knowledge will assist the trier of fact to understand the evidence or to determine a fact in issue, a witness qualified as an expert by knowledge, skill, experience, training, or education may testify thereto in the form of an opinion, or otherwise, if all of the following apply: (1) the testimony is based upon sufficient facts or data. (2) the testimony is the product of reliable principles and methods. (3) the witness has applied the principles and methods reliably to the facts of the case
North Dakota Rule of Evidence 702 (2014)	A witness who is qualified as an expert by knowledge, skill, experience, training, or education may testify in the form of an opinion or otherwise if the expert's scientific, technical, or other specialized knowledge will help the trier of fact to understand the evidence or to determine a fact in issue
Ohio Rules of Evidence 702 (1994)	A witness may testify as an expert if all of the following apply: (A) The witness' testimony either relates to matters beyond the knowledge or experience possessed by laypersons or dispels a misconception common among laypersons; (B) the witness is qualified as an expert by specialized knowledge, skill, experience, training, or education regarding the subject matter of the testimony; (C) the witness' testimony is based on reliable scientific, technical, or other specialized information. To the extent that the testimony reports the result of a procedure, test, or experiment, the testimony is reliable only if all of the following apply: (1) the theory upon which the procedure, test, or experiment is based is objectively verifiable or is validly derived from widely accepted knowledge, facts, or principles; (2) the design of the procedure, test, or experiment reliably implements the theory; (3) the particular procedure, test, or experiment was conducted in a way that will yield an accurate result
Oregon Revised Statutes 40.410, Rule 702 (2015)	If scientific, technical, or other specialized knowledge will assist the trier of fact to understand the evidence or to determine a fact in issue, a witness qualified as an expert by knowledge, skill, experience, training, or education may testify thereto in the form of an opinion or otherwise

(continued)

Table 6.2 (continued)

Pennsylvania Rule of Evidence 702 (2013)	A witness who is qualified as an expert by knowledge, skill, experience, training, or education may testify in the form of an opinion or otherwise if: (a) the expert's scientific, technical, or other specialized knowledge is beyond that possessed by the average layperson; (b) the expert's scientific, technical, or other specialized knowledge will help the trier of fact to understand the evidence or to determine a fact in issue; and (c) the expert's methodology is generally accepted in the relevant field
South Carolina Rule of Evidence 702 (2011)	If scientific, technical, or other specialized knowledge will assist the trier of fact to understand the evidence or to determine a fact in issue, a witness qualified as an expert by knowledge, skill, experience, training, or education may testify thereto in the form of an opinion or otherwise
South Dakota Codified Laws 19-15-2, Rule 702 (2012)	If scientific, technical, or other specialized knowledge will assist the trier of fact to understand the evidence or to determine a fact in issue, a witness qualified as an expert by knowledge, skill, experience, training, or education may testify thereto in the form of an opinion or otherwise, if: (1) the testimony is based upon sufficient facts or data, (2) the testimony is the product of reliable principles and methods, and (3) the witness has applied the principles and methods reliably to the facts of the case
Texas Rule of Evidence 702 (2015)	A witness who is qualified as an expert by knowledge, skill, experience, training, or education may testify in the form of an opinion or otherwise if the expert's scientific, technical, or other specialized knowledge will help the trier of fact to understand the evidence or to determine a fact in issue
Utah Rule of Evidence 702 (2011)	Subject to the limitations in paragraph (b), a witness who is qualified as an expert by knowledge, skill, experience, training, or education may testify in the form of an opinion or otherwise if the expert's scientific, technical, or other specialized knowledge will help the trier of fact to understand the evidence or to determine a fact in issue. b) Scientific, technical, or other specialized knowledge may serve as the basis for expert testimony only if there is a threshold showing that the principles or methods that are underlying in the testimony (1) are reliable, (2) are based upon sufficient facts or data, and (3) have been reliably applied to the facts. (c) the threshold showing required by paragraph (b) is satisfied if the underlying principles or methods, including the sufficiency of facts or data and the manner of their application to the facts of the case, are generally accepted by the relevant expert community
Washington Rule of Evidence 702 (1979)	If scientific, technical, or other specialized knowledge will assist the trier of fact to understand the evidence or to determine a fact in issue, a witness qualified as an expert by knowledge, skill, experience, training, or education may testify thereto in the form of an opinion or otherwise
Wisconsin Statutes 907.02(1) (2011)	If scientific, technical, or other specialized knowledge will assist the trier of fact to understand the evidence or to determine a fact in issue, a witness qualified as an expert by knowledge, skill, experience, training, or education may testify thereto in the form of an opinion or otherwise, if the testimony is based upon sufficient facts or data, the testimony is the product of reliable principles and methods, and the witness has applied the principles and methods reliably to the facts of the case

examination indicated that he was HIV-infected. His functioning improved after he began a regimen of both antiretroviral and antipsychotic medications. The court retained a clinical social worker to examine both defendants. The social worker concluded that the first defendant was competent to stand trial but that the second defendant was not responsible by reason of mental disease or defect. The attorney for the first defendant appealed, arguing that the social worker's assessment was outside of the scope of his practice, that the findings should not be admitted, and that his client should be examined by a psychiatrist.

In reviewing the social worker's qualifications to serve as an expert, the court considered his professional accomplishments, noting specifically that the social worker was the founding chairperson of the Committee on Forensic Clinical Social Work of the National Federation of Societies for Clinical Social Work and the primary author of the standards for forensic social work that had been adopted by the New York State Society for Clinical Social Work (*State v. R.R.*, 2005, p. 3, n.1). In reviewing the admissibility of his testimony, the court found as a matter of law that:

> the evaluation, making and rendering of diagnoses and prognoses, formulating treatment plans and the psychological-psychosocial treatment of mental disorders or of mental, emotional and behavioral symptoms which, either in whole or in part, are or may reasonably be assumed to be organic in nature or which may result to some degree from a concurrent physical ailment or dysfunction, are within the scope of practice of the professions of psychology and licensed clinical social work, whose scopes of practice although described using some different words at times, do not vary in substance and are wholly equal and the same. (*State v. R.R.*, 2005, p. 544)

Determining the Admissibility of Expert Testimony

In addition to finding that an individual qualifies as an expert witness, the court must also decide whether his or her testimony will be admissible. For many years, federal courts utilized the criteria for determining the admissibility of evidence that had been set out by the US Supreme Court in the 1923 case of *Frye v. United States*. The Court in that case held that evidence was reliable and admissible when the methods and procedures employed by the expert had gained "general acceptance in the particular field in which it belongs" (*Frye v. United States*, 1923, p. 1014). This standard changed with the Court holding in the case of *Daubert v. Merrell Dow Pharmaceuticals, Inc.* (1993).

The case of *Daubert v. Merrell Dow Pharmaceuticals, Inc.* involved a lawsuit by two infants and their guardians ad litem against a pharmaceutical company for birth defects that they alleged had been sustained by their mothers' use of an anti-nausea drug, Bendectin, during pregnancy (*Daubert v. Merrell Dow Pharmaceuticals*, 1993). At the trial level, the plaintiffs attempted to submit the testimony of eight experts who had concluded that Bendectin caused birth defects based on their review of animal studies, chemical structure analysis, and the unpublished reanalysis of previously published human statistical studies (*Daubert v. Merrell Dow*

Pharmaceuticals, Inc., 1993). The trial court held this expert testimony inadmissible under the *Frye* standard, reasoning that non-epidemiological studies such as the animal cell studies, live animal studies, and chemical structure analyses were not a "generally accepted" methodology for evaluating Bendectin and were therefore inadmissible (*Daubert v. Merrell Dow Pharmaceuticals*, 1993). The court also found that the plaintiff's epidemiological reanalyses were not generally accepted because they had not been published or subject to peer review (*Daubert v. Dow Merrell Pharmaceuticals*, 1993).

The US Supreme Court determined that Federal Rule of Evidence 702, which had been promulgated after the Court decided the case of *Frye v. United States,* did not contain a "general acceptance" standard for determining the admissibility of expert testimony (*Daubert v. Merrell Dow Pharmaceuticals*, 1993). Instead, Rule 702 required that the trial judge ensure both the reliability and relevance of an expert's testimony (*Daubert v. Merrell Dow Pharmaceuticals*, 1993), permitting expert testimony only when "the expert's scientific, technical or other specialized knowledge will help the trier of fact to understand the evidence or to determine a fact in issue" (Federal Rule of Evidence 702, 2011). The Court found that the use of the term "scientific" in Federal Rule of Evidence 702 "implies a grounding in the methods and procedures of science," while "'knowledge' connotes more than subjective belief or unsupported speculation" (*Daubert v. Merrell Dow Pharmaceuticals*, 1993, p. 590).

The Supreme Court provided a list of factors that should be considered in determining whether evidence that a party seeks have admitted is reliable and relevant and, therefore, admissible. These factors are intended to assist the trial judge in determining whether the methodology employed by the expert is reliable, but they are not to be deemed to be exhaustive (*Daubert v. Merrell Dow Pharmaceuticals*, 1993). In considering these factors, the trial judge is to focus on the methodology employed by the expert rather than his or her conclusions (*Daubert v. Merrell Dow Pharmaceuticals*, 1993). The factors to be considered are:

1. Whether the theory or technique can be (and has been) tested
2. Whether the theory or technique has been subjected to peer review and publication
3. The theory or technique's known potential error rate and the existence and maintenance of standards controlling its operation
4. Whether the theory or technique has attained widespread acceptance within a relevant scientific community (*Daubert v. Merrell Dow Pharmaceuticals*, 1993)

The Supreme Court remanded the case so that the lower courts could apply the newly articulated standard to the proffered expert testimony (*Daubert v. Merrell Dow Pharmaceuticals*, 1993). In applying this standard, the Ninth Circuit Court of Appeals found that the plaintiffs had failed to satisfy the requirements enunciated by the Supreme Court's holding.

The later case of *General Electric v. Joiner* (1997) focused on the question of how an appeals court should review a lower federal court decision regarding the admissibility of evidence. The Supreme Court held that the appeals court was to utilize an "abuse of discretion standard," meaning that a review would entail an assessment of the lower court decision to determine if it was (1) clearly unreasonable, arbitrary, or fanciful; (2) based on an erroneous conclusion of law; (3) clearly erroneous; or (4) premised on a record that contains no evidence upon which the court rationally could have based its decision (Casey, Camara, & Wright, 2001–2002). Additionally, the Supreme Court later decided that, based on its reading of Federal Rule of Evidence 702, the trial judge's gatekeeping role applied to all forms of expert testimony and was not limited to testimony based on "hard" science (*Kumho Tire Co. v. Carmichael*, 1999). Accordingly, the *Daubert* standard of admissibility would apply to all forms of expert testimony (*Kumho Tire Co. v. Carmichael*, 1999).

State requirements governing the admissibility of experts' evidence vary across the states and may take any one of four approaches. These include (1) application of the standard enunciated in *Daubert*, (2) reliance on the earlier *Frye* standard, (3) utilization of a standard that is a hybrid of the *Daubert* and *Frye* standards, and (4) application of a completely different standard. These various standards are reflected in the statutory provisions contained in Table 16.2. Experts are cautioned to ensure they become familiar with the standard for the state in which they are testifying and the manner in which the standard has been applied by the courts. Accordingly, the standard on which the admissibility of a social worker's expert testimony will be assessed will depend, first, on whether the legal action is in state or federal court and, second, if it is in state court, the standard utilized by that state in determining the admissibility of evidence offered by an expert witness.

The Legislative and Policymaking Settings

Many social workers may believe that social work cannot play a role in the development and implementation of new legislation. However, the shift from larger juvenile institutions to smaller, community-based facilities during the 1970s is directly attributable to the efforts of a social worker, Jerome Miller, DSW, who was then Commissioner of the Massachusetts Department of Youth Services (Alexander, 1995). Social workers played a key role in advocating for the passage of the Juvenile Justice and Delinquency Prevention Act of 1974. The implementation of that legislation was led by another social worker, Ira Schwartz. Significant changes that were made included the deinstitutionalization of juvenile status offenders, e.g., truants and runaways, and the establishment of shelters (Roberts & Brownell, 1999).

An understanding of the legislative process is critical if social workers are to continue to be influential with respect to legislation that may affect their client constituents and the profession of social work itself. The process may differ in some respects at the state level across the 50 states, but, in general, the state process most often mirrors to a great degree the federal legislative process. For this reason, the federal legislative process is discussed below.

The formulation of proposed legislation may occur in any of several ways. First, a legislator may draft the legislation on his or her own and seek to have the legislation passed by both houses of Congress. Alternatively, the legislation may originate through the action of a citizen or a concerned group, such as a regional or national social work organization, which then approaches a representative in Congress to have the idea introduced in the form of proposed legislation (Sinclair, 1997). Instead of drafting a specific bill, the ideas can also be incorporated into legislation that is being drafted by a legislative committee or they can be offered as an amendment to someone's legislation.

A member of Congress must introduce the bill, regardless of which process was utilized in its formulation. This can be done in either the House of Representatives or the Senate. The bill will be assigned a number but may also be known by a title (Smith, 1995). The presiding officer of the house into which it was introduced will then send it to the appropriate committee or, if appropriate based on the subject matter of the bill, to several committees, a process known as multiple referral. This occurs where the bill relates to matters over which several committees may share jurisdiction. Often, the legislation will be sent to a subcommittee of a full committee. Committees and subcommittees have the authority to conduct investigations and hearings, during which they may receive testimony from interested parties and experts.

Committees may also perform markups on legislation, that is, they consider the proposed legislation in detail and amend it as they deem necessary. The committee may then report back the measure to the full House or Senate, but can only do so if a majority of the committee's members are present at the time. The committee must provide a report in reporting back the bill. These reports are frequently written by committee staff members and will often include a minority viewpoint (Smith, 1995). Committees also can refuse to act on proposed legislation; when this occurs, the legislation is said to have died in committee.

The general process following committee consideration, amendment, and markup consists of the consideration of the proposed legislation on the floor of the house in which it is being considered. The final version of a bill as it is approved by one house of Congress is known as an engrossed bill (Smith, 1995). The legislation must be approved by the two houses of Congress before it can be forwarded to the president for executive action. The second house can pass the legislation in the same form as it was passed in the house of origin. Alternatively, the two houses may exchange amendments on the legislation until they can agree, or the legislation can be forwarded to a conference committee comprised of representatives of both houses. The representatives on the conference committee are appointed by committee leaders to attempt to resolve the differences between the houses with respect to the proposed legislation. The final version of the bill that is approved by both houses, known as an enrolled bill, is printed on parchment and is certified by either the Clerk of the House or the Secretary of the Senate, based on which house first passed it. It is then signed by the Speakers of the House and the president pro tempore of the Senate, with space reserved for the president's signature.

The procedures for the consideration of legislation on the floor differs between the two houses. In the House of Representatives, when major legislation is being considered, the sponsors of the legislation may request a special rule from the Committee on Rules. If granted, the special rule limits general debate on the legislation to 1 h. The order of voting on amendments to the legislation may be structured. Members may be allowed to vote on more than one version of the legislation.

There is no such committee in the Senate. The scheduling of legislation to be heard on the floor of the Senate is done by making a motion to proceed to consider it. The motion to proceed, however, can be debated, sometimes to the point that the legislation is "talked to death." This is known as a filibuster. A filibuster can be stopped through cloture, meaning that, if all of the senators are present, 60 of the 100 senators must support cloture in order to end a filibuster.

Legislation relating to government agencies may be for authorization or for appropriations. Authorizing legislation relates to the agency's organization and ability to make rules, while appropriations legislation provides the money to carry out these functions.

If Congress is still in session when the legislation is approved by both houses and sent to the president, the president may sign the bill into law, veto the bill and send it back to Congress with a statement detailing his objections to the provisions of the legislation, or do nothing. A two-thirds vote of both houses is necessary to override a presidential veto. If the president chooses to do nothing, the bill will become law at the end of 10 days. If Congress is scheduled to adjourn within the 10 days, the president has the same courses of action available to him. However, because Congress will not be in session, and therefore cannot override a presidential veto, the bill will die if the president vetoes it or if the president does nothing. The veto of a bill in this manner—by doing nothing—is known as a pocket veto.

It has frequently been suggested that lobbyists, special interest groups, and individual or organizational advocates for a particular cause or position wield undue influence because, depending on the specifics of a situation, they may be able to convince a member of Congress to put a specific issue on the legislative agenda or keep an issue off of the agenda. A lobbyist has been defined as "someone who is paid to communicate with Congress on behalf of others" (Smith, 1995, p. 326). The role of lobbyists has been criticized even by members of Congress:

> Unfortunately, there is a widespread perception that Members of the Congress are failing to pursue the public interest and are responding to special interests inside the beltway. In the view of many, Members have lost touch with ordinary Americans, in part because they enjoy an assortment of special perks and privileges that are unavailable to the general public.
>
> Now, I know and I believe deeply that many of my colleagues would not change their view on legislative matters because someone offers to buy them a meal or a gift. But the perception problem is real. And the fact is, many Members of Congress do enjoy special advantages that do not accrue to the ordinary American. And many of these special perks are specifically designed to influence Members in the performance of their official duties.
>
> One prime example ... is the way that many lobbyists shower Members of Congress with gifts. It is not unusual for lobbyists to give Members free tickets to, say, a show, a

concert, a sporting event, and take them out to dinner before the event, buy them a cup of coffee and some nice desserts afterward or maybe a little champagne. Some lobbyists regularly take Members out for lavish meals at expensive restaurants. Let me add that we do not want to hurt the restaurant business, but this needs to be cleaned up.

Sometimes the lobbyists provide Members with free trips, typically involving stays in luxurious hotels in beautiful places, along with various forms of entertainment, whether it is playing tennis, golf, skiing, you name it.

I know that many of my colleagues feel that Members of Congress would not be influenced by a free dinner or even a luxury trip to the Caribbean. And I concur in that. Members of this body are serious, committed public servants who want to do what is right for their constituents and for the country at large.

However, it seems indisputable that these kinds of gifts have contributed to Americans' deepening distrust of Government, and Congress, in particular. And that is a serious problem, for as public trust diminishes, the ability of Congress to address our Nation's serious problems is also diminished. (Lautenberg, 1993, p. S5502)

Special interest groups often include occupational organizations or particular segments of the population. Approximately 20 percent of the interest groups consist of citizens' groups. Such groups:

> usually arise in the wake of broad social movements concerned with such problems as the level of environmental pollution, threats to civil rights, or changes in the status of women. The groups formed to act as representatives of these social movements often are created by political enterpreneurs operating with the support of wealthy individuals, private foundations, or elected political leaders who act as their protectors, financial supporters, and patrons. (Walker, 1991, p. 10)

Research relating to special interest groups has found that many interest groups often formulate their lobbying efforts strategically and may use any or all of the following strategies in their attempts to influence legislation: testifying at hearings, contacting government officials directly, engaging in informal contacts with government officials such as at conventions, presenting research findings or technical information, sending letters to organization members to inform them about activities, entering into coalitions with other organizations, attempting to influence the implementation of policy, interacting with media representatives, consulting with government officials to plan legislative strategy, assisting in drafting legislation, participating in letter writing campaigns, organizing grassroots lobbying efforts, and prevailing upon influential constituents to contact the offices of their local representatives (Denzau & Munger, 1986; Kollman, 1998; Schlozman & Tierney, 1986).

Despite the seemingly negative portrayal of lobbying by many writers, lobbying may serve an important function in that it brings critical issues to the attention of Congressional representatives and provides information and insights to which they might not otherwise have access. The National Association of Social Workers has encouraged its members to become active in advocating individually with their Congressional representatives for legislation that would impact social work clients and/or the social work profession. The organization has enumerated a list of lobbying do's and dont's:

DO
1. Do learn members' committee assignments and where their specialties lie.
2. Do present the need for what you're asking the member of Congress to do. Use data or cases you know.
3. Do relate situations in his/her home state or district.
4. Do ask the representative's or senator's position and why.
5. Do—in case of voting records—ask why he/she voted a particular way.
6. Do show openness to the knowledge of counterarguments and respond to them.
7. Do admit you don't know. Offer to try to find out the answer and send information back to the office.
8. Do spend time with members whose position is against yours. You can lessen the intensity of the opposition and perhaps change it.
9. Do spend time in developing relationships with Congressional staff.
10. Do thank them for stands the member has taken which you support.

DON'T
1. Don't overload a Congressional visit with too many issues.
2. Don't confront, threaten, pressure, or beg.
3. Don't be argumentative. Speak with calmness and commitment so as not to put him/her on the defensive.
4. Don't overstate the case. Members are very busy, and you're apt to lose their attention if you are too wordy.
5. Don't expect members of Congress to be specialists. Their schedules and workloads tend to make them generalists.
6. Don't be put off by smoke screens or long-winded answers. Bring the members back to the point. Maintain control of the meetings.
7. Don't make promises you can't deliver.
8. Don't be afraid to take a stand on the issues.
9. Don't shy away from meetings with legislators with known views opposite your own.
10. Don't be offended if a legislator is unable to meet and requests that you meet with his/her staff (National Association of Social Workers, 2017).

The NASW also provides its members with guidance on how best to approach Congressional representatives through letter writing (https://www.socialworkers.org/ advocacy/resources/writing_congress.asp) and how to arrange a meeting with one's representative (http://www.naswma.org/?page=Lobby101).

The NASW regularly sponsors lobbying days for its members. One such example is provided by the California Chapter of NASW which has proactively arranged lobby days at the state level for March 11 and 12, 2018, almost a year away at the time of this writing. These efforts will focus on the transinstitutionalization of mentally ill persons to jails and prisons, the effects on Californians by recent federal executive immigration-related orders, and the needs of older LGBT individuals in long-term care facilities (National Association of Social Workers California Chapter, n.d.).

Evaluation Research

There are far too many examples of evaluation research conducted by professionals engaged in forensic social work to review them here. Two particular studies can serve as examples of social workers' engagement in this domain.

One such study focused on the evaluation of a mentoring program for children of incarcerated parents that had been established within a youth shelter program (Bruster & Foreman, 2012). The study specifically sought to understand where the children were residing, the effectiveness of the mentoring services being provided, the emotional and psychological status of the children, and the frequency and manner of communication used by the mentoring program. The child and caregiver program participants were asked to complete a survey that focused on the parents' incarceration and family thoughts and feelings. An analysis of the survey responses revealed that the vast majority of program participants derived substantial benefit from the program. The study findings had implications for clinical practice: the authors concluded that clinical providers of services to children should ask them specifically about parental incarceration as they might not otherwise disclose such circumstances.

Yet another evaluation study reviewed outcome evaluation strategies for sexual assault service programs (Sullivan & Coats, 2000), that is, the evaluation evaluated strategies. This review was compiled in a practical guide to program evaluation to assist sexual assault service programs in the design of their own evaluations. Such a review has the potential to impact both the content and the delivery of the services that may be offered to clients of such programs and, indirectly, the infrastructure of the programs themselves in terms of staffing and productivity and accountability features.

Advocacy

The reentry unit social work services program in San Francisco provides an excellent example of the advocacy function that may be a component of forensic social work. The reentry social work services provided to defendants through the Public Defender's Office constitute one component of a holistic program of services intended to provide defendants and their families with needed support. The reentry social workers

> implement this program through their client assessments, treatment plans, referrals, and advocacy in court hearings. Reentry social workers assess clients' social service and legal needs while working with Public Defender attorneys to develop appropriate and viable alternatives to incarceration. The Reentry social workers in the Public Defender's Office have extensive knowledge of San Francisco social services and treatment networks as well as deep relationships with the social services staff and directors to which they connect their clients.

In addition, reentry social workers possess critical knowledge about the legal process and partner with Public Defender attorneys to discuss the best legal course of action for a client. The legal advocacy that reentry social workers provide ranges from supplying documentation in court proceedings to negotiating in a judge's chambers on a client's behalf. The social worker and attorney form a powerful team that works to strategize legal outcomes, finding the best holistic results for the client. The reentry social workers aim to mitigate state prison sentences by helping build legal cases that would offer alternative possibilities to defendants. The Reentry Unit's ultimate goal is to decrease sentence length and severity of sentencing location (from state prison to jail to program placement) by providing alternatives to incarceration that promise better client, family, and community outcomes through decreased recidivism and healthier reentry into defendants' communities (LFA Group, 2009, p. 5).

Clients are referred to the program by the public defender. Clients with a felony conviction and those whose probable sentence would likely entail prison time in a state prison receive priority for services. The reentry social workers often serve as advocates for their clients in the program by referring them to local social service agencies and (re)linking them to programs. The social workers have been found to be key in that they allow the attorneys to focus on the legal issues while ensuring that the clients' social service needs are addressed and they promote judicial understanding of the clients' circumstances. An evaluation of the impact of the reentry social worker services found that the involvement of the social workers was associated with an increased likelihood that the client would receive an alternate sentence in lieu of state prison and/or a reduced sentence; would receive needed treatment, such as for mental health or medical services; and would receive vocation training or education and job referrals (LFA Group, 2009).

Ethical Issues in Forensic Social Work

Various commentators have noted the numerous ethical issues that may arise in the practice of forensic social work (Butter & Vaughan-Eden, 2011; Lanzer, 1948). As Lanzer (1948, pp. 36–37) observed:

Both worker and client have to function in terms of the authoritarian setting, for it is legal authority which brought the relationship into being and which will determine its conditions and its ending. The client's problems have to be handled as basically centering around his definition of, reaction to, use of, and differentiation of authority.

Although Lanzer's discussion focused primarily on the role of the social worker in the prison and probation settings, his perspective is also relevant to situations in which the social worker serves as a consultant to an attorney or a court. Other writers, noting the tensions inherent in the role of a social worker's provision of social work services in the context of service to a court, advised:

The resolution of the treatment and control polarities necessarily has to occur within the individual worker who comes to integrate both dimensions, recognizing and accepting the creative tension between them. (Brennan, Gdrich, Tardy, & McCrea, 1986, p. 343)

The tension between the goals and values of social work and those of the legal system is most apparent with respect to issues surrounding confidentiality and reporting. Social workers retained by attorneys are bound by the attorney-client privilege to maintain as confidential all information that they discover in the course of that employment. However, they are also mandated reporters of child and elder abuse and, in some states, of partner abuse. Their legal and ethical responsibility as a social worker is in direct conflict with their legal responsibility as a contractor for the attorney; divulging abuse violates the attorney-client privilege, but a social worker's failure to report the abuse carries the potential for adverse civil, criminal, and licensing consequences (Butter & Vaughan-Eden, 2011; Galowitz, 1998–1999).

Social workers may also be required to provide the court or a legal authority with periodic reports detailing the client's progress or lack thereof, e.g., if a mental health court judge orders the client to attend a group and/or adhere to a medication regimen. Even if the client signs a release that permits the social worker to divulge the information to the appropriate authorities, the validity of that consent is open to question because the client may feel that he or she is under duress to allow the release of the information. The competency of an individual to provide informed consent may also be in question in some situations, such as when the client's severe mental illness has been the impetus that brought the individual to the attention of the legal system and that serves as the basis for the social worker's involvement (Odiah, 2004). A social worker's failure to file the requisite report or the filing of an incomplete or untruthful report may subject the social worker to legal repercussions (Butter & Vaughan-Eden, 2011). It may be advisable in such circumstances to separate the therapeutic and the evaluative functions so that each is addressed by a different person and the ethical issues associated with a dual relationship can be avoided (Butter & Vaughan-Eden, 2011; Campbell, 1994).

It appears that no practice guidelines or standards exist for the practice of forensic social work (Munson, 2011).[2] This absence creates potential ethical and legal conundrums for the social worker because (1) there are insufficient data to determine what may constitute best practices in any given domain of forensic social work; (2) the lack of guidance may increase the difficulty for social workers and other stakeholders to both enunciate a standard of care and to assess social worker competency in a given subspecialty of forensic practice; and (3) the ability to safeguard client rights and interests is potentially reduced (Munson, 2011). The lack of guidance also impacts licensing boards because they will have no framework from

---

[2] Practice guidelines have been defined as "suggested or recommended voluntary pointers for appropriate and acceptable practice" (Munson, 2011, p. 41). In contrast, practice standards "imply a set of behaviors that are precisely adhered to and mandated" and "should be viewed as directives and as supports for practitioners to use in safeguarding client rights in the context of intervention" (Munson, 2011, pp. 41, 43). Practice standards both guide social workers in the performance of their responsibilities and are relied upon by regulatory agencies in assessing the adequacy and appropriateness of social worker action and inaction. It has been suggested that, although practice standards are mandated, they are actually aspirational.

which to determine whether a social worker has performed inadequately or unethically in a given situation.[3]

It has been suggested that social workers may experience conflict in forensic practice because they are "trained to work toward mutually beneficial outcomes for either side of a dispute, whereas the legal system, at least superficially, seems to promote winners and losers" (Butter & Vaughan-Eden, 2011, p. 63. See also Galowitz, 1998–1999, p. 2142; Odiah, 2004, p. 5). This comparison ignores, however, the strides that have been made in recent years in implementing alternative processes for the resolution of legal disputes, including mediation services; reliance on processes of restorative justice and therapeutic jurisprudence, as discussed above; and the increasing availability of resolution in mental health and substance abuse courts for individuals who meet their eligibility criteria. These approaches do not conceive of resolution as winning or losing, but rather of enabling the individual, as well as other stakeholders, to resolve the presenting issue(s) and move forward productively.

References

32 *Corpus juris secundum*. (2012a). Burden and manner of presenting proof of competency, § 707.
32 *Corpus juris secundum*. (2012b). Generally, § 706.
32 *Corpus juris secundum*. (2012c). Scope of requisite expertise; licensing, § 702.
Alexander, C. A. (1995). Distinctive dates in social welfare history. In R. L. Edwards (Ed.), *Encyclopedia of social work* (Vol. 3, 19th ed., pp. 2631–2647). Washington, DC: NASW Press.
Barker, R. L. (1995). *The social work dictionary*. Washington, DC: NASW Press.
Barker, R. L. (2003). *The social work dictionary* (2nd ed.). Washington, DC: NASW Press.
Bazemore, G., & Maloney, D. (1994). Rehabilitating community service: Toward restorative service sanctions in a balanced justice system. *Federal Probation, 55*, 24–35.
Bazemore, G., & Walgrave, L. (1999). Restorative juvenile justice: In search of fundamentals and an outline for systemic reform. In G. Bazemore & L. Walgrave (Eds.), *Restorative juvenile justice: Repairing the harm of youth crime* (pp. 45–74). New York: Criminal Justice Press.
Benjamin, E., & Settle, R. (1965). Forensic social work. *Australian Journal of Social Work, 18*(1), 21–22.
Braithwaite, J. (1989). *Crime, shame and reintegration*. Cambridge, UK: Cambridge University Press.
Braithwaite, J. (1998). Restorative justice. In M. Tonry (Ed.), *The handbook of crime and punishment* (pp. 323–344). New York: Oxford University Press.
Braithwaite, J. (2002). *Restorative justice and responsive regulation*. New York: Oxford University Press.
Brennan, T. P., Gdrich, A. E., Tardy, M. J., & McCrea, K. T. (1986). Forensic social work: Practice and vision. *Social Casework, 67*(6), 340–350.
Brookbanks, W. (2001). Therapeutic justice: Conceiving an ethical framework. *Journal of Law & Medicine, 8*, 328–341.
Brooks, S. L. (1999). Therapeutic jurisprudence and preventive law in child welfare proceedings: A family systems approach. *Psychology, Public Policy, & Law, 5*, 951–965.

---

[3] For suggested model performance expectations, which refers to various levels of practice guidelines and standards, see Munson (2011).

Brownell, P., & Roberts, A. R. (2002). A century of social work in criminal justice and correctional settings. *Journal of Offender Rehabilitation, 35*(2), 1–17.

Bruster, B. E., & Foreman, K. (2012). Mentoring children of prisoners: Program evaluation. *Social Work in Public Health, 27*(1–2), 3–11.

Butters, R. P., & Vaughan-Eden, V. (2011). The ethics of practicing forensic social work. *Journal of Forensic Social Work, 1*, 61–72.

Campbell, T. (1994). Cross-examining psychologists and psychiatrists as expert witnesses. *Michigan Bar Journal, 73*, 68–72.

Casey, K., Camara, J., & Wright, N. (2001–2002). Standards of appellate review in the federal circuit: Substance and semantics. *Federal Circuit Bar Journal.* http://www.stradley.com/~/media/Files/ResourcesLanding/Publications/2001/01/Standards%20of%20Appellate%20Review%20in%20the%20Federal%20Cir__/Files/krc-standards/FileAttachment/krc-standards.pdf. Accessed 15 May 2017.

Clear, T. R. (1994). *Harm in American penology: Offenders, victims, and their communities*. Albany, NY: State University of New York Press.

Denzau, A. T., & Munger, M. C. (1986). Legislators and interest groups: How unorganized interests get represented. *American Political Science Review, 80*(1), 89–106.

Dore, M. (2012). Expert qualifications. *Law of Toxic Torts, 5*(30), 4. Clark Boardman Callaghan.

Faigman, D., Blumenthal, J., Cheng, E., Mnookin, J., Murphy, E., & Sanders, J. (2011). Bases of exclusion—Lack of qualifications. *Modern Science Evidence: The Law and Science of Expert Testimony, 3*(26), 13.

Galowitz, P. (1998–1999). Collaboration between lawyers and social workers: Re-examining the nature and potential of the relationship. *Fordham Law Review, 67*, 2123–2164.

Green, G., Thorpe, J., & Traupmann, M. (2005). The sprawling thicket: Knowledge and specialization in forensic social work. *Australian Social Work, 58*(2), 142–153.

Guin, C. G., Noble, D. N., & Merrill, T. S. (2003). From misery to mission: Forensic social workers on multidisciplinary mitigation teams. *Social Work, 48*(3), 362–371.

Kollman, K. (1998). *Outside lobbying: Public opinion and interest group strategies*. Princeton, NJ: Princeton University Press.

Kress, K. (1999). Therapeutic jurisprudence and the resolution of value conflicts: What we can realistically expect, in practice, from theory. *Behavioral Science & Law, 17*, 555–588.

Lanzer, I. A. (1948). Forensic social care work: An analytical survey. *Social Case Work, 39*, 34–48.

Lautenberg, F. (1993, May 3). *Congressional record*.

LFA Group. (2009). *Reentry unit social work services program evaluation*. San Francisco: Author. http://sfpublicdefender.org/wp-content/uploads/sites/2/ 2009/05/reentry-unit-program-evaluation.pdf. Accessed 02 June 2017.

Loue, S. (1999). *Forensic epidemiology: A comprehensive guide for legal and epidemiology professionals*. Carbondale, IL: Southern Illinois University Press.

Loue, S. (2009). *Forensic epidemiology: Integrating epidemiology and law enforcement*. New York: Jones and Bartlett.

Loue, S. (2012). Parentally-mandated religious healing for children: A therapeutic jurisprudence approach. *Journal of Law and Religion, 27*(2), 397–422.

Loue, S. (Ed.). (2013). *Forensic epidemiology in the global context*. New York: Springer Science+Business.

Marshall, T. F. (1996). The evolution of restorative justice in Britain. *European Journal on Criminal Policy and Research, 4*(4), 21–43.

Maschi, T., & Killian, M. L. (2011). The evolution of forensic social work in the United States: Implications for 21st century practice. *Journal of Forensic Social Work, 1*, 8–36.

McCold, P. (2000). Toward a holistic vision of restorative juvenile justice: A reply to the maximalist mode. *Contemporary Justice Review, 3*, 357–414.

Munson, C. (2011). Forensic social work practice standards: Definition and specification. *Journal of Forensic Social Work, 1*, 37–60.

References

National Association of Social Workers. (2017). Lobbying "do's" and "don't's." https://www.socialworkers.org/advocacy/resources/do_dont.asp. Accessed 14 May 2017.

National Association of Social Workers California Chapter. (n.d.). Legislative lobby days (LLD event). http://www.naswca.org/?page=164. Accessed 14 May 2017.

National Organization of Forensic Social Work. (n.d.). What is forensic social work? http://nofsw.org/?page_id=10. Accessed 17 May 2017.

Odiah, C. (2004). Impact of the adversary system on forensic social work practice: Threat to therapeutic alliance and fiduciary relation. *Journal of Forensic Psychology Practice, 4*(4), 3–33.

Robbins, S. P., Vaughan-Eden, V., & Maschi, T. (2015). From the editor—It's not CSI: The importance of forensics for social work education. *Journal of Social Work Education, 51*, 421–424.

Roberts, A. R., & Brownell, P. (1999). A century of forensic social work: Bridging the past to the present. *Social Work, 44*(4), 359–369.

Sapir, G. (2007). Qualifying the expert witness: A practical voir dire. *Forensic Magazine*. http://www.forensicmag.com/article/qualifying-expert-witness-practical-voir-dire?page=0,0. Accessed 06 October 2012.

Schlozman, K. L., & Tierney, J. T. (1986). *Organized interest and American democracy*. New York: HarperCollins Publishers.

Schma, W. G. (2003). Therapeutic jurisprudence. *Michigan Bar Journal, 82*, 25–27.

Sinclair, B. (1997). *Unorthodox lawmaking: New legislative processes in the U.S. Congress*. Washington, DC: Congressional Quarterly, Inc.

Slobogan, C. (1995). Therapeutic jurisprudence: Five dilemmas to ponder. *Psychology, Public Policy, & Law, 1*, 193–219.

Smith, S. S. (1995). *The American Congress*. Boston: Houghton Mifflin Company.

Sullivan, C.M., & Coats, S. (2000). *Outcome evaluation strategies for sexual assault service programs: A practical guide*. Michigan Coalition Against Domestic and Sexual Violence. https://www.wcasa.org/file_open.php?id=883. Accessed 02 June 2017.

Van Wormer, K., Roberts, A., Springer, D.W., & Brownell, P. (2008). Forensic social work: Current and emerging developments. In K. M. Sowers, & C. N. Dulmus (Eds.), *Comprehensive handbook of social work and social welfare* (pp. 315–342). John Wiley and Sons, Inc. Online doi: https://doi.org/10.1002/9780470373705. Accessed 17 May 2017.

Walgrave, L. (2000). How pure can a maximalist approach to restorative justice remain? Or can a purist model of restorative justice become maximalist? *Contemporary Justice Review, 3*, 415–432.

Walker, J. L., Jr. (1991). *Mobilizing interest groups in America*. Ann Arbor, MI: University of Michigan Press.

Wenzel, M., Okimoto, T. G., Feather, N. T., & Platow, M. J. (2008). Retributive and restorative justice. *Law and Human Behavior, 32*(5), 375–389.

Wexler, D. (2000). Therapeutic jurisprudence: An overview. *Thomas M Cooley Law Review, 17*, 125–134.

Wexler, D. B. (1990). *Therapeutic jurisprudence: The law as a therapeutic agent*. Durham, NC: Carolina Academic Press.

Wexler, D. B. (1996). Therapeutic jurisprudence and changing conceptions of legal scholarship. In D. B. Wexler & B. J. Winick (Eds.), *Law in a therapeutic key: Developments in therapeutic jurisprudence* (pp. 597–610). Durham, NC: Carolina Academic Press.

Zehr, H. (1990). *Changing lenses: Restorative justice for our times*. Harrisonburg, VA: Herald Press.

Zehr, H. (2002). *The little book of restorative justice*. Intercourse, PA: Good Book.

Legal References

Cases

Daubert v. Merrell Dow Pharmaceuticals, 43 F.3d 1311 (9th Cir. 1995).
Daubert v. Merrell Dow Pharmaceuticals, 509 U.S. 579 (1993).
Frye v. United States, 293 F. 1013 (D.C. Cir. 1923).
General Electric v. Joiner, 522 U.S. 136 (1997).
Kumho Tire Co. v. Carmichael, 526 U.S. 137 (1999).
Pineda v. Ford Motor Co., 520 F.3d 237 (3rd Cir. 2008).
State v. R.R., 807 N.Y.S.2d 516 (2005).
State v. Taylor, 669 So.2d 364 (La., 1996), *rehearing denied*.
United States v. Hicks, 389 F.3d 514 (5th Cir. 2004).

Statutes

Alaska Rule of Evidence 702 (2014).
Arkansas Rule of Evidence 702 (2016).
California Evidence Code §720 (2016).
Connecticut Code of Evidence 7-2 (2000).
Delaware Uniform Rules of Evidence 702 (2001).
Evidence Code, Florida Statutes 90.702 (2013).
Federal Rule of Evidence 702 (2011).
Hawaii Rules of Evidence 702 (2010).
Idaho Rules of Evidence 702 (1985).
Illinois Rules of Evidence 702 (2011).
Juvenile Justice and Delinquency Prevention Act of 1974, Pub. L. No. 93–415.
Kentucky Rules of Evidence 702 (2007).
Louisiana Code of Evidence 702 (1989).
Michigan Rules of Evidence 702 (2012).
Minnesota Rules of Evidence 702 (2006).
Mississippi Rules of Evidence 702 (2003).
Missouri Revised Statutes 490.065 (2017).
Montana Code Annotated, Rule of Evidence 702 (2015).
Nebraska Code §27-702, Rule 702 (1975).
Nevada Revised Statutes 50.275 (1971).
New Hampshire Rules of Evidence 702 (2011).
North Carolina General Statutes 8C-702, Rule 702 (2011).
North Dakota Rules of Evidence 702 (2014).
Ohio Rules of Evidence 702 (1994).
Oregon Revised Statutes 40.410, Rule 702 (2015).
Opinion and Expert Testimony, South Dakota Codified Laws 19-15-2 (2011).
Pennsylvania Rules of Evidence 702 (2013).
South Carolina Rules of Evidence 702 (2011).

South Dakota Codified Laws 19-15-2, Rule 702 (2012).
Texas Rules of Evidence 702 (2015).
Utah Rules of Evidence 702 (2011).
Washington Rules of Evidence 702 (1979).
Wisconsin Statutes 907.02(1) (2011).

Chapter 7
Working with Families

Defining "Family"

The legal concept of family has evolved significantly over time. Although many individuals consider themselves to be members of the same family, the federal government legally recognizes as "family" only those individuals who are united by birth, adoption, and marriage. As an example, same-sex or opposite-sex *un*married couples may view themselves and act for all intents and purposes as family, yet the US government does not recognize them as such. And until the 2015 decision of the US Supreme Court in the case of *Obergefell v. Hodges*, federal law did not confer the same benefits to spouses of same-sex marriages as to opposite-sex marriages.[1]

State laws vary considerably with respect to their legal recognition of relationships as family in situations that do not involve marriage, birth, or adoption. A number of states continue to recognize, at least in some circumstances, common law marriages, i.e., the relationship of two individuals who are unmarried but who hold themselves out as a married couple. These states include:

- Alabama
- Colorado
- District of Columbia
- Georgia (if created before 1/1/97)
- Idaho (if created before 1/1/96)
- Iowa
- Kansas
- Montana

---

[1] Prior to the Supreme Court decision in *Obergefell v. Hodges* (2015), 36 states and the District of Columbia had recognized the right of same-sex couple to marry (Denniston, 2015). In recognizing the right of same-sex couples to marry, the Supreme Court noted the "centrality of marriage to the human condition" (*Obergefell v. Hodges*, 2015, slip op. p. 3) and concluded that the fundamental right to marry under the U.S. Constitution is applicable to same-sex, as well as to opposite-sex, couples.

- New Hampshire (for inheritance purposes only)
- Ohio (if created before 10/10/91)
- Oklahoma (possibly only if created before 11/1/98. Oklahoma's laws and court decisions may be in conflict about whether common law marriages formed in that state after 11/1/98 will be recognized.)
- Pennsylvania (if created before 1/1/05)
- Rhode Island
- South Carolina
- Texas
- Utah (Thomson Reuters, 2017a; Unmarried Equality, 2017).

Courts have played an important role in determining the parameters of family through their interpretation of state laws and state and federal constitutions. As a result of federal court decisions, states may not prohibit or penalize interracial marriages (*Loving v. Virginia*, 1967), prevent individuals with AIDS from marrying (*T.E.P. v. Leavitt*, 1993), or prohibit prisoners, other than those serving life sentences, from entering into marriage (*Turner v. Safley*, 1987).

State court decisions have also defined who is to be considered family, albeit within a specified context. In a case involving rent control regulations in New York City, property owners were prohibited from evicting the surviving spouse or other family member of a deceased tenant who had been living with the tenant (*Braschi v. Stahl*, 1989). The law, however, did not specify who constituted family, and the case arose prior to New York's recognition of same-sex civil unions and marriages. Following the death of his life partner, Miguel Braschi sued for the right to remain in the apartment. The New York Supreme Court, in deciding the case in favor of Braschi, found that the concept of family as contained in the housing regulations should not be restricted to only those relationships evidenced by a birth certificate or marriage certificate.

In yet another case originating out of California, the California Supreme Court awarded custody of a child to the mother's boyfriend who, although not biologically related to the child, had acted as the boy's father by supporting him both emotionally and financially (*In re Nicholas H.*, 2002). In a Rhode Island case, the state Supreme Court found that a written visitation agreement entered into by a lesbian couple with respect to their child was enforceable. The Rhode Island Supreme Court premised its decision on the following facts: (1) the child was conceived through artificial insemination following a joint decision of the women, (2) the majority of the costs associated with the artificial insemination were paid for by the nonbiological mother, (3) the two women had lived together and had raised the child together for 4 years prior to separating, (4) the child's birth certificate displayed a family name that had been created from the last names of both of the mothers, and (5) both women had represented that the child was theirs (*Rubano v. Dicenzo*, 2000).

The Growing Family

Marriage and Domestic Partnerships

Marriage is deemed to be a contractual relationship, controlled by state law. All states mandate that the parties intending to marry obtain a marriage license, which generally requires that individuals provide evidence of their identity and of the termination of any previous marriages. The prerequisites to marriage and/or obtaining a license, such as age or a blood test for specified sexually transmitted disease, vary across states.

Some prospective marriages are considered to be void under state law, meaning that the law will not recognize them, e.g., marriage between a parent and a child, a grandparent and a grandchild, between siblings, and between uncles and nieces and aunts and nephews. As an example, a woman in Oklahoma who married her mother was charged by the state with the crime of incest (Associated Press, 2017). Some states will also not recognize marriages between first cousins (Paul & Spencer, 2008).

Other marriages may be considered to be voidable under state law, that is, the marriage will be recognized but may be annulled if so requested. This may occur if one of the parties was under the legal age of consent to marry at the time the marriage occurred, if one or both of the parties lacked the mental capacity to enter into marriage, if either party lacked the physical capacity to enter into a sexual relationship, or if the parties entered into the marriage due to force or duress (Goda, 1967; Tolstoy, 1964). In general, a marriage may be annulled by either an ecclesiastical declaration or a judicial decision in situations in which one or both parties lacked the capacity to consent, was under the legal age to marry, or failed to consummate the marriage.

Article 4 of the US Constitution requires that states recognize the validity of a marriage that is validly entered into in another state. Known as the full faith and credit clause, Section 1 of this Article provides "Full Faith and Credit shall be given in each State to the public Acts, Records, and judicial Proceedings of every other State." Accordingly, a couple that is married under the common laws of one state may be able to obtain a divorce from a court in another state, even though that state does not recognize common law marriages (*Anderson v. Anderson*, 1991) .

Prior to the recognition of same-sex marriages, many states had promulgated laws recognizing same-sex domestic partnerships. Although the requirements to establish a domestic partnership varied across states, in general state laws required that both parties have attained a minimum age of 18, share a principal residence, agree to be responsible for each other's living expenses, share a committed relationship, and not be related by blood or be a partner in another domestic partnership or marriage. The benefits available to domestic partners also varied across states, e.g., the right to make medical decisions for one's partner in the event the partner no longer had capacity to do so and the right to adopt a partner's child. Following the US Supreme Court's recognition of same-sex marriages, some states automatically converted then-existing same-sex civil unions to marriages, while others continue to recognize civil unions or domestic partnerships (National Center for Lesbian Rights, 2017).

Adoption

Social workers may play a critical role in law-related aspects of the adoption process in response to a request from a court, an attorney, or an agency. Depending upon their qualifications and position, they may be asked to conduct a preadoption home study, serve as a consultant, or testify as an expert. Additionally, a social worker who is employed as an accredited representative by an agency authorized by the Office of Legal Access Programs of the Executive Office for Immigration Review to provide immigration services may be involved in helping prospective adoptive parents complete the necessary paperwork and process required for an intercountry adoption. (See Chap. 12 for a discussion of accredited representatives.)

An adoption may be domestic, that is, conducted entirely in one's own country, or international, meaning that the US-based parent or parents wish to adopt a child from another country (Child Welfare Information Gateway, 2015). Domestic adoptions may take one of four different forms.

Public agency adoptions are those that occur through public agencies. In general, many of the children waiting to be adopted through public adoption agencies have been in foster care and have been removed from their birth families for any number of reasons, which may include neglect or abuse. The agency will consider the needs of both the child and the intending adoptive parents in making a decision about the adoption (Child Welfare Information Gateway, 2015). In some states, an employee of a public agency or the agency may refuse to consider an individual or couple for prospective adoption based on the employee's/agency's religious beliefs. (See Appendix A for a listing of states and their provisions that permit such refusal.)

Domestic adoption may also occur through a private licensed agency. In such cases, the birth parents have relinquished the child to the agency. The agency may encourage the parent(s) to specify the characteristics of the individual(s) who they would like to be the adoptive parents and there may be arranged meetings between the birth parents and potential adoptive parents. Because the adoption is not final until after the birth of the infant, there remains the possibility that one or both parents will ultimately decide not to relinquish the child to the intending adoptive parents.

Independent adoptions are frequently arranged through an attorney. Generally, the intending adoptive parents will identify the biological parents, although an attorney may identify intending adoptive parents to individuals wishing to place their newborn for adoption. Like adoptions through private licensed agencies, independent adoptions offer several advantages in that the adoptive and biological parents have the opportunity to exchange information, thereby providing the adoptive parents with a more detailed family medical history than might otherwise be available; the biological parents may feel more confident about the adoption because they have had the opportunity to meet with the adoptive family; and the birth and adoptive parents can discuss and negotiate the possibility of ongoing contact between the child and the biological parents. However, independent adoptions tend to be much more expensive, and there remains the risk that one or both of the birth parents will ultimately decide against relinquishment (Child Welfare Information Gateway, 2015).

Adoptions may also be arranged through facilitators or unlicensed adoption agencies. Facilitators and unlicensed adoption agencies link the expectant mother with the intending adoptive parents. Because such agencies and facilitators are not well-regulated, the adoptive parents may have few avenues of recourse if the process does not go as planned or represented.

An adoption may be open or closed. An open adoption refers to one in which the birth parents and the adoptive parents may know of or know each other; birth parents may maintain contact with the adoptive family, including their birth child (Thomson Reuters, 2017b). A closed adoption is one in which there is no contact between the birth and adoptive parents and child following the adoption. Closed adoptions are increasingly rare in the United States, but they are relatively common in the context of international adoptions. Some states have made provisions to allow individuals to have access to the information concerning the birth families, despite the closed nature of the adoption (Thomson Reuters, 2017b). Open adoptions offer several advantages: the adoptive family and the child have access to the medical history of the child and his or her family and knowing the birth parents may help the adopted child to resolve some issues relating to the reasons for his or her adoption. However, there are also several disadvantages of an open adoption, such as in situations involving abuse, repetitive criminal behavior and incarceration, and possible confusion on the part of the child.

The processing of an international, also known as an intercountry adoption, varies depending upon the country in which the child is located and the specific situation of the intending adoptive families. Some countries do not permit foreigners to adopt children from their country. Others will not allow adoptions of children by single parents, same-sex parents, or parents over a specified age. While some agencies will match adoptive parents with a child as soon as a child becomes available, taking into account the child's needs, others may allow the prospective adoptive parents to meet with a child prior to committing to the adoption.

Intercountry adoptions may occur through an agency that is situated in either a Hague Convention country or a non-Hague Convention country, generally referred to as a non-Convention country. The United States ratified the Hague Convention on Protection of Children and Cooperation in Respect of Intercountry Adoption in 2008. This Convention sets forth specific requirements for adoption agencies, home studies, and parent training. The child must be adoptable within the terms of the Convention and must obtain an immigrant visa. Adoption from a Convention country requires that the child be:

1. Under the age of 16 at the time the Petition to Classify Convention Adoptee as Immediate Relative (Form I-800) is filed with the United States Citizenship and Immigration Service (USCIS) on his or her behalf (taking into account special rules on filing dates for children aged 15–16), or the child is under the age of 18 and is a sibling of a child (under the age of 16) who has been or will be adopted by the same adoptive parents.
2. The child will be adopted by a married US citizen and spouse jointly or by an unmarried US citizen at least 25 years of age, habitually resident in the United States, whom USCIS has found suitable and eligible to adopt (Form I-800A approval) with the intent of creating a legal parent-child relationship. (Note: at this stage, the child must not have been adopted yet.)
3. The Central Authority of the child's country of origin has determined that the child is eligible for intercountry adoption and has proposed an adoption placement which has been accepted, and the child has not yet been adopted or been placed in the custody of the prospective adoptive parents.
4. The child's birth parents (or parent, if the child has a sole or surviving parent), or other legal custodian, individuals, or entities whose consent is necessary for adoption have freely given their written, irrevocable consent to the termination of their legal relationship with the child and to the child's emigration and adoption.
5. If the child's last legal custodians were two living birth parents who signed the irrevocable consent to adoption, those parents must be incapable of providing proper care for the child (Bureau of Consular Affairs, United States Department of State, 2017).

A listing of Convention countries that includes both countries from which adoption is possible and those from which they are not can be found at the intercountry adoption website of the Bureau of Consular Affairs of the United States Department of State: https://travel.state.gov/content/adoptionsabroad/en/hague-convention/convention-countries.html.

Individuals who elect to adopt from a non-Convention country can have a home study conducted prior to choosing the country from which they wish to adopt, as long as the agency performing the study is licensed under state law and meets all state and federal requirements. A child adopted from a non-Convention country must qualify as an orphan under the laws of the United States and must obtain an immigrant visa. The US immigration law currently provides that a child who is to be adopted from a non-Convention country must:

1. Be under the age of 16 at the time the Petition to Classify Orphan as an Immediate Relative with the USCIS (Form I-600) is filed on his or her behalf or be under the age of 18 and a sibling of a child (under the age of 16) who has been or will be adopted (by the same adoptive parents)
2. Either have no parents because of the death or disappearance of, abandonment or desertion by, or separation or loss from, both parents or have a sole or surviving parent who is incapable of providing proper care for the child and has, in writing, irrevocably released the child for emigration and adoption

3. Have been or will be adopted by a married US citizen and spouse jointly or by an unmarried US citizen at least 25 years of age, with the intent of forming a bona fide parent-child relationship (Bureau of Consular Affairs, United States Department of State, 2017)

Additionally, the adopting parents must have completed a final adoption in the child's country of origin or obtained legal custody of the child for purposes of emigration and adoption in the United States (Bureau of Consular Affairs, U.S. Department of State, 2017).

Many of the children who are available through an intercountry adoption process will have lived in an orphanage and/or foster home for a period of time prior to the adoption. The level of care while the child is in foster care or an orphanage varies greatly depending upon the country, the specific institution, and the child's caregivers. In some situations, the child may have suffered severe abuse or neglect which will adversely impact his or her future development and ability to form a close emotional attachment (Human Rights Watch, 1998, 2014; Joyce, 2017; Silver, 2014). Adoptive parents often will have relatively little information about the child's social and medical history.

Family Ruptures: Separation, Divorce, and Termination of Parental Rights

Separation, Divorce, and Custody Proceedings

Social workers may become involved in legal proceedings in a number of ways in situations in which married couples or couples living together decide to either suspend temporarily or terminate their relationship permanently. Social workers may be asked to evaluate each of the potential options for custody of any children involved or to interpret evaluations done by others, to serve as an expert witness with respect to the fitness of one or more individuals seeking custody of a child, to assist in locating a parent who has not met his or her support obligation or, if qualified as a mediator, to provide mediation services in an effort to help the parties reach an agreement with respect to property division and/or custody.

It is critical that social workers be aware of and attempt to avoid the insertion of any bias into their evaluation, interpretation, or mediation efforts. The Code of Ethics governing social workers holding US licenses charges them with the ethical obligation of promoting sensitivity to cultural and ethnic diversity and respecting the inherent dignity and worth of each individual (National Association of Social Workers, 2008).

The Supreme Court of the United States has held that the parental right to care for, control, and have custody of their children is guaranteed by the Fourteenth Amendment of the United States Constitution (*Meyer v. Nebraska*, 1923). Custody may be physical, legal, or both and may be held by either or both parents. Custody arrangements entered into in connection with a separation or divorce may vary, so that both parents may share physical and legal custody; one parent may hold physical custody, with the other parent holding legal custody and visitation rights; or one parent may hold both legal and physical custody, with the other parent having visitation rights.

Generally, the court will assess the "best interest of the child" in determining the award of custody (Charlow, 1986; Kohn, 2008). However, state laws may also delineate the parameters within which courts may make custody decisions. Alaska, for example, provides that custody is to be determined in the best interest of the child while considering all factors; domestic violence is considered to be contrary to the best interests of the child (Alaska Statutes § 25.24.150, 2015). In comparison, Iowa has a presumption in favor of joint custody if either party requests joint custody. In determining the best joint custody arrangement, the court will consider:

- Whether each parent would be a suitable custodian for the child
- Whether the psychological and emotional need and development of the child will suffer due to lack of active contact with and attention from both parents
- Whether the parents can communicate with each other concerning the child's needs
- Whether both parents have actively cared for the child before and since the separation
- Whether each parent can support the other's relationship with the child
- Whether the custody arrangement is in accord with the child's wishes or whether the child has strong opposition, taking into account the child's age and maturity
- Whether one or both parents agree or are opposed to joint custody
- The geographic proximity of the parents
- The safety of the child or other children or the other parent would be jeopardized by an award of joint custody or by unsupervised or unrestricted supervision
- Whether a history of domestic abuse exists (Iowa Judicial Branch, 2017)

If the court does not award joint custody, it must specify the reasons for denying this arrangement and why it is not in the best interests of the child. Additionally, joint custody does not encompass joint physical custody; the award of physical care will be made according to the best interests of the child.

In the past, state laws generally awarded custody to the mother in situations in which the parents were not legally married. This, however, is no longer the case. In some situations, a nonmarital biological father may be awarded custody and/or has the right to maintain a paternal relationship if he is not found to be unfit as a parent (*Caban v. Mohammed*, 1979; *Lehr v. Robertson*, 1983; *Quilloin v. Wolcott*, 1978; *Stanley v. Illinois*, 1969). Whether a biological father might be found to be an unfit parent in situations characterized by past violence or the threat of future violence, substance use, or criminal behavior would potentially be decided by the relevant agency charged with the responsibility of making such a determination or by a court. However, the biological father of a child who is born during the marriage of the mother to another man does not have the right to have a paternity test or to a paternal relationship with the child (*Michael H. v. Gerald D.*, 1989). Rather, there is a presumption that a child born to a woman in a marital relationship is the product of that marriage; to allow otherwise would disrupt the existing family relationship.

This raises the question of who is deemed to be the father of a child. Twenty-three states and the Northern Mariana Islands provide that a man will be presumed to be the father of a child in any of the following circumstances:

- He and the child's mother are or were married to each other, and the child is born during the marriage or within 300 days after the marriage ended.
- Before the birth of the child, he and the child's mother attempted to marry, and the marriage is or could be declared invalid, and the child is born during the marriage or within 300 days after the marriage is terminated.
- With his consent, he is listed as the father on the child's birth certificate.
- He has acknowledged his paternity in writing.
- He is obligated to support the child, either by voluntary agreement or court order.
- While the child is a minor, he has resided with the child and openly claimed the child as his biological child (Child Welfare Information Gateway, 2014).

A state may, however, have established procedures that would allow a putative father to challenge his paternity (Finley, 2002). Although many states limit a judge's exercise of discretion, requiring him or her to consider only those factors that bear some relationship to the welfare of the children, other states permit judges to exercise broad discretion in awarding custody. In some such situations, lower court judges charged with the initial responsibility for custody decisions have premised their awards of custody based on stereotypes associated with particular individual characteristics including disability (*Carney v. Carney*, 1979), HIV/AIDS (*Doe v. Roe*, 1988), and race (*Palmore v. Sidoti*, 1984).

Interstate custody disputes are often particularly challenging for everyone involved. Such disputes can arise in a variety of circumstances including parental relocation due to employment demands or family illness, kidnapping by the noncustodial parent, and a desire by a nonparent family member to continue to care permanently for a child who has been left temporarily in their care. Under the Uniform Child Custody Jurisdiction and Enforcement Act, any state that is not the child's home state will defer jurisdiction to the child's home state with respect to the custody issue (Uniform Child Custody Jurisdiction and Enforcement Act, 1997).[2] In addition, once a state has taken jurisdiction over a custody dispute, it will retain jurisdiction as long as that state determines that it continues to have "a significant connection" with the parties who are in dispute or until those parties have left that state (National Conference of Commissioners on Uniform State Laws, 2017). However, a state that does not have jurisdiction may enter an emergency custody order if the child is believed to be in danger and in need of immediate protection. If there is already a custody order in effect and the child is kidnapped by a noncusto-

---

[2] The Uniform Child Custody Jurisdiction and Enforcement Act (UCCJEA) replaces the Uniform Child Custody Jurisdiction Act of 1968 (National Conference of Commissioners on Uniform State Laws, 2017). As of January 2016, the UCCJEA had been adopted by 49 states and the District of Columbia. Only Massachusetts and Puerto Rico had not adopted the Act as of that date.

dial parent or other family member, the courts must give full faith and credit to the custody determination that has already been rendered in another state (Parental Kidnapping Prevention Act of 1981).

Custody orders may be subject to modification if there is a change in circumstances that may affect the well-being of the child. Judges will often consider factors such as the length of time that the current custody arrangement has been in place, the quality of the living situation that can be provided to the child by each of the parents, the extent to which each parent has provided for the child, and the ability of each parent to provide the child with the necessary guidance (*Friederwitzer v. Friederwitzer*, 1982). Just as with an initial custody determination, a social worker may be called upon to serve as an evaluator, an expert witness, or a mediator, depending upon the specific situation and the social worker's credentials and expertise.

Termination of Parental Rights

Parental rights may be terminated voluntarily through their relinquishment, involuntarily as the result of legal action against the parent(s), or as the result the child's emancipation. A social worker may become involved in such situations through a request by a court or an attorney to provide an independent evaluation of one or more aspects of the situation or to serve as an expert witness or consultant. In some instances, the social worker may have been responsible for the preparation of the report that serves, at least in part, as the basis for the proceeding to terminate parental rights. In such situations, it is possible that the social worker will be called as a witness to provide clarification about the content of the report or the process that was used to develop the report. The voluntary relinquishment of parental rights, discussed above in connection with adoption, will not be addressed here.

Involuntary Termination The state may seek to terminate an individual's parental rights in situations involving abandonment, neglect, and/or abuse of a child. (State efforts to remove a child from a pregnant woman, prior to or immediately following birth, due to the woman's substance use during pregnancy are discussed in Chap. 10.) That said, as can be seen from the discussion below, a state's definitions of abandonment, neglect, and abuse may overlap. Whether a situation involving abandonment, neglect, or abuse will rise to such a level that a court will involuntarily terminate a parent's rights depends upon both the specific circumstances, including the available evidence that supports either termination or non-termination and existing state law. A decision to terminate an individual's parental rights cannot be taken lightly, as parental rights are protected by the US Constitution.

Although the definition of abandonment varies across states, in general, abandonment involves leaving a child "without provision for reasonable and necessary care or supervision" (Connecticut General Statutes § 46b-115a(1), 2015). One court has stated:

> A parent abandons a child if the parent has failed to maintain a reasonable degree of interest, concern or responsibility as to the welfare of the child .... Abandonment focuses on the parent's conduct .... Abandonment occurs where a parent fails to visit a child, does not display love or affection for the child, does not personally interact with the child, and demonstrates no concern for the child's welfare.... (*In re Justin F*, 2012)

A minimum time period may not be necessary to find that a parent has abandoned the child *(In re Paul M., Jr.*, 2014). Incarceration, in and of itself, may be found to be an insufficient basis for a determination of abandonment *(In re Brian T., Jr.*, 2013).

As indicated above, the concepts of abandonment, neglect, and abuse as used in a state's law be overlap, so that abandonment, for example, may also constitute neglect. As an example, Connecticut defines a neglected child as follows:

> (9) a child or youth may be found *'neglected'* who (A) has been *abandoned,* or (B) is being denied proper care and attention, physically, educationally, emotionally or morally, or (C) is being permitted to live under conditions, circumstances or associations injurious to the well-being of the child or youth, or (D) has been abused.... (Connecticut General Statutes § 46b-120(8), 2015) (emphasis added)

A child will be deemed to be uncared for if he or she:

> is homeless or whose home cannot provide the specialized care that the physical, emotional or mental condition of the child requires. For the purposes of this section, the treatment of any child by an accredited Christian Science practitioner in lieu of treatment by a licensed practitioner of the healing arts, shall not of itself constitute neglect or maltreatment. (Connecticut General Statutes § 46b-120(10), 2015)

Like abandonment and neglect, the definition of abuse varies across states' statutes and court decisions. Connecticut, as one example, defines an abused child as one who:

> (A) has been inflicted with physical injury or injuries other than by accidental means, or (B) has injuries that are at variance with the history given of them, or (C) is in a condition that is the result of maltreatment such as, but not limited to, malnutrition, sexual molestation or exploitation, deprivation of necessities, emotional maltreatment or cruel punishment. (Connecticut General Statutes § 46b-120(4), 2015)

Abuse need not be physical and can involve severe emotional abuse (In re Sean H., 1991). Because of the apparent overlap in Connecticut's definitions of abandonment, neglect, and abuse, the deprivation of necessities that falls within the definition of abuse may also constitute abandonment and/or neglect.

Because of the fundamental nature of parental rights, an individual whose parental rights may be terminated is entitled to due process rights. These include the right to receive notice of the charges that form the basis for the state's efforts to terminate parental rights (*Loveheart v. Long*, 1988), the right to prepare and respond to the charges, and the right to be represented by an attorney. Although there is a right to have an attorney, there is no right under the US Constitution to have a court-appointed attorney if the parent is unable to afford one or locate one (*In re Isaiah J*, 2013). However, some states may statutorily provide that an indigent individual in such circumstances may be provided with court-appointed counsel or a judge may decide in a particular case that court-appointed representation is warranted (e.g., Connecticut General Statutes § 45a-717(b), 2015). The US Supreme Court has indicated that lower courts should consider various factors in deciding whether or not to appoint counsel: (1) the nature of the specific action in question, e.g., the termination of the parent-child relationship; (2) the risk that an erroneous deprivation will result from the procedure utilized and whether additional safeguards may be valuable; and (3) the government's interest, including any associated administrative and financial burden (*Lassiter v. Department of Social Services*, 1981; *Mathews v. Eldridge*, 1976).

Some states provided that the state must only prove its case by a preponderance of the evidence, the lowest burden of proof, because the termination of parental rights involves a civil, rather than a criminal action (Cressler, 1994). However, in recognition of the serious nature of an involuntary loss of parental rights and the constitutional rights involved, the higher standard of clear and convincing evidence is required on the part of the state (*Santosky v. Kramer*, 1982) As an example, the State of Connecticut must prove its case for the termination of parental rights by clear and convincing evidence (*In re Emmanuel*, 1994).

The Emancipated Minor Parental rights are also terminated, in whole or in part, when a minor child becomes emancipated while still under the state-determined age of majority. In general, children remain under the legal control of their parents until they reach the age of majority under the laws of their state, which ranges, depending upon the state, from the age of 18 to the age of 21. A minority of states recognize specified circumstances under which a child will be deemed to have been emancipated from his or her parents, even though still under the age of majority. (See Table 7.1 below.)

Table 7.1 Select state law provisions for emancipation of minors

State	Requirements	Source
Alabama	An emancipation order serves to expand the rights of minors over the age of 18 and under the age of 19, the age of majority in Alabama. An emancipation petition may be filed by the parents of a minor or by the minor if the minor does not have parents or if a living parent has abandoned the minor or is insane. The court will evaluate whether emancipation is in the best interest of the minor	Alabama Code § 26-13-1 (2016)
Arizona	Judicial order of emancipation requires minimum age of 16; minor must demonstrate that he or she can provide for his/her own housing, food, and medical care; is not a ward of the state; and understands the rights and obligation associated with emancipation. Nonjudicial emancipation occurs through marriage	Arizona Revised Statutes § 12-2451 (2005); Superior Court, Maricopa County (n.d.)
Arkansas	Nonjudicial emancipation through marriage or military service. Judicial emancipation requires proof by a preponderance of the evidence that the minor is at least 17 years of age; is willing to live separate and apart from his or her parent, legal guardian, or legal custodian; has an appropriate place to live; has been managing or has the ability to manage his or her own financial affairs; has a legal source of income, such as employment or a trust fund; has health-care coverage or a realistic plan on how to meet his or her health needs; and agrees to comply with the compulsory school attendance laws; and emancipation is in the best interest of the juvenile. The court will consider the wishes of the parent, legal guardian, or legal custodian in making its decision	Arkansas Code § 9-27-362 (2016); Arkansas Legal Services Partnership (2014)
California	A minor who is married, a member of the armed forces, or has previously been declared emancipated by a California court is deemed to be emancipated. Court-ordered emancipation requires minimum age of 14, residence apart from parents, and ability to support oneself financially. The minor must also demonstrate that he or she is not receiving income from illegal or criminal activity. The court-ordered emancipated minor may sign contracts; approve medical care; buy, lease, and sell real property; be the plaintiff or defendant in a law suit; write a will; live in their own home; go to school; and get a work permit. The court may terminate the minor's emancipated status if the minor's situation changes and advise the minor's parents that they are once again responsible for the minor	California Courts, n.d.; California Family Code § 7000 et seq. (2016); Legal Services for Children, Inc. (2014)

(continued)

Table 7.1 (continued)

State	Requirements	Source
Connecticut	Nonjudicial emancipation through marriage (even if the child has since divorced) or active US military service. Judicial emancipation requires a showing that minor is willingly living apart from his parents or guardians (with or without their consent) and is managing his own financial affairs, regardless of the lawful source of his income or good cause showing that emancipation is in the best interests of the minor or his child or the minor's parents or guardian. Petition may be filed by 16- or 17-year-old or parent or guardian.	Connecticut General Statutes §§ 46b-150 – 150e (2016); Price-Livingston, 2002
Florida	Nonjudicial emancipation through marriage. Court order of emancipation requires statement of the minor's character, habits, education, income, and mental capacity for business and an explanation of how the needs of the minor with respect to food, shelter, clothing, medical care, and other necessities will be met; whether the minor is a party to or the subject of a pending judicial proceeding in this state or any other jurisdiction or the subject of a judicial order of any description issued in connection with such pending judicial proceeding; statement of the reason why the court should remove the disabilities of nonage. Notice to parent/guardian required. Court will determine if emancipation is in the best interest of the minor	Florida Statutes § 743.015 (2017)
Georgia	Nonjudicial emancipation occurs through marriage or active service in the military. Judicial emancipation requires demonstration of ability to financially support self and manage personal affairs; names and contact information of enumerated individuals with personal knowledge of minor and ability to verify that emancipation is in minor's best interest; absence of parental objection or judicial finding that emancipation is in the best interest of the minor	Official Code of Georgia Annotated §§ 15-11-200 to -208 (2014); Southern Judicial Circuit (n.d.)
Illinois	Court order of emancipation may be granted to a "mature minor who has demonstrated the ability and capacity to manage his (or her) own affairs and to live wholly or partially independent of his (or her) parents." Requires age of 16 but less than 18; residence in Illinois; explanation from minor as to why he or she is seeking emancipation; demonstration that minor is "mature minor"; evidence that minor has lived on his or her own; and absence of objections from the minor or the parents to an order of emancipation. The court may grant full or partial emancipation and will tailor the order to meet the needs of the minor	Emancipation of Minors Act [Illinois], 750 Illinois Compiled Statutes 30/1 et seq. (2017).
Louisiana	Emancipation may occur as the result of marriage, court order of emancipation for good cause of a minor 16 years of age or older, or limited emancipation "by authentic act" of a parent	Louisiana Civil Code, tit. VIII, arts. 366, 368 (2009)

Maryland	There is no clear statutory provision; process must be initiated by child protective services or parent. Requires minimum age of 15; minor must demonstrate ability to care for self; parent must provide valid reason for terminating parent-child relationship with accompanying responsibilities	Johns Hopkins School of Public Health (n.d.)
Michigan	Requirements for emancipation without court order: marriage, reaching the age of majority (18 years of age), joining the armed forces, and temporarily while in police custody in order to consent to needed medical treatment Requirements for petition with court order: Minor must provide information indicating that he or she can care for self financially without seeking state assistance and that they can care for personal needs. The emancipation petition must include a statement from an adult familiar with the minor that explains why emancipation would be in the best interest of the minor. One or both parents may object to the proceeding, in which case the court will dismiss the proceedings A granting of the petition represents "termination of the rights of the parents to the custody, control, services, and earnings of a minor." The minor will not, however, be able to perform functions that are legally limited by age, e.g., voting and purchasing of alcohol. The court may rescind the order of emancipation if the minor's situation changes	Emancipation of Minors Act [Michigan], Michigan Compiled Laws § 722.4c (1998)
Mississippi	Petition must be filed by someone other than the minor. The petition must state the age of the minor, join as defendants his or her parent(s) then living (and if neither are living, two of his/her adult relatives within the third degree), and the reasons for seeking emancipation. Emancipation may be granted at any age	Mississippi Code Annotated § 93-11-65 (2001)
Montana	Requires minimum age of 16; that limited emancipation is in minor's best interests; minor desires limited emancipation; there is no public interest compelling denial of limited emancipation; minor has or will obtain money to pay for financial obligations incurred as a result of limited emancipation; understands and will exercise rights and responsibilities associated with limited emancipation; has graduated or will continue to pursue graduation from high school; will undergo periodic counseling with an appropriate advisor if court deems it necessary	Montana Code Annotated § 41-1-501 (2017) (limited emancipation)
New Mexico	Requires minimum age of 16, residence outside of home of guardian, minor's ability to manage own financial affairs, and demonstration that emancipation is in minor's best interest	Emancipation of Minors Act [New Mexico], New Mexico Statutes Annotated §§ 32A-21-1 to 32A-21-7 (1978)

(continued)

Table 7.1 (continued)

State	Requirements	Source
North Carolina	Minimum age of 16; requires court order of emancipation. Minor must demonstrate that he or she is able to support self and assume adult responsibilities. Court must determine that emancipation is in the best interest of the minor	North Carolina General Statutes §§ 7B-3500 to -3509 (1998)
Oregon	Minimum age of 16; requires court order of emancipation. Court will consider: whether the parent of the minor consents to the proposed emancipation, whether the minor has been living away from the family home and is substantially able to be self-maintained and self-supported without parental guidance and supervision, and whether the minor can demonstrate that he or she is sufficiently mature and knowledgeable to manage his or her affairs without parental assistance	Oregon Revised Statutes §§ 419B.550 to 419B.558 (2015)
South Dakota	Emancipation occurs through marriage, active duty in U.S. armed forces, or through court order of emancipation. Court order requires minimum age of 16, residence apart from parents or guardian with the consent or acquiescence of parents or guardian, management of own financial affairs, and showing that income is not derived from any activity declared to be a crime by the laws of the state of South Dakota or the laws of the United States	South Dakota Codified Laws § 25-5-26 (1993).
Texas	Requires residence in state, minimum age of 17 or 16 if living separately from guardian, and ability to be self-supporting and manage own financial affairs	Texas Family Code § 31.001 (1995)
Vermont	Minimum age of 16; requires court order of emancipation unless the minor is married or has entered the armed forces, in which case the minor will be considered to have been emancipated. Court-ordered emancipation requires that minor be 16 years of age or older but under the age of majority; has lived apart from his or her parents, custodian, or legal guardian for 3 months or longer; is managing his or her own financial affairs; has demonstrated the ability to be self-sufficient in financial and personal affairs; holds a high school diploma or its equivalent or is earning passing grades in a court-approved educational program; is not under a legal guardianship or in the custody of the Commissioner for Children and Families; and is not under the supervision or in the custody of the Commissioner of Corrections	Vermont Statutes Annotated, tit. 12, 7151 (2003)

Virginia	Minimum age of 16; petition may be filed by minor or parent or guardian. Court may issue order of emancipation upon finding that minor has entered into a valid marriage, whether or not that marriage has been terminated by dissolution; or is on active duty with U.S. armed forces; or willingly lives apart from parents or guardian, with the consent or acquiescence of the parents or guardian, and is or is capable of supporting himself or herself and competently managing own financial affairs	Code of Virginia § 16.1-331 -334.1 (2016)
Washington	Requires declaration by minor that he/she has the ability to manage his/her financial affairs; ability to manage his/her personal, social, educational, and nonfinancial affairs. Requires notice of petition to parent(s) or guardian(s)	Washington Revised Code §§ 13.64.010 to -080 (1995)
West Virginia	Nonjudicial emancipation if over 16 years of age and married. Judicial emancipation requires minimum age of 16 and under 18; demonstrated ability to provide for self, maintain physical and emotional well-being, and make decisions. Parental notice of petition required	West Virginia Code § 49-4-115 (2016)
Wyoming	Minor is emancipated if he or she is or has been married, is in the US military service, or has received a court order of emancipation. Court order requires minimum age of 17; living separate from parents; parents' consent; minor is financially self-supporting and income is lawfully derived	Wyoming Statutes § 14-1-201 et seq. (2016)

References

Arkansas Legal Services Partnership. (2014). Emancipation packet. https://www.arlegalservices.org/files/PROSEFORM-EmancipationPacket.pdf. Accessed 06 November 2017.

Associated Press. (2017, November 10). Oklahoma woman who married mother pleads guilty to incest. *ABC News*. http://abcnew.go.com/Us/wireStory/oklahoma-woman-married-mother-pleads-guilty-incest-51061162. Accessed 10 November 2017.

Bureau of Consular Affairs, United States Department of State. (2017). Intercountry adoption: Who can be adopted. https://travel.state.gov/content/adoptions abroad/en/adoption-process/how-to-adopt/who-can-be-adopted.html. Accessed 07 November 2017.

California Courts. (n.d.). How-to guide: Getting a declaration of emancipation. http://www.courts.ca.gov/1221.htm. Accessed 06 November 2017.

Charlow, A. (1986). Awarding custody: The best interests of the child and other fictions. *Yale Law & Policy Review, 5*(2), 267–290.

Child Welfare Information Gateway. (2014). *The rights of unmarried fathers*. Washington, DC: United States Department of Health and Human Services, Administration for Children and Families, Administration on Children, Youth, and Families, and Children's Bureau. https://www.childwelfare.gov/pubPDFs/ putative.pdf. Accessed 05 November 2017.

Child Welfare Information Gateway. (2015). *Adoption options: Where do I start?* Washington, DC: U.S. Department of Health and Human Services, Administration for Children and Families, Administration on Children, Youth, and Families, and Children's Bureau. https://www.childwelfare.gov/pubPDFs/ f_adoptoption.pdf. Accessed 07 November 2017.

Cressler, D. E. (1994). Requiring proof beyond a reasonable doubt in parental rights termination cases. *University of Louisville Journal of Family Law, 32*(4), 785–816.

Denniston, L. (2015, June 26). Opinion analysis: Marriage now open to same-sex couple. *SCOTUSblog*. http://www.scotusblog.com/2015/06/opinion-analysis-marriage-now-open-to-same-sex-couples/. Accessed 05 November 2017.

Finley, G. E. (2002). Birth father rights and legislative interventions. *Adoption Quarterly, 6*(1), 1–5.

Goda, P. J. (1967). The historical evolution of the concepts of void and voidable marriages. *Journal of Family Law, 7*, 297–308.

Human Rights Watch. (1998). Report documents brutal treatment in Russian orphanages. https://www.hrw.org/news/1998/12/15/report-documents-brutal-treatment-russian-orphanages. Accessed 14 November 2017.

Human Rights Watch. (2014). Disabled children face violence, neglect in Russian orphanages. https://www.youtube.com/watch?v=hH6Li7Dg4Bc. Accessed 14 November 2017.

Iowa Judicial Branch. (2017). Child custody. http://www.iowacourts.gov/For_the_Public/Representing_Yourself_in_Court/DivorceFamily_Law/Child_Custody/. Accessed 05 Nov 2017.

Johns Hopkins School of Public Health. (n.d.). Maryland minor consent laws. https://www.jhsph.edu/.../Maryland_Minor_Consent_Laws_10.26.12.docx. Accessed 06 November 2017.

Joyce, K. (2017, July 22). Why adoption plays such a big, contentious role in US-Russia relations. *Vox*. https://www.vox.com/the-big-idea/2017/7/21/16005500/adoption-russia-us-orphans-abuse-trump. Accessed 14 November 2017.

Kohm, L. M. (2008). Tracing the foundations of the best interests of the child standard in American jurisprudence. *Journal of Law & Family Studies, 10*(2), 337–376.

Legal Services for Children, Inc. (2014). *Questions and answers about emancipation for teenagers*. San Francisco: Author. http://www.courts.ca.gov/documents/ emancipation_manual.pdf. Accessed 06 November 2017.

National Association of Social Workers. (2008). Code of ethics. https://www.socialworkers.org/pubs/code/code.asp. Accessed 11 February 2016.

National Center for Lesbian Rights. (2017). Marriage, domestic partnerships, and civil unions: Same-sex couples within the United States. www.nclrights.org/wp-content/uploads/2013/07/Relationship_Recognition.pdf. Accessed 14 November 2017.

National Conference of Commissioners on Uniform State Laws. (2017). Uniform Child Custody Jurisdiction and Enforcement Act Summary. http://www.uniformlaws.org/ActSummary.aspx?title=Child%20Custody%20Jurisdiction%20and%20Enforcement%20Act. Accessed 06 November 2017.

Paul, D. B., & Spencer, H. G. (2008). "It's OK, we're not cousins by blood": The cousin marriage controversy in historical perspective. *PLoS Biology, 6*(12), e320. https://www.ncbi.nlm.nih.gov/pmc/articles/PMC2605922/. Accessed 13 November 2017.

Price-Livingston, S. (2002). Emancipation procedures. https://www.cga.ct.gov/2002/ rpt/2002-R-0008.htm. Accessed 06 November 2017.

Silver, K. (2014, June 23). Romania's lost generation: Inside the Iron Curtain's orphanages. *ABC*. http://www.abc.net.au/radionational/programs/allinthemind/inside-the-iron-curtain%E2%80%99s-orphanages/5543388. Accessed 14 November 2017.

Southern Judicial Circuit. (n.d.) Emancipation packet: General information about emancipation. http://www.southernjudicialcircuit.com/selfhelp/miscforms/ emancipationminor.pdf. Accessed 06 November 2017.

Superior Court, Maricopa County. (n.d.). Emancipation. http://www.superiorcourt. maricopa.gov/SuperiorCourt/JuvenileCourt/emancipation.asp. Accessed 06 November 2017.

Thomson Reuters. (2017a). Findlaw: Common law marriage states. http://family.findlaw.com/marriage/common-law-marriage-states.html. Accessed 05 November 2017.

Thomson Reuters. (2017b). Findlaw: Open vs. closed adoption. http://family.findlaw.com/adoption/open-vs-closed-adoption.html. Accessed 13 November 2017.

Tolstoy, D. (1964). Void and voidable marriages. *Modern Law Review, 27*(4), 385–394.

Unmarried Equality. (2017). Common law marriage fact sheet. http://www.unmarried.org/common-law-marriage-fact-sheet/. Accessed 05 November 2017.

Legal References

Cases

Anderson v. Anderson, 577 So. 2d 658 (Fla. Dist. Ct. App. 1991).
Braschi v. Stahl, 543 N.E.2d 49 (N.Y. 1989).
Caban v.Mohammed, 441 U.S. 380 (1979).
Carney v. Carney, 598 P.2d 36 (Cal. 1979).
Doe v. Roe, 526 N.Y.S.2d 718 (N.Y. Supr. Ct. New York County 1988).
Friederwitzer v. Friederwitzer, 432 N.E.2d 765 (N.Y. 1982).
In re Brian T., Jr., 38 A.3d 114 (2013).
In re Emmanuel, 648 A.2d 904 (1994).
In re Isaiah J, 59 A.3d 892 (Conn. 2013).
In re Justin F, 45 A.3d 94 (2012).
In re Nicholas H., 46 P.3d 932 (Cal. 2002).
In re Paul M., Jr., 85 A.3d 1263 (Conn. 2014).
In re Sean H., 586 A.2d 1171 (1991), *cert. denied*, 218 Conn. 904.
Lassiter v. Department of Social Services, 452 U.S. 18 (1981).
Lehr v. Robertson, 463 U.S. 268 (1983).
Loveheart v.Long, 762 S.W.2d 32 (Mo. 1988).
Loving v. Virginia, 388 U.S. 1 (1967).

Mathews v. Eldridge, 424 U.S. 319 (1976).
Meyer v.Nebraska, 262 U.S. 390 (1923).
Michael H. v. Gerald D., 491 U.S. 110 (1989).
Obergefell v. Hodges, 576 U.S. ___ (2015).
Palmore v. Sidoti, 466 U.S. 429 (1984).
Quilloin v Wolcott, 434 U.S. 246 (1978).
Rubano v. DiCenzo, 759 A.2d 959 (R.I. 2000).
Santosky v. Kramer, 455 U.S. 745 (1982).
Stanley v. Illinois, 405 U.S. 645 (1969).
T.E.P. v. Leavitt, 840 F. Supp. 110 (d. Utah 1993).
Turner v. Safley, 482 U.S. 78 (1987).

Statutes

Alabama Code § 26-13-1 (2016).
Arizona Revised Statutes § 12-2451 (2005).
Arkansas Code § 9-27-362 (2016).
California Family Code § 7000 et seq. (2016).
Code of Virginia § 16.1-331 -334.1 (2016).
Connecticut General Statutes § 45a-717(b), 46b-115a(1), 46b-120(8), 46b-120(10) (2015).
Connecticut General Statutes §§ 46b-150 – 150e (2016).
Emancipation of Minors Act [Illinois], 750 Illinois Compiled Statutes 30/1 et seq. (2017).
Emancipation of Minors Act [Michigan], Michigan Compiled Laws § 722.4c (1998).
Florida Statutes § 743.015 (2017).
Louisiana Civil Code, tit. VIII, arts. 366, 368 (2009).
Mississippi Code Annotated § 93-11-65 (2001).
Montana Code Annotated § 41-1-501 (2017).
Emancipation of Minors Act [New Mexico], New Mexico Statutes Annotated §§ 32A-21-1 to 32A-21-7 (1978).
North Carolina General Statutes §§ 7B-3500 to -3509 (1998).
Official Code of Georgia Annotated §§ 15-11-200 to -208 (2014).
Oregon Revised Statutes §§ 419B.550 to 419B.558 (2015).
Parental Kidnapping Prevention Act of 1981, 28 U.S.C.A § 1738-A (West 20002).
Texas Family Code § 31.001 (1995).
Uniform Child Custody Jurisdiction and Enforcement Act. (1997). http://www.uniform laws.org/shared/docs/child_custody_jurisdiction/uccjea_final_97.pdf. Accessed 13 November 2017.
Vermont Statutes Annotated, tit. 12, § 7151 (2003).
Washington Revised Code §§ 13.64.010 to -080 (1995).
West Virginia Code § 49-4-115 (2016).
Wyoming Statutes § 14-1-201 et seq. (2016).

Other Sources

United States Constitution, 14th Amendment.
United States Constitution, Article 4, section 1.

Chapter 8
School Social Work

The Role of the School Social Worker

Depending upon state law and regulations and the particular public school district, school social workers may be responsible for a broad range of activities. These may include any of the following:

- Involvement in school services including, but not limited to, committees, in-services, or supervision
- Evaluations on either a case basis or program basis
- Intervention with individuals, groups, or families
- Assessment at the individual case level or the program level
- Development and implementation of school-wide prevention programs, e.g., psychoeducation
- Case-finding
- The provision or organization of or advocacy for community-focused services, such as referrals and wraparound services
- Involvement in local, regional, and national professional associations
- Legislative activities at the local, state, and/or national levels (Greenberg, 2014; Illinois State Board of Education, 2007)

Clearly, social workers may fulfill a broad range of functions; the specific functions often depend upon the needs of their school districts, the numbers of students in the schools, the characteristics of the surrounding community, the number of social workers, and the particular perspective and budget of the school district. Accordingly, it is critical that school social workers develop a working knowledge of both the legal and ethical provisions that are relevant to their diverse functions.

Social Worker Involvement in Access to School and School Services

Several US Supreme Court decisions govern issues related to access to school and school services. The Supreme Court has ruled that children cannot be required to attend public school (*Pierce v. Society of Sisters*, 1939), students may receive their education in a language other than English (*Meyer v. Nebraska*, 1923), and the maintenance of separate schools based on race is unconstitutional (*Brown v. Board of Education*, 1955). However, the Court has also held that education is not a fundamental right and, accordingly, the Court held that the funding of public schools based on local property tax revenues does not violate the Equal Protection Clause of the Fourteenth Amendment, even though it may result in the allocation of fewer resources to poor districts (*San Antonio v. Rodriguez*, 1973).

The Supreme Court case of *Wisconsin v. Yoder* (1972) dealt with a dispute between Amish parents and the state of Wisconsin with respect to the state's requirement that children remain in the educational system overseen by the state until the age of 16. The parents contended that this requirement infringed on their practice of their faith and their desire in accordance with their religious beliefs to have their children remain apart from more worldly influences beyond a specified age. The court found that the parents were sincere in their religious beliefs and their desire to remove their children from the state-overseen schools was consistent with those beliefs and the practice of their religion.

The Court considered the state's contention that an additional 2 years of high school was necessary to prepare the children to be productive citizens and acquire the necessary skills that would enable them to do so. The Court found, however, that in view of the children's likely future as members of the Amish community, an additional 2 years of high school education would not help them to develop the skills that they would need to be productive members of the Amish community. It is critical to note that the genuineness of the parents' religious beliefs and the congruence between those beliefs and their actions were significant factors in the Court's decision in favor of the parents and its finding that the state's requirement was an infringement on the parents' free exercise of their religion. A philosophical or secular belief that the children should not continue with their high school education likely would have yielded a different result.

The case of *Plyler v. Doe* (1982) involved a challenge to a Texas law that withheld from any local school districts state funding for the education of children who had not been legally admitted into the United States and authorized school districts to deny enrollment to such students. The US Supreme Court expressly found that this statute violated the Equal Protection Clause of the Fourteenth Amendment to the US Constitution. The Court concluded that the statute would impose a lifetime of hardship on a class of children for a situation that was not of their making and over which they had no control, while their presence in the schools did not impose a special burden on Texas' ability to provide high-quality public education.

It is unlikely that many school social workers would become involved in the litigation of such issues. However, it is important that school social workers be aware of these court decisions and their relevance to both school policies and practices at the local level and to legislation at the state level. School social workers may become involved in advocacy efforts at the local, state, or regional levels to ensure that laws, regulations, policies, and practices are consistent with these court decisions and that children are able to access the services to which they are entitled.

The Every Student Succeeds Act

This legislation replaced the No Child Left Behind Act (2002), which was a reauthorization of the Elementary and Secondary Education Act of 1965. The Elementary and Secondary Education Act of 1965 permitted the federal government to provide financial support for primary and secondary education and had been reauthorized in 1994 as the Improving America's Schools Act. This, in turn, was repealed in 2001 when the legislation was reauthorized as the No Child Left Behind Act.

The No Child Left Behind Act delineated a level of performance that schools would be required to attain. These include:

- The development and implementation of system of annual student testing and assessment
- The development of state standards for and assessments of students' adequate yearly progress
- The provision of specified information to parents
- A prohibition against the exclusion of any child from a federally assisted educational program on the basis of his or her surname or language minority status
- The provision of supplemental educational services to children in schools that have been identified as failing to achieve adequate annual progress

In addition, the law permits parents to transfer their child to another school from one that has been identified as failing to make yearly progress. Particular emphasis is placed on assessing and improving the achievement of students who may be economically disadvantaged, those from major ethnic and racial groups, those with limited English proficiency, and those with disabilities.

The Every Student Succeeds Act narrowed the role of the federal government in elementary and secondary education. Although the law retained the requirement of standardized testing, it shifted much of the accountability from the federal to the state government. States must address proficiency on tests, English language proficiency, and graduation rates. States are also required to identify and intervene with schools that perform in the bottom 5 percent, in high schools in which the graduation rate is 67 percent or less, and in districts where students appear to be struggling. States are no longer required to evaluate teachers on the basis of student outcomes.

School social workers may be involved in the evaluation of student outcomes, as well as the design and/or evaluation of programs to support students who appear to be struggling. In some cases, the requirements of the legislation may impact students on an individual level, requiring social worker intervention. As an example, the mandate for standardized testing may impact students with test-taking anxiety, and some of these students may need or seek out social work services in an effort to reduce their test-related anxiety.

The Equal Access Act

The Equal Access Act was passed in 1984 with the intent that public high schools that receive federal funding provide student-initiated religious groups with the same access to school resources, such as space, as those groups that are nonreligious. The law provides:

> It shall be unlawful for any public secondary school which receives Federal financial assistance and which has a limited open forum to deny equal access or a fair opportunity to, or discriminate against, any students who wish to conduct a meeting within that limited open forum on the basis of the religious, political, philosophical, or other content of the speech at such meetings. (20 U.S.C. § 4071(a) 2002)

Accordingly, the Equal Access Act protects student groups that are voluntary; that have been initiated and controlled by students; that are not sponsored by the school, a government unit, or a government employee; and that are religious in nature and are not officiated by either a school employee or government official. A school cannot deny student access because it disagrees with the student group's perspective or message, regardless of whether it is religious, political, or philosophical in nature. Additionally, nonschool personnel cannot be in regular attendance, and the actions of the group cannot be such that they materially and substantially interfere with the orderly conduct of the school's educational activities (20 U.S.C. § 4071, 2002). However, a school can deny student access in situations in which the student group's guidelines for membership conflict with the school district's policy. For example, a school can deny student access if the group's membership policy contravenes the school district's antidiscrimination policy (*Truth v. Kent School District*, 2008).

School social workers may be called upon by student groups to assist with their efforts to establish a student group. As an example, this author is aware of a situation in which students approached a teacher and a social worker to assist and support them in their efforts to establish a gay-straight alliance in their high school, intending to foster greater understanding. In another instance, a school social worker assisted students in their efforts to develop a school-based club devoted to the provision of voluntary services in the surrounding neighborhood, e.g., free tutoring and nursing home visitation.

Title IX of the Education Amendment Act of 1972

Title IX prohibits discrimination on the basis of sex by educational programs that receive federal financial assistance. The protections extend to participation in athletic programs, to employment, and to protection from sexual harassment by peers, teachers, or colleagues. The provisions are applicable to both public and private schools that receive federal funding, including elementary and secondary schools, college, universities, and vocational and professional schools; an exemption is provided only for religious schools for which the Title IX requirements would conflict with their religious principles. At the time of this writing, the Trump administration had withdrawn guidelines that had been issued by the Obama administration to protect transgender students under Title IX, which had asserted that the law's provisions applied to gender identity as well as to gender (Battle & Wheeler, 2017; Kreighbaum, 2017).

Discrimination is defined broadly to include sexual harassment and sexual violence, including rape, sexual assault, sexual battery, and sexual coercion (United States Department of Education, Office for Civil Rights, n.d.). The law requires that all schools have a policy against discrimination; respond efficiently and effectively if it suspects that sexual harassment or sexual violence is occurring, including an investigation into its cause and the formulation of strategies to prevent its recurrence; develop and implement a grievance procedure that permits students to file grievances related to complaints of sexual harassment and sexual violence; and disclose to the complainant the imposition of any sanctions against the alleged offender if the sanctions involve the complainant, e.g., a prohibition against contact of the victim by the perpetrator. Schools are also required to designate a specific individual who is charged with the responsibility for compliance with Title IX provisions.

There have been a number of lawsuits filed against school for violations of Title IX provisions. *In J.K. v. Arizona Board of Regents* (2008), the court rejected the university's assertion that it bore no responsibility for the rape of a student by a school athlete, even though it had expelled the athlete for his severe sexual harassment of other women on campus. In ruling on a motion for summary judgment,[1] the court found that there was sufficient evidence to conclude that the coach had acted

---

[1] A motion for summary judgment is a judgment entered by a court for one party against another without a full trial. The party that moves (asks) the court to enter judgment on a motion for summary judgment is essentially arguing that there is no genuine dispute with respect to any material fact and that they are entitled to a judgment in their favor as a matter of law. In moving for summary judgment, the party is most frequently trying to avoid the time and expense that the discovery process and a trial would require. In ruling on a motion for summary judgment, the court must consider all facts in the light most favorable to the party who is opposing the motion for summary judgment. For example, if a plaintiff is suing a social worker and the plaintiff moves for summary judgment, the court must view all facts in the light most favorable to the social worker when deciding on the motion. In ruling on a motion for summary judgment, the judge may rule in favor of the moving party with respect to all, some, or none of the legal issues or may rule in favor of the party opposing the motion with respect to some, all, or none of the legal issues (see Federal Rule of Civil Procedure 56).

"deliberately and indifferently to the danger that he was creating" (J.K. v. Arizona Board of Regents, 2008, p. 8). In the case of *Simpson v. University of Colorado* (2007), a federal court found that the university had acted with "deliberate indifference" in its response to the sexual assault of two female students by athletes and recruits. The court concluded that the university "had an official policy of showing high school football recruits a 'good time' on their visits to the CU campus," that it "failed to provide adequate supervision and guidance to player-hosts chosen to show the recruits a 'good time'," and that "the likelihood of such misconduct was so obvious that CU's failure was the result of deliberate indifference" (American Civil Liberties Union, 2006). In both cases, the universities involved reached a financial settlement with the plaintiffs and instituted measures aimed at the prevention of future such occurrences (American Civil Liberties Union, 2017).

It is not unlikely that a social worker employed by a school district, college, or university would be consulted by a student who has been victimized in a similar situation. The student may be seeking information, counseling, or advocacy services, depending upon the particular circumstances and his or her emotional and physical needs at the time. Depending upon the age of the student and state law, the social worker may be legally required to report the occurrence of child abuse or partner violence. In some cases, the social worker may not be permitted to provide counseling in the absence of parental consent. In all such situations, the social worker should inform the student of his or her legal obligation to make such a report. And in order to avoid any misunderstandings at the time of student disclosure, the social worker may wish to consider posting a notice that informs visitors to his or her office of the legal reporting requirement.

Individuals with Disabilities Education Act

The Individuals with Disabilities Education Act, previously known as the Education for All Handicapped Children Act, seeks to ensure that all children with disabilities are afforded the same educational opportunities as those without disabilities. Key elements of the law include the Individualized Education Program (IEP), Free and Appropriate Public Education (FAPE), Least Restrictive Environment (LRE), Appropriate Evaluation, Parent and Teacher Participation, and Procedural Safeguards. Schools are required to develop an individualized education program that addresses the child's unique needs in the least restrictive environment possible. (United States Department of Education, Office for Civil Rights, 2010). The team that works to develop the plan must include the child's parents, one of the child's teachers, a professional who can interpret the educational implications of the evaluations that have been conducted, and an administrator or Committee of Special Education that has adequate knowledge of the resources available in the school district and is empowered to commit the provision of those services to the child. Not infrequently, a school social worker will participate in the formulation of an individualized education program.

The law provides that parents have the following rights:

- The ability to participate
- Access to the child's records
- Prior notification if there is to be a change in the child's Individualized Education Plan
- Receipt of a notice detailing procedural safeguards
- Language interpreter services, if needed
- The maintenance of the child in a status quo situation during ongoing attempts to resolve a dispute (the "stay-put rule")
- Due process protections
- The ability to utilize mediation as a strategy to resolve disputes, prior to commencing litigation
- An express right to file a lawsuit if they are dissatisfied (Individuals with Disabilities Education Act, 2015)

There are significant limitations to the impact of this law. First, to be eligible for coverage under its provisions, the child's disability must adversely affect his or her performance in such a way that special education is required (34 C.F.R. § 300.8, 2007). Accordingly, a child with a disability that does not affect his or her educational performance would not need special education and would consequently not be covered under the provisions of the law. Second, a state may choose whether or not to participate in the Individuals with Disabilities Education Act. The benefits and protections available under the Act in one state may be unavailable to a child in another. Many parents may be unaware of this situation when they contemplate the possibility of relocation, e.g., for employment opportunities. It would be important that the school social worker provide them with such information if he or she becomes aware of a potential move.

Scholars have noted that there appears to be a disproportionate representation of minority students in special education classes (Skiba et al., 2008). Under the Individual with Disabilities Education Act, states are required to:

- Have policies and procedures to prevent the inappropriate overidentification of or disproportionate representation by race or ethnicity of students with disabilities (20 U.S.C. § 1412(a)(24), 2015; 34 C.F.R. § 300.173, 2015)
- If receiving funding under Part B of the Act, collect and evaluate special education data to determine whether race- or ethnicity-related disproportionality is occurring at the state or local level in regard to disability, placement, or disciplinary actions (20 U.S.C. § 1418(d), 2015; 34 C.F.R. § 300.646, 2016)
- Provide for a review and, as appropriate, revision of policies, procedures, and practices for the identification and placement of students if significant disproportionality is found (20 U.S.C. § 1418(d), 2015; 34 C.F.R. § 300.646, 2016)
- Disaggregate data relating to suspension and expulsion rates by race and ethnicity and compare these rates to those of local educational agencies in the state or the rates of nondisabled children within those agencies (20 U.S.C. § 1418(d), 2015; 34 C.F.R. § 300.646, 2016)

- Monitor local education agencies with quantifiable indicators of disproportionate representation of racial and ethnic groups in special education (20 U.S.C. § 1416(a)(3), 2015; 34 C.F.R. § 300.600(d), 2008)

Social workers may be involved at various levels with these mandates depending upon their individual skills, assigned responsibilities, and the needs of the school system or state. They may participate in a review of the relevant policies, procedures, and practices; the revision of such policies, procedures, and practices; and/or the interpretation of the data that are collected.

Americans with Disabilities Act of 1990

The Americans with Disabilities Act prohibits discrimination against individuals with disabilities in employment, public services, public accommodations, and telecommunications, whether or not the specific entity receives federal funding. The definition of disability for the purposes of eligibility under this legislation is significantly broader than that utilized by the Individuals with Disabilities Education Act, in that it does not require a nexus between the disability and educational implications. Disability under the Americans with Disabilities Act is defined as follows:

(1) Disability. The term "disability" means, with respect to an individual:
   (A) A physical or mental impairment that substantially limits one or more major life activities of such individual
   (B) A record of such an impairment
   (C) Being regarded as having such an impairment (as described in paragraph (3))

(2) Major life activities
   (A) In general. For purposes of paragraph (1), major life activities include, but are not limited to, caring for oneself, performing manual tasks, seeing, hearing, eating, sleeping, walking, standing, lifting, bending, speaking, breathing, learning, reading, concentrating, thinking, communicating, and working.
   (B) Major bodily functions. For purposes of paragraph (1), a major life activity also includes the operation of a major bodily function, including, but not limited to, functions of the immune system, normal cell growth, digestive, bowel, bladder, neurological, brain, respiratory, circulatory, endocrine, and reproductive functions.

(3) Regarded as having such an impairment. For purposes of paragraph (1)(C):
   (A) An individual meets the requirement of "being regarded as having such an impairment" if the individual establishes that he or she has been subjected to an action prohibited under this chapter because of an actual or perceived physical or mental impairment whether or not the impairment limits or is perceived to limit a major life activity.
   (B) Paragraph (1) (C) shall not apply to impairments that are transitory and minor. A transitory impairment is an impairment with an actual or expected duration of 6 months or less (Americans with Disabilities Act, 42 U.S.C. § 12102 (2002).

School social workers may become involved in the assessment of a child for a disability within the meaning of the Americans with Disabilities Act. They may also be consulted by parents and/or school administrators seeking an evaluation of the nature of the services that may be required in order to comply with the law and/or the adequacy of the services being provided.

Vocational Rehabilitation Act of 1973

Section 504 of the Vocational Rehabilitation Act of 1973 provides in pertinent part:

> No otherwise qualified individual with a disability ... shall, solely by reason of his or her disability, be excluded from the participation in, be denied the benefits of, or be subjected to discrimination under any program of activity receiving Federal financial assistance.... (29 U.S.C. § 794 (a), 2015)

Eligibility for services under Section 504 requires the existence of an identified mental or physical condition that substantially limits a major life activity. Major life activities include such things as walking, seeing, hearing, speaking, breathing, learning, working, and caring for oneself. The school district must determine whether a child's impairment "substantially limits" one or more major life activities.

Various differences exist between this Act and the Individuals with Disabilities Education Act. Unlike the eligibility requirements under the Individuals with Disabilities Education Act, the Vocational Rehabilitation Act does not require that the student's disability or handicap adversely affect his or her educational performance. Under the Vocational Rehabilitation Act, a periodic reevaluation is required, but unlike the Individuals with Disabilities Education Act, it need not be conducted every 3 years at a minimum. Additionally, the Vocational Rehabilitation Act does not provide for an independent evaluation at the school's expense (deBettencourt 2002). The Vocational Rehabilitation Act lacks a "stay-put" provision and does not require days' notice prior to a change in the child's placement. And enforcement of the provisions of the Individuals with Disabilities Education Act falls to the United States Department of Education, Office of Special Education, whereas enforcement of the Vocational Rehabilitation Act is within the purview of the United States Department of Education, Office of Civil Rights (deBettencourt 2002).

Regulations promulgated to implement the statute require that all recipients of federal funding that operate a public elementary or secondary education program or activity must provide "a free appropriate public education to each qualified handicapped person who is in the recipient's jurisdiction, regardless of the nature or severity of the person's handicap" (34 C.F.R. § 104.33(a) 2000). An appropriate education is one that meets "the individual education needs of students with disabilities as adequately as the needs of nondisabled students are met" and may include regular or special education (United States Department of Education 2010). Social workers may be called upon to assist with the development, implementation, and/or evaluation of the educational services provided to a student to ensure that they are adequate to meet a student's individual education needs.

Intervention with Individuals, Groups, or Families

As noted above, social workers may be called upon to provide individual counseling to students who have experienced sexual harassment within the meaning of Title IX of the Education Amendment Act of 1972. Depending upon the individual situation and the nature of a student's disability, social workers may also be asked to develop and/or provide student-level interventions.

At the time of this writing, the United States is experiencing an upsurge in the deportation of individuals who have entered the United States illegally, including the deportation of parents with US citizen children (Cooke & Rosenberg, 2017; Hesson & Kim, 2017; Shear & Nixon, 2017). Officers of the Immigration Customs and Enforcement (ICE) agency have been moving against individuals with no history of wrongdoing apart from their illegal entry, even at public schools (Castillo, 2017). This situation may likely be traumatic not only to the children's whose lives may be disrupted as a result of their parents' deportation but also to those children who witness the arrest of their friends' and schoolmates' family members. In such situations, school social workers may need to be available to provide counseling services to children who are experiencing distress and to help arrange suitable living arrangements for those children who remain in the United States following the deportation of their parents.

Considerations Relating to Confidentiality, Privacy, and the Release of Information

The Family Educational Rights and Privacy Act (FERPA)

The Family and Educational Rights and Privacy Act, often referred to as FERPA, requires that schools receiving federal funding provide parents access to their children's school records (United States Department of Education, 2015). It is important to remember that this applies only to minor children; once a child attains the age of 18, parents can no longer access their children's educational records, even in circumstances in which they are paying for that education, e.g., for an adolescent or young adult attending college.

There are very limited circumstances under which information contained in educational records can be disclosed without parental consent if the child is a minor or without the consent of the student if he or she is 18 years of age or older. Such circumstances include federal audits, requests by the juvenile justice system, requests for information pursuant to a subpoena or court order, and when the disclosure is necessary in order to safeguard the health or safety of the child or of others (20 U.S.C. § 1232 g (b), (h), 2013; 34 C.F.R. §§ 99.30–0.36, 2017).

However, despite the provisions of FERPA, parents may not be entitled to access all information relating to their minor children that is generated within the context of a school setting. First, many states provide that minor children of a specified age may receive some services confidentially, without the knowledge or the consent of their parents. These often include services related to substance use and mental health assessment and treatment; contraceptive services; testing and treatment for sexually transmitted infections, including HIV; and legal counsel in juvenile and court proceedings (Dibble, n.d.).

Second, FERPA defines an educational record as

those records, files, documents, and other materials which:
(i) Contain information directly related to a student
(ii) Are maintained by an educational agency or institution or by a person acting for such agency or institution (20 US.C. § 1232(a)(4)(A), 2010)

Educational records do not include treatment records, such as those made by a school social worker, *as long as they are not shared with others*. As one attorney has advised:

FERPA applies to 'education records.' FERPA does not apply to medical records used only for treatment, (let's call those 'unshared treatment records.') Once the medical records are shared outside the treatment sphere (let's call those 'shared treatment records'), they become education records and are subject to FERPA. So, FERPA applies to education records, including shared treatment records, and does not apply to unshared treatment records.

HIPAA specifically excludes both education records, including shared treatment records, and unshared treatment records. (See 45 C.F.R. 160.103 definition of 'Protected Health Information') It does not apply to any of the three.

So, neither FERPA nor HIPAA applies to unshared treatment records. (Lavoie, 2016)

This necessarily raises both ethical and legal issues if the social worker is engaging students in a group treatment. Maintaining one record for all of the group participants raises concerns with respect to confidentiality. As an example, if it were to become necessary to disclose something in the record for the purpose of protecting a particular student or others, the disclosure of the record containing information pertaining to that student would result in the disclosure of information pertaining to each of the individual students. Accordingly, it has been recommended that school social workers maintain separate records for each student participating in a group, rather than a record for the group as a whole (Luepker, 2003).

As indicated above in another context, issues of confidentiality may arise in situations in which a student discloses that he or she has been the victim of abuse, sexual harassment, or sexual assault. Most, if not all, states require that social workers report suspected abuse of a minor child to the designated state agency. A failure to report abuse may have implications not only for the health and well-being of the minor child but for the social worker's license as well. In some states, social workers may also be obligated to report partner violence to a designated state authority, regardless of whether the victim is a minor or of an age to be considered an adult. FERPA specifically provides that information that would otherwise be confidential may be disclosed in an emergency when necessary to protect the health or safety of the student or others (20 U.S.C. §§ 1232 g (b), (h),; 34 C.F.R. § 99.36, 2017).

Additionally, many states impose a duty to warn on mental health-care providers, including social workers. The concept of duty to warn derives from the California case of *Tarasoff v Regents of the University of California* (1976). In that case, a university student disclosed to a psychologist on the university campus that he intended to kill his girlfriend. The psychologist notified his supervisor and the campus police; the police determined from a brief conversation with the student that he was not intending to carry out the threat. However, the student did kill his former girlfriend as he had threatened to do. The psychologist defended his actions on the basis of the need to maintain confidentiality in the context of a therapeutic relationship. Although the court recognized the need for confidentiality, the court held that "the public policy favoring protection of the confidential character of patient-psychotherapist communications must yield to the extent to which disclosure is essential to avert danger to others. The protective privilege ends where the public peril begins" (*Tarasoff v. Regents of the University of California*, 1976, p. 346). Accordingly, it appeared that a mental health provider would be required to breach confidentiality in situations in which it appeared that there was an immediate threat of harm that could be carried out against an identifiable victim.

States vary in the extent to which they have adopted this perspective, either by case law through the courts or by statute. (For additional discussion of the duty to warn and varying state interpretations and applications, see Chaps. 2 and 5.) School social workers will want to familiarize themselves with their state's law relating to duty to warn. It is possible that questions regarding the existence of a duty to warn may arise even if there exists the possibility, as indicated by word or deed, that a student or students are contemplating either hazing others, which has been known to lead to fatalities (Bacon & Baskin, 2015; Turpin, 2017), or committing other acts of violence against others (*Tarasoff v. Regents of the University of California,* 1976).

References

American Civil Liberties Union. (2006, August 24). Simpson v. University of Colorado. https://www.aclu.org/cases/simpson-v-university-colorado. Accessed 03 May 2017.

American Civil Liberties Union. (2017). Title IX and sexual violence in schools. https://www.aclu.org/title-ix-and-sexual-violence-schools. Accessed 19 April 2017.

Bacon, J., & Baskin, M. (2015, September 15). 37 fraternity members face charges in hazing death of pledge. *USA Today*. https://www.usatoday.com/story/news/nation-now/2015/09/15/fraternity-deaths-hazing-pledges-charges/72299808/. Accessed 03 May 2017.

Battle, S., Acting Assistant Secretary for Civil Rights, United States Department of Education, & Wheeler, T.E. II, Acting Assistant Attorney General for Civil Rights, United States Department of Justice. (2017, February 22). Dear colleague letter. http://www.justice.gov/press-release/file/941551/download. Accessed 18 April 2017.

Castillo, A. (2017, March 3). Immigrant arrested by ICE after dropping daughter off at school, sending shock waves through neighborhood. *Los Angeles Times*,. http://www.latimes.com/local/lanow/la-me-immigration-school-20170303-story.html. Accessed 10 May 2017.

Cooke, K., & Rosenberg, M. (2017, March 4). Parents fearing deportation pick guardians for U.S. children. *Reuters*, http://www.reuters.com/article/us-usa-immigration-parents-idUSKBN16A16V. Accessed 10 May 2017.

deBettencourt, L. U. (2002). Understanding the differences between IDEA and Section 504. *Teaching Exceptional Children, 34*(2), 16–23.

Dibble, N. (n.d.). Minor students' rights to confidentiality, self-determination, and informed consent in Wisconsin. Wisconsin Department of Public Instruction. https://dpi.wi.gov/sites/default/files/imce/sspw/pdf/sswpgethicsrights.pdf. Accessed 29 March 2017.

Greenberg, J. P. (2014). Significance of after-school programming for immigrant children during middle childhood: Opportunities for school social work. *Social Work, 59*(3), 243–251.

Hesson, T., & Kim, H. M. (2017, May 3). Casey blasts Trump administration over child deportation. *Politico,* http://www.politico.com/story/2017/05/03/bob-casey-tweets-halt-deportation-237939. Accessed 10 May 2017.

Illinois State Board of Education. (2007). School social work: Student services providers recommended practices and procedures manual. https://www.isbe.net/Documents/social_work_manual.pdf. Accessed 29 March 2017.

Kreighbaum, A. (2017, February 23). Transgender protections withdrawn. *Inside Higher Ed*, http://www.insidehighered.com. Accessed 18 April 2017.

Lavoie, N. (2016). Definition of educational record. In Office of General Counsel, Catholic University of America. http://counsel.cua.edu/ferpa/questions/. Accessed 18 April 2017.

Luepker, E. T. (2003). *Record keeping in psychotherapy and counseling*. New York: Brunner-Routledge.

Shear, M. D., & Nixon, R. (2017, February 26). New Trump deportation rules allow far more expulsions. *New York Times*, https://www.nytimes.com/2017/02/21/us/politics/dhs-immigration-trump.html. Accessed 10 April 2017.

Skiba, R. J., Simmons, A. B., Ritter, S., Giss, A. C., Rausch, M. K., Cuadrado, J., & Chung, C.-S. (2008). Achieving equity in special education: History, status, and current challenges. *Exceptional Children, 74*(3), 264–288.

Turpin, C. (2017, February 13). Police probe hazing, excessive drinking in Penn State frat death. *NJ.com.* http://www.nj.com/hunterdon/index.ssf/2017/02/police_probe_hazing_excessive_drinking_in_penn_sta.html. Access 3 May 2017.

United States Department of Education. (2015, June 26). Family Educational Rights and Privacy Act (FERPA). https://www2.ed.gov/policy/gen/guid/fpco/ferpa/index.html? src=rn. Accessed 03 May 2017.

United States Department of Education. (2010, June). Family Educational and Privacy Rights Act (FERPA) and the disclosure of student information related to emergencies and disasters. https://www2.ed.gov/policy/gen/guid/fpco/pdf/ferpa-disaster-guidance.pdf. Accessed 18 April 2017.

United States Department of Education, Office for Civil Rights. (2010). Free appropriate public education for students with disabilities: Requirements under Section 504 of the Rehabilitation Act of 1973. https://www2.ed.gov/about/offices/list/ocr/docs/edlite-FAPE504.html. Accessed 10 May 2017.

United States Department of Education, Office for Civil Rights. (n.d.). Know your rights: Title IX prohibits sexual harassment and sexual violence where you go to school. https://www2.ed.gov/about/offices/list/ocr/docs/title-ix-rights-201104.pdf. Accessed 19 April 2017.

Legal References

Cases

Brown v. Board of Education, 347 U.S. 483 (1954) (Brown I); Board v. Board of Education, 349 U.S. 294 (1955) (Brown II).
J.K. v. Arizona Board of Regents, 2008 LEXIS 83855 (No. CV 06–916-PHX-MHM, D. Ariz. Sep. 29, 2008).
Meyer v. Nebraska, 262 U.S. 390 (1923).
Pierce v. Society of Sisters, 268 U.S. 510 (1925).
Plyler v. Doe, 457 U.S. 202 (1982).
San Antonio v. Rodriguez, 411 U.S. 1 (1973).
Simpson v. University of Colorado, 500 F.3d 1170 (10th Cir. 2007).
Tarasoff v. Regents of the University of California, 17 Cal. 3d 425 (1976).
Truth v. Kent School District, 542 F.3d 634 (9th Cir. 2008).
Wisconsin v. Yoder, 406 U.S. 205 (1972).

Statutes

Americans with Disabilities Act, 42 U.S.C. § 12101 et seq. (West 2002).
Americans with Disabilities Amendments Act, Pub. L. No. 110–325 (2009).
Elementary and Secondary Education Act of 1965, Pub. L. No. 89–10, 79 Stat. 27 (1965).
Equal Access Act, 20 U.S.C.A. § 4071 (2002).
Every Student Succeeds Act, Pub. L. No. 114–95, 129 Stat. 1802 (2015).
Family Education Rights and Privacy Act (FERPA), 20 U.S.C. §§ 1232(a)(4)(A), 1232g (b), (h) (2013).
Federal Rule of Civil Procedure 56.
Improving America's Schools Act, Pub. L. No. 103–381, 108 Stat. 3518 (1994).
Individuals with Disabilities Education Act (IDEA), Pub. L. No. 101–476, 104 Stat. 1142 (1990).
No Child Left Behind Act, Pub. L. No. 107–110, 115 Stat. 145 (2002).
Vocational Rehabilitation Act of 1973 § 504, 29 U.S.C. § 794 (a) (2015).

Regulations

46 C.F.R. § 99.30-.36 (2017).
34 C.F.R. § 104.33(a) (2000).
34 C.F.R. § 300.8 (2007).
34 C.F.R. § 300.173 (2015).
34 C.F.R. § 300.600(d) (2008).
34 C.F.R. § 300.646 (2016).

Chapter 9
Social Work in the Context of Health Care

Documentation Issues

The maintenance of adequate documentation, whether in private practice or as an employee of a health-care facility or agency, is critical to accountability and credibility (Kagle & Kopels, 2008) and as a risk management tool (Reamer, 2005). The production of documentation may be required in a variety of circumstances, including in response to a subpoena or a retrospective audit of health records by an insurer or a third party acting on its behalf (Felton, 2015). Such audits, which are an exception to the confidentiality provisions of the Health Insurance Portability and Accountability Act (HIPAA) of 1996, may be requested randomly or as part of an effort to detect fraudulent billing practices, errors in processing claims, or coding problems.

One writer has urged consideration of four separate aspects of documentation in developing a risk management strategy and standards for recordkeeping: content, language, credibility, and access (Reamer, 2005). The documentation *content* must be sufficient both to facilitate the delivery of client services and to protect the social worker in the event that a lawsuit or ethics complaint may be filed (Reamer, 2005). Accordingly, the content of the documentation must strike a balance between having too much detail, which could be read as an indication that the matter was handled in an unusual way (Simon, 1998), and too little detail, which could lead to decreased credibility if the social worker was asked to defend his or her approach or actions (Bergstresser, 1998).

It has been suggested that the following elements be included in any record as a means of both facilitating service delivery and as a strategy to manage risk. These include:

- An assessment of the client and his or her needs and situation
- A diagnosis, if appropriate, that is premised on the guidelines delineated in the American Psychiatric Association's most recent edition of the *Diagnostic and Statistical Manual of Mental Disorders* (2013)

- A description of the social worker's approach and an explanation for its selection
- Decisions and actions taken by the social worker and others that affect the client and/or his or her situation
- Service goals, plans, and timeline, as well as any modifications and the reasons for those changes
- Indicators of movement and the measures utilized
- Appointment logs
- Critical events and the actions taken by the social worker in addressing them
- The status of the client and his or her situation and needs at closing, the reason(s) for termination, and any referrals provided
- A description of efforts and referrals to ensure that a client who needs continued service has not been abandoned (Kagle & Kopels, 2008)

The National Association of Social Workers (NASW) has issued ethical standards specific to practice in a health-care setting. While these ethical standards do not constitute legal requirements, they may be relevant in actions involving malpractice claims. (See Chap. 4 for a discussion of civil lawsuits and malpractice.) The guidelines define "high-quality social work documentation" in the health-care context including:

> The client's identifying information
> Screening results
> Initial and subsequent biopsychosocial-spiritual assessments
> A client care plan, with procedures for monitoring and quantifying progress toward accomplishment of client goals, services provided, and other information about plan implementation
> Referrals to or from other provider organizations or resources, including rationale for referrals, and other collaboration on behalf of the client
> Dates, times, and descriptions of contact with the client, the client's support system, and other health-care provider organizations
> Quantifiable service outcomes
> Supervision or consultation sought or provided to enhance social work services
> Transfer or termination of services
> When indicated, written permission from the client too release and obtain information
> Documentation of compliance with confidentiality and privacy rights and responsibilities
> Accounting of receipts and disbursements related to client service provision (National Association of Social Workers, 2016, p. 36)

Because supervisors are responsible and are potentially liable for decisions that they have made and actions that they have taken, they should also maintain adequate documentation of supervision sessions (Reamer, 2005). Records should reflect the date and content of the supervision session, the persons who were present, and any recommendations that were made.

It is important to remember that multiple parties may have a legal right to *access* the social work record, including supervisors, health insurance auditors, utilization review personnel, a payer, an attorney, a court, or the client. Care should be taken in maintaining personal notes and in maintaining records for families and couples.

Personal notes may be subject to subpoena, and the maintenance of a single record for interactions with both members of a couple or multiple members of a family similarly risks disclosure of confidential details pertaining to one individual.

The *language* used should be clear, concise, and unambiguous. Conclusions and defamatory language are to be avoided. As an example, it would be inappropriate for a social worker to knowingly and falsely indicate in a record that a client abused her child or to conclude, in the absence of a formal assessment, that a client was confused.

In order to enhance *credibility*, documentation should be entered into the record as soon as possible after a meeting or event; lengthy delay will potentially diminish the credibility of any claim and raise doubts about the accuracy of the social worker's memory. However, documentation of an event before it has occurred is to be avoided (Reamer, 2005).

Patient Rights in the Health-Care Context

By virtue of their status as a patient, an individual has various rights that are specified in law. These include the right to provide informed consent to treatment, the right to refuse treatment, the right to privacy, and the right to have one's medical records remain confidential (United States Department of Health and Human Services n.d.-b). Privacy and confidentiality rights are discussed in detail in Chap. 2 and that discussion will not be repeated here. The discussion below focuses on legal issues associated with access to treatment and health-care decisionmaking.

The Right to Treatment and Access to Care

Despite what many people may believe, there is no legal right in the United States to receive health care in general. An exception exists, however, for medical emergencies. Known as the antidumping law, the federal Emergency Medical Treatment and Active Labor Act (EMTALA) requires that a hospital that has an emergency department and that receives federal funding provides medical screening and sufficient medical care to stabilize persons who are experiencing a medical emergency or are in active labor, regardless of their ability to pay for such services. The statute defines an emergency as:

> a medical condition (including emergency labor and delivery) manifesting itself by acute symptoms of sufficient severity (including severe pain) such that the absence of immediate medical attention could reasonably be expected to result in: (A) placing the patient's health in serious jeopardy, (B) serious impairment to bodily functions: or (C) serious dysfunction of any bodily organ or part. (Social Security Act § 1903(v)(3), 42 U.S.C. § 1396b(v)(3))

The law also sets forth the conditions under which a patient will be said to have been stabilized:

> The term 'to stabilize' means, with respect to an emergency medical condition described in paragraph (1)(A), to provide such medical treatment of the condition as may be necessary to assure, within reasonable medical probability, that no material deterioration of the condition is likely to result from or occur during the transfer of the individual from a facility, or, with respect to an emergency medical condition described in paragraph (1)(B), to deliver (including the placenta).
> (B) The term 'stabilized' means, with respect to an emergency medical condition described in paragraph (1)(A), that no material deterioration of the condition is likely, within reasonable medical probability, to result from or occur during the transfer of the individual from a facility, or, with respect to an emergency medical condition described in paragraph (1)(B), that the woman has delivered (including the placenta).
> (4) The term 'transfer' means the movement (including the discharge) of an individual outside a hospital's facilities at the direction of any person employed by (or affiliated or associated, directly or indirectly, with) the hospital, but does not include such a movement of an individual who (A) has been declared dead, or (B) leaves the facility without the permission of any such person. (42 U.S.C. § 1395dd(e), 2012)

Hospitals are not legally obligated to provide care to a patient beyond the care needed to achieve stabilization, even if additional care is medically recommended. This clearly presents difficulties for patients lacking adequate funds or health-care insurance to cover such costs. However, funding for care may be available to individuals under any of the existing federal programs funding health care if the individual meets the eligibility criteria.

Medicare and Medicaid The Medicare program is a federally funded program established by Title XVIII of the federal Social Security Act. This program provides health-care insurance for those who are 65 years of age or older, for individuals under the age of 65 years who are disabled and receive Social Security Supplemental Income, and for people of any age who have end-stage renal disease (for Medicare & Medicaid Services, 2014). Social workers in private practice may choose through the "opt-in" process to become Medicare providers (Groshong, 2010). As a Medicare provider, the social worker is considered available to receive Medicare patients; a refusal to do so is considered to be a violation of federal law.

A social worker who is enrolled as a Medicare provider but has not submitted a claim for payment from Medicare for 12 consecutive months will be disenrolled from the program. Reenrollment is possible following reapplication.

Social workers who are Medicare providers may choose to opt out of the program. In general, an opt-out is effective for a 2-year period, which may be renewable. In order to opt out, the social worker must opt out of Medicare for all beneficiaries and services, except emergency or urgent care situations. The social worker can then contract privately with clients to provide services that would have been covered by Medicare, but the contract entered into between the social worker and the beneficiary must state explicitly that neither will seek reimbursement from Medicare.

Eligibility criteria for the receipt of medical care coverage under the Medicaid program include age, disability, membership in a family with dependent children, or pregnancy. Unlike the Medicare program, eligibility for health-care coverage under Medicaid requires that individuals' income fall below a specified level. Some states have established Medicaid programs that extend health insurance coverage to those who would otherwise be eligible for Medicaid, but whose incomes are too high to qualify; these individuals are referred to as medically needy.

Individuals who are not citizens of the United States may in some circumstances be barred from accessing Medicare or Medicaid funding for their care, even if they would otherwise be eligible. The Illegal Immigration Reform and Immigrant Responsibility Act (IIRAIRA) of 1996 and the welfare law known as the Personal Responsibility and Work Opportunity Reconciliation Act (PRWORA) of 1996 together severely restrict the eligibility of immigrants, both those who are legally present in the United States and those who are undocumented, from receiving publicly funded benefits, such as federally funded medical care. The PRWORA established two classes of noncitizens for the purpose of receiving publicly funded benefits, those who are deemed to be "qualified" and those who are considered "not qualified." Individuals must fall into one of the following categories in order to be considered qualified:

- Lawfully admitted permanent resident aliens ("green card" holders)
- Refugees
- People who have been granted asylum
- Conditional entrants
- People granted withholding of deportation
- Cuban and Haitian entrants
- People who have been granted parole status by the Department of Homeland Security for a period of at least 1 year
- Abused immigrants, their parents, and/or children who meet specific criteria
- Survivors of trafficking and their derivative beneficiaries, e.g., children, who have obtained a T visa or whose application for a T visa indicates that they have a prima facie case of eligibility for a T visa. (See Chap. 12 for additional detail relating to eligibility as a battered spouse or child or a victim of trafficking.)

In addition to undocumented immigrants, the PRWORA also bars individuals who are permanent residents from receiving some public-funded benefits if they entered after the effective date of the law, August 22, 1996. Most immigrants who entered the United States on or after that date cannot obtain "federal means-tested public benefits" for a period of 5 years after they become "qualified" immigrants. "Federal means-tested public benefits" include benefits under Medicaid other than for emergency care. There are some categories of immigrants who are exempted from this 5-year bar: asylees and refugees, individuals granted withholding of deportation or removal, Cuban and Haitian entrants, specified Amerasian immigrants, Iraqi and Afghan Special Immigrants, qualified immigrant veterans and their dependents, survivors of trafficking, qualified immigrants active duty military and their dependents, and children who are receiving federal foster care. (See Chap. 12 for additional detail relating to health-care coverage by some states to pregnant women and children and access to public health programs regardless of individuals' immigration status.)

Individuals with disabilities may not be discriminated against in their efforts to obtain care on the basis of their disability if they are otherwise qualified to receive the services that they seek (United States Department of Health and Human Services n.d.-a; United States Department of Justice and United States Department of Health and Human Services, 2010). In one case, the US Supreme Court concluded that a dentist had discriminated against a woman with HIV infection in violation of the Americans with Disabilities Act by requiring that she receive her routine dental care in a hospital, which would have resulted in additional expense to her (*Bragdon v. Abbott*, 1998).

Hospitals and other health-care providers that provide services to Medicare and Medicaid patients are required to provide services that are medically necessary. The law defines "medically necessary" as:

> health care services or supplies needed to diagnose or treat an illness, injury, condition, disease, or its symptoms and that meet accepted standards of medicine. (United States Center for Medicare and Medicaid Services n.d.-b)

This does not mean, however, that the characterization of a procedure or treatment as medically necessary by a physician or other health-care provider will be judged to be medically necessary by Medicare or Medicaid. For example, Medicare may authorize specified services at only predesignated time intervals, such as annually. Medicare might deny payment for more frequent utilization of such a service, even if recommended by a physician, because the frequency falls outside of Medicare's established usage limit.

Access to Care and Extrajudicial Medical Removal Despite the legal requirement (and the medical need) that a patient be stabilized before he or she can be transferred and "that no material deterioration of the condition is likely to result from or occur during the transfer of the individual from a facility," some hospitals may attempt to send patients to another country in order to avoid the costs associated with their care, a practice that has been variously called medical deportation, medical repatriation, international patient dumping, extrajudicial deportation, and extralegal deportation, among others (Associated Press, 2013; Furth, 2015; Seton Hall Law School and New York Lawyers for the Public Interest, 2012; Loue, 2016, 2018; O'Connell, 2010). Such an attempt may occur even without the consent of the patient or their family members. Additionally, some hospitals have attempted to send US citizens to countries from which their families originated, even if the child had never been in that country and without the knowledge or consent of the family (Sontag, 2008). Immigration, however, is a function reserved to the federal government, and neither hospitals nor state governments have the legal authority to attempt or effectuate the deportation of any person from the United States (United States Constitution, Article 1; *Montejo v. Martin Memorial Hospital*, 2004). In such situations, the patient and/or the patient's family may decide to pursue a lawsuit against the hospital for false imprisonment[1]; medical malpractice; violations of federal statutory provisions, such as the Emergency Medical Treatment and Active Labor Act; and/or violations of state law, including antidiscrimination statutes.

The extent to which social workers may become involved in such circumstances remains unclear. However, it is not unlikely that a family confronted with the prospective involuntary transport of their loved one to another country would seek information from the hospital social worker. The social worker may face an ethical dilemma in such situations, as he or she may be torn between a responsibility to uphold the decision of his or her hospital employer and the simultaneous recognition of an ethical obligation to correct or intervene to prevent a likely social injustice. Additionally, should the family decide to bring a lawsuit against the hospital, the social worker as well as the patient's health-care providers may be called as a witness.

Consent to and Refusal of Treatment

Informed Consent to Treatment The legal principle of informed consent was enunciated over a quarter of a century ago in the case of *Schloendorff v. Society of New York Hospital* (1914). That case involved the admission of a woman with a stomach disorder into a New York hospital. Surgery was recommended for what was found to be a fibroid tumor. The patient refused the surgery but consented to have an examination performed under anesthesia. During that procedure, the surgeons removed the tumor. The woman later developed gangrene in her left arm, which ultimately led to the loss of several fingers. The woman sued, claiming that the surgery had been responsible for the gangrene and loss of her fingers. The court found that the operation constituted medical battery because the physicians did not have the patient's consent to proceed. In reaching its conclusion, the court stated:

> Every human being of adult years and sound mind has the right to determine what shall be done with his own body; and a surgeon who performs an operation without his patient's consent commits an assault for which he is liable in damages. This is true except in cases of emergency where the patient is unconscious and where it is necessary to operate before consent can be obtained. (*Schloendorff v. Society of New York Hospital,* 1914, p. 93)

This principle protects patients from assaults and from being subjected to procedures that they do not want.

The principle of informed consent is also one of the foundational concepts of bioethics. The ethical principle conceives of informed consent as a process of

---

[1] Although the Florida court in *Montejo v. Martin Memorial Hospital* (2004) found that there was no legitimate basis for the discharge of the patient from the hospital, an Iowa court ruled that the defendant hospital was not liable for false imprisonment of the comatose patient who they had sent to Mexico despite his family members' objections (*Cruz v. Central Iowa Hospital Corporation*, 2012).

communication between the health-care provider and the patient and, in some circumstances, the patient's agent, surrogate, or family members. That process requires the provision by the health-care provider to the individual of sufficient relevant information to allow the individual to make a decision. The information must be understandable; technical/medical language may not be understandable to many people, so the health-care provider may be required to simplify the language used. In general, the individual must be apprised of the likely risks and benefits of the treatment or procedure and of any alternative treatments that may be available, even if that specific provider does not make them available. The patient must also have the capacity to provide consent, meaning that the individual has the cognitive ability to weigh the information as it pertains to him or to her and arrive at a decision. In most circumstances, individuals are presumed to be competent to make their own decisions; an individual will not be deemed to lack decisionmaking capacity merely because his or her decision seems to be illogical (*In re Claire C. Conroy*, 1985). Finally, the individual's consent must be given voluntarily, and he or she must be told that they may withdraw their consent.

It is important to recognize that a signature on an informed consent form does not constitute adequate informed consent. Individuals may feel pressured to sign the form, even when they do not wish to do so (Dixon-Woods et al., 2006). Providers may unknowingly inject their own bias into the process (Fowler et al., 2000).

There are a number of exceptions to the presumption of patient capacity to consent. Some individuals are clearly unable by virtue of their medical condition to provide informed consent, such as individuals who are in a persistent vegetative state. In general, children are deemed to lack competence to consent, largely due to their age and lack of experience. However, children who have been emancipated or found to be "mature minors" are in many cases able to consent to their own treatment. (See Chaps. 1 and 7 for discussion regarding processes for and status of emancipation.) Additionally, a court may appoint a guardian or conservator to make health-care decisions for an individual who the court has determined lacks competence to make health-care decisions for themselves. In most such circumstances, the guardian or conservator will have the authority to make most health care-related decisions for the individual.

Refusal of Treatment The corollary to consent to treatment is the right to refuse treatment (*In re Claire C. Conroy*, 1985). Individuals may refuse treatment for any number of reasons, including religious belief, a determination that the risks associated with a particular treatment outweigh the anticipated benefits, and/or a belief that the treatment or procedure would be futile.

Although courts will not override an individual's refusal of treatment merely because they may disagree with the individual's decision or because the decision seems illogical (*In re Yetter*, 1973), some circumstances do exist in which a court may decide to override an individual's decision to refuse treatment. This has occurred in situations involving a parental refusal of life-saving treatment for a child (*Custody of a Minor*, 1978; *Jehovah's Witnesses of Washington v. King County Hospital*, 1968). As an example, a Massachusetts court allowed the state to intervene when the parents of a child suffering from acute lymphocytic leukemia refused to authorize chemotherapy for the child, despite the fact that uncontroverted medical evidence suggested that it was the only then-known treatment for the disease and that the treatment would provide the child with a "substantial chance for a cure and a normal life" (*Custody of a Minor*, 1978, p. 737).

In some situations, courts have upheld actions taken by health authorities to reduce the risks to public health that may ensue from an individual's refusal of treatment, but have not ordered individuals to comply with the treatment that they have refused. This has occurred in situation in which public health authorities have attempted to effectuate the quarantine of individuals whose refusal of treatment for infectious tuberculosis may expose others to the risk of infection (*Application of Halko*, 1966; City *of New York v. Antoinette R.*, 1995; *City of Newark v. J.S.*, 1993). Courts have also upheld state requirements for tuberculosis screening of students despite a student's religious objections, finding that the student's First Amendment interest was outweighed by the public health interest of students and employees (*State ex rel. Holcombe v. Armstrong*, 1952).

Health-Care Decisionmaking

Surrogate Decisionmakers in the Absence of Advance Directives.

A surrogate is "an adult family member who has priority over other family members in making health-care decisions for an individual when incapacity occurs" (American Bar Association Commission on Law and Aging, 2015). The issues of who may serve as a surrogate and the extent of their authority often arise when an individual loses the capacity to make decisions for him- or herself, and decisions are needed with respect to medication administration, surgery, and/or the initiation or withdrawal of one or more forms of life-sustaining treatment. Approximately one-third of states have failed to promulgate legislation indicating who shall serve as a surrogate if one is needed to make health-care decisions, a situation that could well lead to family conflict should the need for a surrogate arise. Even in those states that have statutorily designated who may serve as a surrogate and in what order of priority, family members may contest through lawsuits the decision of a surrogate. Several court cases have raised public awareness about the role of a surrogate and the issues that may be confronted in such situations. The sequence of events in these cases serves to underscore the importance of having an advance directive, discussed further below.

The case of Karen Quinlan involved a request by a father to a court to appoint him as the surrogate for his daughter, who had been in a persistent vegetative state for a year (*In re Karen Quinlan*, 1976). As her surrogate, he wished to have the respirator that had been maintaining her breathing removed. The court found that

Karen would have had the right to refuse the use of the respirator had she had the capacity to decide for herself and communicate her wishes. The evidence presented indicated that there was no reasonable chance that she would ever regain consciousness and that there was agreement between the family, the physicians, and the hospital's ethics committee that removal of the respirator was the appropriate course of action. The court found that Quinlan's interest, voiced through her surrogate, in refusing the bodily intrusion that was required by the respirator outweighed any state interest.

The later case of *Cruzan v. Director, Missouri Department of Health* (1990), involved an effort by the parents of Nancy Cruzan to prevent the hospital from continuing to administer artificial hydration and nutrition to their daughter, who was in a persistent vegetative state following a car accident. The Supreme Court held that the hospital was not under an obligation to adhere to the patient's wishes, there was no evidence that she would want the treatment terminated if she were able to decide for herself, and, although it was unlikely that she would ever regain consciousness, the hospital could continue to administer the artificial hydration and nutrition.

More recently, the case of Terri Schiavo centered on the competing desires of the patient's spouse and parents with respect to the removal of her feeding tube. Schiavo had suffered a heart attack, from which she was resuscitated. However, she experienced a lack of oxygen to her brain and, as a result, had severe brain damage that left her comatose. Her husband indicated that she would not wish to be maintained in her persistent vegetative state and wanted the life support treatment withdrawn. Her parents disagreed with both the diagnosis of a persistent vegetative state and with her husband's assessment of her desires (CBS News, 2005). The dispute ultimately involved 14 appeals in Florida courts, 5 suits in federal district courts, denials of certiorari by the US Supreme Court, and efforts to intervene by then-Florida Governor Jeb Bush, then-US President George W. Bush, and the US Congress, as well as pro-life groups, right to die groups, and disability rights groups (ABC News, 2006; Johnson, 2006; Sanburn, 2015). The feeding tube was withdrawn 15 years after her cardiac arrest.

Advance Directives

Durable Power of Attorney for Health Care Social workers employed in hospitals and other health-care settings are often called upon to provide patients with basic information about advance directives and to inquire of a patient whether he or she already has one or would like to have one. Advance directives can take any one of several forms including durable power of attorney for health care, also known as health-care proxies, medical power of attorneys, and appointment of a health-care agent (United States Center for Medicare and Medicaid Services, n.d.-a). The obligation of a hospital or other health-care facility to make such information available derives from the Patient Self-Determination Act, which provides that health-care providers participating in Medicare or Medicaid must advise all competent patients about state law relating to advance directives (42 U.S.C. §§ 1395cc(f), 1396a(w), 2002). Although the social worker cannot give legal advice, it is important that he or she understand the purpose and the basic provisions of a durable power of attorney for health care (DPAHC).

A DPAHC permits an individual to designate an agent to make health-care decisions for him or for her in the event that they are no longer able to do so. The specific requirements for a valid DPAHC vary across states. In general, the individual appointed as the person's agent may not be a minor and may not be the individual's health-care provider. Additionally, the document must either be signed by the individual making the document (the principal) and witnessed by one or more persons or signed in the presence of a notary public and then notarized. A DPAHC offers several advantages in that it is durable, meaning that it continues to be valid even if the principal becomes incompetent, and the maker of the document can indicate his or her wishes regarding care as explicit as he or she might like.

An individual who executes a durable power of attorney can specify in the document when it should take effect, e.g., if two physicians certify that he or she no longer has the capacity to make health-care decisions; place limits on the authority of his or her designated agent, such as indicating that he or she does not want to be resuscitated under specified conditions; and indicate when the authority of the named agent is to end. Because a durable power or health-care proxy can be tailored to the needs of the individual, the individual may also indicate that he or she would like more than one health-care agent and whether the agents are to make decisions in the alternative, so that one can make decisions only if the first is not available, or whether the named agents are to consult with each other and reach consensus about what is to be done.

How the agent is to make a decision on behalf of the appointing person, known as the principal, varies depending upon the state law and the particular circumstances. In situations in which the desires of the principal are known, the agent will often be asked to make decisions that are consistent with the principal's preferences. In cases in which the principal's wishes and desires are not clear or are not known and cannot be ascertained, the agent will often be asked to make decisions that are consistent with the patient's best interests (American Bar Association, 2015).

Living Wills Unlike a durable power of attorney for health care or health-care proxy, a living will does not involve the appointment of another person to make decisions on behalf of an individual who no longer has the capacity to do so him- or herself. Rather, it permits the maker of the document to indicate the nature of the medical care that he or she would want and whether life-sustaining measures are to be utilized and under what circumstances, if any. Like durable power of attorney, the requirements for a valid living will vary across states.

References

ABC News. (2006). Terri Schiavo timeline. http://abcnews.go.com/Health/Schiavo/story?id=531632&page=1. Accessed 18 November 2017.

American Bar Association Commission on Law and Aging. (2015). Health care decision-making authority: What is the decision-making standard? https://www.americanbar.org/content/dam/aba/administrative/law_aging/What_is_the_Decision_Making_Standard.authcheckdam.pdf. Accessed 18 November 2017.

American Psychiatric Association. (2013). *Diagnostic and statistical manual of mental disorders* (5th ed.). Washington, DC: Author.

Associated Press. (2013, April 23). Report: U.S. hospitals deported hundreds of immigrants. *CBS News*, https://www.cbsnews.com/news/report-us-hospitals-deported-hundreds-of-immigrants/. Accessed 18 November 2017.

Bergstresser, C. (1998). The perspective of the plaintiff's attorney. In L. Lifson & R. Simon (Eds.), *The mental health practitioner and the law: A comprehensive handbook* (pp. 329–343). Cambridge, MA: Harvard University Press.

CBS News. (2005). A look back: The Terri Schiavo case. https://www.cbsnews.com/pictures/look-back-in-history-terri-schiavo-death/. Accessed 18 November 2017.

Centers for Medicare & Medicaid Services. (2014). Medicare program—general information. https://www.cms.gov/Medicare/Medicare-General-Information/MedicareGenInfo/index.html. Accessed 22 December 2017.

Dixon-Woods, H., Williams, S. J., Jackson, C. J., Akkad, A., Kenyon, S., & Habiba, M. (2006). Why do women consent to surgery, even when they don't want to an interactionist and Bourdieusian analysis. *Social Science and Medicine, 62*(11), 2742–2753.

Felton, E.M. (2015). Legal issues in health insurance audits. *National Association of Social Workers California News*. http://nascwcanews.org/legal-issues-in-health-insurance-audits/. Accessed 29 March 2017.

Fowler, F. J., Jr., McNaughton Collins, M., Albertsen, P. C., Zielman, A., Elliott, D. B., & Barry, M. J. (2000). Comparison of recommendations by urologists and radiation oncologists for treatment of clinically localized prostate cancer. *Journal of the American Medical Association, 283*(24), 3217–3222.

Furth, S. (2015). Medical repatriation: The intersection of mandated emergency care, immigration consequences, and international obligations. *Journal of Legal Medicine, 36*, 45–72.

Groshong, L. (2010). Medicare—Opting in or out. https://www.clinical socialworkassociation.org/Legislative-Alerts/3740167. Accessed 29 March 2017.

Johnson, M. (2006). Terri Schiavo: A disability rights case. *Death Studies, 30*(2), 163–176.

Kagle, J. D., & Kopels, S. (2008). *Social work records* (3rd ed.). Long Grove, IL: Waveland Press.

Loue, S. (2016, February 27). *Medical deportation: Legal and ethical issues*. Presented at the 56th Annual Meeting of the American College of Legal Medicine, Austin, TX. http://c.ymcdn.com/sites/www.aclm.org/resource/collection/2E2DE1DA-FB17-4974-B6EA 3CEDDFD9A6A7/_Saturday_Breakout_Session_IV_Sana_Loue2.ppt.pdf. Accessed 18 November 2017.

National Association of Social Workers. (2016). Standards for social work practice in health care settings. Washington, DC: Author. https://www.socialworkers.org/practice/naswstandards/Healthcarestandardsfinal draft.pdf. Accessed 29 March 2017.

O'Connell, C. (2010). Return to sender: Evaluating the medical repatriations of uninsured immigrants. *Washington University Law Review, 87*, 1429–1459.

Reamer, F. G. (2005). Documentation in social work: Evolving ethical and risk-management standards. *Social Work, 10*(4), 325–334.

Sanburn, J. (2015, March 31). How Terri Schiavo shaped the right-to-die movement. *Time*, http://time.com/3763521/terri-schiavo-right-to-die-brittany-maynard/. Accessed 18 November 2017.

Seton Hall Law School, & New York Lawyers for the Public Interest. (2012). Discharge, deportation, and dangerous journeys: A study on the practice of medical repatriation. https://law.

shu.edu/ProgramsCenters/PublicIntGovServ/CSJ/upload/final-med-repat-report-2012.pdf. Accessed 18 November 2017.
Simon, R. (1998). Litigation hot spots in clinical practice. In L. Lifson & R. Simon (Eds.), *The mental health practitioner and the law: A comprehensive handbook* (pp. 117–139). Cambridge, MA: Harvard University Press.
Sontag, S. (2008, November 8). Deported in a coma, saved back in U.S. *New York Times*, http://www.nytimes.com/2008/11/09/us/09deport.html. Accessed 18 November 2017.
United States Center for Medicare and Medicaid Services. (n.d.-a). Advance directives & long-term care. https://www.medicare.gov/manage-your-health/advance-directives/advance-directives-and-long-term-care.html. Accessed 18 November 2017.
United States Center for Medicare and Medicaid Services. (n.d.-b). Glossary: Medically necessary. https://www.medicare.gov/glossary/m.html. Accessed 18 November 2017.
United States Department of Health and Human Services. (n.d.-a). Discrimination on the basis of disability. https://www.hhs.gov/civil-rights/for-individuals/disability/index.html. Accessed 22 December 2017.
United States Department of Health and Human Services. (n.d.-b). What are my health care rights and responsibilities? https://www.hhs.gov/answers/health-care/what-are-my-health-care-rights/index.html. Accessed 18 November 2017.
United States Department of Justice, Civil Rights Division, Disability Rights Section and United States Department of Health and Human Services, Office for Civil Rights. (2010). Americans with Disabilities Act: Access to medical care for individuals with mobility disabilities. https://www.ada.gov/medcare_mobility_ta/medcare_ta.htm#part1. Accessed 22 December 2017.

Legal References

Cases

Application of Halko, 54 Cal. Rptr. 661, 246 Cal. App. 2d 553 (Cal. Ct. App. 1966).
Bragdon v. Abbott, 524 U.S. 624 (1998).
City of New York v. Antoinette R., 630 N.Y.S.2d 1008, 165 Misc. 2d 1014 (N.Y. Sup.Ct. 1995).
City of Newark v. J.S., 652 A.2d 265 (N.J. Super. Ct. Law Div. 1993).
Cruz v. Central Iowa Hospital Corporation, 820 N.W.2d 516 (Iowa Ct. App. 2012).
Cruzan v. Director, Missouri Department of Health, 497 U.S. 261 (1990).
Custody of a Minor, 379 N.E.2d 1053 (Mass. 1978).
In re Claire C. Conroy, 486 A.2d 1209 (N.J. 1985).
In re Karen Quinlan, 355 A.2d 647 (N.J. 1976), *cert. denied, sub nom.*, Gerger v. New Jersey, 429 U.S. 922 (1976), *overruled for other reasons*, In re Claire C. Conroy, 486 A.2d 1209 (N.J. 1985).
In re Yetter, 62 Pa. D. & C.2d 619 (Pa. Comm. Pl. 1973).
Jehovah's Witnesses of Washington v. King County Hospital, 278 F. Supp. 488 (W.D. Wash. 1968), affirmed 390 U.S. 598 (1968).
Montejo v. Martin Memorial Hospital, 874 So. 2d 654 (Fla. App. Ct. 2004).
Schloendorff v. Society of New York Hospital, 105 N.E. 92 (1914).
State ex rel. Holcombe v. Armstrong, 239 P.2d 545 (Wash. 1952).

Statutes

42 U.S.C. §§ 1395cc(f), 1396a(w) (2002).
Americans with Disabilities Act, 42 U.S.C.A. § 12102 (West 2002).
Emergency Medical Treatment and Active Labor Act, 42 U.S.C.A. § 1395dd (West 2002).
Health Insurance Portability and Accountability Act of 1996, Pub. L. 104–191.
Illegal Immigration Reform and Immigrant Responsibility Act of 1996 (IIRIRA), enacted as Division C of the Defense Department Appropriations Act, 1997, Pub. L. No. 104–208, 110 Stat. 3008 (Sept. 30, 1996).
Personal Responsibility and Work Opportunity Reconciliation Act, Pub. L. 104–193, 110 Stat. 2105 (1996), codified in United States Code Title 8.
Social Security Act §1903(v)(3), 42 U.S.C. § 1396b(v)(3).

Other Sources

United States Constitution, Article 1.
Loue, S. (2018). The "passport biopsy" and de facto deportation: Hospitals' involuntary international transfer of patients. Immigration Briefings, 18(3), 1–29

Chapter 10
Mental Health and Substance Use

Mental Illness and Involuntary Outpatient Civil Commitment

Involuntary outpatient commitment of individuals for mental illness, also known as "outpatient commitment" and "assisted outpatient commitment" (Treatment Advocacy Center, n.d.), refers to the procedure through which a court mandates a specific treatment plan for an individual with a severe mental illness (National Coalition for Mental Health Recovery, n.d.). It has been described as:

> [a] civil court procedure wherein a judge orders a person with severe mental illness to adhere to an outpatient treatment plan designed to prevent relapse and dangerous deterioration. Persons appropriate for this intervention are those who need ongoing psychiatric care owing to severe illness but who are unable or unwilling to engage in ongoing, voluntary, outpatient care. (American Psychiatric Association, 2015)

The court often requires that the individual adheres to a prescribed medication plan and may also include restrictions or directions on where the individual can reside and the activities in which he or she is to participate. However, forcible medication is not allowed under an involuntary commitment order in most states (Ridgely, Borum, & Petrila, 2001).

Involuntary outpatient civil commitment is seen as an alternative to the more restrictive possibility of involuntary hospitalization (Ridgely, Borum, & Petrila, 2001). In general, the procedure may utilize any of the three following approaches to require the individual's participation in community-based mental health treatment:

1. The individual meets criteria for involuntary hospitalization, e.g., is mentally ill and a danger to him- or herself or others, and the court requires the individual to receive outpatient mental health treatment at a community-based provider.
2. The individual has been involuntarily committed to a hospital for the treatment of mental illness and continues to meet the criteria for continued hospitalization, but the court releases the individual conditionally. If the individual does not adhere to the court-ordered outpatient treatment, he or she can be returned to the hospital without the need for an additional court order because the original order mandating hospitalization is still in effect.

3. The individual has a severe mental illness and, in the absence of treatment, his or her condition is likely to deteriorate to the point where he or she becomes severely disabled or a threat. The court can order the individual to participate in community-based treatment, and if the individual fails to do so, the mental health provider can ask that law enforcement transport the individual to the treatment center for evaluation (Ridgely, Borum, & Petrila, 2001).

As of 1999, 40 states and the District of Columbia had instituted involuntary civil commitment laws (National Conference of State Legislatures, 1999). As of the date of this writing, it appears that all states with the exception of Connecticut, Maryland, and Massachusetts have adopted legislation permitting the use of involuntary outpatient treatment (Treatment Advocacy Center, n.d.). However, the extent to which the laws are actually utilized varies greatly across states. As of 1999, for example, the states of Arizona, Michigan, North Dakota, Washington, and Wisconsin used involuntary outpatient treatment laws frequently, whereas they were very rarely utilized in Illinois, Indiana, Minnesota, Mississippi, Montana, Oregon, South Dakota, Texas, and Kentucky (National Conference of State Legislatures, 1999).

The use of involuntary outpatient commitment has been fraught with controversy. Proponents of the laws argue that the procedure reduces arrest and incarceration, homelessness, victimization, suicide, and the commission of violent acts by mentally ill persons against others (Treatment Advocacy Center, n.d.). Critics, however, have raised significant concerns regarding the associated infringement on individuals' civil liberties, the costs of monitoring individuals, the potential increase in the need for hospital beds due to individuals' nonadherence to the court-ordered treatment, the lack of enforcement, the extent to which coerced treatment is actually effective (National Coalition for Mental Health Recovery, n.d.; Ridgely, Borum, & Petrila, 2001), and the inability to accurately predict a specific individual's future behavior, such as his or her future proclivity to harm him- or herself or others (Bazelon Center on Mental Health Law, 2004).

Coercion, in particular, has been and continues to be an issue of concern, with respect to not only the individual who is ordered to comply with a treatment plan but also to the community through the extension of mandated treatment to the community (Ridgely, Borum, & Petrila, 2001). The American Psychiatric Association (2015) has expressed concerns regarding the infringement of the process on individual autonomy, the conflict between a patient's interest in self-determination and his or her medical best interest, and the difficulties in achieving a balance between the ethical principles of respect for persons (autonomy) and beneficence (maximizing good) (See Zilber, 2016). In recognition of these challenges, it supports the use of involuntary outpatient treatment only when specified conditions are met, including the systematic and resourced implementation of the procedure, the provision of a range of needed medication management and psychosocial services, the provision of treatment over a sustained period of time, clinical attention to individuals' comorbidities, efforts to engage patients and their families, and avoidance of the disproportionate use of such procedures with minority and disenfranchised groups.

Other organizations have also issued position statements regarding involuntary outpatient commitment. Mental Health America is opposed to involuntary outpatient commitment because:

> allocating scarce resources from people on waiting lists to a civilly committed class of people who are resisting treatment seems self-defeating ... Moreover, intervening to compel treatment of people not deemed so seriously ill as to need custodial care imposes enforcement costs and contradicts the recovery principles that are essential to community integration. (Mental Health America, 2013)

Although the American Psychological Association (2004) has issued a position statement on outpatient civil commitment, it fails to provide guidance on the use of the process. The National Association of Social Workers appears to have not issued a position statement, despite the apparent conflict between mandated treatment participation and social work's emphasis on client self-determination and empowerment (Dewees, 2002).

Additionally, and importantly, the extent to which a court order is even necessary is questionable. An extensive 2001 review study of research relating to outcomes of involuntary outpatient commitment concluded that three elements are critical to the process: having an adequate infrastructure to support outpatient commitment, having an adequate range and quantity of services in the community to meet the needs of the mentally ill persons, and having a service system that is able to deliver the needed services rationally (Ridgely, Borum, & Petrila, 2001). That study also found that research did "*not* prove that treatment works better in the presence of coercion or that treatment will not work in the absence of coercion" (Ridgely, Borum, & Petrila, 2001, p. 99; emphasis in original). A recent study concluded that the procedure "does not appear to reduce health service use or improve patients' social functioning. It also does not significantly reduce perceived coercion" (Kisely, Campbell, & Preston, 2012, p. 21). Research also suggests that the use of involuntary outpatient commitment may be disproportionately utilized with minority individuals (Swanson et al., 2009).

It is important that social workers providing direct services to clients and those working with the courts be at least aware of the concerns associated with the use of involuntary outpatient treatment. First, individuals who feel that they are being coerced and their wishes not considered may be less willing to engage in treatment. In such instances, the social worker will need to be aware of the power dynamic and, additionally, may need to emphasize with the client that he or she has the ability to set goals within the process. Second, in circumstances in which the need for community-based resources for mental health services exceeds the availability, advocacy efforts by social workers to expand the range and increase the availability of services will be critical, not only to those who are part of the court-mandated system but to the community in general. Finally, advocacy efforts can be made to ensure that involuntary outpatient commitment is utilized only as a last resort in view of the inability to accurately predict individuals' future behavior, the relatively limited availability of mental health services in the community, and the disproportionate use of involuntary outpatient commitment procedures with minority individuals and those who may be otherwise disenfranchised or marginalized.

Mental Illness and Involuntary Emergency Inpatient Commitment

All states provide for the involuntary hospitalization of individuals for a limited period of time if, in general, there is a determination that the individual is exhibiting symptoms or behaviors that indicate that he or she poses an immediate danger to themselves or to others. Such hospitalization of an individual is variously known as detention, emergency admission, a hold, a pickup, temporary detention, or emergency hospitalization, depending upon the wording in the particular state law allowing such action.

The person authorized under state law to either request such admission or to conduct the necessary assessment varies across states. Appendix B provides a listing of the standard for emergency hospitalization for observation in each of the 50 states and the District of Columbia. Social workers should be familiar with the law of the state(s) in which they practice, as not all states permit social workers to fulfill these roles. As an example, Colorado permits a licensed clinical social worker to effectuate a 72-h hold (Colorado Revised Statutes § 27-5-105(1), 2016), but the District of Columbia provides that only specified agents of the Department of Mental Health, officers with arresting authority, physicians, or psychologists may have the individual detained (D.C. Code Annotated § 21-521, 2016).

Pregnancy, Substance Use, and Law

It is not at all clear from research findings that *any* use of legal or illegal substances during the course of a pregnancy, regardless of the frequency, timing, amount, or manner of ingestion, will result in short-term or long-term harm to the as yet unborn child (Chavkin, 2001; Frank, Augustyn, Knight, Pell, & Zuckerman, 2001; Phelps & Cottone, 1999), particularly in view of the interplay between numerous biological, psychological, and environmental factors (Singer, et al., 2002). Variations in study design across research studies increase the difficulty inherent in efforts to decipher the effects of each individual variable. Nevertheless, at the time of this writing, women have been prosecuted for drug use during pregnancy in all but five states, Delaware, Iowa, Maine, Rhode Island, and Vermont (Miranda, Dixon, & Reyes, 2015), and the rate of such prosecutions appears to have been increasing (Khazan, 2015a, b; Paltrow, 1998). These prosecutions have proceeded on any one or more of various theories: that a fetus is a child and the use of substances, even legal ones, during pregnancy constitutes child abuse, neglect, and/or endangerment or subjects the child to the risk of endangerment, that the woman's ingestion of a substance constitutes the delivery of a drug to another because it may be passed through the umbilical cord to the unborn child, or that the death of fetus constitutes fetal homicide (National Conference of State Legislatures, 2017; Paltrow, 1998; Paltrow & Flavin, 2013). Not only can women be prosecuted for prenatal substance use, but three states—Minnesota, South Dakota, and Wisconsin—provide that they may be civilly committed for substance use during pregnancy (Guttmacher Institute, 2017).

Many state courts have dismissed charges, vacated convictions, or overturned decisions permitting civil commitment, finding that the statutes governing child abuse and neglect most often do not apply to fetuses and/or that the statute relied upon for the prosecution is unconstitutional (see Table 10.1). One court observed:

> Many types of prenatal conduct can harm a fetus, causing physical or mental abnormalities in a newborn. For example, medical researchers have stated that smoking during pregnancy may cause, among other problems, low birth weight, which is a major factor in infant mortality. Drinking alcoholic beverages during pregnancy can lead to fetal alcohol syndrome, a condition characterized by mental retardation, prenatal and postnatal growth deficiencies, and facial [sic] anomalies.
>
> A pregnant woman's failure to obtain prenatal care or proper nutrition can also affect the status of the newborn child. Poor nutrition can cause a variety of birth defects… Poor prenatal care can lead to insufficient or excessive weight gain, which also affects the fetus. Some researchers have suggested that consuming caffeine during pregnancy also contributes to low birth weight.
>
> Other factors not involving specific conduct also can affect the fetus and, eventually, the status of the newborn… A couple may pass to their children an inheritable disorder, such as TaySachs disease or sickle-cell anemia. Occupational or environmental hazards, such as exposures to solvents used by painters and dry cleaners, can cause adverse outcomes. The contraction of or treatment for certain diseases, such as diabetes and cancer, also can affect the health of the fetus.
>
> Allowing the state to define the crime of child abuse according to the health or condition of the newborn child would subject many mothers to criminal liability for engaging in all sorts of legal or illegal activities during pregnancy. We cannot, consistent with the dictates of due process, read the statute that broadly. (*Reneisto v. Superior Court,* 1995, p. 736)

Indeed, there is increasing evidence to indicate that in utero exposure to illegal drugs does not invariably produce the harm to children that is often the basis for seeking incarceration or commitment (Khazan, 2015a, b). The literature suggests that prosecution, imprisonment, and/or civil commitment may, in fact, do more harm than good (Mohapatra, 2011; Schroedel & Fiber, 2001; Schwartz, 2015). Too, such policies may discourage women from seeking the prenatal care or substance use treatment that they need and desire.

Social workers, including those employed by hospitals and child protective services, were responsible for 17 percent of the 413 instances of forced legal interventions against pregnant women, the majority of which were associated with illicit substance use, which occurred between 1973 and 2005 (Khazan, 2015a; Paltrow & Flavin, 2013). The cases were distributed across 44 of the 50 states and the District of Columbia, but the largest proportion originated in the southern states (56%), particularly South Carolina, Florida, Missouri, Georgia, and Tennessee. Although illicit substance use is at least as common among White women as women of color, more than one-half of the women for whom racial/ethnic data were available were women of color, including African Americans, Hispanics/Latinos, Native Americans, and Asian Pacific Islanders (Paltrow & Flavin, 2013), raising the issue in this writer's mind of bias in the decision to initiate law enforcement or reporting

Table 10.1 State laws relating to substance abuse during pregnancy

State/venue	Prenatal substance abuse considered child abuse/neglect[a]	Court cases
Alabama	Yes	Fetal exposure to cocaine held to constitute chemical endangerment of a child under statute, consistent with the public policy of Alabama to protect unborn life (*Ankrom v. State*, 2011)
Alaska	No	Woman convicted of criminally negligent homicide and sentenced to prison and probation for cocaine use during pregnancy, where infant died 2 weeks after birth of a heart attack caused by prenatal cocaine use (*State v. Grubbs*, 1989)
Arizona	No specific law	State child abuse statute held not to encompass fetus in case involving woman's use of heroin during pregnancy (*Reinesto v. Superior Court*, 1995)
Arkansas	Yes	Court reversed conviction and dismissed case against woman sentenced to 20 years in prison following conviction for introducing controlled substance into the body of another premised on her use of methamphetamine during pregnancy, finding that statute did not apply to fetuses or unborn children (*Arms v. State*, 2015. See also Jeltsen, 2015)
		Statute pertaining to juveniles found not to encompass fetus so that order from circuit court placing fetus in the custody of the Department of Human Services found to be invalid (*Arkansas Department of Human Services v. Collier*, 2003)
California	No	Court dismissed charges of felony endangerment of child against mother who used heroin during pregnancy, finding that statute did not encompass unborn child (*Reyes v. Superior Court of San Bernardino County*, 1977)
Colorado	Yes	
Connecticut	No	Mother's parental rights cannot be terminated for prenatal cocaine use, finding that statute pertaining to "child" did not encompass fetus (*In re Valerie*, 1992)
Delaware	No	No prosecutions
District of Columbia		Woman arrested and charged with theft subjected to court-ordered drug test and detained in jail until conclusion of pregnancy (*United States v. Vaughn*, 1988)
Florida	Yes	State statute providing for criminal prosecution for delivery of drug found not to encompass delivery of illegal drug from womb to placenta to umbilical cord to newborn in case of mother who ingested a controlled substance prior to giving birth (*Johnson v. State*, 1992)
		Court dismissed charges against woman who used cocaine during pregnancy, finding that statute did not apply to pregnant women (*State v. Gethers*, 1991)

Georgia	No specific law	Court held that woman cannot be prosecuted for delivery of narcotics to fetus because "deliver" applies to transfer from one person to another and fetus is not considered a person at common law (*State v. Luster*, 1992).
Hawaii	No specific law	Court dismissed manslaughter charge against woman who used methamphetamine while pregnant, finding that statute not intended to protect fetus from drug exposure (*State v. Aiwohi*, 2005).
Idaho	No specific law	
Illinois	Yes	Court reversed decision of lower court that sentenced woman to 7 years in prison to prevent her from becoming pregnant, finding that she had used cocaine during pregnancy (*People v. Bedenkop*, 1993)
Indiana	Yes	Court found that statute criminalizing neglect of a dependent could not be applied prior to birth in case involving woman who ingested cocaine while pregnant (*Herron v. State*, 2000)
Iowa	Yes	No prosecutions
Kansas	No	No cases found
Kentucky	No	Criminal abuse statutes do not apply to a woman's use of drugs or alcohol during pregnancy (*Cochran v. Commonwealth*, 2010)
		State supreme court affirmed appellate court decision vacating mother's conviction for criminal abuse premised on her use of illicit drug while pregnant, finding that criminal abuse statute does not apply to use of drugs or alcohol by pregnant women (*Commonwealth v. Welch*, 1993)
Louisiana	Yes	No cases found
Maine	No	No prosecutions
Maryland	Yes	Criminal law provision making it a misdemeanor for a person to recklessly engage in conduct creating a substantial risk of death or serious physical injury to another person found to not apply to prenatal drug ingestion by a pregnant woman (*Kilmon v. State*, 2006)
Massachusetts	No	Court held that prenatal exposure to controlled substance is probative of maternal neglect; case remanded (*Commonwealth v. Pellegrini*, 1993)
Michigan	No	Woman's use of cocaine during pregnancy that may result in postpartum transfer of cocaine metabolites through the umbilical cord to the infant found not to be encompassed in statute prohibiting delivery of cocaine (*People v Hardy*, 1991)
Minnesota	Yes	No cases found
Mississippi	No specific law	No cases found

(continued)

Table 10.1 (continued)

State/venue	Prenatal substance abuse considered child abuse/neglect[a]	Court cases
Missouri	Yes	Court found that state statute defining first-degree child endangerment as knowingly acting in a manner that created a substantial risk to a child less than 17 years old does not apply to pregnant woman who caused indirect harm to her fetus by ingesting illicit drugs during pregnancy (*State v. Wade*, 2007)
Montana	No	No cases found
Nebraska	No	Court found that child abuse statute did not apply to unborn children, where mother ingested alcohol while pregnant (*State v. Arandus*, 1993)
Nevada	Yes	Statute criminalizing child endangerment found not to encompass mother's prenatal substance abuse that results in transmission of illegal substance to child through the umbilical cord (*Sheriff v. Encoe*, 1994)
New Hampshire	No	No cases found
New Jersey	No	Mother's positive urine test for cocaine upon admission to the hospital to give birth found not to constitute actual harm or demonstrate imminent danger or substantial risk of harm to the newborn child and held not to constitute child abuse or neglect (*New Jersey Department of Children and Families v. A.L.*, 2013)
New Mexico	No	Mother's prenatal use of illicit drug found insufficient to establish child neglect where newborn had negative toxicology screen and no evidence of neglect (*State v. Amanda H.*, 2007)
New York	No	Court can issue order prohibiting pregnant woman from using illegal drugs during pregnancy in order to protect unborn child from substantial risk of harm (*In re Unborn Child*, 1998) Court found fetus not encompassed in statute pertaining to endangering the welfare of a child in case involving woman's use of cocaine while pregnant (*People v. Morabito*, 1992) Court held that an unborn child is a person within the meaning of the state statute, that a failure to obtain prenatal care and to refrain from the use of alcohol during pregnancy constituted child neglect, where medical record indicated that child was born with "a small possibility" of fetal alcohol syndrome (*Matter of Smith*, 1985)
North Carolina	No	Court dismissed charges against woman for delivery of controlled substance to a person based on her use of crack during pregnancy, finding that fetus is not a person within the meaning of the statute (*State v. Inzar*, 1991)

Pregnancy, Substance Use, and Law 191

North Dakota	Yes	No cases found
Ohio	Yes	Court held that mother's positive toxicology screen at time of child's birth, indicating use of illicit drugs during pregnancy, was inadequate to support state assumption of guardianship over child (*In re V.R.*, 2008) Court held that a fetus is a child for the purpose of statute relating to child neglect, abuse, dependency, and constitutionally applicable where mother and newborn test positive for cocaine (*In re Baby Boy Blackshear*, 2000) State statute penalizing child endangerment found not to encompass fetus in case involving woman's ingestion of illicit substance during pregnancy (*State v. Gray*, 1992)
Oklahoma	Yes	Supreme court of Oklahoma vacated lower court order that fetus remains in custody of Department of Human Services due to pregnant woman's use of methamphetamines during pregnancy (*In re Unborn Child Julie Starks*, 2001)
Oregon	No	No cases found
Pennsylvania	No	Charges of recklessly endangering another person, recklessly endangering the welfare of children, and delivery of cocaine lodged against expectant mother for delivery of cocaine to fetus through the umbilical cord dismissed based on court finding that statute did not encompass prenatal conduct (*Commonwealth v. Kemp*, 1992)
Rhode Island	Yes	No prosecutions
South Carolina	Yes	Woman convicted of homicide by child abuse for killing unborn fetus by smoking crack during pregnancy; sentenced to 12 years in prison (*State v. McKnight*, 2001) Court held that fetus is a person and that pregnant woman's conduct that endangers or is likely to endanger a viable fetus constitutes child abuse (*Whitner v. State*, 1997)
South Dakota	Yes	No cases found
Tennessee	No	No cases found
Texas	Yes	Court reversed conviction of woman who used cocaine during pregnancy and child born addicted, finding that criminal statute did not encompass fetus in definitions of child or person (*Collins v. Texas*, 1994)
Utah	Yes	Juvenile court granted petition of division of child and family Services to place child in custody on basis of neglect where infant born prematurely and tested positive for cocaine (*State ex. rel. M.E.C.*, 1997)

(continued)

Table 10.1 (continued)

State/venue	Prenatal substance abuse considered child abuse/neglect[a]	Court cases
Vermont	No specific law	No prosecutions
Virginia	Yes	Court dismissed child abuse charges against woman who used drugs during pregnancy, finding that child abuse statute did not apply to fetuses or prenatal conduct (*Commonwealth v. Smith*, 1991)
Washington	Yes	Charges against woman for criminal mistreatment of viable unborn child for use of cocaine during pregnancy dismissed, court finding that unborn child was not a "child" under criminal mistreatment statute (*State v. Dunn*, 1996)
West Virginia	No	A pregnant woman who ingests a controlled substance during pregnancy with resulting harm to her subsequently born child is not criminally liable for child neglect leading to death based on statute because the reference to "child" in the law does not include reference to "unborn child" or "fetus"; defendant could not have known of possible prosecution for child neglect based on her prenatal use of methamphetamine (*State v. Louk*, 2016)
Wisconsin	Yes	Wisconsin supreme court found that statute allowing state to assume custody of child does not apply to fetus in case involving effort by county Department of Health and Human Services to assume custody over viable fetus (and pregnant woman) where woman tested positive for cocaine during pregnancy (*Wisconsin ex. rel. Angela M.W. v. Kruzicki*, 1997)
Wyoming	No specific law	No cases found

[a]Sources: Guttmacher Institute (2017), Miranda et al. (2015).

procedures. Indeed, reports suggest that African Americans compared to those of other racial/ethnic groups are more likely to be subjected to drug testing, to be reported, and to be subjected to court-ordered interventions (Anderson, 2008; Chasnoff, Landres, & Barrett, 1990; Ellsworth, Stevens, & D'Angio, 2010; Roberts & Nuru-Jeter, 2011; Rotzoll, 2001). Additionally, almost three-quarters of the women involved were economically disadvantaged, suggesting that many may have not been able financially to access legal representation experienced with such cases.

In all cases, but particularly in those states that do not mandate social worker reporting of substance use by a pregnant woman, social workers should consider whether their reporting of the substance use comports with their ethical obligations to the pregnant woman, who is their client. In such circumstances, social workers may find it helpful to refer to the *Code of Ethics* of the National Association of Social Workers (2008) as a guide and to ask themselves the following questions as they consider the wisdom, or lack thereof, of reporting the woman's substance use:

- Does reporting/not reporting advance the social work value of helping people in need to address social problems?
- Is reporting/not reporting consonant with the social work value of challenging social injustice?
- How does reporting/not reporting demonstrate respect for the inherent worth and dignity of the client?
- How does reporting/not reporting promote the right of the client to self-determination?
- Has the client been informed by the social worker that he or she may report substance use that occurs while the client is pregnant? Does the reporting violate the ethical responsibility to maintain client confidentiality?
- Does reporting recognize the addiction as an illness and will it lead to the provision of the type and scope of care that the client needs?
- Does a decision to report/not report reflect bias? Would the social worker make exactly the same determination if the pregnant client were of a different race, ethnicity, sexual orientation, gender identity, socioeconomic status, or religion? Would the social worker report the substance use if the client were a man?

Drug and Mental Health Courts

Substance Use, Incarceration, and Drug Courts

Reports indicate that an extraordinarily high proportion of individuals incarcerated in US jails and prisons meet criteria for substance use or dependence (Center for Prisoner Health and Human Rights, n.d.). Many are incarcerated for crimes that they committed while under the influence of a drug or alcohol. By 2010, 1.5 million individuals of the 2.3 million incarcerated in US prisons and jails met medical criteria for substance abuse or dependence; an additional 458,000 had histories of substance use and/or were under the influence of drugs or alcohol at the time of their criminal offense or were incarcerated for an alcohol or drug violation. Together, this constitutes 85% of the country's prison population (National Center in Addiction and Substance Abuse, 2010). However, the same study found that only 11% of inmates with substance abuse and addiction disorders receive any treatment during the period of their incarceration, despite the potential health benefits to the inmate and the likely cost savings to the government.

In the absence of treatment, the substance abuse-involved inmates are more likely than those who do not have such issues to re-offend and be re-incarcerated. Estimates suggest that more than one-half of individuals who are incarcerated for drug use or drug-related offenses will re-offend within 3 years of their release (Marlowe, 2002). With appropriate treatment and monitoring through a drug court program, the recidivism rate may drop to as low as 16.4% after 1 year (Huddleston III, Freeman-Wilson, & Boone, 2005).

Drug courts were first established in Miami, Florida, in 1989 in an effort to reduce recidivism among those brought before the courts for drug-related offenses and lessen the backlog of such cases then pending in courts (Lloyd & Brook, 2014). By 1999, 492 drug courts had been established in the United States; this number increased to 2734 by mid-2012 (Lloyd & Brook, 2014) and to 3142 by June 2015 (United States Department of Justice, Office of Justice Programs, National Institute of Justice, n.d.).

Although drug courts differ depending upon the population served, e.g., violent or nonviolent crime, the program design, and the availability of service resources, they all provide screening and assessment of risk, needs, and responsivity, judicial interaction, monitoring and supervision, sanctions and incentives, and treatment and rehabilitation (United States Department of Justice, Office of Justice Programs, National Institute of Justice, n.d.). The Drug Court Standards Committee of the National Association of Drug Courts Professionals (2004) has enumerated 10 key components of drug courts:

1. Drug courts integrate alcohol and other drug treatment services with justice system case processing.
2. Using a nonadversarial approach, prosecution and defense counsel promote public safety while protecting participants' due process rights.
3. Eligible participants are identified early and promptly placed in the drug court program.
4. Drug courts provide access to a continuum of alcohol, drug, and other related treatment and rehabilitation services.
5. Abstinence is monitored by frequent alcohol and other drug testings.
6. A coordinated strategy governs drug court responses to participants' compliance.
7. Ongoing judicial interaction with each drug court participant is essential.
8. Monitoring and evaluation measure the achievement of program goals and gauge effectiveness.
9. Continuing interdisciplinary education promotes effective drug court planning, implementation, and operations.

10. Forging partnerships among drug courts, public agencies, and community-based organizations generates local support and enhances drug court program effectiveness.

Critically, drug courts utilize a team approach that includes the prosecutor, the defense team, the clinical team, and, often, professionals within a local agency.

Family drug courts have been developed in an effort to address substance abuse and dependence associated with child maltreatment and to improve the likelihood of family reunification and stability (Lloyd & Brook, 2014). Although reunification with a sober parent is the preferred route, the courts will terminate parental rights on a timely basis if the parent(s) is/are unable or unwilling to improve the situation (Pach, 2009).

Family drug courts are said to rest on two approaches: therapeutic jurisprudence and restorative justice. Therapeutic jurisprudence uses "social science to study the extent to which a legal rule or practice promotes the psychological and physical well-being of the people it affects" (Slobogin, 1995, p. 196). Courts are viewed as a social force capable of producing behaviors and consequences (Hora, 2002).

Restorative justice provides "a process whereby all the parties with a stake in a particular offence come together to resolve collectively how to deal with the aftermath of the offence and its implications for the future" (Marshall, 1996, p. 37). Restorative justice seeks to balance the need to hold offenders accountable for their actions with the need to accept and reintegrate them into the community (Braithwaite, 1989; Zehr, 2002). This approach addresses the needs of the victims (Clear, 1994; Zehr, 1990), in this case the child, by shifting the focus from the offender to include the victim(s) and communities as well (Bazemore & Maloney, 1994), and empowers the victims, the offenders, and the community through a process of negotiation, mediation, and reparation. The process emphasizes healing the victim and community, the offender's moral and social self, and repairing relationships (Braithwaite, 1998, p. 2002). Although punishment is frequently a component of restorative justice, its inclusion is not central to the resolution of a situation. In contrast to the unilateral imposition of punishment that occurs within the retributive justice framework, restorative justice "is a collective effort shared between victim, offender, and community," whereby moral meaning "is restored through consensus with the offender" (Wenzel, Okimoto, Feather, & Platow, 2008, pp. 379–380) (see Chap. 6 for additional discussion relating to therapeutic jurisprudence and restorative justice).

Although the operation of family drug courts differs widely, Lloyd & Brooks (2014) have identified five key elements:

1. An underpinning in comprehensive law (restorative justice and therapeutic jurisprudence)
2. An interdisciplinary team approach
3. Intensive court involvement
4. Extensive collaboration with community service providers
5. An integrated focus on the well-being and safety of the entire family

Mental Illness, Criminal Offense, and Mental Health Courts

Like drug courts, mental health courts are problem-oriented courts. The first mental health court opened in 1997 in Broward County, Florida; by 2004, 98 mental health courts had been established in 33 states, and by June 2005, 125 mental health courts were operating in 36 states (Bureau of Justice Assistance Mental Health Courts Program, n.d.). A 2004–2005 survey of mental health courts found that more than one-third of the courts functioning at that time were located in the western states (37%) and the southern states (37%), with more than 40% of all adult mental health courts situated in only four states (California, Ohio, Florida, and Washington) (Bureau of Justice Assistance Mental Health Courts Program, n.d.). The court can be utilized at the pre-sentencing stage in order to divert mentally ill defendants from the criminal justice system, or alternatively, they may be used at the post-sentencing phase to prevent their imprisonment and to reduce the length of their probation (Goldkamp & Irons-Guynn, 2000). A majority of mental health courts accept both misdemeanor and felony cases (Bureau of Justice Assistance Mental Health Courts Program, n.d.; Redlich, Steadman, Monahan, Robbins, & Petrila, 2006) and also require that the defendant enter a guilty plea (Bureau of Justice Assistance Mental Health Courts Program, n.d.).

Mental health courts were thought to be necessary due to the high proportion of individuals with mental health problems, oftentimes in addition to substance use issues, who are confined to US jails and prisons. A 2006 special report of the Bureau of Justice Statistics indicated that at midyear 2005, more than one-half of all prison and jail inmates had a mental health problem—56% of state prisoners, 45% of federal prisoners, and 64% of jail inmates (James and Glaze, 2006). These numbers had not decreased by 2015 (Khazan, 2015b; Swanson, 2015). By 2015, the largest prison in each of the 44 of the 50 states and the District of Columbia held more mentally ill inmates than did the largest state psychiatric hospital in each of these venues (Swanson, 2015). Exceptions were Kansas, New Jersey, North Dakota, South Dakota, Washington, and Wyoming.

Prevalence estimates vary widely across various diagnoses. A recent review of studies that compared the prevalence of specific disorders in the prison population with those of community-based samples found a particularly high prevalence in the prison population of attention deficit hyperactivity, generalized anxiety, major depression, panic, posttraumatic stress disorder, and schizophrenia (Prins, 2014).

The high prevalence of mental illness among inmates is believed to be related to the deinstitutionalization of psychiatric services that began during the 1960s (Lamb & Weinberger, 1998; Roberts, 2010; Smiley, 2001; Tyuse & Linhorst, 2005). Deinstitutionalization was undertaken to alleviate the poor conditions in which mentally ill persons were housed for psychiatric care and to transition them to community-based quality mental health care. However, a lack of adequate funding for such care rendered the goal more aspirational than actual, resulting in a high prevalence of homelessness, a lack of care, and a revolving door of mental health treatment and criminal incarceration (Bachrach, 1983; Denckla & Berman, 2001).

Like drug courts, mental health courts are premised on therapeutic jurisprudence, with the expectation that the courts will provide an opportunity for offenders to achieve psychiatric stability and a mechanism to enhance public safety (Boothroyd, Poythress, McGaha, & Petrila, 2003; Fisler, 2005; Slate & Johnson, 2008). Researchers have suggested that although mental health courts utilize a variety of designs (Bernstein & Seltzer, 2003), they generally reflect common elements that include:

- A specific docket that is set aside for individuals with a mental illness
- A team, consisting of both criminal justice and mental health professionals, that develops a recommended treatment and supervision plan and identifies a responsible party
- Assurances to the defendant that the recommended treatment services will be provided to him or her
- Court monitoring of the implementation of the plan to assess (non)compliance and the need to impose sanctions (Steadman, Davidson, & Brown, 2001)

Position Statement 53 of the Mental Health America (2017), effective until December 31, 2019, focuses specifically on issues related to mental health courts. The statement enunciates 17 guidelines for the development and operation of mental health courts. These include:

1. Comprehensive mental health outreach to ensure access to community-based mental health treatment services
2. Maximum diversion, specifically pre-booking diversion in situations in which a voluntary mental health treatment plan would provide a reasonable alternative to the imposition of criminal sanctions
3. Meaningful diversion, meaning that no charges would be filed, when appropriate
4. The absence of a requirement of a guilty plea
5. Voluntary participation, such that a decision about participation should not be required until and unless the individual has been provided with all of the terms of the proposed treatment plan
6. Treatment of the individual by the least restrictive means possible
7. The right of the individual to refuse treatment
8. Availability of an advocate or counselor
9. Confidentiality
10. Cultural and linguistic competence of treatment services
11. Development of community coalitions, including partnerships between the criminal justice, mental health, and substance use treatment networks and agencies
12. Comprehensive outreach and training of criminal justice personnel
13. Integrated treatment for those with co-occurring disorders
14. A convening role for the mental health courts
15. Consolidation and coordination of cases to ensure that the individual remains the focus, rather than a specific case and to maintain a coordinated case management and treatment plan

16. Avoidance of extensions of time under mental health court jurisdiction in situations in which the client relapses
17. The monitoring of court processes, waiting lists, and outcomes (Mental Health America, 2017)

Individuals participating in a mental health court system generally progress through three phases (Hodges and Anderson, 2005). The first phase is geared toward orienting, stabilizing, and engaging the individual. During the second phase, the individual engages in treatment. The third phase focuses on helping the individual to transition back to and integrate to the community. A graduation ceremony is often held for those who complete their program. Movement through these phases may range from 6 months to several years, depending on numerous factors, including the severity of the individual's mental illness and substance use and the severity and history of criminal charges (Bureau of Justice Assistance, 2004).

Research suggests that mental health courts are both effective and cost-effective (Bazelon Center for Mental Health Law, 2004). They have been found to reduce costs by helping to avoid inpatient hospitalizations (Swartz et al., 2001), reduce incarceration in jails or prisons and recidivism (McNiel and Binder, 2007), lessen the public's need for law enforcement services needed for crimes committed by individuals with mental illness (McNiel & Binder, 2007), and improve mental health outcomes (Cosden, Ellens, Schnell, Yamini-Diouf, & Wolfe, 2003).

Social Workers in Drug and Mental Health Court Settings

Social Worker Roles Social workers may fulfill a variety of roles in both drug and mental health courts. In mental health courts, they may work in any of the following capacities, depending upon their educational level, experience, and licensure:

- Clinical director, with responsibility for the supervision of a team of social workers
- Social worker, whose principal task is the conduct of initial assessments
- Treatment coordinator, responsible for maintaining daily contact with the offender and mental health providers (Roberts, 2010)
- Case manager to assist the individual in achieving his or her goals related to housing, employment, and education (Roberts, Phillips, Bordelon, & Seif, 2014)
- Program evaluator (Hodges & Anderson, 2005; cf. Wolff & Pogorzelski, 2005)

It has been suggested that drug courts, and family drug courts in particular, are consistent with a strengths-based approach in social work. A strengths-based approach comprises six specific features:

- Goal orientation
- Systematic assessment of strengths
- Perceptions of the individual's environment as resource-laden

- Explicit methods that rely on client strengths for the attainment of goals
- Hope-inducing relationship
- Provision of meaningful choices and client authority to choose (Rapp, Saleebey, & Sullivan, 2005)

These features suggest that every individual, group, family, and community possesses strengths; injuries and trauma may serve as sources of resilience; every client has the potential for growth and the limits of that growth are not knowable; and the social worker-client relationship should reflect collaboration, shared decisionmaking, and reciprocity (Lloyd & Brook, 2014). Accordingly, both the strengths-based perspective and the foundational framework for family drug courts emphasize the well-being of all involved participants, the delineation of goals and a path forward, the development of supportive linkages within the community, and the avoidance of a deficit focus (Lloyd & Brook, 2014).

Ethical Issues for Consideration Social workers practicing in the drug and mental health court settings may be faced with any number of ethical issues. Although these issues may arise in the context of any social work practice, they are particularly likely to occur in this context due to the nature of the context itself.

Concerns have been raised relating to the capacity of individuals who are asked to choose between participation in a drug or mental health court and appearance in the usual court in which their offense might be heard (Erickson, Campbell, & Lamberti, 2006; Watson, Luchins, Hanrahan, Heyrman, & Lurigio, 2000). This may be of particular concern in situations in which the client is suffering from a psychosis or other serious mental illnesses that may adversely impact their ability to think and make reasoned judgments or a client who may be intoxicated due to recent substance use. Social workers in the community and those working with drug and mental health courts will want to assess the client's ability to understand the benefits and risks associated with each option and how it applies to their own situation prior to making an election. It is recognized, though, that in some cases, the client will have made his or her choice before they ever see a social worker.

Similar concerns have been raised with respect to coercion: if the client is faced with a choice between treatment and prison or jail, is it truly a voluntary choice (Goldkamp & Irons-Guynn, 2000)? Again, it will be important that the risks and benefits of each option be presented to the client and that he or she be provided with sufficient opportunity to consider the ramifications of each possible choice.

Confidentiality is a particular concern due to the nature of the drug and mental health courts (cf. Bernstein & Seltzer, 2003). Because the approach in these courts is team-based and is premised on the concept of therapeutic jurisprudence, the social worker may, depending on his or her role, need to share information with other professionals within the team in order to effectuate the treatment plan and achieve the treatment goals for the client. However, disclosure of client noncompliance with a term of his or her program during participation in the court program may result in dismissal from the program, imposition of a jail or prison term, or other adverse consequences. Clearly, a social worker in such situations may experience a conflict in his or her responsibilities as an advocate for the client and as a collaborator with the court (cf. Erickson, Campbell, & Lamberti, 2006). It is critical that the social worker advise the client that his or her responsibility may devolve not only to him or to her but to the court as well.

Ethical issues have also been raised regarding the use by mental health court and drug court judges of incarceration as punishment for a client's failure to comply with all of the terms of their program (Bernstein & Seltzer, 2003). The social worker does not have any direct control over a judge's propensity to use incarceration as a stick to encourage individuals to adhere to their agreed-upon treatment. However, depending upon their role vis-à-vis the court, the social worker may be able to advocate for the client by providing the court with his or her insights regarding the (in) advisability of incarceration for a nonadherent client and the circumstances underlying the nonadherence.

Mental Illness and the Americans with Disabilities Act

The Americans with Disabilities Act is a federal law that prohibits discrimination against those with disabilities in employment, state and local government services, public accommodations, commercial facilities, and transportation (United States Department of Justice, Civil Rights Division, n.d.). Originally promulgated in 1990, the law was revised in 2008, and these revisions became effective in 2009 (ADA Amendments Act of 2008). The provision related to employment applies to employer with 15 or more employees and requires that the employer:

> provide qualified individuals with disabilities an equal opportunity to benefit from the full range of employment-related opportunities available to others. For example, it prohibits discrimination in recruitment, hiring, promotions, training, pay, social activities, and other privileges of employment. It restricts questions that can be asked about an applicant's disability before a job offer is made, and it requires that employers make reasonable accommodation to the known physical or mental limitations of otherwise qualified individuals with disabilities, unless it results in undue hardship. (United States Department of Justice, Civil Rights Division, Disability Rights Section, 2009)

The term "disability" has a specific legal meaning under the Americans with Disabilities Act. "Disability" means:

> (A) A physical or mental impairment that substantially limits one or more major life activities of such individual
> (B) A record of such an impairment
> (C) Being regarded as having such an impairment (as described in Paragraph (3)) (42 U.S.C. § 12102(1))

Major life activities include, but are not limited to, caring for oneself, performing manual tasks, seeing, hearing, eating, sleeping, walking, standing, lifting, bending, speaking, breathing, learning, reading, concentrating, thinking, communicating, and working (42 U.S.C. § 12,102(2)).

The provisions do not apply in situations in which the disability lasts or is expected to last 6 months or less. In such circumstances, it will be considered to be transitory. However, a disability need not be permanent; a temporary disability may require only a temporary accommodation (*Summers v. Altarum Institute Corp.*, 2014). The provisions are also inapplicable where the individual's condition does not prevent him or her from "performing either a class of jobs or a broad range of jobs" but only restricts their ability to perform a "unique aspect" of a "single specific job" (*Carothers v. County of Cook*, 2015).

Individuals who have a disability must be able to perform the essential functions of their employment, but they may request a reasonable accommodation in order to assist them to maintain and enhance their performance. Examples of accommodations include flexible breaks or working hours, situation in an area that has reduced noise or distractions, and telecommuting from home. Individuals are not legally required to disclose a disability. However, it must be disclosed if they wish to request a reasonable accommodation (ADA National Network, n.d.).

Awareness of the ADA provisions may be important not only in the context of providing direct client services and client advocacy, but also in situations in which the social worker him- or herself has a mental illness diagnosis. As an example, a social worker may be suffering from depression and, while able to carry out the essential tasks of their position, finds it more difficult to focus on work in an area of the office that borders on a relatively busy, noisy lobby. A reasonable accommodation might be to have their office moved to a quieter area in the building.

References

ADA National Network. (n.d.). Mental health conditions in the workplace and the ADA. https://adata.org/factsheet/health. Accessed 19 October 2017.

American Psychiatric Association. (2015). Position statement on involuntary outpatient commitment and related programs of assisted outpatient treatment. https://www.psychiatry.org/.../Position-2015-Involuntary-Outpatient-Commitment.pdf. Accessed 20 October 2017.

American Psychological Association. (2004, July 28). APA resolution on outpatient civil commitment. http://www.apa.org/about/policy/outpatient.pdf. Accessed 20 October 2017.

Anderson, T. (2008, June 30). Race tilt in foster care hit; hospital staff more likely to screen minority mothers. *L.A. Daily News*. http://www.dailynews.com/2008/06/30/hospital-staff-more-likely-to-screen-minority-mothers/. Accessed 13 October 2017.

Bachrach, L. L. (1983). *Deinstitutionalization*. San Francisco: Jossey-Bass.

Bazelon Center on Mental Health Law. (2004). Position statement on involuntary commitment. http://www.bazelon.org/wp-content/uploads/2017/04/Position-Statement-on-Involuntary-Commitment.pdf. Accessed 20 October 2017.

Bazelon Center for Mental Health Law. (2004). The role of mental health courts in system reform. http://www.courts.ca.gov/documents/MHCtsSysReform.pdf. Accessed 12 October 2017.

Bazemore, G., & Maloney, D. (1994). Rehabilitating community service: Toward restorative service sanctions in a balanced justice system. *Federal Probation, 55*, 24–35.

Bernstein, R., & Seltzer, T. (2003). Criminalization of people with mental illnesses: The role of mental health courts in system reform. *University of District Columbia Law Review, 7*, 143–162.

Boothroyd, R. A., Poythress, N. G., McGaha, A., & Petrila, J. (2003). The Broward mental health court: Process, outcomes, and service utilization. *International Journal of Law and Psychiatry, 26*, 55–71.

Braithwaite, J. (1998). Restorative justice. In M. Tonry (Ed.), *The handbook of crime and punishment* (pp. 323–344). New York: Oxford University Press.

Braithwaite, J. (1989). *Crime, shame and reintegration*. Cambridge, UK: Cambridge University Press.

Bureau of Justice Assistance. (2004). Mental health courts program grantee meeting. January 22–23, Cincinnati, OH. Cited in Hodges, J.Q., & Anderson, K.M. (2005). What do social workers need to know about mental health courts? *Social Work in Mental Health, 4*(2), 17–30.

Bureau of Justice Assistance Mental Health Courts Program. (n.d.). Mental health courts: A national snapshot. https://www.bja.gov/Programs/MHC_National_Snapshot.pdf. Accessed 11 October 2017.

Center for Prisoner Health and Human Rights. (n.d.). *Incarceration, substance abuse, and addiction*. Providence, RI: Author. http://www.prisonerhealth.org/educational-resources/factsheets-2/incarceration-substance-abuse-and-addiction/. Accessed 08 October 2017.

Chasnoff, I. J., Landress, H. J., & Barrett, M. E. (1990). The prevalence of illicit-drug or alcohol use during pregnancy and discrepancies in mandatory reporting in Pinellas County, Florida. *New England Journal of Medicine, 322*(17), 1202–1206.

Chavkin, W. (2001). Cocaine and pregnancy: Time to look at the evidence. *Journal of the American Medical Association, 285*(12), 1626–1628.

Clear, T. R. (1994). *Harm in American penology: Offenders, victims, and their communities*. Albany, NY: State University of New York Press.

Cosden, M., Ellens, J. K., Schnell, J. L., Yamini-Diouf, Y., & Wolfe, M. M. (2003). Evaluation of a mental health treatment court with assertive community treatment. *Behavioral Sciences & the Law, 21*(4), 415–427.

Dewees, M. (2002). Contested landscape: The role of critical dialogue for social workers in mental health practice. *Journal of Progressive Human Services, 13*(1), 73–91.

Denckla, D., & Berman, G. (2001). *Rethinking the revolving door: A look at mental illness in the courts*. State Justice Institute, New York State Unified Court System, Center for Court Innovation. https://www.courtinnovation.org/sites/default/files/rethinkingtherevolvingdoor.pdf. Accessed 01 May 2018.

Ellsworth, M. A., Stevens, T. P., & D'Angio, C. T. (2010). Infant race affects application of clinical guidelines when screening for drugs of abuse in newborns. *Pediatrics, 125*(6), e1379–e1385.

Erickson, S. K., Campbell, A., & Lamberti, J. S. (2006). Variations in mental health courts: Challenges, opportunities, and a call for caution. *Community Mental Health Journal, 42*(4), 335–344.

Fisler, C. (2005). Building trust and managing risk: A look at a felony mental health court. *Psychology, Public Policy, and Law, 11*(4), 587–604.

Frank, D. A., Augustyn, M., Knight, W. G., Pell, T., & Zuckerman, B. (2001). Growth, development, and behavior in early childhood following prenatal cocaine exposure: A systematic review. *Journal of the American Medical Association, 285*(12), 1613–1625.

Goldkamp, J. S., & Irons-Guynn, C. (2000). *Emerging judicial strategies for the mentally ill in the criminal caseload: Mental health courts in Fort Lauderdale, Seattle, San Bernardion, and Anchorage* [NCJ 182504]. Washington, DC: United States Department of Justice, Office of Justice Programs, Bureau of Justice Assistance.

Guttmacher Institute. (2017). Substance use during pregnancy. https://www.guttmacher.org/print/state-policy/explore/substance-use-during-pregnancy. Accessed 12 October 2017.

Hodges, J. Q., & Anderson, K. M. (2005). What do social workers need to know about mental health courts? *Social Work in Mental Health, 4*(2), 17–30.

Hora, H. P. (2002). A dozen years of drug treatment courts: Uncovering our theoretical foundation and the construction of a mainstream paradigm. *Substance Use & Misuse, 37*(12–13), 1469–1488.

Huddleston, C. W., III, Freeman-Wilson, K., Marlowe, D. B., & Roussell, A. (2005). Painting the current picture: A national report card on drug courts and other problem solving court programs in the United States. *National Drug Court Institute, 1*(2), 1–22. https://www.ndci.org/wp-content/uploads/PCPI.2.2005.pdf. Accessed 08 October 2017.

James, D. J., & Glaze, L. E. (2006). *Mental health problems of prison and jail inmates* [NCJ 213600]. Washington, DC: United States Department of Justice, Office of Justice Programs.

Jeltsen, M. (2015, October 13). Relief for woman sentenced to 20 years for using meth while pregnant. *Huffington Post*. https://www.huffingtonpost.com/entry/melissa-mccann-arms-sentence-reversed_us_561bbb8fe4b0e66ad4c872f1. Accessed 13 October 2017.

Khazan, O. (2015a, May 8). Into the body of another. *The Atlantic*. https://www.theatlantic.com/health/archive/2015/05/into-the-body-of-another/392522/. Accessed 13 October 2017.

Khazan, O. (2015b, April 7). Most prisoners are mentally ill. *The Atlantic*. https://www.theatlantic.com/health/archive/2015/04/more-than-half-of-prisoners-are-mentally-ill/389682/. Accessed 08 October 2017.

Kisely, S. R., Campbell, L. A., & Preston, N. J. (2012). Compulsory community and involuntary outpatient treatment for people with severe mental disorders. *Cochrane Database System Review, 2*: CD00408.pub.3.

Lamb, H. R., & Weinberger, L. E. (1998). Persons with severe mental illness in jails and prisons: A review. *Psychiatric Services, 49*, 483–492.

Lloyd, M. H., & Brook, J. P. (2014). Strengths based approaches to practice and family drug courts: Is there a fit? *Journal of Family Strengths, 14*(1), 15. http:digitalcommons.library.tmc.edu/jfs/vol14/iss1/15. Accessed 08 October 2017.

Marlowe, D. B. (2002). Effective strategies for intervening with drug abusing offenders. *Villanova Law Review, 47*, 988–995.

Marshall, T. F. (1996). The evolution of restorative justice in Britain. *European Journal on Criminal Policy and Research, 4*(4), 21–43.

McNiel, D. E., & Binder, R. L. (2007). Effectiveness of a mental health court in reducing criminal recidivism and violence. *American Journal of Psychiatry, 164*(9), 1395–1403.

Mental Health America. (2013). Position statement 22: Involuntary mental health treatment. http://www.mentalhealthamerica.net/positions/involuntary-treatment. Accessed 20 October 2017.

Mental Health America. (2017). Position statement 53: Mental health courts. http://www.mentalhealthamerica.net/positions/mental-health-courts. Accessed 11 October 2017.

Miranda, L., Dixon, V., & Reyes, C. (2015). How states handle drug use during pregnancy. *Propublica: Journalism in the Public Interest*. https://projects.propublica.org/graphics/maternity-drug-policies-by-state. Accessed 12 October 2017.

Mohapatra, S. (2011). Unshackling addiction: A public health approach to drug use during pregnancy. *Wisconsin Journal of Law, Gender & Society, 26*, 241–274.

National Association of Drug Court Professionals, Drug Court Standards Committee. (2004). Defining drug courts: The key components. https://www.ncjrs.gov/pdffiles1/bja/205621.pdf. Accessed 08 October 2017.

National Association of Social Workers. (2008). Code of ethics. https://www.socialworkers.org/pubs/code/code.asp. Accessed 11 February 2016.

National Center on Addiction and Substance Abuse, Columbia University. (2010). *Behind bars II: Substance abuse and America's prison population*. New York: Author. https://www.centeronaddiction.org/newsroom/press-releases/2010-behind-bars-II. Accessed 08 October 2017.

National Coalition for Mental Health Recovery. (n.d.). Involuntary outpatient commitment myths and facts. https://www.ncmhr.org/downloads/NCMHR-Fact-Sheet-on-Involuntary-Outpatient-Commitment-4.3.14.pdf. Accessed 20 October 2017.

National Conference of State Legislatures. (2017). Fetal homicide laws. http://www.ncsl.org/research/health/fetal-homicide-state-laws.aspx. Accessed 13 October 2017.

National Conference of State Legislatures. (1999, July 15). Health policy tracking service. Fact sheet: Outpatient civil commitment. http://www.courts.state.ny.us/reporter/webdocs/HPTS.htm. Accessed 20 October 2017.

Pach, J. N. M. (2009). An overview of operational family dependency treatment courts. *National Drug Court Institute, 6*(1), 67–122.

Phelps, L., & Cottone, J. W. (1999). Long-term developmental outcomes of prenatal cocaine exposure. *Journal of Psychoeducational Assessment, 17*, 343–353.

Paltrow, L. M. (1998). Punishing women for their behavior during pregnancy: An approach that undermines the health of women and children. In C. L. Wetherington & A. D. Roman (Eds.), *Drug addiction research on the health of women* (pp. 467–501). Rockville, MD: United States Department of Health and Human Services, National Institutes of Health, National Institute on Drug Abuse.

Paltrow, L. M., & Flavin, J. (2013). Arrests of and forced interventions on pregnant women in the United States, 1973–2005: Implications for women's legal status and public health. *Journal of Health Politics, Policy and Law, 38*(2), 299–343.

Prins, S. J. (2014). The prevalence of mental illnesses in US state prisons: A systematic review. *Psychiatric Services, 65*(7), 862–872.

Rapp, C. A., Saleebey, D., & Sullivan, W. P. (2005). The future of strengths-based social work. *Advances in Social Work, 6*(1), 79–90.

Redlich, A. D., Steadman, H. J., Monahan, J., Robbins, P. C., & Petrila, J. (2006). Patterns of practice in mental health courts: A national survey. *Law and Human Behavior, 30*(3), 347–362.

Ridgely, M. S., Borum, R., & Petrila, J. (2001). *The effectiveness of involuntary outpatient treatment: Empirical evidence and the experience of eight states*. Santa Monica, CA: Rand. https://www.rand.org/content/dam/rand/pubs/monograph_reports/2007/MR1340.pdf. Accessed 19 October 2017.

Roberts, L. (2010). Mental health courts: An interface between social work and criminal justice. *Columbia Social Work Review, 1*, 36–44.

Roberts, S. C., & Nuru-Jeter, A. (2011). Universal alcohol/drug screening in prenatal care: A strategy for reducing racial disparities? Questioning the assumptions. *Maternal and Child Health Journal, 15*(8), 1127–1134.

Roberts, M. R., Phillips, I., Bordelon, T. D., & Seif, L. (2014). A social worker's role in drug court. *Sage Open, 4*(2). https://doi.org/10.1177/2158244014535413.3.

Rotzoll, B. W. (2001, March 16). Black newborns likelier to be drug-tested: Study. *Chicago Sun-Times*, https://www.highbeam.com/doc/1P2-4579175.html. Accessed 13 October 2017.

Schroedel, J. R., & Fiber, P. (2001). Punitive versus public health oriented approaches to drug use by pregnant women. *Yale Journal of Policy, Law & Ethics, 1*, 217–236.

Schwartz, A. R. (2015). Dangerousness or just pregnant? How sanism & biases infect the dangerousness determination in the civil commitment of pregnant women. *Indiana Journal of Law and Social Equality, 3*(2.) article 4.

Singer, L. T., Salvator, A., Arendt, R., Minnes, S., Farkas, K., & Kliegman, R. (2002). Effects of cocaine/polydrug exposure and maternal psychological distress on infant birth outcomes. *Neurotoxicology and Teratology, 24*, 127–135.

Slate, R. N., & Johnson, W. W. (2008). *Criminalization of mental illness*. Durham, NC: Carolina Academic Press.

Slobogin, C. (1995). Therapeutic jurisprudence: Five dilemmas to ponder. *Psychology, Public Policy, and Law, 1*(1), 193–219.

Smiley, A. (2001). Forensic mental health in the United Sates—An overview. In G. Landsberg & A. Smiley (Eds.), *Forensic mental health: Working with offenders with mental illness* (pp. 1–16). Kingston, NJ: Civil Research Institute.

Steadman, H. J., Davidson, S., & Brown, C. (2001). Mental health courts: Their promise and unanswered questions. *Psychiatric Services, 52*, 457–458.

Swanson, A. (2015, April 30). A shocking number of mentally ill Americans end up in prison instead of treatment. *Washington Post*. https://www.washingtonpost.com/news/wonk/wp/2015/04/30/a-shocking-number-of-mentally-ill-americans-end-up-in-prisons-instead-of-psychiatric-hospitals/?utm_term=.a0345d7bf333. Accessed 08 October 2017.

Swanson, J., Swartz, M., Van Dorn, R. A., Monahan, J., McGuire, T. G., Steadman, H. J., & Robbins, P. C. (2009). Racial disparities in involuntary outpatient commitment: Are they real? *Health Affairs, 28*(3), 816–826.

Swartz, M. S., Swanson, J. W., Hiday, V. A., Wagner, H. R., Burns, B. J., & Borum, R. (2001). A randomized controlled trial of outpatient commitment in North Carolina. *Psychiatric Services, 52*, 325–329.

Treatment Advocacy Center. (n.d.). Promoting assisted outpatient treatment. http://www.treatmentadvocacycenter.org/fixing-the-system/promoting-assisted-outpatient-treatment. Accessed 20 October 2017.

Tyuse, S. W., & Linhorts, D. M. (2005). Drug courts and mental health courts: Implications for social work. *Health & Social Work, 30*(3), 233–240.

United States Department of Justice, Civil Rights Division (n.d.). Information and technical assistance on the Americans with Disabilities Act. https://www.ada.gov/2010_regs.htm. Accessed 19 October 2017.

United States Department of Justice, Civil Rights Division, Disability Rights Section. (2009). *A guide to disability rights laws*. https://www.ada.gov/cguide.htm#anchor62335. Accessed 19 October 2017.

United States Department of Justice, Office of Justice Programs, National Institute of Justice. (n.d.) Drug courts. http://www.nij.gov/topics/courts/drug-courts/Pages/welcome.aspx. Accessed 01 October 2017.

Watson, A., Luchins, D., Hanrahan, P., Hyerman, M. J., & Lurigio, A. (2000). Mental health courts: Promises and limitations. *Journal of the American Academy of Psychiatry and the Law, 28*, 476–482.

Wenzel, M., Okimoto, T. G., Feather, N. T., & Platow, M. J. (2008). Retributive and restorative justice. *Law and Human Behavior, 32*(5), 375–389.

Wolff, N., & Pogorzelski, W. (2005). Measuring the effectiveness of mental health courts: Challenges and recommendations. *Psychology, Public Policy, and Law, 11*(4), 539–569.

Zehr, H. (1990). *Changing lenses: Restorative justice for our times*. Harrisonburg, VA: Herald Press.

Zehr, H. (2002). *The little book of restorative justice*. Intercourse, PA: Good Book.

Zilber, C. (2016, November 29). Ethics considerations of involuntary outpatient treatment. *Psychiatric News*. http://psychnews.psychiatryonline.org/doi/full/10.1176/appi.pn.2016.12a16. Accessed 20 October 2017.

Legal References

Cases

Arkansas Department of Human Services v. Collier, 95 S.W.3d 772 (Ark. 2003).
Ankrom v. State, 152 So. 3d 373 (Ct. Crim. App. 2011).
Carothers v. County of Cook, 808 F.3d 1140 (7th Cir. 2015).
Cochran v. Commonwealth, 315 S.W.3d 325 (Ky. 2010).
Collins v. Texas, 890 S.W.2d 893 (Tex. App. 1994).
Commonwealth v. Kemp, 1992 Pa. Dist. & Cty. Dec. LEXIS 35 (1992).
Commonwealth v. Pellegrini, 608 N.E.2d 717 (Mass. 1993).
Commonwealth v. Welch, 864 S.W.2d 280 (Ky. 1993).
Herron v. State, 729 N.E.2d 1008 (Ind. Ct. App. 2000).
In re Baby Boy Blackshear, 736 N.E.2d 462 (2000), *affirming* 1999 Ohio App. LEXIS 4274 (Ohio Ct. App. 1999).

In re Unborn Child, 683 N.Y.S.2d 366 (N.Y. Fam. Ct. 1998).
In re Unborn Child Julie Starks, 18 P.3d 342 (Okla. 2001).
In re Valerie, 613 A.2d 748 (Conn. 1992).
In re V.R., 2008 Ohio App. LEXIS 1285 (Ct. App. Ohio 2008).
Johnson v. State, 602 So. 2d 1288 (1992).
Kilmon v. State, 905 A.2d 306 (Md. Ct. App. 2006).
Matter of Smith, 492 N.Y.S.2d 331 (Monroe Co. Fam. Ct. 1985).
New Jersey Department of Children and Families v. A.L., 59 A.3d 576 (N.J. 2013).
People v. Bedenkop, 625 N.E. 2d 123 (Ill. App. Ct. 1993).
People v. Hardy. 469 N.W.2d 50 (Mich. Ct. App. 1991).
People v. Morabito, 151 Misc.2d 259 (Geneva Cty. Ct. 1992).
Reinesto v. Superior Court, 894 P.2d 733 (Ariz. Ct. App. 1995).
Reyes v. Superior Court of San Bernardino County, 141 Cal. Rptr. 912 (Cal. Ct. App. 1977).
Sheriff v. Encoe, 885 P.2d 596 (1994).
State v. Aiwohi, 123 P.3d 1210 (Hawaii 2005).
State v. Amanda H., 154 P.3d 674 (N.M. Ct. App. 2007).
State v. Arandus, No. 93072, slip. Op. (D. Neb. June 17, 1993).
State v. Dun, 916 P.2d 952 (Wash. Ct. App. 1996).
State v. Gethers, 595 So. 2d 1140 (Fla. Dist. Ct. App. 1991).
State v. Grubbs, No. 4 FA S89–415 (Alaska Super. Ct. Oct. 2, 1989).
State v. Inzar, 90CRS6960, 90CRS696, slip op. (N.C. Super. Ct. Apr. 9, 1991).
State v. Louk, 786 S.E.2d 219 (West Va. 2016).
State v. Luster, 419 S.E.2d 32 (Ga. Ct. App. 1992).
State v. McKnight, Indictment No. 2000 GS26432 (Horry Co. Ct. May 17, 2001).
State v. Wade, 232 S.W.3d 663 (Mo. Ct. App. 2007).
State ex. rel. M.E.C., 942 P.2d 955 (1997).
Summers v. Altarum Institute Corp., 740 F.3d 325 (4th Cir. 2014).
United States v. Vaughn, No. F-2172-88B (D.C. Super. Ct. Aug. 23, 1988).
Whitner v. State, 492 S.E.2d 777 (S.C. 1997).
Wisconsin ex. rel. Angela M.W. v. Kruzicki, 561 N.W.2d 729 (Wis. 1997).

Statutes

42 U.S.C. § 12102.
ADA Amendments Act of 2008, P.L. 110–325.
Colorado Revised Statutes § 27-5-105(1) (2016).
D.C. Code Annotated § 21-521 (2016).

Chapter 11
Abuse and Neglect Issues Across the Lifespan

Child Maltreatment

Incidence

Various writers believe that child maltreatment in high-income countries, such as the United States and Europe, now constitutes "a major public-health and social-welfare problem" (Gilbert, Widom, et al., 2009, p. 68). In 2012, a total of 3.4 million reports of child abuse were made to child protective services in the United States alone (United States Department of Health and Human Services, Administration for Children and Families, Administration on Children, Youth and Families, Children's Bureau, 2012). Of the 1640 children who died from child maltreatment, 70% suffered from neglect and 44% experienced physical abuse; almost three-quarters of the children who died were under the age of 3 (United States Department of Health and Human Services, Administration for Children and Families, Administration on Children, Youth and Families, Children's Bureau, 2012). Data from the National Incidence Study of Child Abuse and Neglect (NIS), which includes data from both child protective services (CPS) agencies and non-CPS sources, indicate that almost 1.25 million children experienced maltreatment during 2005–2006 (Sedlak et al. 2010). Nevertheless, these figures are believed to represent an underestimate of the incidence of child abuse and neglect in the United States (Gilbert, Kemp, et al., 2009; Melton, 2005).

The effects of maltreatment have been well-documented. Physical abuse may lead to severe injury, such as fractures, hemorrhage, burns, bruises, lacerations, inflammation, scars, and death (Gilbert, Kemp, et al., 2009). Such injuries have resulted from beatings, burns, and attempted or completed drowning, smothering, and poisoning. Child maltreatment has been found to be associated with anxiety, depression, posttraumatic stress, dissociation, oppositional behavior, substance misuse, aggression, self-injurious or risk-taking behavior, age-inappropriate sexual behavior, and suicide attempts (Ford, 2002; Friedrich et al., 2001; Johnson et al., 2002).

Definitional Issues and Reporting Dilemmas

Although all states mandate the reporting of child abuse and neglect (Alvarez, Kenny, Donohue, & Carpin, 2004; King, Reece, Bendel, & Patel, 1998; Melton, 2005; Zellman, 1990), research suggests that a significant proportion of mandated professionals either occasionally or consistently fail to report suspected child maltreatment during their careers (Alvarez et al., 2004; King et al., 1998). The (un)willingness of human service providers, such as social workers, to report possible abuse or neglect has been found to be associated with the amount of training they have received, the extent to which their identity as a reporter will be protected, a desire to avoid involvement with the legal system, a belief that reporting will ultimately harm the child, the provider's personal experiences, the existence of institutional barriers to reporting, and the extent of their own professional autonomy in decisionmaking (King et al., 1998; National Research Council, 2002). Research further suggests that social workers are more likely to file a report if they wish to avoid the legal consequences for failing to do so, desire to obtain additional help for the family involved, and believe that child protective services has the expertise to intervene effectively (Zellman, 1990).

In part, the failure to report suspected abuse or neglect may be somewhat attributable to varying understandings of what behaviors constitute "abuse," "neglect," and "maltreatment" across subgroups within the larger society (Korbin & Spilsbury, 1999), even among professionals. One US-based study found that significant variability exists in the severity ratings of specific acts across the lawyers, pediatricians, social workers, and police officers who had been surveyed (Giovannoni & Becerra, 1979). Yet another study found large differences between therapists and child protective workers with respect to the identification of situations requiring reporting (Deisz, Doueck, George, & Levine, 1996). Factors such as the frequency or chronicity of an act, the seriousness of any injury resulting from that act, the age and developmental level of the child, and the historical time period in which the act occurs are often critical in judging the nature of an act (National Research Council, 1993; Portwood, 1999; Straus & Mathur, 1996; Zellman, 1992). As an example, Whitney and colleagues found that child welfare practitioners surveyed in 2001 rated some behaviors, such as spanking and shaking, as more severe than practitioners who had been similarly surveyed in 1977 (Whitney, Tajima, Herrenkohlm, & Huang, 2006).

It may also be difficult to distinguish reportable situations, apart from those that involve severe harm to the child, because the laws that define child maltreatment are situated within a cultural context that both accepts physical force as a solution to problems (DeLey, 1988) and corporal punishment as a means of disciplining children (Wauchope & Straus, 1995). Religious belief, as well, may serve as a basis and/or justification for the use of corporal punishment as a means of discipline (Pagelow & Johnson, 1988). As one writer observed, "There is an ill-defined line between legal, socially sanctioned parental discipline, and illegal abuse" (Ashton, 1999, p. 540). Indeed, a vignette-based study involving upper-level undergraduates majoring in professional programs, including social work, found that those who approved of corporal punishment for children were less likely to perceive maltreatment and less willing to endorse reporting (Ashton, 2001).

Social worker understandings of what may constitute abuse may also vary due to the differing definitions of abuse and neglect that are utilized by states. Although many states frame their mandate to require reporting only in situations in which there exists "reasonable cause to suspect" child maltreatment, that standard is ill-defined (Deisz et al., 1996) and subject to varying interpretation due to more specifically delineated requirements that coexist with this more general standard. As an example, as of July 2012, statutes of 19 states and the District of Columbia contained reporting procedures where there was evidence of children's exposure to drugs, alcohol, or controlled substances at the time of their births; 12 states and the District of Columbia addressed such exposure in their definitions of child abuse and neglect (Child Welfare Information Gateway, 2012, p. 3).

A social worker may also experience confusion regarding the need to report a situation that might constitute medical neglect due to religious exemptions in some states. Although parental withholding of medical treatment in favor of various forms of religious healing may lead to preventable child deaths (Asser & Swan, 1998), some states continue to exempt parents from prosecution for abuse or neglect. As of 2005, 39 states had statutes that provided religious exemptions from civil child abuse or neglect charges in such cases, and 33 allowed religious defenses to criminal charges, such as abuse, manslaughter, or homicide, when the child's death resulted from the lack of medical care (Hickey & Lyckholm, 2004; Hughes, 2005). Ohio law provides one such example:

> Nothing in this chapter shall be construed as subjecting a parent, guardian, or custodian of a child to criminal liability when, solely in the practice of religious beliefs, the parent, guardian, or custodian fails to provide adequate medical or surgical care or treatment for the child. This division does not abrogate or limit any person's responsibility under section 2151.421 of the Revised Code to report child abuse that is known or reasonably suspected or believed to have occurred, child neglect that is known or reasonably suspected or believed to have occurred, and children who are known to face or are reasonably suspected or believed to be facing a threat of suffering abuse or neglect and does not preclude any exercise of the authority of the state, any political subdivision, or any court to ensure that medical or surgical care or treatment is provided to a child when the child's health requires the provision of medical or surgical care or treatment. (Ohio Revised Code § 2151.03(B), 2006)

A social worker might interpret the law to mean that a situation potentially constituting abuse or neglect must be reported and the issue of a religious basis for the (in) action is relevant only to potential prosecution. Alternatively, the social worker might understand the provision to mean that no reporting is necessary if the (in) action is premised upon religious beliefs.

State definitions may also vary with respect to their congruence with the language of the federal Child Abuse Prevention and Treatment Act (2010), which defines child abuse and neglect as "Any recent failure or act on the part of a parent or caretaker which results in death, serious physical or emotional harm, sexual abuse or exploitation; or an act or failure to act which presents and imminent risk of serious harm." Such variations in definitions, their application, and the resulting reporting of incidents have led to disagreement with respect to the actual numbers of children who are subjected to maltreatment during any given time period (Manly, 2005). Accordingly, the Centers for Disease Control and Prevention (Leeb, Paulozzi, Melanson, Simon, & Arias, 2008) has recommended that standardized definitions be adopted (see Table 11.1).

Despite the guidance provided by these guidelines, confusion with respect to the need to report is likely to continue due to their vagueness and continuing inconsistency with the provisions of state laws. For example, in providing examples of inadequate hygiene, the Centers for Disease Control and Prevention lists "dirty dishes and spoiled food are left on the kitchen table and counter" (Leeb, Paulozzi, Melanson, Simon & Arias, 2008, p. 17). However, this example is without context; a social worker must still determine if *any* such incident constitutes neglect or whether the situation must be severe and continuous (Deisz et al., 1996). The social worker's ultimate conclusion may depend heavily on his or her subjective opinion and cultural expectations, which are often a function of educational level, age, socioeconomic status, and gender (cf. Alvarez et al., 2004; Ashton, 1999; Korbin & Spilsbury, 1999). Additionally, the use by some national agencies of other categories and definitions may lead to confusion. For example, the National Council on Child Abuse and Family Violence (2015) also utilizes the category of "emotional abuse," defining it as including "both verbal assaults and the withholding of positive emotional support." As such, it overlaps with the two categories of psychological abuse and emotional neglect that are suggested by Leeb et al. (2008).

Similarly, medical neglect may be difficult to identify first, because of its various forms and, second, because of the importance of the context in which the failure to act occurs. Medical neglect may be due to a failure to address symptoms of an illness or a failure to follow the instructions of a health-care provider after such advice has been sought (Jenny and the Committee on Child Abuse and Neglect, 2007). Various factors must be present in order to establish medical neglect:

1. The child is either being harmed or is at risk of being harmed due to the lack of health care.
2. The child would receive a net benefit from the recommended health care.
3. The anticipated benefit of the recommended care or treatment is significantly greater than the morbidity, so that reasonable caregivers would generally prefer the treatment rather than the nontreatment.
4. Access to health care is available and is not being utilized.
5. The caregiver understands the medical advice that he or she obtained (Jenny and the Committee on Child Abuse and Neglect, 2007).

Accordingly, the child's caregiver who receives the advice must be cognitively able to understand the risks associated with the illness and with the recommended treatment, must share the same values as the individual providing the treatment recommendation and/or assessing the situation for neglect, and must have "access to health care." However, exactly what constitutes "access to health care" is itself unclear; it may mean that the needed health care exists and is accessible without impediment, or it may mean that the health care exists and is deemed to be accessible

Table 11.1 Definitions of types of abuse (acts of commission) and neglect (acts of omission)*

Term	Definition	Examples and exceptions
Child maltreatment	"Any act or series of acts of commission or omission by a parent or other caregiver that results in harm, potential for harm, or threat of harm to a child"	Includes physical abuse, sexual abuse, psychological abuse, physical neglect, emotional neglect, medical/dental neglect, educational neglect, and failure to supervise
Physical abuse	"The intentional use of physical force against a child that results in, or has the potential to result in, physical injury." acts that constitute physical abuse range from those that do not leave a mark on a child to those that can cause permanent disability, disfigurement, or death. "Physical abuse can result from discipline or physical punishment" (emphasis added) "Physical injuries are physical harm, including death, occurring to the body from exposure to thermal, mechanical, electrical, or chemical energy interacting with the body in amounts or rates that exceed the threshold of physiological tolerance, or from the absence of such essentials as oxygen or heat. Physical injuries can include physical marks, burns, lacerations, contusions, abrasions, broken bones, internal injuries, organ damage, poisoning, asphyxiation, or death because of physical injuries sustained"	Hitting, punching, kicking, beating, biting, pushing, shoving, throwing, pulling, dragging, dropping, shaking, strangling or choking, smothering, burning, scalding, poisoning Injuries that are encompassed by the definition of sexual abuse (see below) do not constitute acts of physical abuse
Sexual abuse	"Any completed or attempted (non-completed) sexual act, sexual contact with, or exploitation (i.e., noncontact sexual interaction) of a child by a caregiver" A *sexual act* involves contact involving penetration between the mouth, penis, vulva, or anus of a child and another individual; penetration of the anal or genital opening by a hand, finger, or other object and includes contact between the penis and vulva, penis and anus, penis and penis, mouth and penis, mouth and anus, and mouth and vulva *Abusive sexual contact* does not involve penetration but does involve the intentional touching, either directly or through the clothing, of any of the following parts of the body: Genitalia, anus, groin, breast, inner thigh, and buttocks. Abusive sexual contact can be performed by the caregiver on the child, by the child on the caregiver, or with the involvement of another person due to the force or coercion of the caregiver *Noncontact sexual abuse* encompasses acts that expose a child to sexual activity, such as pornography, filming a child in a sexual manner, sexual harassment of a child, and prostitution or transporting a child by deception across an international border for the purpose of forced sexual activity (trafficking)	Abusive sexual contact does not encompass acts that are required to fulfill the child's daily needs or care

(continued)

Table 11.1 (continued)

Term	Definition	Examples and exceptions
Psychological abuse	Intentional behavior by the caregiver that communicates to the child that he or she is unworthy, unloved, unwanted, endangered, or valued only for the purpose of fulfilling the needs of another. The abuse may be chronic and pervasive or episodic or harmful, potentially harmful, or insensitive to the child's developmental needs and may lead to psychological or emotional damage	Blaming, belittling, degrading, intimidating, restraining, confining, corrupting, exploiting, spurning. Isolating behavior is that which prevents the child from having contact with others or minimizes contact. Terrorizing behavior causes the child to feel unsafe, e.g., threat of abandonment, violence, or death if expectations are not met
Physical neglect	Caregiver failure to provide adequate nutrition, hygiene, shelter, or clean and appropriately sized clothing that is adequate for the weather	Denial of meals as punishment; roach-infested residence; lack of coat in winter
Emotional neglect	Caregiver inattention to child, emotional unresponsiveness, inadequate mental health care	
Medical/dental neglect	Caregiver failure to provide adequate access to medical, vision, or dental care	Caregiver failure to administer prescribed medications or seek medical attention for child's illness
Educational neglect	Caregiver failure to provide adequate education	Child absence from school for ≥ 25 days/year
Failure to supervise	Caregiver failure to ensure that child engages in safe activities and uses appropriate safety devices; fails to protect child from recognized maltreatment by another caregiver	Child regularly left along in dangerous situations
Exposure to violent environments	Caregiver failure to protect the child from "pervasive violence" occurring in the home, neighborhood, or community	Caregiver sale of illicit drugs from the home; child exposure to violence between the caregivers, e.g., partner violence

*All definitions and examples are from Leeb et al. (2008, pp. 11–19).

because of its existence regardless of the existing barriers, which may include language differences, lack of transportation, and/or lack of funds or insurance to cover the cost of medication.

Reporting Procedures

Just as with state definitions of abuse and neglect, reporting procedures vary across states. States may impose specific time requirements for both the filing of oral reports of suspected maltreatment, e.g., within 24 h after abuse is suspected, and the permissible lapse of time between the filing of an oral report and the later filing of a written one (Alvarez et al., 2004). The mechanism of transmitting a written report may also differ, e.g., by faxed or mailed statement or by completion of a specific form. Depending upon the state, the report must be filed with a designated agency, through a central hotline, or with law enforcement. In some jurisdictions, mandated reporters, including social workers, must provide their names and contact information (Child Welfare Information Gateway, 2016). A number of jurisdictions provide that the identity of the reporter may be disclosed.

Although the specific content of the report may vary across states, it appears that there is some standardization with respect to basic information. Necessary elements of the report generally include the child's identifying information, such as age or date of birth and race/ethnicity, the name and address of the child's parent or caregiver, the facts and circumstances that have led to the making of the report, and in most states, the provider's name and contact information (Alvarez et al., 2004; Child Welfare Information Gateway, 2016).

Variation across states also exists with respect to the responsibility of individual mandated reporters to make a report in situations in which their agency organization is required to report and/or has established review procedures prior to the filing of a report. Some states do not relieve individuals of filing a report even where their organizations are also required to report (Child Welfare Information Gateway, 2016). Seventeen states prohibit an employer from taking any action to dissuade an individual from making a report.

Most, if not all, states provide immunity for social workers and other providers who report suspected abuse. Almost all states impose penalties for a mandated reporter's failure to knowingly or willfully fail to make a report of suspected abuse or neglect. Depending upon the specific state law, the severity of the abuse, and the frequency of the failure to report, the violation may be punishable as either a misdemeanor or a felony (Child Welfare Information Gateway, 2015; *People v. Cavaiana*, 1988; *State v. Brown*, 2004; *State v. Grover*, 1989; *State v. Hurd*, 1986). Mandated reporters who fail to report may face jail sentences and/or heavy financial penalties. Penalties may be imposed in many jurisdictions for obstructing the filing of a report and for false reporting.

In addition to facing potential fines and/or imprisonment for failing to report suspected abuse or neglect, social workers may also be sued by clients, their family members, or their legal representatives for failing to report. As an example, the case of *DeShaney v. Winnebago County Department of Social Services* (1989) involved a mother's Fourteenth Amendment claim against social workers and their agency administrators for the brain damage suffered by her son as a result of abuse inflicted by his father, who had custody of the child. The US Supreme Court ultimately found against the mother's claim, holding that the Fourteenth Amendment protected people from the actions of the state; accordingly, the agency and the social workers had no legal duty to protect the child from his father, despite the social workers' and agency's knowledge of repeated acts of abuse so severe that they required the child's hospitalization. The Court left open the question as to whether to social workers and/or the agency might have been found liable had the child been in state custody at the time of the abuse.

Social workers and their agencies may also be subject to suit under the federal Child Abuse Prevention and Treatment Act (2016). This Act provides federal funding and guidance to states in their efforts to prevent, investigate, and prosecute child abuse. In addition, the Act sets forth the federal definitions of child abuse and neglect and sexual abuse. Although two federal Courts of Appeal have held that the provisions of the statute fail to provide a sufficient basis upon which to claim that a social worker's actions were deficient or that a specific duty was owed to a client (*Doe v. District of Columbia*, 1996; *Tony L. By and Through Simpson v. Childer*, 1995), one federal court judge agreed with the plaintiffs' claim in that case that children have a right under the statute to sue the city for its failure to conduct an investigation promptly and to protect at-risk children (*Marisol v. Giuliani*, 1996). Publicly employed social workers and their agencies may also be subject to a lawsuit under similar state statutes for wrongful death for their failure to adequately investigate reported child abuse (*Jensen v. Anderson County Department of Social Services*, 1991).

In some situations, the agency responsible for taking the reports of abuse and neglect will report the abuse or neglect to other agencies that may also be charged with investigating the investigation. In some states, such interagency reporting is mandated by statute under specific circumstances, e.g., death or serious injury.

Research suggests that a large number of reports of suspected child maltreatment are later determined to be "unsubstantiated" (Drake, 1996; Gilbert, Kemp et al., 2009). The lack of substantiation of many reported incidents of abuse may lead some providers to believe that families are unjustly disrupted by unnecessary and fruitless investigations (Besharov, 1991, 1992). A decision by child protective services to halt further action should not, however, be taken to mean that maltreatment did not occur or that a report should not have been filed. In some situations, there may be inadequate evidence to substantiate the report, or the harm was not sufficiently severe to meet the legal standard imposed by state law. Accordingly, instances of abuse that are later unsubstantiated may be nonconfirmable, rather than being ruled out (Giovannoni, 1989, 1991; Jason, Andereck, Marks, & Tyler, 1982; Zuravin, Orme, & Hegar, 1995).

Partner Violence

Incidence and Consequences

Women in the United States are at higher risk of homicide victimization than are women in any other high-income societies (Hemenway, Shinoda-Tagawa, & Miller, 2002). In the United States, an average of 20 people suffer physical abuse at the hands of an intimate partner every minute (Black et al., 2011). Estimates indicate that during their lifetimes, 22.23% of all women experience severe physical violence by an intimate partner, 8.8% are raped by an intimate partner, and 15.8% experience other forms of sexual violence perpetrated against them by an intimate partner (Breiding et al., 2014). Among men, lifetime estimates indicate that 14.8% suffer severe physical violence by an intimate partner, while 0.8% are raped and 8.5% have other forms of sexual violence perpetrated against them by an intimate partner (Breiding et al., 2014). The prevalence of intimate partner violence appears to be high regardless of sexual orientation and may be even higher among bisexual women compared to those who self-identify as lesbian or straight/heterosexual (Shwayder, 2013).

Intimate partner violence may result in serious health consequences and a resulting need for medical attention. In the United States, one or both partners in approximately 500,000 couples sustain injuries from violence each year (Sorenson, Upchurch, & Shen, 1996). Women in the United States make almost three times as many visits to medical providers for the treatment of injuries associated with partner violence as they do for injuries related to motor vehicle accidents (National Committee for Injury Prevention and Control, 1989). Outcomes of partner violence may include damage to joints, partial loss of vision or hearing, burns, bites, hematomas, fractures, cuts or abrasions, inflammation, penetrating puncture wounds, dislocation, sprains, and death (Balakrishnan, Imell, Bandy, & Prasad, 1995; Bates, Redman, Brown, & Hancock, 1995; Beck, Freitag, & Singer 1996; Browne & Williams, 1993; Hartzell, Botek, & Goldberg, 1996). Women in abusive relationships have been found to be less likely to use condoms and more likely to experience threats of violence when they discussed condoms, resulting in an increased risk of HIV infection (Wingood & DiClemente, 1997).

Initial psychological responses to partner violence often include shock, denial, withdrawal, confusion, numbing, fear, and depression (Browne, 1987; Dutton, 1992; Hilberman, 1980; Symonds, 1979; Walker, 1979). Long-term effects may include anxiety, fear, fatigue, sleeping and eating disorders, and feelings of loss, betrayal, and/or helplessness (Walker, 1979). Post-traumatic stress disorder is one of the most common psychological consequences (Herman, 1997).

Death is the most severe consequence of intimate partner violence. Research indicates that of all adult women who are murdered, the majority are killed by an intimate or former intimate; of these, the majority were battered before their deaths (Campbell, 1992). A study of the homicides of women in New Mexico found that 46% of the deaths that were investigated were attributable to a male intimate

(Arbuckle et al., 1996). Studies conducted in New York and Chicago indicate that the leading cause of maternal mortality is trauma; the highest proportion of these traumatic deaths was attributable to homicide (Fildes, Reed, Jones, Martin, & Barrett, 1992). Additionally, intimate partner violence has been implicated in women's commission of suicide (Olson et al., 1999).

Third parties may also experience serious consequences. Several studies have suggested that low infant birthweight may be associated with physical abuse during pregnancy, although the causal pathway remains unclear (Bullock & McFarlane, 1989; Campbell et al., 1999; Parker, McFarlane, & Soeken, 1994). Children who witness the violence may themselves experience anxiety, depression, preoccupation with aggression, suicidal ideation, sleep disorders, headaches, bed-wetting, and digestive difficulties, sometimes resulting in social withdrawal and truancy (Attala, Bauza, Pratt, & Viera, 1995; Holden & Ritchie, 1991; Hughes, 1986, 1988; Humphreys, 1993).

Definitional Issues and Reporting Dilemmas

Just as with child maltreatment, definitions are often inconsistent across writers and legal jurisdictions, despite efforts to formulate and adopt uniform definitions (Breiding Basile, Smith, Black, & Mahendra, 2015). For example, although some definitions include intentionality as a critical element, others do not. Reiss and Roth (1993) define violence as "behavior by persons against persons that intentionally threatens, attempts, or actually inflicts physical harm." Similarly, Brown (1992, p. 1) defines "wife beating" as the intentional infliction of pain by man on a woman, "within a non-transient, male-female relationship, whether or not the partners are officially married." Wife beating, Brown asserts, is often culturally expected, tolerated by the recipient female partners, and not at all seen as deviant. Wife battering, in contrast, refers to extraordinary behavior that is neither usual nor acceptable within the referent society and may result in serious injury, disability, and even death.

In contrast, Kornblit (1994, p. 1181) distinguishes between abuse and violence:

The former refers to actions which are harmful for the victim, both physically as well as mentally, committed or resulting from omission, carried out intentionally or not.

Violence in a limited sense is used to refer to physical aggression.

Maltreatment includes abuse (physical, sexual, and/or emotional) and neglect (physical, educational, and/or affective).

Yet another definition is offered by Loseke (1992), who limits the term "wife abuse" to encompass only women, regardless of marital status, who can be perceived as "pure victims" of their male offenders. According to Loseke's perceptions of how wife abuse is constructed in the United States, the term does not encompass single incidents, but rather refers only to situations in which there exists a pattern of terrifying physical violence or a continuing series of terrifying abusive and degrading acts that are characterized by increasing severity and frequency and necessarily result in physical injury.

Additionally, those who suffer violence may not identify their experiences as such until they have been able to gain some distance from their experience (van der Kolk, 2014). Kelly (1990) found from her interviews with 60 women that 60% did not initially identify their own experiences as a form of violence, but 70% did so as the violence became more frequent and as their understandings of what had happened to them changed over time. Ultimately, the characterization of each individual's experience and what he or she might do in response to the situation in which they find themselves may depend upon beliefs about the nature of the incident and the underlying reasons for such experiences.

Legal Procedures for the Social Worker

In contrast to the past practice of ignoring incidents of partner violence on the part of many police departments, individuals experiencing partner violence may now file a complaint with their police and expect that it will be taken seriously. They may also bring a civil suit against the partner for injuries suffered, and may seek a protective order from a court, which would place legal limitations on the batterer's ability to contact the battered partner. (It should be noted here that, depending upon the state, a restraining order generally will not provide the same level of legal protection as a protective order. For example, violation of a prohibition contained in a restraining order may not be criminally enforceable, whereas the provisions listed in a protective order are. See Soulé and Gustafson (2013) for additional detail.) The specific nature of a criminal charge brought against the batterer by the district attorney or the specific basis of a civil suit by the battered partner depends on the law of each state. Similarly, the elements that must be demonstrated in order to obtain an order of protection from a court vary across states. The protection order may be temporary; often, a formal hearing will be required before court will order a permanent order of protection.

Despite the potential availability of such remedies, it is clear that there are systemic difficulties that limit their effectiveness. As an example, the protective order issued by a judge in one county of a state may not be available to law enforcement located in an adjacent county (see, e.g., Virginia Department of Criminal Justice Services, n.d.).

A social worker who has provided direct client services to an individual who was the victim of partner violence may be asked by the client to testify in his or her behalf at a hearing or to prepare an affidavit that sets forth details about the harm suffered by the client that are directly known by the social worker. In jurisdictions that recognize social worker-client privilege, such a request constitutes a waiver of that privilege, at least with respect to information that may be deemed relevant to the action. It is important that the social worker explain the broader implications of such a waiver to the client and that he or she also seek input on the advisability of complying with the client's request from an agency supervisor if in an agency-based practice or from colleagues. It is also possible in some circumstances that the social worker would be served with a subpoena for his or her records and/or testimony. In such instances, the social worker will want to confer with the client to understand the client's wishes with regard to the release of the information. Absent client consent to provide the material demanded in the subpoena, it would be advisable for the social worker to confer with his or her own attorney, the agency administrator, and/or the agency's legal counsel prior to responding to the subpoena (see Chap. 2 for additional discussion relating to subpoenas and social worker-client privilege).

Social workers who provide direct services to immigrant women, as well as those who have become accredited representatives within agencies recognized by the Executive Office for Immigration Review, may also be called upon by clients to assist with the preparation of documentation to support an application for a remedy that may be available under the Violence Against Women Act (2000). Details relating to such remedies are discussed in Chap. 12.

Elder Abuse and Neglect

Incidence

Elder abuse and neglect have been variously referred to as granny battering (Baker, 1975), elder mistreatment (Beachler, n.d., cited in Biggs, 1995, p. 37), the battered elder syndrome (Block and Sinnott, 1979), elder maltreatment (Douglass, Hickey, & Noél, 1980), granny bashing (Eastman & Sutton, 1982), old age abuse (Eastman, 1984), inadequate care of the elderly (Fulmer and O'Malley, 1987), granny abuse (Eastman, 1988), and miscare (Hocking, 1988). Whatever the term used, mistreatment may occur in any of the settings in which the individual receives care—in their own home with a relative or other caregiver; in an institutional setting such as a nursing home, assisted living facility, or senior residence; or in a public place (Quinn & Tomita, 1997; Uekert, Keilitz, & Sanders, 2012)—and may assume one or more of 43 different forms, ranging from abandonment, threats of institutionalization, and misuse of the individual's resources to sexual molestation and use of a weapon against the individual (Hall, 1989).

It has been estimated that 1 out of every 10 Americans over the age of 60 years has experienced some form of elder abuse (National Council on Aging, 2017), but only 1 out of every 14 cases of abuse is reported to legal authorities (Bonnie & Wallace, 2003). Close to one-half of individuals who have some form of dementia have experienced elder abuse (National Council on Aging, 2017). In 60% of cases of elder abuse, the abuser is a family member; two-thirds of the perpetrators are adult children or spouses.

Definitional Issues and Reporting Dilemmas

As of January 2015, almost every state had promulgated legislation to mandate the reporting of elder abuse by specified professionals (Felton & Polowy, 2016). As in the cases of child maltreatment and partner violence, varying definitions may create doubt as to the need or advisability of reporting (see Steinmetz, 1990), as suggested by the following definitions:

> Elder abuse is an intentional act, or failure to act, by a caregiver or another person in a relationship involving an expectation of trust that causes or creates a risk of harm to an older adult. (Centers for Disease Control and Prevention, 2017)

> [Elder mistreatment is] destructive behavior which is directed toward an older adult, occurs within the context of a relationship denoting trust, and is of sufficient intensity and/or frequency to produce harmful physical, psychological, social, and/or financial effects of unnecessary suffering, injury, pain, loss and/or violation of human rights and decreased quality of life for the older adult. (Hudson, Armachain, Beasley, & Carlson, 1998, p. 540)

> Elder abuse shall mean an act or omission which results in harm or threatened harm to the health or welfare of an elderly person. Abuse includes intentional infliction of physical or mental injury; sexual abuse; or withholding of necessary food, clothing and medical care to meet the physical and mental health needs of an elderly person by one having the care, custody, or responsibility of an elderly person. (American Medical Association, Council on Scientific Affairs, 1987, p. 966)

As can be seen from these definitions, there are divergent views regarding the requirements of intentionality, frequency, and the nature of the relationship, e.g., whether trust is a requisite element of the relationship for abuse to have occurred. The definitions also differ with respect to whether the omission of an action falls within the parameters of abuse. Table 11.2 provides additional examples of the variation in both the typology of abuse and the definitions utilized for each such category.

Some researchers have suggested that violence committed by one elderly partner against another should be considered as a separate category of abuse, arguing that some elder abuse is actually partner abuse that "has grown old" (Phillips, 1986, p. 212). Others have recognized medical abuse as a distinct form of abuse, rather than encompassing it within the broader category of neglect. When viewed separately, it has been defined as:

> withholding or improper administration of medications or necessary medical treatments for a condition, or the withholding of aids the person would medically require such as false teeth, glasses, [and] hearing aids. (American Medical Association, Council on Scientific Affairs, 1987, p. 968)

State laws differ with respect to not only how they define elder abuse and neglect but also with respect to the individuals encompassed by the provisions. Depending upon the state, individuals may be deemed to be elderly and encompassed within the statute at the age of 60 or 65. The criteria enunciated by the Centers for Disease Control and Prevention and set forth in Table 11.2 above apply only to adults

Table 11.2 Categories and definitions of elder abuse and neglect

Source	Category	Definition
Centers for Disease Control and Prevention (2017)	Physical abuse	The intentional use of physical force that results in acute or chronic illness, bodily injury, physical pain, functional impairment, distress, or death. Physical abuse may include, but is not limited to, violent acts such as striking (with or without an object or weapon), hitting, beating, scratching, biting, choking, suffocation, pushing, shoving, shaking, slapping, kicking, stomping, pinching, and burning
	Sexual abuse or abusive sexual contact	Forced or unwanted sexual interaction (touching and non-touching acts) of any kind with an older adult. This may include but is not limited to forced or unwanted completed or attempted contact between the penis and the vulva or the penis and the anus involving penetration, however slight. It might also include forced or unwanted contact between the mouth and the penis, vulva, or anus; forced or unwanted penetration of the anal or genital opening of another person by a hand, finger, or other object; or forced or unwanted intentional touching, either directly or through the clothing, of the genitalia, anus, groin, breast, inner thigh, or buttocks. These acts also qualify as sexual abuse if they are committed against an incapacitated person who is not competent to give informed approval
	Emotional or psychological abuse	Verbal or nonverbal behavior that results in the infliction of anguish, mental pain, fear, or distress. Examples of tactics that may exemplify emotional or psychological abuse of an older adult include behaviors intended to humiliate (e.g., calling names or insults), threaten (e.g., expressing an intent to initiate nursing home placement), isolate (e.g., seclusion from family or friends), or control (e.g., prohibiting or limiting access to transportation, telephone, money, or other resources)
	Neglect	Failure by a caregiver or other responsible person to protect an elder from harm or the failure to meet needs for essential medical care, nutrition, hydration, hygiene, clothing, basic activities of daily living, or shelter, which results in a serious risk of compromised health and safety. Examples include not providing adequate nutrition, hygiene, clothing, shelter, or access to necessary health care or failure to prevent exposure to unsafe activities and environments
	Financial abuse or exploitation	The illegal, unauthorized, or improper use of an older individual's resources by a caregiver or other person in a trusting relationship, for the benefit of someone other than the older individual. This includes, but is not limited to, depriving an older person of rightful access to information about, or use of, personal benefits, resources, belongings, or assets. Examples include forgery, misuse or theft of money or possessions, use of coercion or deception to surrender finances or property, or improper use of guardianship or power of attorney

National Council on Aging (2017)	Physical abuse	Inflicting physical pain or injury upon an older adult
	Sexual abuse	Touching, fondling, intercourse, or any other sexual activities with an older adult, when the older adult is unable to understand, unwilling to consent, threatened, or physically forced
	Emotional abuse	Verbal assaults, threats of abuse, harassment, or intimidation
	Confinement	Restraining or isolating an older adult, other than for medical reasons
	Passive neglect	A caregiver's failure to provide an older adult with life's necessities, including, but not limited to, food, clothing, shelter, or medical care
	Willful deprivation	Denying an older adult medication, medical care, shelter, food, a therapeutic device, or other physical assistance and exposing that person to the risk of physical, mental, or emotional harm—Except when the older, competent adult has expressed a desire to go without such care
	Financial exploitation	The misuse or withholding of an older adult's resources by another
American Health Care Association (2001), Levine (2003) (definitions for nursing homes)	Abuse	Willful infliction of injury, unreasonable confinement, intimidation, or punishment with resulting physical harm, pain, or mental anguish
	Verbal abuse	The use of oral, written, or gestured language that willfully includes disparaging and derogatory terms to residents or their families, or within their hearing distance, regardless of their age, ability to comprehend, or disability
	Sexual abuse	Includes but is not limited to sexual harassment, sexual coercion, or sexual assault
	Physical abuse	Includes hitting, slapping, pinching, kicking, and controlling behavior through corporal punishment
	Mental abuse	Includes but is not limited to humiliation, harassment, threats of punishment, or deprivation
	Involuntary seclusion	Separation of a resident from other residents or from his or her room, or confinement to his or her room, with or without roommates, against his or her will or the will of the resident's legal representative
Pillemer and Finkelhor (1989, p. 53)	Physical abuse	At least one act of physical violence
	Psychological abuse	[repeated insults and threats] termed "chronic verbal aggression." this form of maltreatment was defined as the elderly person being insulted, sworn at, or threatened
	Neglect	The deprivation of some assistance that the elderly person needed for important activities of daily living, etc. the ten activities of daily Living included meal preparation, housework, and shopping, as well as personal care activities such as dressing and toileting

60 years of age and older. Some states protect only residents of that state, while others provide protection for any otherwise qualifying individual who is located within its jurisdiction. The complexity of the criteria under state statutory provisions for coverage within its protections may potentially add an additional dimension to filing a report.

Over one-half of states mandate the reporting of "self-neglect" by mandated reporters. Self-neglect is one of the most frequent grounds for referral to an ombudsman and protective services (Shiferaw et al., 1994; Lachs, Williams, O'Brien, Hurst, & Horwitz, 1996). However, this category of mistreatment is also one of the most controversial. It has been asserted that mandatory reporting of elder abuse and neglect has been inappropriately modeled after child abuse reporting laws that are premised on the concept of *parens patriae*. This concept refers to the power of the state to act as guardian for those unable to speak for themselves (Faulkner, 1982). In the case of elder self-neglect, a behavior that might be viewed as merely eccentric in a younger person could be perceived as self-neglect merely because of the individual's age (Loue, 2001).

In some such situations, a social worker is potentially confronted with an ethical dilemma. Reporting even suspected self-neglect is consonant with the state's legal mandate, but the reporting may violate the core principle of client self-determination: "Social workers promote clients' socially responsible self-determination. Social workers seek to enhance clients' capacity and opportunity to change and to address their own needs" (National Association for Social Workers, 2008). Consider, as an example, the definition of neglect of an elderly person provided by Texas law:

> the failure to provide for oneself the goods or services, including medical services, which are necessary to avoid physical or emotional harm or pain or the failure of a caretaker to provide such goods or services. (Texas Human Resources Code § 48.002(a)(4), 2015)

The statute as written gives no consideration to external factors that may be beyond the control of the individual, such as income level, availability of appropriate medical providers, or neighborhood characteristics. Rather, the social worker must use his or her best judgment to consider whether a particular situation rises to the level of reportable self-neglect while also bearing in mind the client's need to maintain autonomy to the extent possible and the ethical principles governing the practice of social work. This legislative provision contrasts sharply with the provisions of various other states, which explicitly recognize that what appears to be neglect or self-neglect may, in fact, have resulted from external factors that are beyond the control of either the individual or his or her caregiver (see, e.g., Pennsylvania Older Adults Protective Services Act, 35 P.S. Health and Safety § 10225.103, 2002).

Reporting Procedures

Depending upon the particular state, a mandated reporter is required to report suspected abuse or neglect to the agency dedicated to Adult Protective Services, a state department of health, law enforcement, and/or a state's Medicaid agency. Failure of a mandated reporter to file a report can result in substantial penalties. As an example, under the Elder Justice Act (2010), a mandated reporter who works in or with a long-term care facility who fails to report a reasonable suspicion of a crime committed against an elderly person faces a maximum civil penalty of $200,000 for their failure to report. That penalty increases to $300,000 if their failure to report a reasonable suspicion exacerbates the harm to the elderly resident or another person.

The report of suspected abuse generally must include the following elements:

- The names and the relationship of the individual and the person who is reporting the abuse
- The age and physical and mental condition of the person who is being abused or neglected
- The specific observations and concerns of the reporter, including the dates of the events involved and timeline, if possible
- Any concerns of immediate harm to the elderly client
- A summary of the client's assets that may be exploited
- The client's location and the best means of contacting them
- Other potential witnesses and their contact information
- Copies of any relevant documents (Thomson Reuter, 2017)

Other Roles for Social Workers in the Context of Abuse and Neglect

In the event that a district attorney chooses to pursue criminal charges against a person or persons for the abuse or neglect of a child or an elder individual, a social worker employed with an adult or child protective services agency may be called upon as a witness, depending upon the nature of the abuse or neglect that is alleged. In the case of physical abuse, financial abuse, or neglect, the social worker-adult protective services worker may be able to provide information regarding any prior allegations against the accused and the mental and physical state of the abused/neglected client. As an example, a social worker who has been providing counseling or therapy to the elderly person may be able to provide information about the impact of a physical assault on his or her elderly client, the interaction between the client and the alleged perpetrator, and the client's statements about the incident and its impact (Uekert et al., 2012).

In some situations, the ability of an elderly client to manage his or her financial affairs, to handle the affairs of daily living, or to care for themselves may be in doubt. Social workers providing direct client services may be involved in evaluating the capacity of the individual to handle financial or other matters. (Capacity is to be distinguished from competence, which is a judicial determination relating to whether and to what extent an individual has or lacks capacity with respect to specified functions.) In such circumstances, the social worker may be asked to provide information in the context of court proceedings related to the potential appointment of a guardian or conservator—which of these depends on state law—to manage the individual's financial affairs or to serve as a substitute decisionmaker for such issues as place of residence and medical care. The court may limit the powers of the guardian or conservator to only specified matters in order to preserve the autonomy of the client to the greatest extent possible. These circumstances may give rise to an ethical dilemma for the social worker, who by virtue of his or her professional ethics will want to both maximize the client's autonomy and empowerment but will also be cognizant of the need to safeguard the client's welfare.

In the examples provided above, the social worker is acting as a fact witness, in that he or she is testifying about factual information of which he or she has knowledge. In some circumstances, however, the social worker may be called upon to serve as an expert witness, e.g., to provide testimony about the traumatic effects of assaults generally or, in cases involving sexual abuse, about rape trauma syndrome. In order to be qualified as an expert, the social worker must meet the legal requirements set forth within the specific jurisdiction. The criteria for expert witnesses and the admissibility of testimony are detailed in Chap. 6.

It is critical that prior to responding to requests for additional information beyond the initial report to the appropriate agency, assuming that such further responses are not legally mandated by statute, the social worker consider his or her ethical and legal responsibility to maintain client confidences. In states that recognize a social worker-client privilege, the information that is being sought may also fall within that privilege. Although privilege is discussed more fully in Chap. 6, it is worth reiterating here that:

- The client, not the social worker, holds the privilege.
- In the absence of a subpoena signed by a judge that mandates the disclosure of the requested information, the client must provide consent to disclose the requested information or waive the privilege.
- The social worker should consult with an attorney prior to releasing information, even if a judge has issued a subpoena, in order to better understand the legal implications of (not) releasing the information and, in the event that the client opposes its disclosure, to seek ways in which the information sought can be limited.
- Privilege does not apply if the client provides information in the context of the legal proceeding that would otherwise be considered privileged.
- Privilege does not apply to information obtained outside the scope of the social worker-client relationship, e.g., the social worker sees the client's caregiver

berating and punching the client at the grocery store while the social worker is buying his or her own groceries.
- The laws of some states specifically provide that privilege does not exist in situations involving child and/or elder maltreatment.

Many states' laws provide that anyone may serve as a guardian or conservator with the approval of the court. In these jurisdictions, it is possible that a social worker who is not involved in the provision of direct services to a specific client may serve as a guardian after complying with all state qualifying procedures and receiving the approval of the court hearing such matters. The Uniform Guardianship and Protective Proceedings Act, followed in some states, provides a listing of persons who may be designated to serve as guardian, in order of priority: anyone acting for the benefit of the individual, anyone nominated by the individual while competent to serve in that capacity, spouse, adult child, parent, or friend/relative with whom the individual resided for at least 6 months prior to the filing of the guardianship petition (National Conference of Commissioners on Uniform State Laws, 2017).

Title VII of the Older Americans Act of 1965, reauthorized in 2016 (Older Americans Act Reauthorization Act, 2016), provides funding to states that may be used for various enumerated functions, including the establishment of an ombudsman program and the delivery of outreach services. The ombudsman program is charged with the responsibility of protecting residents of nursing homes and other long-term care facilities by identifying, investigating, and resolving complaints that are filed by or on behalf of residents in those facilities. The complaints must relate to inaction, action, or decisions that negatively impact the health, safety, welfare, or rights of a facility's residents. A social worker employed as the state ombudsperson will be involved in representing the rights of residents in long-term care facilities, educating the public about issues related to long-term care services, and advocating for policy and legislative changes that will benefit the health, safety, and welfare of long-term care residents.

References

American Health Care Association. (2001). *The long-term care survey.* Washington, DC: Author. Cited in J.M. Levine. (2003). Elder abuse and neglect: A primer for primary care physicians. *Geriatrics, 58*(10), 37–44.

American Medical Association, Council on Scientific Affairs. (1987). Elder abuse and neglect. *Journal of the American Medical Association, 257*, 966–971.

Arbuckle, J., Olson, L., Howard, M., Brillman, J., Anctil, C., & Sklar, D. (1996). Safe at home? Domestic violence and other homicides among women in New Mexico. *Annals of Emergency Medicine, 27*, 210–215.

Ashton, V. (1999). Worker judgments of seriousness about and reporting of child maltreatment. *Child Abuse & Neglect, 23*(6), 539–548.

Ashton, V. (2001). The relationship between attitudes toward corporal punishment and the perception and reporting of child maltreatment. *Child Abuse & Neglect, 25*, 389–399.

Asser, S., & Swan, R. (1998). Child fatalities from religion-motivated medical neglect. *Pediatrics, 101,* 625–629.

Attala, J. M., Bauza, K., Pratt, H., & Viera, D. (1995). Integrative review of effects on children of witnessing domestic violence. *Issues in Comprehensive Pediatric Nursing, 18,* 163–175.

Baker, A. A. (1975). Granny battering. *Modern Geriatrics, 8,* 20–24.

Balakrishnan, C., Imell, L. L., Bandy, A. T., & Prasad, J. K. (1995). Perineal burns in males secondary to spouse abuse. *Burns, 21,* 34–35.

Bates, L., Redman, S., Brown, W., & Hancock, L. (1995). Domestic violence experienced by women attending an accident and emergency department. *Australian Journal of Public Health, 19,* 292–299.

Beachler, M. A. (n.d.). *Mistreatment of elderly persons in the domestic setting,* Unpublished manuscript. Cited in Biggs, S., Phillipson, C., & Kingston, P. (1995). *Elder abuse in perspective.* Buckingham, UK: Open University Press.

Beck, S. R., Freitag, S. K., & Singer, N. (1996). Ocular injuries in battered women. *Ophthalmology, 103,* 148–151.

Besharov, D. (1991). Child abuse and neglect reporting and investigations: Policy guidelines for decision making. *Children and Youth Services, 15*(2), 35–49.

Besharov, D. (1992). A balanced approach to reporting child abuse. *Child, Youth, and Family Services Quarterly, 15*(1), 1–2.

Black, M. C., Basile, K. C., Breiding, M. J., Smith, S. G., Walters, M. L., Merrick, M. T., … Stevens, M. (2011). *The national intimate partner and sexual violence survey: 2010 summary report.* http://www.cdc.gov/violenceprevention/pdf/nisvs_report2010-a.pdf. Accessed 26 Feb 2016.

Block, M., & Sinnott, J. D. (1979). *The battered elder syndrome.* Baltimore: University of Maryland, Center on Aging.

Bonnie, R. J., & Wallace, R. B. (Eds.). (2003). *Elder mistreatment: Abuse, neglect, and exploitation in aging America.* Washington, DC: National Academies Press.

Breiding, M. J., Basile, K. C., Smith, S. G., Black, M. C., & Mahendra, R. (2015). *Intimate partner surveillance uniform definitions and recommended data elements, version 2.0.* Atlanta, GA: Center for Disease Control and Prevention. http://www.cdc.gov/violenceprevention/pdf/intimatepartnerviolence.pdf. Accessed 22 Feb 2016.

Breiding, M. J., Smith, S. G., Basile, K. C., Walters, M. L., Chen, J., & Merrick, M. Y. (2014). Prevalence and characteristics of sexual violence, stalking, and intimate partner violence victimization—National Intimate Partner and sexual violence survey, United States, 2011. *Morbidity and Mortality Weekly Report, 63*(8), 1–108. http://www.cdc.gov/mmwr/pdf/ss/ss6308.pdf. Accessed 22 Feb 2016.

Brown, J. K. (1992). Introduction: Definitions, assumptions, themes, and issues. In D. A. Counts, J. K. Brown, & J. C. Campbell (Eds.), *Sanctions and sanctuary: Cultural perspectives on the beating of wives* (pp. 1–18). Boulder, CO: Westview Press.

Browne, A., & Williams, K. R. (1993). Gender, intimacy, and lethal violence: Trends from 1976 through 1987. *Gender & Society, 7,* 78–98.

Bullock, L. F., & McFarlane, J. (1989). The birthweight/battering connection. *American Journal of Nursing, 89,* 1153–1155.

Campbell, J. C. (1992). "If I can't have you, no one can." power and control in homicide of female partners. In J. Radford & D. Russell (Eds.), *Femicide: The politics of woman killing* (pp. 99–113). Boston: Twain.

Campbell, J. C., Torres, S., Ryan, J., King, C., Campbell, D. W., Stallings, R. Y., & Fuchs, S. C. (1999). Physical and nonphysical partner abuse and other risk factors for low birthweight among full term and preterm babies: A multiethnic case-control study. *American Journal of Epidemiology, 150,* 714–726.

Centers for Disease Control and Prevention. (2017). *Elder abuse: Definitions.* https://www.cdc.gov/violenceprevention/elderabuse/definitions.html. Accessed 01 Sept 2017.

Child Welfare Information Gateway. (2012). *Parental drug use as child abuse*. Washington, DC: Author. https://www.childwelfare.gov/pubPDFs/drugexposed.pdf. Accessed 25 Dec 2015.

Child Welfare Information Gateway. (2015). *Penalties for failure to report and false reporting of child abuse and neglect*. https://www.childwelfare.gov/topics/systemwide/laws-policies/statutes/report/. Accessed 31 Aug 2017.

Child Welfare Information Gateway. (2016). *Mandatory reporters of child abuse and neglect*. Washington, DC: United States Department of Health and Human Services Administration, Children's Bureau. https://www.childwelfare.gov/pubPDFs/manda.pdf#page=3&view=Standards for making a report. Accessed 31 Aug 2017.

Deisz, R., Doueck, H. J., George, N., & Levine, M. (1996). Reasonable cause: A qualitative study of mandated reporting. *Child Abuse & Neglect, 20*(4), 275–287.

DeLey, W. W. (1988). Physical punishment of children in Sweden and the United States. *Journal of Comparative Family Studies, 19*, 410–431.

Douglass, R. L., Hickey, T., & Noël, C. (1980). *A study of maltreatment of the elderly and other vulnerable adults*. Ann Arbor: University of Michigan, Institute on Aging.

Drake, B. (1996). Unraveling "unsubstantiated". *Child Maltreatment, 1*(3), 261–271.

Dutton, M. A. (1992). *Empowering and healing the battered women: A model for assessment and intervention*. New York: Springer.

Eastman, M. (1984). *Old age abuse*. Mitcham, England: Age Concern England.

Eastman, M. (1988). Granny abuse. *Community Outlook, Oct*., 15.

Eastman, M., & Sutton, M. (1982). Granny battering. *Geriatric Medicine, 12*, 11–15.

Faulkner, L. A. (1982). Mandating the reporting of suspected cases of elder abuse: An inappropriate, ineffective and ageist response to the abuse of older adults. *Family Law Quarterly, 16*(1), 69–91.

Felton, E.M., & Polowy, C.I. (2016). Social workers and elder abuse. *National Association of Social Workers California News*. http://naswcanews.org/social-workers-and-elder-abuse/. Accessed 1 Sep 2017.

Fildes, J., Reed, L., Jones, N., Martin, M., & Barrett, J. (1992). Trauma: The leading cause of maternal death. *Journal of Trauma, 32*, 643–645.

Ford, J. D. (2002). Traumatic victimization in childhood and persistent problems with oppositional defiance. *Journal of Aggression, Maltreatment and Trauma, 6*, 25–58.

Friedrich, W. N., Fisher, J. L., Dittner, C. A., Acton, R., Berliner, L., Butler, J., …, Wright, J. (2001). Child sexual behavior inventory: Normative, psychiatric, and sexual abuse comparisons. *Child Maltreatment, 6*, 37–49.

Fulmer, T., & O'Malley, T. (1987). *Inadequate care of the elderly: A health care perspective on abuse and neglect*. New York: Springer.

Gilbert, R., Kemp, A., Thoburn, J., Sidebotham, P., Radford, L., Glaser, D., & MacMillan, H. L. (2009). Recognising and responding to child maltreatment. *Lancet, 373*, 167–180.

Gilbert, R., Widom, C. S., Browne, K., Fergusson, D., Webb, E., & Janson, S. (2009). Burden and consequences of child maltreatment in high-income countries. *Lancet, 373*, 68–81.

Giovannoni, J. (1989). Substantiated and unsubstantiated reports of child maltreatment. *Child and Youth Services Review, 11*, 299–318.

Giovannoni, J. (1991). Unsubstantiated reports: Perspectives of child protection workers. *Child and Youth Services, 15*(2), 51–62.

Giovannoni, J. M., & Becerra, R. M. (1979). *Defining child abuse*. New York: Free Press.

Hall, P. A. (1989). Elder maltreatment items: Subgroups and types: Policy and practical implications. *International Journal of Aging and Human Development, 28*(3), 191–205.

Hartzell, K. N., Botek, A. A., & Goldberg, S. H. (1996). Orbital fractures in women due to sexual assault and domestic violence. *Ophthalmology, 103*, 953–957.

Hemenway, D., Shinoda-Tagawa, T., & Miller, M. (2002). Firearm availability and female homicide rates among 25 populous high-income countries. *Journal of the American Medical Women's Association, 57*, 100–104.

Herman, J. L. (1997). *Trauma and recovery: The aftermath of violence: From domestic abuse to political terror.* New York: Basic Books.

Hickey, K. S., & Lyckholm, L. (2004). Child welfare versus parental autonomy: Medical ethics, the law, and faith-based healing. *Theoretical Medicine, 25,* 265–276.

Hilberman, E. (1980). Overview: The "wife-beater's wife" reconsidered. *American Journal of Psychiatry, 2,* 460–470.

Hocking, D. (1988). Miscare—A form of abuse in the elderly. *Hospital Update, May, 15,* 2411–2419.

Holden, G. W., & Ritchie, K. L. (1991). Linking extreme marital discord, child rearing, and child behavior problems: Evidence from battered women. *Child Development, 62,* 311–327.

Hudson, M. F., Armachain, W. D., Beasley, C. M., & Carlson, J. R. (1998). Elder abuse: Two native American views. *The Gerontologist, 38*(5), 538–548.

Hughes, H. M. (1986). Research with children in shelters: Implications for clinical services. *Children Today, 15,* 21–25.

Hughes, H. M. (1988). Psychological and behavioral correlates of family violence in child witnesses and victims. *American Journal of Orthopsychiatry, 58,* 77–90.

Hughes, R. A. (2005). The death of children by faith-based medical neglect. *Journal of Law and Religion, 20,* 247–265.

Humphreys, J. (1993). Children of battered women. In J. C. Campbell & J. Humphreys (Eds.), *Nursing care of survivors of family violence.* St. Louis: Mosby.

Jason, J., Andereck, N., Marks, J., & Tyler, C. (1982). Child abuse in Georgia: A method to evaluate risk factors and reporting bias. *American Journal of Public Health, 72*(12), 1353–1358.

Jenny, C., & Committee on Child Abuse and Neglect. (2007). Recognizing and responding to medical neglect. *Pediatrics, 120*(6), 1385–1389.

Johnson, J. G., Cohen, P., Gould, M. S., Kasen, S., Brown, J., & Brook, J. S. (2002). Childhood adversities, interpersonal difficulties, and risk for suicide attempts during late adolescence and early childhood. *Archives of General Psychiatry, 59,* 741–749.

Kelly, L. (1990). How women define their experiences of violence. In K. Yllo & M. Bograd (Eds.), *Feminist perspectives on wife abuse* (pp. 114–132). Newbury Park, CA: Sage.

King, G., Reece, R., Bendel, R., & Patel, V. (1998). The effects of sociodemographic variables, training, and attitudes on the lifetime reporting practices of mandated reporters. *Child Maltreatment, 3*(3), 276–283.

Korbin, J. E., & Spilsbury, J. C. (1999). Cultural competence and child neglect. In H. Dubowitz (Ed.), *Neglected children: Research, practice and policy* (pp. 69–88). Thousand Oaks, CA: Sage Publications, Inc.

Kornblit, A. L. (1994). Domestic violence—An emerging health issue. *Social Science & Medicine, 39,* 1181–1888.

Lachs, M. S., Williams, C., O'Brien, S., Hurst, L., & Horwitz, R. (1996). Older adults: An 11-year longitudinal study of adult protective service use. *Archives of Internal Medicine, 156,* 449–453.

Leeb, R. T., Paulozzi, L. J., Melanson, C., Simon, T. R., & Arias, I. (2008). *Child maltreatment surveillance: Uniform definitions for public health and recommended data elements.* Atlanta, GA: Centers for Disease Control and Prevention.

Levine, J. M. (2003). Elder abuse and neglect: A primer for primary care physicians. *Geriatrics, 58*(10), 37–44.

Loseke, D. R. (1992). *The battered woman and shelters: The social construction of wife abuse.* Albany, NY: State University of New York Press.

Loue, S. (2001). Elder abuse and neglect in medicine and law: The need for reform. *Journal of Legal Medicine, 22,* 159–209.

Manly, J. T. (2005). Advances in research definitions of child maltreatment. *Child Abuse & Neglect, 29,* 425–439.

Melton, G. B. (2005). Mandated reporting: A policy without reason. *Child Abuse & Neglect, 29,* 9–18.

References

National Association for Social Workers. (2008). *Code of ethics*. https://www.socialworkers.org/pubs/code/code.asp. Accessed 11 Feb 2016.
National Committee for Injury Prevention and Control. (1989). *Injury prevention: Meeting the challenge*. New York: Oxford University Press.
National Conference of Commissioners on Uniform State Laws. (2017). *Uniform Guardianship, Conservatorship, and Other Protective Arrangements Act*. http://www.uniformlaws.org/shared/docs/Guardianship%20and%20Protective%20Proceedings/2017mar_UGCOPPAA_Mtg%20draft_Clean_2.pdf. Accessed 7 Sept 2017.
National Council on Aging. (2017). *What is elder abuse?* http://ncoa.org. Accessed 2 Sept 2017.
National Council on Child Abuse & Family Violence. (2015). *Child abuse information*. http://www.nccafv.org/child-abuse. Accessed 01 May 2015.
National Research Council. (1993). *Understanding child abuse and neglect*. Washington, DC: National Academy Press.
National Research Council. (2002). *Confronting chronic neglect: The education and training of health professionals on family violence*. Washington, DC: National Academy Press.
Olson, L., Huylar, F., Lynch, A. W., Fullerton, L., Werenko, P., Sklar, D., & Zumwalt, R. (1999). Guns, alcohol, and intimate partner violence: The epidemiology of female suicide in New Mexico. *Crisis, 20*, 121–126.
Pagelow, M. D., & Johnson, P. (1988). Abuse in the American family: The role of religion. In A. L. Horton & J. A. Williamson (Eds.), *Abuse and religion: When praying isn't enough* (pp. 2–11). Lexington, MA: Lexington Books.
Parker, B., McFarlane, J., & Soeken, K. (1994). Abuse during pregnancy: Effects of maternal complications and birthweight in adult and teenage women. *Obstetrics & Gynecology, 84*, 323–328.
Phillips, L. R. (1986). Theoretical explanations of elder abuse: Competing hypotheses and unresolved issues. In K. A. Pillemer & R. S. Wolf (Eds.), *Elder abuse: Conflict in the family* (pp. 197–217). Dover, MA: Auburn House.
Pillemer, K., & Finkelhor, D. (1989). Causes of elder abuse: Caregiver stress versus problem relatives. *American Journal of Orthopsychiatry, 59*(2), 179–187.
Portwood, S. G. (1999). Coming to terms with a consensual definition of child maltreatment. *Child Maltreatment, 4*(1), 56–68.
Quinn, M. J., & Tomita, S. K. (1997). *Elder abuse and neglect: Causes, diagnosis, and intervention strategies* (2nd ed.). New York: Springer.
Reiss, A. J., Jr., & Roth, J. A. (Eds.). (1993). *Understanding and preventing violence*. Washington, DC: National Academy Press.
Sedlak, A. J., Mettenburg, J., Bassena, M., Petta, I., McPherson, K., Greene, A., & Li, S. (2010). *Fourth national incidence study of child abuse and neglect (NIS-4): Report to congress*. Washington, DC: United States Department of Health and Human Services, Administration for Children and Families.
Shiferaw, B., Mittelmark, M. B., Wofford, J. L., Anderson, R. T., Walls, P., & Rohrer, B. (1994). The investigation and outcome of reported cases of elder abuse: The Forsyth County aging study. *Gerontologist, 34*, 123–125.
Shwayder, M. (2013, November 5). A same-sex domestic violence epidemic is silent. *The Atlantic*. http://www.theatlantic.com/health/archive/2013/11/a-same-sex-domestic-violence-epidemic-is-silent/281131. Accessed 23 Feb 2016.
Sorenson, S. B., Upchurch, D. M., & Shen, H. (1996). Violence and injury in marital arguments: Risk patterns and gender differences. *American Journal of Public Health, 86*, 35–40.
Soulé, K., & Gustafson, C. (2013). Myths about protective orders. *The Prosecutor, 43*(6.) https://www.tdcaa.com/journal/myths-about-protective-orders. Accessed 10 Sept 2017.
Steinmetz, S. K. (1990). Elder abuse: Myth and reality? In T. H. Brubaker (Ed.), *Family relationships in later life* (pp. 193–211). New York: Springer.
Straus, M. A., & Mathur, A. K. (1996). Social change and the trends in approval of corporal punishment by parents from 1968 to 1994. In D. Frehsee, W. Horn, & K. D. Bussmann (Eds.),

Family violence against children: A challenge for society (pp. 91–105). New York: Walter de Gruyter.

Symonds, A. (1979). Violence against women. The myth of masochism. *American Journal of Psychotherapy, 33*, 161–173.

Thomson Reuters. (2017). Reporting elder abuse. *FindLaw*. http://elder.findlaw.com/elder-abuse/reporting-elder-abuse.html. Accessed 4 Sept 2017.

Uekert, B. K., Keilitz, S., & Sanders, D. (2012). *Prosecuting elder abuse cases: Basic tools and strategies*. Williamsburg, VA: National Center for State Courts. https://wwwazab@bgu.ac.il.bja.gov/Publications/NCSC-Prosecuting-Elder-Abuse-Cases-Basic-Tools-and-Strategies.pdf. Accessed 2 Sept 2017.

United States Department of Health and Human Services, Administration for Children and families, Administration on Children, Youth and Families, Children's Bureau. (2012). *Child maltreatment 2012*. Washington, DC: Government Printing Office. http://www.acf.hhs.gov/sites/default/files/cb/cm2012.pdf. Accessed 25 Dec 2015.

van der Kolk, B. A. (2014). *The body keeps the score: Brain, mind, and body in the healing of trauma*. New York: Penguin Books.

Virginia Department of Criminal Justice Services. (n.d.). *General order 2–32, domestic violence*. https://www.dcjs.virginia.gov/sites/dcjs.virginia.gov/files/law-enforcement/files/model-policy/domestic_violence.docx. Accessed 10 Sept 2017.

Walker, L. E. (1979). *The battered woman*. New York: Harper and Row.

Wauchope, B. A., & Straus, M. A. (1995). Physical punishment and physical abuse of American children: Incidence rates by age, gender, and occupational class. In M. A. Straus & R. J. Gelles (Eds.), *Physical violence in American families* (pp. 133–143). New Brunswick, NJ: Transaction Publishers.

Whitney, S. D., Tajima, E. A., Herrenkohl, T. I., & Huang, B. (2006). Defining child abuse: Exploring variations in ratings of discipline severity among child welfare practitioners. *Child and Adolescent Social Work Journal, 23*(3), 316–342.

Wingood, G. M., & DiClemente, R. J. (1997). The effects of an abusive primary sexual partner on the condom use and sexual negotiation practices of African-American women. *American Journal of Public Health, 87*, 1016–1018.

Zellman, G. L. (1990). Child abuse reporting and failure to report among mandated reporters. *Journal of Interpersonal Violence, 5*(1), 3–22.

Zellman, G. L. (1992). The impact of case characteristics on child abuse reporting decisions. *Child Abuse & Neglect, 16*, 57–74.

Zuravin, S., Orme, J., & Hegard, R. (1995). Disposition of child physical abuse reports: Review of the literature and test of a predictive model. *Children and Youth Services Review, 17*(4), 547–566.

Legal References

Cases

DeShaney v. Winnebago County Department of Social Services, 489 U.S. 189 (1989).

Doe v. District of Columbia, 93 F.3d 861 (D.C. Cir. 1996).

Jensen v Anderson County Department of Social Services, 403 S.E.2d 615 (S. Ct. SC 1991).

Marisol v. Giuliani, 929 F. Supp. 662 (S.D.N.Y. 1996), *cert. denied*, 520 U.S. 1211 (1997), *affirmed*, 126 F.3d 372 (1997).

People v. Cavaiani, 432 N.W.2d 409 (Mich. Ct. App. 1988).

State v. Grover, 437 N.W.2d 60 (Minn. 1989).
State v. Brown, 140 S.W.3d 51 (Mo. 2004).
State v. Hurd, 400 N.W.2d 42 (Wis. App. Ct. 1986).
Tony L. By and Through Simpson v. Childer, 71 F.3d 1182 (6th Cir. 1995).

Statutes

Alvarez, K.M., Kenny, M.C., Donahue, B., & Carpin, K.M. (2004). Why are professionals failing to initiate mandated reports of child maltreatment and are there any empirically based training programs to assist professionals in the reporting process? *Aggression and Violent Behavior,* 9(5), 563–578.
Browne, A. (1987). When battered women kill. New York: Free Press.
Child Abuse and Prevention and Treatment Act, P.L. 93–247 (1974), as amended by the Justice for Victims of Trafficking Act, P.L. 114–22 (2015), and the Comprehensive Addiction and Recovery Act, P.L. 114–198 (2016), currently found at 42 U.S.C. chap. 67.
Elder Justice Act. Patient Protection and Affordable Care Act ("Health Care Reform"), Pub. L. No. 111–148, 124 Stat. 119 (Mar. 23, 2010).
Ohio Revised Code § 2151.03(B) (2006).
Older Americans Act, Pub. L. 89–73, 79 Stat. 218 (1965).
Older Americans Reauthorization Act, Pub. L. 114–144 (April 19, 2016).
Pennsylvania Older Adults Protective Services Act, 35 P.S. Health and Safety § 10225.103 (2002).
Texas Human Resources Code § 48.002(a)(4) (2015).

Chapter 12
Legal Issues Working with Immigrants, Refugees, and Asylees

Immigrants in the USA

The United States Census Bureau classifies all individuals who are not US citizens at birth as "foreign born." This includes individuals who are legal permanent residents ("green card holders"), individuals who acquired US citizenship through naturalization, temporary migrants, humanitarian migrants, and unauthorized migrants (United States Census Bureau, n.d.). As of 2015, foreign-born persons in the USA accounted for approximately 13.5 percent of the country's population, with the majority of foreign-born individuals arriving from Latin America and the Caribbean (Zong & Batalova, 2017). (It is important to remember here that individuals born in Puerto Rico are US citizens by birth.) States with the largest foreign-born proportions of their populations include California, Florida, Massachusetts, Nevada, New Jersey, New York, and Texas (United States Census Bureau, n.d.).

Data indicate that almost one-half of foreign-born individuals had become naturalized citizens (Zong & Batalova, 2017). Forty-four percent of the more than one million new permanent residents in 2015 received their permanent resident status as immediate relatives (spouses or children under the age of 18) of US citizens. An additional 20 percent entered on the basis of a family-sponsored preference, e.g., unmarried sibling over the age of 21 of a US citizen, and an additional 14 percent obtained their status on the basis of their employment. Fourteen percent became permanent residents after having gained admission as refugees or asylees, and just 5 percent won the diversity lottery (Zong & Batalova, 2017).

More than two-thirds of foreign-born individuals are actively participating in the labor force (United States Census Bureau, n.d.). In 2015, approximately 6% of the foreign-born population was under the age of 18, and an additional 15% were 65 years of age or older (Zong & Batalova, 2017). In 2015, almost one-half of all immigrants 5 years of age and older had limited English proficiency (Zong & Batalova, 2017).

Despite what is often a popular belief, the number of undocumented/unauthorized immigrants in the USA has declined from previous years (Krogstad, Passel, & Cohn, 2017). Additionally, the majority of unauthorized immigrants are not now from Mexico, but are from Asia and Central America. The states of California, Florida, Illinois, New Jersey, New York, and Texas are home to 59 percent of unauthorized immigrants. It has been estimated that at least two-thirds of all unauthorized immigrants have lived in the USA for a decade or longer. Contrary to the view of unauthorized immigrants as criminals, data suggest that less than 3 percent of unauthorized immigrants have committed a felony, compared with 6 percent in the overall US population (Yee, Davis, & Patel, 2017).

Immigration Law: The Basics

US immigration law divides the world into citizens and "aliens," that is, individuals who are not US citizens. "Aliens" are further classified according to their intended length of stay in the USA and their intended role when here.

Nonimmigrants

Those who are entering temporarily for a temporary purpose are classified as nonimmigrants. This category of persons includes students, tourists, entertainers, business persons, crewmen, and temporary workers. Immigrants are those who apply to enter the USA with the intent to remain indefinitely. A few visa categories allow individuals to enter with dual intent, meaning that they can simultaneously have the intent to remain in the USA temporarily but may also apply for status as a permanent resident which, if granted, would allow them to remain permanently. Table 12.1 below provides an overview of the various nonimmigrant categories, together with a brief description of each.

Legal entry as a nonimmigrant requires that the individual have a passport; depending upon the country from which the individual is from, he or she may also need a visa. Visa applications are filed at the US consulate or embassy, usually in the country from which the individual is from. The specific category of the visa depends on the individual's purpose for travel to the USA. In some cases, the individual is required to appear for an interview before a decision will be made on the visa application.

Upon arrival at a port of entry into the USA, e.g., an airport or seaport, the border office of the Department of Homeland Security reviews the individual's documentation to ensure that he or she holds the category of visa congruent with the individual's purpose for travel to the USA or to confirm that the individual does not need a visa. The officer will stamp the individual's passport, indicating that he or she has entered into the USA. This may be confusing for many individuals; arrival at a port of entry does not mean that the individual has legally entered into the USA. Legal entry occurs only if the individual is "inspected and admitted" by the officer.

Immigration Law: The Basics 235

Table 12.1 Nonimmigrant visa categories, USA

Visa	Category	Description/basic requirements
A	Diplomats and their relatives and attendants	A-1: Ambassador, public minister, diplomat or consular officer, cultural attaché or trade representative, or other foreign government official or employee A-2: Family members of A-2 visa holders; foreign military personnel stationed in the USA A-3: Attendants, servants, and personal employees of A-1 and A-2 visa holders and members of their families
B	Tourists; business persons	B-1: Amateur or professional athlete competing for prize money only; business visitor; domestic employee or nanny accompanying a foreign national employer B-2: Visitor for medical treatment; tourist; pleasure visitor
C	Transit visa	Transiting immediately and continuously through the US maximum validity of 29 days
D	Crewmember	Individuals serving as crewmen on a vessel or aircraft while in port
E	Treaty trader/ treaty investor	E-1: Treaty trader—enters the USA in furtherance of the provisions of a Treaty of Commerce and Navigation between the USA and the foreign country of which the alien (and the alien's employer) is a national. In the context of an E visa, a person is considered to be a national of the country whose passport he or she carries regardless of their birthplace. Requires that the individual be coming to the USA solely to carry on substantial trade principally between the USA and the foreign country of which he/she is a national E-2: Treaty investor—an alien who is coming to the USA pursuant to the provisions of a Treaty of Commerce and Navigation between the USA and the foreign country of which he/she is a national, solely to develop and direct the operations of an enterprise in which he or she has invested or is actively in the process of investing a substantial amount of capital; executives, managers, and essential specialized employees of foreign firms from a treaty country which have made a substantial investment E-3: Professional—Australian national coming to perform services in a "professional specialty occupation." The job must be one that generally requires a related baccalaureate degree, the individual must have the appropriate credentials for the job, the US employer must file a labor condition application attesting that it will pay the prevailing wage for the job offered, the benefits and working conditions offered to the E-3 professional must be similar to those offered to US workers
F	Students	Academic students who enter the USA temporarily and solely for the purpose of pursuing a full course of study in an educational program at an established institution of learning which has been approved by US Citizenship and Immigration Services for attendance by foreign students. Not available to students who are to be enrolled in public elementary schools or publicly funded adult education programs F-2: Alien spouse and children of a F-1 visa holder

(continued)

Table 12.1 (continued)

Visa	Category	Description/basic requirements
G	Employee of designated international organization or NATO	G-1: Permanent mission member of a recognized government to a designated international organization and their immediate family members G-2: Representatives of a recognized government traveling temporarily to the USA to attend meetings of a designated international organization and their immediate family members G-3: Representatives of nonrecognized or nonmember governments and their immediate family members G-4: Individuals coming to the USA to take up an appointment at a designated international organization, including the United Nations, and their immediate family members G-5: Personal employees or domestic workers of G-1–G-4 visa holders
H		H-1B: An alien coming to the USA temporarily to perform services in specialty occupations in fields requiring highly specialized knowledge. "Qualified occupation" requires at least a 4-year baccalaureate degree related to the job (or its equivalent) as a prerequisite to entry-level employment. A qualified alien is a person who has the appropriate education and training for the offered position. An H-1B position is offered to the alien for a temporary period, but the position itself may be ongoing. Requires that the employer file both a H-1B petition for the individual and a Labor Condition Application with the US Department of Labor H-2: For aliens coming temporarily to perform services or labor that meet a temporary need, provided that unemployed persons capable of performing such services cannot be found in the USA. Requires that employer file for temporary labor certification from US Department of Labor H-2A: Temporary agricultural worker H-2B: Temporary worker performing nonagricultural services or labor of a temporary or seasonal nature H-3: Training in a program not primarily for employment. To be qualified as a trainee, the alien must be coming to the USA temporarily at the invitation of an individual, organization, firm, or other trainer in any field of endeavor, e.g., agriculture, commerce, communications, finance, government, transportation, and the professions. The employer petitioner must describe the type of training to be given, the source of remuneration of the trainee, whether or not any benefit will accrue to the petitioner, and why it is necessary for the alien to be trained in the USA, why such training is unavailable in the alien's home country abroad, and why the US employer is willing to incur the cost of training. The trainee is not allowed to engage in productive employment unless it is incidental and necessary to the training and may not engage in employment which will displace a US worker

(continued)

Table 12.1 (continued)

Visa	Category	Description/basic requirements
I	Media/journalist	For bona fide representatives of a foreign press, radio, film, or other foreign information media organization, who will be entering the USA solely to engage in this professional activity, and the spouse and children of the media representative. The media representative may be required to have press credentials and a signed contract of employment with the foreign media organization or its US bureau, affiliate, or branch office
J	Exchange visitor	J-1: Trainees/fellows. Trainee is required to have completed a bachelor's degree abroad and have 1 year of experience in the field or have 5 years of experience in the field. Some J-1 visa holders are often subject to a 2-year foreign residency requirement before they may apply for a change in visa status or seek permanent residence (green card), e.g., doctors who receive postgraduate medical training in the USA, trainees whose programs receive government funding, and any scholars or trainees whose exchange program is in a field designated by the home country as a skill set that country wishes to retain J-2: Aliens who are bona fide students, scholars, trainees, teachers, professors, research assistants, specialists, or leaders in a field of specialized knowledge or skill, coming temporarily as a participant in a program designated by the Department of State for the purpose of teaching, instructing, lecturing, studying, observing, conducting research, practical training, etc. in an approved exchange program, and their spouse and minor children
K	Fiancé(e)	K-1: Individuals engaged to be married to a US citizen who seeks entry into the USA to enter into a valid marriage with that US citizen within 90 days after their entry into the USA K-3: Individuals and their minor unmarried children for whom a US citizen spouse has filed an immigrant visa petition which is pending
L	Intracorporate transferees	L-1: During the 3 years prior to the application for admission to the USA, has been employed abroad for 1 year by a multinational firm, corporation, or other legal entity and who wishes to enter the USA temporarily in order to continue to provide services to the same employer, or a subsidiary, commonly held affiliate, or branch office of the same legal entity, in a capacity which is managerial or executive or involves specialized knowledge which is not readily available in the US job market L1-B: Specialized knowledge L1-A: Executive or managerial
M	Nonacademic students	Nonacademic students seeking to pursue a full-time course of study at a vocational or other recognized nonacademic institution
N	Relatives of employees of specified international organizations	Specified relatives of long-term employees of the United Nations and other international organizations

(continued)

Table 12.1 (continued)

Visa	Category	Description/basic requirements
O	Extraordinary ability in arts, science, education, or business	O-1: Aliens of "extraordinary ability" in the sciences, education, business, and athletics, who have demonstrated "sustained national or international acclaim and recognition for achievements in the field of expertise" showing that the alien "is one of the small percentage who have risen to the very top of the field" O-2: Assistants to aliens of extraordinary ability who are an integral part of the performance because of critical skills or a long-standing relationship with the principal performing alien
P	Performing athlete, artist, or entertainer	P-1: Athletes and entertainers—Artists performing as part of an internationally recognized entertainment group that is based abroad and of which at least 75 percent of its members have been with the group for at least 1 year. Requires that a petition be filed with the immigration service, by a US agent, presenter, or employer, including a contract and itinerary stating where and when the group will perform or compete P-2: Athletes and entertainers (reciprocal exchange) (generally between a US-based union and one abroad) P-3: Athletes and entertainers seeking entry into the USA to perform in a culturally unique program. Individuals must demonstrate evidence of distinction in the art form or sport. A majority of the group must have worked together for at least 1 year. Additionally, a petition must be filed with the immigration service by a US agent, presenter, or employer, including a contract and itinerary stating where and when the group will perform or compete, and a labor advisory opinion from a union or peer group is required
Q	International cultural exchange visitor	Aliens entering the USA to participate in designated international cultural exchange programs that provide practical training, employment, and sharing of culture
R	Religious worker	Certain religious workers entering the USA to perform work in a religious vocation, religious profession, or traditional religious occupation for a bona fide nonprofit religious organization in the USA, who have had membership in the same religious denomination as the sponsoring US organization for at least 2 years preceding the application, and their spouses and children. The US sponsor is required to file a petition with the USCIS prior to the filing of a visa application by the individual
S	Specified witness and informants	Aliens who will be serving as witnesses in federal or state court in relation to "criminal enterprises" if the Attorney General has determined that they possess "critical and reliable information" and if it is determined by both the Attorney General and the Secretary of State that they will provide "critical and reliable information" regarding terrorist organizations or operations to federal law enforcement authorities or a federal court. In some cases, the spouse, the married or unmarried sons and daughters, and the parents of S visa holders may also be accorded an S visa

(continued)

Table 12.1 (continued)

Visa	Category	Description/basic requirements
T	Trafficking victims	Individuals who have been victims of trafficking who are physically present on the mainland of the USA or in American Samoa, the Commonwealth of the Mariana Islands, or at a port of entry thereto, specifically because of such trafficking and the individual has received a reasonable request to provide assistant to a federal, state, or local investigation or prosecution and has provided this requested assistance
U	Victim of criminal activity	Individuals who have suffered physical or mental abuse as the result of criminal activity and have been helpful to a local, state, or federal investigation or prosecution of this criminal activity
V	Specified relatives of lawful permanent resident alien	Nonimmigrant visa for spouse and children of lawful permanent resident
W	Specified beneficiaries of petition	Beneficiary of a petition according preference status that was filed with the Attorney General on or before December 21, 2000
TD/TN	NAFTA-related	NAFTA professional worker from Canada/Mexico
NATO	NATO-related	NATO-1, NATO-2, NATO-3, NATO-4, NATO-5, NATO-6: Traveling to the USA under the applicable provision of the Agreement on the Status of the North Atlantic Treaty Organization of the Protocol on the Status of International Military Headquarters Set Up pursuant to the North Atlantic Treaty, including national representatives, international staff, and immediate family members NATO-6, NATO-7: Personal employees or domestic workers of a NATO-1–NATO-6 visa holder

Sources: Immigration and Nationality Act § 101, 8 US.C. § 1101; United States Department of State, Bureau of Consular Affairs (n.d.)

In some instances, an individual may enter with a visa but overstay his or her visa, that is, stay beyond the date on which the visa expires. Alternatively, an individual may enter the country without permission to do so. In a small proportion of these situations, the individual may be potentially eligible to obtain a nonimmigrant visa if he or she meets specified requirements of the immigration law. Three of the nonimmigrant categories—the S, T, and U—may be particularly relevant to social workers in such circumstances and especially those social workers who are employed in an agency setting.

The S visa allows noncitizens who are not immigrants to remain in the USA temporarily if they will be serving as witnesses in federal or state court in relation to "criminal enterprises" if the Attorney General has determined that they possess "critical and reliable information" and if it is determined by both the Attorney General and the Secretary of State that they will provide "critical and reliable information" regarding terrorist organizations or operations to federal law enforcement authorities or a federal court. In some cases, the spouse, the married or unmarried sons and daughters, and the parents of S visa holders may also be accorded an S visa.

T visas are potentially available to individuals who have been victims of trafficking. In order to qualify for such a visa, the individual must be physically present on the mainland of the USA or in American Samoa, the Commonwealth of the Mariana Islands, or at a port of entry thereto, specifically because of such trafficking. Additionally, eligibility for this type of visa requires that the individual have received a reasonable request to provide assistant to a federal, state, or local investigation or prosecution and has provided this requested assistance.

Individuals may be eligible for a U visa if they have suffered physical or mental abuse as the result of criminal activity and have been helpful to a local, state, or federal investigation or prosecution of this criminal activity. Examples of physical or mental injury that is encompassed under this provision are rape, murder, assault, felonious assault, witness tampering, obstruction of justice, perjury, false imprisonment, slave trade, kidnapping, blackmail, extortion, prostitution, abduction, unlawful criminal restraint, being held hostage, peonage, female genital mutilation, domestic violence, torture, incest, sexual assault, and attempt, conspiracy, or solicitation to commit any of these offenses.

Immigrants

Individuals may obtain permanent resident status through a family or employment relationship that is legally recognized for the purpose of immigration, through qualification as a woman who is a victim of violence, through the diversity visa program, or as a refugee or asylee. Immigration as a victim of violence or a refugee/asylee is addressed in greater detail below.

Table 12.2 sets forth the categories of persons who are eligible to apply for permanent resident (immigrant/green card) status based on a family relationship. Table 12.3 provides a similar listing of the employment-based preferences that may provide the basis for an immigrant visa ("green card").

Table 12.2 Categories for immigration on the basis of family relationship

Category	Description
Immediate relatives	Spouse, widow(er), and unmarried children under the age of 21 of a US citizen who is 21 years of age or older
First preference	Unmarried sons and daughters of US citizens who are 21 years of age or older and their minor children
Second preference	Spouses and minor children and unmarried sons and daughters age 21 years and older of US permanent residents
Third preference	Married sons and daughters of US citizens and their spouses and minor children
Fourth preference	Brothers and sisters of US citizens and their spouses and minor children if the US citizen is 21 years of age or older

Table 12.3 Basic categories for immigration on the basis of employment relationship

Category	Description
First preference	Priority workers, i.e., persons of extraordinary ability in the sciences, arts, education, business, or athletics
Second preference	Professionals holding advanced degrees or persons of exceptional ability in the arts, sciences, or business
Third preference	Skilled workers, professionals holding baccalaureate degrees or the equivalent, and other workers
Fourth preference	Special immigrants: Amerasians, widow(er)s, battered spouses, or children of US citizens or other special immigrant juveniles
Fifth preference	Employment creation investors

Asylees and Refugees

The US Immigration and Nationality Act provides:

> Any alien who is physically present in the United States or who arrives in the United States (whether or not at a designated port of arrival and including an alien who is brought to the United States after having been interdicted in international or United States waters), irrespective of such alien's status, may apply for asylum in accordance with this section or, where applicable, section 235(b). (Immigration and Nationality Act § 208(a)(1), 8 U.S.C. § 1158(a)(1))

The application for asylum status must be filed within 1 year of the individual's arrival in the USA, unless the individual can demonstrate that there have been changed circumstances that justify a delay in their application (Immigration and Nationality Act § 208(a)(2)(B), (D), 8 U.S.C. § 1158(a)(2)(B)). The burden of proof is on the individual applying for such status to prove that he or she filed the application within 1 year or that there were changed circumstances justifying the delay.

A successful application for asylum status must demonstrate that race, religion, nationality, membership in a particular social group, or political opinion was at least one central reason for the persecution of the individual in the country from which he or she is seeking asylum (Immigration and Nationality Act § 208(b)(1)(B)(i), 8 U.S.C. § 1158(b)(1)(B)(i)). The evaluation of the individual's claim to asylum status rests, as well, on a credibility determination. The relevant section of the Immigration and Nationality Act explains:

> Considering the totality of the circumstances, and all relevant factors, a trier of fact may base a credibility determination on the demeanor, candor, or responsiveness of the applicant or witness, the inherent plausibility of the applicant's or witness's account, the consistency between the applicant's or witness's written and oral statements (whenever made and whether or not under oath, and considering the circumstances under which the statements were made), the internal consistency of each such statement, the consistency of such statements with other evidence of record (including the reports of the Department of State on country conditions), and any inaccuracies or falsehoods in such statements, without regard to whether an inconsistency, inaccuracy, or falsehood goes to the heart of the applicant's claim, or any other relevant factor. There is no presumption of credibility, however, if no adverse credibility determination is explicitly made, the applicant or witness shall have a rebuttable presumption of credibility on appeal. (Immigration and Nationality Act § 208(b)(1)(B)(iii), 8 US.C. § 1158(b)(1)(B)(iii))

By statute, some individuals are ineligible for asylum status. This includes individuals who have been convicted of a particularly serious crime or aggravated felony, as defined by the immigration law; those who were firmly resettled in another country prior to arriving in the USA; those for whom there are reasonable grounds to believe would be a danger to the security of the USA; and individuals who "ordered, incited, assisted, or otherwise participated in the persecution of any person on account of race, religion, nationality, membership in a particular social group, or political opinion" (Immigration and Nationality Act § 208(b)(2)(A)(i), 8 U.S.C. § 1158(b)(2)(A)(i)).

Removal Proceedings

Individuals who the government believes have entered the USA without authorization or who have entered legally but have violated the terms of their stay, e.g., by staying beyond the expiration date of their permission to remain or by committing a crime or working without authorization, may be subject to removal proceedings. A removal proceeding is a hearing that occurs before an Immigration Judge in Immigration Court, during which both the government and the individual (called an "alien" in such proceedings) can provide evidence in support of their case. Immigration Courts are part of the Executive Office for Immigration Review (EOIR) of the United States Department of Justice. EOIR also includes the Board of Immigration Appeals (BIA), which hears appeals from decisions of Immigration Court judges, and the Office of Legal Access Programs (OLAP).

The removal proceeding is initiated by the issuance of a Notice to Appear by the United States Department of Homeland Security through its Immigration and Customs Enforcement (ICE) Division. The Notice to Appear sets forth the date and time of the hearing and the charges that the government is lodging against the individual as the basis for the removal proceeding. The first hearing is known as the master calendar hearing; subsequent hearings will be set during which time the merits of the government's and alien's cases will be heard by the Immigration Judge (Immigration and Nationality Act § 239, 8 U.S.C. § 1229).

At the time of the removal proceeding, the government, through its lawyers, must first prove by clear and convincing evidence that the individual is an alien; US citizens cannot be deported (Immigration and Nationality Act § 240, 8 U.S.C. § 1229a). If the alien can establish that he or she is present in the USA legally, the government must prove that the individual is deportable on one or more of the many grounds listed in the immigration statute. Grounds of removal include the commission of specified types of crimes, such as domestic violence or a crime of moral turpitude committed within 5 years after being admitted to the USA or receiving lawful permanent residence ("green card"); the commission of marriage fraud; assisting in the smuggling or trafficking of other aliens into the USA; the commission of document fraud; falsely claiming US citizenship; and having been convicted of most drug-related violations (Immigration and Nationality Act § 237, 8 U.S.C. § 1227).

If the individual is an applicant for admission to the USA, e.g., he or she entered the country without authorization but is now applying for a benefit that will allow them to remain in the USA, he or she must establish entitlement to remain in the country (Immigration and Nationality Act § 240, 8 US.C. § 1229a).

Depending upon the circumstances of a particular case, the Immigration Judge must decide whether the individual is inadmissible, meaning that he or she never should have been admitted to the USA, or deportable, meaning the person may have been admitted legally but is now subject to expulsion due to a violation of law.

Individuals subject to removal proceedings have numerous rights under the law. These include the right to be represented by an attorney, although there is no right to have the Immigration Court or the government pay for the attorney; the right to have the case heard by an impartial Immigration Judge; the right to cross-examine witnesses and examine evidence against him or her; the use of a qualified interpreter; the right to receive sufficient notice about the date and time of the hearing; and the right to be informed about charges against them (Immigration and Nationality Act, §§ 239, 240, 8 U.S.C. §§ 1229, 1229a).

Immigration and Public Support

Qualifying for Benefits

The Illegal Immigration Reform and Immigrant Responsibility Act of 1996 (IIRAIRA) and the welfare law known as the Personal Responsibility and Work Opportunity Reconciliation Act of 1996 (PRWORA) together severely restrict the eligibility of immigrants, both those who are legally present in the USA and those who are undocumented, from receiving publicly funded benefits. The PRWORA established two classes of noncitizens for the purpose of receiving publicly funded benefits, those who are deemed to be "qualified" and those who are considered "not qualified." Individuals must fall into one of the following categories in order to be considered qualified:

- Lawfully admitted permanent resident aliens ("green card" holders)
- Refugees
- People who have been granted asylum
- Conditional entrants
- People granted withholding of deportation
- Cuban and Haitian entrants
- People who have been granted parole status by the Department of Homeland Security for a period of at least 1 year
- Abused immigrants, their parents, and/or children who meet specific criteria, discussed further below
- Survivors of trafficking and their derivative beneficiaries, e.g., children, who have obtained a T visa or whose application for a T visa indicates that they have a prima facie case of eligibility for a T visa

In order for an abused immigrant to be considered qualified as a battered spouse or child, he or she must have (1) filed the necessary paperwork (petition) for themselves under the Violence Against Women Act (2000) and it has been approved or indicates a prima facie case warranting the relief; (2) had a petition filed on their behalf by a spouse or child, and the filed petition has been approved; or (3) filed and received approval of their application for cancelation of removal under the Violence Against Women Act. To qualify, the battered spouse or child must have been the victim of extreme cruelty in the USA by a family member with whom they resided, or the immigrant's parent or child must have been the victim of such treatment. The immigrant seeking the benefit must demonstrate a "substantial connection" between the violence and the need for the benefit and must not be living with the abuser.

Additional criteria also exist for individuals who have been trafficked. In order for survivors of trafficking to be considered qualified for the purpose of receiving benefits, they must demonstrate that they were victims of a "severe form of trafficking" and must be under 18 years of age or the US Department of Health and Human Services has certified that the individual is willing to assist in the investigation and prosecution of severe forms of trafficking in persons (Broder & Neville, 2015; Victims of Trafficking and Violence Protection Act of, 2000).

Access to Benefits

All immigrants, regardless of their legal status, are eligible to receive emergency medical services if they are otherwise qualified under their state's Medicaid law. The law defines an emergency medical condition as:

> a medical condition (including emergency labor and delivery) manifesting itself by acute symptoms of sufficient severity (including severe pain) such that the absence of immediate medical attention could reasonably be expected to result in: (A) placing the patient's health in serious jeopardy, (B) serious impairment to bodily functions: or (C) serious dysfunction of any bodily organ or part. (Social Security Act §1903(v)(3), 42 U.S.C. § 1396b(v)(3))[1]

All immigrants, regardless of their legal status, may also receive the benefit of public health programs that provide immunizations for the prevention of communicable diseases and treatment of communicable disease symptoms. Children can participate in the school breakfast and lunch programs regardless of their immigration status. Additionally, all states provide services under the Special Supplemental Nutrition Program for Women, Infants, and Children (WIC) (Personal Responsibility and Work Opportunity Reconciliation Act of 1996 § 742).

In addition to undocumented immigrants, the PRWORA bars even individuals who are permanent residents from receiving some public funded benefits if they entered after the effective date of the law, August 22, 1996. Most immigrants who entered the USA on or after that date cannot obtain "federal means-tested public benefits" for a period of 5 years after they become "qualified" immigrants. "Federal means-tested

---

[1] For a summary of the various state provisions relating to emergency Medicaid for nonqualified immigrants, see Andrews et al. (2016).

public benefits" includes benefits under the following programs: Medicaid other than for emergency care, the Supplemental Nutrition Assistance Program (SNAP, previously known as the Food Stamp Program), Temporary Assistance for Needy Families (TANF) and its previous program iteration of Aid to Families with Dependent Children (AFDC), and Social Security Insurance (SSI). There are some categories of immigrants who are exempt from this 5-year bar: asylees and refugees, individuals granted withholding of deportation or removal, Cuban and Haitian entrants, specified Amerasian immigrants, Iraqi and Afghan special immigrants, qualified immigrant veterans and their dependents, survivors of trafficking, qualified immigrant active duty military and their dependents, and children who receive federal foster care.

A number of states, such as New York, provide health care to pregnant women and children regardless of their immigration status. Additionally, since 2009, states are able to use federal Medicaid and CHIP funds to provide benefits to women and children who are lawfully residing in the USA regardless of the date on which they entered the USA (Children's Health Insurance Program Reauthorization Act of 2009 § 214, 2009). Various exceptions also exist for the receipt of SNAP benefits, and a few states use state funding to provide assistance to families that would be ineligible for SNAP benefits. Immigrants who would otherwise be ineligible to receive SSI benefits may qualify to receive them for the first 7 years after they gain their immigration status if they fall into the category of "humanitarian" immigrants, e.g., survivors of trafficking, refugees, asylees, and a few other classes of immigrants.

Some otherwise qualified immigrants may not be able to access benefits even after the expiration of the 5-year bar. Under the 1996 IIRAIRA and PRWORA, individuals who immigrated on the basis of a family relationship and, in some cases, an employment-based application would have had to have been "sponsored" by a family member or employer, respectively. The sponsor would have had to complete and sign an Affidavit of Support (Form I-864), indicating that they would provide support to the immigrant and promising to repay the benefits that the immigrant might use. The affidavit is enforceable. Consequently, the income of the sponsor could be "deemed" to the immigrant in some situations in which an otherwise qualified immigrant applies for the federally funded public benefit. Such "deeming" could result in the immigrant's ineligibility for the desired benefit; the immigrant's income would be above the requisite threshold for the benefit due to the additional income deemed to be available to him or to her. Survivors of domestic violence and indigent immigrants, i.e., those who would otherwise be homeless or without food, may not be subject to the deeming requirement for a period of 12 months.

Public Charge Concerns

Some individuals may be concerned that reliance on any form of publicly funded support could result in their removal or a denial of their admission to the United Sates on the grounds that they are "likely to become a public charge." As explained by the United States Citizenship and Immigration Services, "public charge" refers to an individual:

who is likely to become primarily dependent on the government for subsistence, as demonstrated by either the receipt of public cash assistance for income maintenance or institutionalization for long-term care at government expense. (United States Citizenship and Immigration Services, 2009)

Immigration law provides that an individual who is seeking entry into the United Sates or wishes to adjust their status to that of a permanent resident may be found inadmissible if, at the time that they apply for admission or to change their status, they are likely at any time to become a public charge (Immigration and National Act § 212(a)(4), 8 U.S.C. § 1182(a)(4)). A variety of factors are to be considered in assessing whether or not an individual is likely to become a public charge, including the individual's age, health, family status, assets, resources, financial status, education, skills, and the availability of any affidavit of support (United States Citizenship and Immigration Services, 2009). The officer adjudicating the application is to consider the totality of the circumstances, rather than utilizing only one or a few factors. Receipt of cash assistance provided through Temporary Assistance for Needy Families, General Assistance programs, Supplemental Security Income (SSI), and programs supporting long-term institutionalized care may often lead to a finding that the individual is likely to become a public charge.

Neither short-term institutionalization for the purpose of rehabilitation nor many noncash benefits are to be considered in assessing likelihood of becoming a public charge. Examples of publicly funded benefits that may not be considered for public charge purposes include noncash benefits other than institutionalization for long-term care; Medicaid and other health insurance and health-related services, such as emergency medical services; Children's Health Insurance Program (CHIP); nutrition programs, including the Supplemental Nutrition Program for Women, Infants, and Children (WIC), emergency food assistance programs, and others; housing benefits; child care services; energy assistance; emergency disaster relief; foster care and adoption assistance; educational assistance, including public school attendance and benefits under the Head Start program; job training programs; and in-kind community-based programs, services, or assistance, such as through food banks and crisis counseling (United States Citizenship and Immigration Services, 2009).

The following groups of individuals are exempt from public charge or may be eligible for a waiver:

- Refugees
- Asylum applicants
- Refugees and asylees who are applying for adjustment to permanent resident status ("green card")
- Applicants for a T visa
- Applicants for a U visa
- Holders of a T visa who are applying for permanent resident status
- Holders of a U visa who are applying for permanent resident status
- Individuals who have received immigration relief under various provisions specific to Nicaraguans, Central Americans, and Haitian refugees or who fall within several other specific categories of persons (United States Citizenship and Immigration Services, 2009)

Roles of the Social Worker in the Immigration Law Context

Case Management and Public Benefits

Many social workers employed by social service agencies may provide case management services, including application assistance for publicly funded benefits, to authorized and/or unauthorized immigrants, depending upon the mission of their agency, its funding source, and other factors. Some social workers may also be employed by law firms to assist clients in navigating the complexities of public benefits systems, such as Social Security, Medicare, and Medicaid, whether the firm is focused on immigration or other legal issues.

The previous discussion relating to public benefits underscores the complexities involved in providing advice and services to immigrants with respect to their potential eligibility for and receipt of publicly funded benefits. In some cases, the receipt of specific types of benefits may have long-lasting, adverse consequences on their ability to obtain or retain legal status in the USA. Social workers will want to be sure that they are not assisting a client with an application that may ultimately be to his or her detriment or, conversely, is not recommending against application for a benefit to which the client may be legally eligible and which will not have a detrimental effect on his or her current or future immigration status.

The Social Worker as Expert Witness

Depending upon the specific details of an individual's situation, he or she may have one or more potential remedies available in the context of a removal hearing. In some cases, reliance on a qualified, reliable expert witness may bolster his or her case before the Immigration Court. For example, a social worker with particular expertise in the diagnosis and/or treatment of posttraumatic stress disorder may be qualified to address the effects that torture has had on an applicant for asylum status, including the resulting posttraumatic stress disorder. An individual who is facing removal from the USA, where he has lived since he was a small child, might benefit from expert testimony that details the emotional trauma that he will face returning to a country with which he is unfamiliar, where he no longer has any family, and whose language he does not speak.

In general, a potential expert witness is contacted by the attorney for the individual in removal proceedings. The attorney may discuss the case with several potential expert witnesses in an effort to determine which one has the greatest expertise with respect to the issues involved in a particular case. The attorney will often make available to the expert witness copies of any paperwork that has been filed on behalf of the immigrant facing removal, so that the expert witness can become acquainted with the charges against the individual and the facts of the case. In many, if not most, cases, the expert witness will meet at least once, and often more, with the individual facing removal. In some cases, the expert witness will perform standardized assessments or recommend that they be conducted by a trained professional.

The attorney will often request that the expert witness provide him or her with a written report of their findings. In addition, the attorney may also request that the expert witness appear at the removal hearing to provide oral testimony. Sometimes, that "appearance" occurs telephonically. In either case, the attorney will ask the expert witness questions that relate directly to the content of the written report and the expert's findings. The Immigration Judge may also ask questions of the expert, in an effort to clarify points made or elicit an opinion. The attorney for the government often wants to cross-examine the expert witness or may attempt to cast doubt on their credibility or qualifications. It is important that the social worker who serves as an expert witness provide information and an opinion that is clearly within the realm of their expertise and not embellish with a legal or political opinion or perspective.

The Social Worker as Accredited Representative

Social workers employed by organizations authorized by the Office of Legal Access Programs of the Executive Office for Immigration Review may seek accreditation as a representative to represent individuals in immigration-related matters. Individuals who are partially accredited have authority to practice before the Department of Homeland Security; those who are fully accredited can represent individuals before the Department of Homeland Security, the Immigration Courts, and the Board of Immigration Appeals (BIA) (8 C.F.R. § 1291.1(a)(4), as amended by 81 Fed. Reg. 92,346, 2016). In order for an organization to be eligible for recognition, it must be:

> a non-profit religious, charitable, social service, or similar organization that provides immigration legal services primarily to low-income and indigent clients within the United States, and, if the organization charges fees, has a written policy for accommodating clients unable to pay fees for immigration legal services;
>
> (2) The organization is a Federal tax-exempt organization established in the United States;
>
> (3) The organization is simultaneously applying to have at least one employee or volunteer of the organization approved as an accredited representative by the OLAP Director and at least one application for accreditation is concurrently approved, unless the organization is seeking renewal of recognition and has an accredited representative or is seeking renewal of recognition on inactive status as described in § 1292.16(i);
>
> (4) The organization has access to adequate knowledge, information, and experience in all aspects of immigration law and procedure; and
>
> (5) The organization has designated an authorized officer to act on behalf of the organization. (8 C.F.R. § 1292.11(a), as amended by 81 Fed. Reg. 92346, 2016)

Recognition of an organization is valid for 6 years, once granted.

A successful application for accreditation requires that the applicant demonstrate that he or she is employed by or is a volunteer of the authorized organization, is not an attorney, and also:

> (1) Has the character and fitness to represent clients before the Immigration Courts and the Board, or DHS, or before all three authorities. Character and fitness includes, but is not limited to, an examination of factors such as: Criminal background; prior acts involving dishonesty, fraud, deceit, or misrepresentation; past history of neglecting professional, financial, or legal obligations; and current immigration status that presents an actual or perceived conflict of interest; ...
>
> (4) Has not resigned while a disciplinary investigation or proceeding is pending and is not subject to any order disbarring, suspending, enjoining, restraining, or otherwise restricting the individual in the practice of law or representation before a court or any administrative agency;
>
> (5) Has not been found guilty of, or pleaded guilty or nolo contendere to, a serious crime, ... in any court of the United States, or of any State, possession, territory, commonwealth, or the District of Columbia, or of a jurisdiction outside of the United States; and
>
> (6) Possesses broad knowledge and adequate experience in immigration law and procedure. If an organization seeks full accreditation for an individual, it must establish that the individual also possesses skills essential for effective litigation. (8 C.F.R. §§ 1292.12(a) (1), (4)-(6), as amended by 81 Fed. Reg. 92346, 2016)

If approved, accreditation is valid for a period of 3 years.

As indicated, full accreditation allows a social worker to represent individuals in matters before the United States Citizenship and Immigration Services (USCIS), the Immigration Courts, and the Board of Immigration Appeals. A recent job posting for an accredited representative at an authorized organization described the individual's responsibilities as follows:

1. Provides information regarding immigration benefits under Administrative Relief and citizenship laws, the appropriate federal and state regulations, federal immigration procedures, forms and fees.
2. Provide legal representation to clients before the USCIS.
    Assess immigration needs of clients and determines eligibility for available Administrative Relief immigration remedies.
3. Prepares applications, petitions and forms as required by law within the jurisdiction of the US Citizenship and Immigration Service (USCIS), Board of Immigration Appeals (BIA) and US consulates.
4. Signs G-28's.
5. Reviews applications prior to submission to USCIS.
6. Maintains accurate, complete and confidential case files.
7. Provides referral to other community agencies.
8. Prepares and submits program reports in a timely manner.
9. Studies and analyzes immigration laws and regulations.
10. Conducts outreach activities and participate in advocacy efforts

11. Perform duties as assigned or approved by the program director.
12. Performs office duties as assigned. (Catholic Charities of Santa Clara County, 2016)

In this capacity, a social worker would be authorized to assist clients of the agency with their immigration petitions and applications and to represent them in deportation and exclusion proceedings.

Such a position brings with it significant responsibility, as the actions of an accredited representative may determine the course of an individual's future life. As an example, Father Vitalglione, a Roman Catholic priest, represented many intending immigrants in his capacity as an accredited representative. His failure to advise one of his clients to appear in court resulted in a deportation order against her. Later investigation found that he had failed to appear or had come unprepared in more than 221 of the 761 cases in which he was listed as the individual's representative. Although he has since been barred from appearing in Immigration Court, his actions and inactions may have adversely affected the lives of hundreds of individuals (Dolnick, 2011).

References

Andrews, S., Brown, D., Dee, L. A., Carter, C., Hayes, B., Leonard, J., ... & Reardon, M. (2016). *Emergency Medicaid for non-qualified immigrants—Medicaid coverage and services for immigrants*. Available at http://library.niwap.org/wp-content/uploads/2015/pdf/PB-Man-Ch17.1-EmergencyMedicaid.pdf. Accessed 02 Aug 2017.

Broder, T., & Neville, S. (2015). *Benefits for immigrant survivors of trafficking, domestic violence, and other serious crimes in California*. California: National Immigration Law Center, Legal Aid Foundation of Los Angeles, and California Immigrant Policy Center. https://www.nilc.org/wp-content/uploads/2015/11/TraffickingReport-2015-09.pdf. Accessed 24 Dec 2017.

Catholic Charities of Santa Clara County. (2016). *BIA Accredited Rep (2016–79)*. https://catholic-charitiesscc.org/jm/jobs/job_1653.html. Accessed 31 July 2017.

Dolnick, S. (2011, July 7). Removal of priest's cases exposes deep holes in immigration courts. *New York Times*. http://www.nytimes.com/2011/07/08/nyregion/priests-former-caseload-exposes-holes-in-immigration-courts.html?_r=0. Access 31 July 2017.

Krogstad, J. M., Passel, J. S., & Cohn, D. (2017). *5 facts about illegal immigration in the U.S. Pew Research Center, April 27*. http://www.pewresearch.org/fact-tank/2017/04/27/5-facts-about-illegal-immigration-in-the-u-s/. Accessed 31 July 2017.

United States Census Bureau. (n.d.). *The foreign-born population in the United States*. https://www.census.gov/newsroom/pdf/cspan_fb_slides.pdf. Accessed 31 July 2017.

United States Citizenship and Immigration Services. (2009). *Public charge*. https://www.uscis.gov/greencard/public-charge. Accessed 31 July 2017.

United States Department of State, Bureau of Consular Affairs. (n.d.). *U.S. visas*. https://travel.state.gov/content/visas/en.html. Accessed 02 Aug 2017.

Yee, V., Davis, K., & Patel, J. K. (2017, March 6). Here's the reality about illegal immigrants in the United Sates. *New York Times*. https://www.nytimes.com/interactive/2017/03/06/us/politics/undocumented-illegal-immigrants.html. Accessed 31 July 2017.

Zong, J., & Batalova, J. (2017, March 8). *Frequently requested statistics on immigrants and immigration in the United States*. Migration Policy Institute. http://www.migrationpolicy.org/article/frequently-requested-statistics-immigrants-and-immigration-united-states. Accessed 31 July 2017.

Legal References

11 C.F.R. §§ 1292.11, 1292.12, as amended by 81 Fed. Reg. 92346, December 19, 2016, effective January 18, 2017.

Children's Health Insurance Program Reauthorization Act of (2009 § 214, 2009) (CHIPRA) (H.R.2), Public Law 111-3 (Feb. 4, 2009).

Illegal Immigration Reform and Immigrant Responsibility Act of 1996 (IIRIRA), enacted as Division C of the Defense Department Appropriations Act, 1997, Pub. L. No. 104–208, 110 Stat. 3008 (Sept. 30, 1996).

Immigration and Nationality Act, §§ 101, 208, 237, 239, 240, 8 US.C. §§ 1101, 1158, 1227, 1229, 1229a.

Personal Responsibility and Work Opportunity Reconciliation Act of 1996 (PRWORA), Pub. L. No. 104– 193, 110 Stat. 2105 (Aug. 22, 1996).

Social Security Act §1903(v)(3), 42 U.S.C. § 1396b(v)(3).

Victims of Trafficking and Violence Protection Act of 2000, Pub. L. No. 106–386, § 107 (Oct. 28, 2000).

Violence Against Women Act (VAWA), Violent Crime Control and Law Enforcement Act of 1994, Title IV, Pub. L. No. 103-22, 103d Cong., 2d Sess., 108 Stat. 1796, reauthorized 2000.

William Wilberforce Trafficking Victims Protection Reauthorization Act of 2008, Pub. L. 110–457, § 211 (Dec. 23, 2008).

Chapter 13
International Social Work

Social Work in an International Context: Preliminary Considerations

Various definitions of international social work have been proffered over time and reflect the development of social work in this context. Table 13.1 below provides a sample of these perspectives.

Just as in the national context, international social work encompasses research, community organization and/or development, and educational endeavors and initiatives. Social workers have led or participated in research teams internationally in the areas of child development, welfare, and adoption (e.g., Brown & Groza, 2013; Groza & Bunkers, 2014; Groza & Muntean, 2015; Groza, Park, Oke, Kalyanvala, & Shetty, 2014); HIV risk and prevention (Weine, Bahromov, Loue, & Owens, 2012; Weine, Bahromov, Loue, & Owens, 2013; Zabrocki et al., 2013); mental illness (e.g., Loue, 2002; Loue & Chiscop, 2014); substance use (Wu, El-Bassel, Gilbert, Piff, & Sanders, 2004); and partner violence (e.g., El-Bassel, Gilbert, Witte, Wu, & Chang, 2011; Loue, 2001). Educational initiatives, often in collaboration with US schools of social work, have included at the student level exchange programs, field experiences, and research projects. (See, e.g., those programs currently ongoing at the time of this writing at Boston College School of Social Work <http://www.bc.edu/schools/gssw/academics/international.html>, the University of Chicago School of Social Service Administration <http://www.ssa.uchicago.edu/international-program>, and Case Western Reserve University's Jack, Joseph, and Morton Mandel School of Applied Social Sciences intensive international courses <http://msass.case.edu/studyabroad/>.) At the faculty level, international education efforts have included faculty exchanges, the development of social work educational programs (e.g., http://msass.case.edu/european-union-changes-allow-mandel-school-faculty-exchange-with-romanian-university/), consultancies, and the dissemination and exchange of information through participation in international conferences and publication (e.g., Loue, 2013, 2014; Loue, Stucker, & Karges, 2015). Direct social

Table 13.1 Definitions of international social work

Definition	Reference
A term loosely applied to (1) international organizations using social work methods or personnel, (2) social work cooperation between countries, and (3) transfer between countries of methods or knowledge about social work	Barker (1999, p. 250)
[I]nternational social work is defined as international professional action and the capacity for international action by the social work profession and its members. International action has four dimensions: internationally related domestic practice and advocacy, professional exchange, international practice and international policy development and advocacy	Healy (2001, p. 7)
International social work is the promotion of social work education and practice globally and locally, with the purpose of building a truly integrated international profession that reflects social work's capacity to respond appropriately and effectively, in education and practice terms, to the various global challenges that are having a significant impact on the well-being of large sections of the world's populations. This global and local promotion of social work education and practice is based on an integrated perspectives approach that synthesizes global, human rights, ecological, and social development perspective of international situations and responses to them	Cox and Pawar (2006, p. 20)
International social work is concerned with the development, administration, implementation, research and evaluation, in and through global social institutions and organizations, of policies and programs that promote human rights, human diversity, the well being and empowerment of people worldwide, and global social and economic justice. In the post-modern era, international social work values difference and diversity in human experience and seeks to engage with and to learn and adapt from people creating indigenous solutions to socio-economic problems around the world. International social work subscribes to ideologies, value systems and theoretical approaches that support these directions	Elliott and Segal (2008, p. 346)

work services may be provided internationally through participation in or employment with nongovernmental organizations and international organizations and on US military bases. In the national or local context, social work activities that focus on immigrant and refugee resettlement efforts and international adoptions and post-adoption support also require a knowledge and understanding of the international arena (e.g., Nandi, Loue, & Galea, 2009; Weine et al., 2009).

Mayadas and Elliott (1997) have argued that this internationalism in social work has existed since the beginning of the social work profession. They have suggested that it is evident through four phases of development:

- Phase I (1880s–1930s), a period characterized by paternalism and ethnocentrism that relied on social control, charity, and philanthropy
- Phase II (1930s–1970s), which was similarly paternalistic and ethnocentrist but also reflected strands of colonialism and universalism, with service delivery effectuated through a medical, remedial, or crisis-oriented model
- Phase III (1970s–1990s), premised on regionalization, localization, and polarization
- Phase IV, with an emphasis on globalization and transcultural interchange and a developmental model of service delivery.

A global perspective may be particularly important at this time due to the increasing globalization of business and food (Inglis & Gimlin, 2009; Shimoda, 2017), the transnational movement of employees, the record numbers of refugees seeking sanctuary from violence and/or famine in their countries of origin (Edwards, 2016), and the growing incidence of situations with international underpinnings and/or implications, such as international adoptions and abductions and human trafficking (Turmann, 2003; United Nations Office on Drugs and Crime, 2016; United States Department of State, Bureau of Consular Affairs, 2015). However, various factors impede the development of a more global perspective in social work including a continuing primary emphasis on individual-level work rather than a community focus (Tan, 2009), limited funding for social work services generally and international social work in particular (cf. Payne & Askeland, 2016), and an increasingly isolationist and protectionist perspective within the USA (Bump, 2016; Suri, 2017).

Human Rights as a Basis for International Social Work

The concept of human rights suggests that there are rights that are universal to all individuals, regardless of their nationality or citizenship or personal characteristics. Many of the provisions embedded in international documents relating to human rights are congruent with the ethical principles that guide the practice of social work. Table 13.2 provides a comparison between the Code of Ethics of the National Association of Social Workers (2008) and provisions of various international agreements relating to human rights.

Readers may notice that the international human rights documents are sometimes titled declarations and sometimes called covenants. It is important to understand the differences between such documents. A declaration, such as the Universal Declaration of Human Rights, is a formal, nonbinding statement that lists general principles and obligations of nation-states. In that sense, the provisions of a declaration can be considered to be aspirational in nature; there are no legal consequences to a country for failing to abide by the terms of the declaration. Additionally, a country must be a signatory to a declaration for it to even apply to that country.

In contrast, a covenant represents an agreement between the signatory countries that they will enforce the provisions of that covenant. A convention is an international agreement between countries to promote specified rights. Additionally, countries that sign on to a covenant or a convention are agreeing to be bound by their provisions. However, the provisions of these documents do not automatically become the law in the countries that are signatories to them. Rather, a country must pass laws incorporating the provisions of these agreements into their national laws. For example, in order for the USA to agree to be bound by a convention, the US Senate must ratify the convention by a two-thirds majority vote. Following that ratification, Congress must in most circumstances pass a law that integrates the convention's provisions into the laws of the USA. Table 13.3 provides a listing of those international instruments that have been ratified by the USA. The USA is a signatory to

Table 13.2 Comparison of provisions of NASW Code of Ethics and provisions of international human rights documents

Provision(s) of NASW Code of Ethics (applicable to social workers as individual professionals)	Provision(s) of international human rights documents (applicable to nation-states)
The primary mission of the social work profession is to enhance human well-being and help meet the basic human needs of all people, with particular attention to the needs and empowerment of people who are vulnerable, oppressed, and living in poverty. A historic and defining feature of social work is the profession's focus on individual well-being in a social context and the well-being of society. Fundamental to social work is attention to the environmental forces that create, contribute to, and address problems in living The mission of the social work profession is rooted in a set of core values. These core values, embraced by social workers throughout the profession's history, are the foundation of social work's unique purpose and perspective: Service Social justice Dignity and worth of the person Importance of human relationships Integrity Competence (preamble)	**Universal Declaration of Human Rights** **Article 1**: All human beings are born free and equal in dignity and rights. They are endowed with reason and conscience and should act towards one another in a spirit of brotherhood **United Nations Millennium Declaration (2000)** 1.2. We recognize that in addition to our separate responsibilities to our individual societies, we have a collective responsibility to uphold the principles of human dignity, equality, and equity at the global level. As leaders we have a duty therefore to all the world's people, especially the most vulnerable and, in particular, the children of the world, to whom the future belongs
Value: dignity and worth of the person **Ethical Principle:** Social workers respect the inherent dignity and worth of the person. Social workers treat each person in a caring and respectful fashion, mindful of individual differences and cultural and ethnic diversity. Social workers promote clients' socially responsible self-determination. Social workers seek to enhance clients' capacity and opportunity to change and to address their own needs. Social workers are cognizant of their dual responsibility to clients and to the broader society. They seek to resolve conflicts between clients' interests and the broader society's interests in a socially responsible manner consistent with the values, ethical principles, and ethical standards of the profession **Standard 1.02 Self-determination** Social workers respect and promote the right of clients to self-determination and assist clients in their efforts to identify and clarify their goals. Social workers may limit clients' right to self-determination when, in the social workers' professional judgment, clients' actions or potential actions pose a serious, foreseeable, and imminent risk to themselves or others	**International Covenant on Civil and Political Rights** **Part I, Article 1 (in part):** 1. All people have the right of self-determination. By virtue of that right they freely determine their political status and freely pursue their economic, social, and cultural development

Standard 4.02 Discrimination

Social workers should not practice, condone, facilitate, or collaborate with any form of discrimination on the basis of race, ethnicity, national origin, color, sex, sexual orientation, gender identity or expression, age, marital status, political belief, religion, immigration status, or mental or physical disability

Universal Declaration of Human Rights

Article 2 (in part): Everyone is entitled to all the rights and freedoms set forth in this Declaration, without distinction of any kind, such as race, colour, sex, language, religion, political or other opinion, national or social origin, property, birth or other status

International Covenant on Civil and Political Rights
Part II, Article 2 (in part):

1. Each State Party to the present Covenant undertakes to respect and to ensure to all individuals within its territory and subject to its jurisdiction the rights recognized in the present Covenant, without distinction of any kind, such as race, colour, sex, language, religion, political or other opinion, national or social origin, property, birth, or other status

International Convention on the Elimination of All Forms of Racial Discrimination
Part 1. Article 2 (in part):

1. States Parties condemn racial discrimination and undertake to pursue by all appropriate means and without delay a policy of eliminating racial discrimination in all its forms and promoting understanding among all races, and, to this end:

(a) Each State Party undertakes to engage in no act or practice of racial discrimination against persons, groups of persons or institutions and to ensure that all public authorities and public institutions, national and local, shall act in conformity with this obligation;

(b) Each State Party undertakes not to sponsor, defend or support racial discrimination by any persons or organizations;

(c) Each State Party shall take effective measures to review governmental, national and local policies, and to amend, rescind or nullify any laws and regulations which have the effect of creating or perpetuating racial discrimination wherever it exists;

(d) Each State Party shall prohibit and bring to an end, by all appropriate means, including legislation as required by circumstances, racial discrimination by any persons, group or organization;

(e) Each State Party undertakes to encourage, where appropriate, integrationist multiracial organizations and movements and other means of eliminating barriers between races, and to discourage anything which tends to strengthen racial division

2. States Parties shall, when the circumstances so warrant, take, in the social, economic, cultural and other fields, special and concrete measures to ensure the adequate development and protection of certain racial groups or individuals belonging to them, for the purpose of guaranteeing them the full and equal enjoyment of human rights and fundamental freedoms. These measures shall in no case entail as a consequence the maintenance of unequal or separate rights for different racial groups after the objectives for which they were taken have been achieved

Table 13.3 International instruments ratified by the USA

International instrument	Date ratified
International Convention on the Prevention and Punishment of Crimes Against International Protected Persons	October 26, 1976
International Convention Against the Taking of Hostages	December 7, 1984
Convention on the Prevention and Punishment of the Crime of Genocide	November 25, 1988
Abolition of Forced Labour Convention	September 25, 1991
International Covenant on Civil and Political Rights	June 8, 1992
International Convention on the Elimination of All Forms of Racial Discrimination	October 21, 1994
Convention Against Torture and Cruel, Inhuman, or Other Degrading Treatment or Punishment	October 21, 1994
Convention Concerning the Prohibition and Immediate Action for the Elimination of the Worst Forms of Child Labour	December 2, 1999
International Convention for the Suppression of Terrorist Bombing	June 26, 2002
Optional Protocol to the Convention on the Rights of the Child on the Involvement of Children in Armed Conflicts	December 23, 2002

From University of Minnesota, Human Rights Library (n.d.)

various other conventions and covenants, such as the Convention on the Elimination of All Forms of Discrimination against Women, but has never ratified them.

As indicated, the mere ratification of an international instrument does not ensure that its provisions will have the force of law within the country that signed and ratified its provisions unless that country passes laws to integrate its provisions into its national laws. A rare exception is when a country signs and ratifies an instrument that is self-executing, meaning that it is effective in that country without the need to pass additional laws. Additionally, a country may have signed and ratified an international instrument but, in actuality, pursues policies and/or utilizes processes that contravene the provisions it has agreed to uphold. This is why a country may be accused of committing human rights violations even though it has agreed to be obligated under the instruments provisions.

Whether or not a specific country has signed or ratified a particular international instrument, the provisions of an instrument may, under some circumstances, be considered to be customary international law. As an example, although neither the Nuremberg Code (1946) nor the Helsinki Declaration (World Medical Association, 2013) is an international convention or covenant, a US court has found that, for various reasons, they can be considered to be international law (*Abdullahi v. Pfizer*, 2009). (For further discussion on this case, see Chap. 5 relating to research.)

Further, social workers employed in an international context are expected to act in a manner consistent with the ethics of the profession, whether or not the USA or a country in which the social worker may be working has signed and ratified the provisions of a specific international instrument. This professional ethical expectation may or may not be consistent with the expectations of the social worker's employer. As an example of how this may occur, consider the involvement of psychologists in the torture of detainees at Guantanamo Bay, where they were held as part of the US effort against terrorism (Hoffman et al., 2015). A report by an independent former prosecutor found that officials of the American Psychological Association had colluded with the US Department of Defense to allow psychologists to participate in the conduct of prisoner interrogations as long as they did not violate US law, although it was clear that they violated medical ethics (Hoffman et al., 2015; See also American Psychological Association Presidential Task Force on Psychological Ethics and National Security, 2005). One writer observed:

> The APA's permissive ethical stance allowed psychologists to participate in interrogations, providing necessary cover for dubious so-called enhanced techniques to continue.... If the APA had .... prohibited psychologists from participating, harsh interrogations and torture would have come to a screeching halt because their presence, as health professionals, provided an air of legitimacy to interrogations. And this was needed (at least in part) to confer protection against future prosecutions of the interrogators. Any interrogators who were questioned could easily point to the psychologists then present to illustrate that their methods had to be safe and ethical. (Boyd, 2015)

The "enhanced interrogation techniques" that the psychologists helped to devise led to persistent mental health problems for the detainees on whom they were used (Apuzzo, Fink, & Risen, 2016).

Clearly, the psychologists were engaged in employment specifically to lend credibility to the use of "enhanced interrogation techniques" that were recognizable as forms of torture. The actions of the psychologists would have clearly been contrary to the ethical principles and values of the social work profession.

Issues at the Intersection of Law, Ethics, and Systems

Social work in an international context is likely to bring the social worker into contact with ideas and ways of doing things that are quite different from those that he or she may be accustomed to hearing or seeing. In any situation, it is important to understand the context of ideas and practices, some of which may conflict with the idea of universality, that all people are entitled to specified rights because they are human. As an example, many countries believe that health care is a human right, but health care is not recognized as a human right by the USA. Even when governments subscribe to the idea that something is a universal right, a particular right may not constitute a priority in the context of limited resources.

In any situation in which the social worker does not understand the basis for particular behaviors or ideas, or when they differ from what the social worker believes would be optimal, it may be important to examine the situation in light of the following questions.

- What should be the approach of a social worker to the variation in cultural practices?
- What should be the approach of a social worker to the variation in moral beliefs people hold about the acceptability of such practices?
- Is the particular practice harmful, beneficial, or neutral to the individual, a group, or the community?
- What are the potential consequences of the social worker's refusal to accept the local practice or standard? Of the social worker's effort to intervene/change the local practice or standard?

Consider the following situations:

- You are assisting on a research study designed to assess HIV risk behaviors among street children in an Eastern European country. One of your colleagues is consistently late for meetings and spends a great deal of his time getting drunk. He is openly critical of the country's government and frequently maligns his in-country colleagues, claiming that they are incompetent and corrupt. The principal investigator of the study appears to be either oblivious to the situation or is ignoring it.
- You are the team leader for a group of American volunteers conducting an observational study to assess the impact of HIV on family dynamics and economies. Several individuals on the team are medical doctors. You have been informed by the Ministry of Health in that country that a condition of the research approval is that no one provides medical care to the study participants or their family members because the volunteers have not been assessed for their competence to provide care. You learn that without your knowledge or consent, one of the volunteer MDs on the project has been surreptitiously immunizing infants against some childhood diseases. These immunizations are otherwise available to children free of cost through the local village health center.
- You are employed by a religious organization that is providing community services in the country in which you are working. The country has a high rate of child abuse, which culturally is not perceived to be abuse, but rather is viewed as the discipline that is necessary to raise a child. You learn through interviews with families that several children are being disciplined in a manner that you would consider abusive. If you were in the USA, you would be a mandated reporter of child abuse, but there is no such system in the country in which you are working. Additionally, it is not clear that the police would do anything if you were to report the "discipline" to law enforcement. It is also uncertain whether a report to the police would further endanger the children involved.

Unfortunately, there are no easy answers in any of these and other situations. Identifying an optimal resolution in each situation is an extremely complex undertaking due to differences in culture, legal mandates, ethical requirements, and, often, language as well.

In each of these situations, a decision must be made about the best course of action to be taken among alternative possibilities. Although the situations are quite different, they share similar dilemmas. In the first scenario, there are no legal issues immediately involved, but there is clearly an element of disrespect on the part of the one individual toward the guest country. In the second scenario involving the volunteer MD, the reasoning underlying the MD's actions are unclear: an effort to be helpful? arrogance? Regardless of the reason, the actions are clearly in violation of the laws of that country and the explicit conditions under which the team was permitted to proceed and are problematic ethically, since it is unclear whether the parents gave informed consent for the immunizations. The third scenario does not involve a violation of that country's laws, but does raise significant ethical issues and, depending on how the social worker proceeds, may also raise legal issues, e.g., if he or she were to file a report with the police. Additionally, the approach taken to address each such issue may have long-term consequences, e.g., government refusal to allow this and/or any other research team to proceed in the future, revocation of the permission granted to the religious organization to remain, deportation of the MD from that country if the violation were to be reported, lawsuits for negligent supervision of the volunteers, and others.

References

American Psychological Association Presidential Task Force on Psychological Ethics and Security. (2005). *Report of the Presidential Task Force on Psychological Ethics and Security*. https://www.apa.org/pubs/info/reports/pens.pdf. Accessed 01 May 2018.

Apuzzo, M., Fink, S., & Risen, J. (2016, October 9). How U.S. torture left a legacy of damaged minds. *New York Times*. https://www.nytimes.com/2016/10/09/world/cia-torture-guantanamo-bay.html. Accessed 18 May 2017.

Barker, R. L. (1999). *Dictionary of social work*. Washington, DC.: National Association of Social Workers Press.

Boyd, J.W. (2015, July 18). How the largest association of U.S. psychologists colluded in torture. *Newsweek*. http://www.newsweek.com/how-largest-association-us-psychologists-colluded-torture-354870. Accessed 18 May 2017.

Brown, S., & Groza, V. (2013). A comparison of adoptive parents' perceptions of their child's behavior among Indian children adopted to Norway, the United States, and within country: Implications for adoption policy. *Child Welfare, 92*(3), 119–143.

Bump, P. (2016, March 22). The Brussels attacks and the increasing isolationism of Donald Trump. *The Washington Post*. https://www.washingtonpost.com/news/the-fix/wp/2016/03/22/the-brussels-attacks-and-the-increasing-isolationism-of-donald-trump/?utm_term=.6b650c272cf4. Accessed 06 May 2017.

Cox, D., & Pawar, M. (2006). *International social work: Issues, strategies, and programs*. Thousand Oaks, CA: Sage.

Edwards, A. (2016, June 20). *Global forced displacement hits record high*. http://www.unhcr.org/afr/news/latest/2016/6/5763b65a4/global-forced-displacement-hits-record-high.html. Accessed 07 May 2017.

El-Bassel, N., Gilbert, L., Witte, S., Wu, E., & Chang, M. (2011). Intimate partner violence and HIV among drug-involved women: Contexts linking these two epidemics – Challenges and implications for prevention and treatment. *Substance Use and Misuse, 46*(2-3), 295–306.

Elliott, D., & Segal, U. A. (2008). International social work. In K. M. Sowers, C. N. Dulmus (Eds.), International social work. Comprehensive handbook of social work and social welfare, 1:16. Boston, MA: John Wiley and Sons, Inc. Published online: DOI: https://doi.org/10.1002/9780470373705.chsw001020. Accessed 06 May 2017.

Groza, V., & Bunkers, K. M. (2014). Adoption policy and evidence-based domestic adoption practice: A comparison of Romania, Ukraine, India, Guatemala and Ethiopia. *Infant Mental Health Journal, 35*(2), 160–171.

Groza, V., & Muntean, A. (2015). A description of attachment in adoptive parents and adoptees in Romania during early adolescence. *Child and Adolescent Social Work Journal, 32*(3), 1–12.

Groza, V., Park, H., Oke, M., Kalyanvala, R., & Shetty, M. (2014). Adoption and birth family issues: Adult adoptees in India placed through BSSK in Pune. *Indian Journal of Social Work, 75*(2), 285–300.

Healy, L. M. (2001). *International social work*. New York, NY: Oxford University Press.

Hoffman, D. H., Carter, D. J., Lopez, C. F. V., Benzmiller, H. L., Guo, A. X., Latifi, S. Y., & Craig, D. C. (2015, July 2). *Report to the Special Committee of the Board of Directors of the American Psychological Association, Independent review relating to APA ethics guidelines, national security interrogations, and torture*. Chicago, IL. http://www.apa.org/independent-review/APA-FINAL-Report-7.2.15.pdf. Accessed 18 May 2017.

Inglis, D., & Gimlin, D. (Eds.). (2009). *The globalization of food*. New York, NY: Oxford University Press.

Loue, S. (2001). *Intimate partner violence: Societal, medical, legal and individual responses*. New York, NY: Plenum Publishing/Kluwer Academic.

Loue, S. (2002). The involuntary civil commitment of mentally ill persons in the United States and Romania: A comparative analysis. *Journal of Legal Medicine, 23*, 211–250.

Loue, S. (2013). Social work, advocacy, and ethics: Opportunities and challenges in Romania. *Procedia—Social and Behavioral Sciences, 92*, 1039–1043.

Loue, S. (2014). Bridge to the unconscious: The combined use of Kalffian sandplay and vocal psychotherapies. *Logos Universality Mentality Education Novelty; Section Social Sciences, 3*(1), 85–93.

Loue, S., & Chiscop, E. (2014). Mental illness research in Romania: A review of author attention to ethical norms. *Revista Română de Bioetică, 12*(4), 84–95.

Loue, S., Stucker, V., & Karges, R. R. (2015). Core values in action: Therapeutic farms for persons with severe mental illness. *Revista Romaneasca pentru Educatie Multidimensionala: Rethinking Social Action and Sustainable Development: Values for Multidimensional Education, 7*(1), 11–23.

Mayadas, N. S., & Elliott, D. (1997). Lessons from international social work: Policies and practices. In M. Reisch & E. Gambrill (Eds.), *Social work in the 21st century* (pp. 175–185). Thousand Oaks, CA: Pine Forge Press.

Nandi, A., Loue, S., & Galea, S. (2009). Expanding the universe of universal coverage: The population health argument for increasing health coverage for immigrants. *Journal of Immigrant and Minority Health, 11*(6), 433–436.

National Association of Social Workers. (2008). *Code of ethics*. https://www.socialworkers.org/pubs/code/code.asp. Accessed 11 Feb 2016.

Nuremberg Code. (1946). In K. Lebacqz & R.J. Levine. (1982). Informed consent in human research: Ethical and legal aspects. In W. T. Reich (Ed.), *Encyclopedia of bioethics* (p. 757). New York, NY: The Free Press.

Payne, M., & Askeland, G. (2016). *Globalization and international social work: Postmodern change and challenge*. London, UK: Routledge.

Shimoda, Y. (2017). *Transnational organizations and cross-cultural workplaces*. New York, NY: Palgrave Macmillan.

Suri, J. (2017, February 20). Trump is repeating the isolationism that led to the Great Depression and World War II. *Dallas News*. https://www.dallasnews.com/opinion/commentary/2017/02/20/trump-repeating-isolationism-lead-great-depression-wwii. Accessed 06 May 2017.

Tan, A. (2009). *Community development theory and practice: Bridging the divide between "micro" and "macro" levels of social work*. Paper presented at NACSW Convention, Indianapolis, IN. https://www.nacsw.org/Publications/Proceedings2009/TanACommunity.pdf. Accessed 24 Dec 2017.

Turmann, A. (2003). *International adoption rate in U.S. doubled in the 1990s*. Washington, DC: Population Reference Bureau. http://www.prb.org/Publications/Articles/2003/InternationalAdoptionRateinUSDoubledinthe1990s.aspx. Accessed 06 May 2017.

United Nations Office on Drugs and Crime. (2016). *Global report on trafficking in persons 2016* [United Nations publication, Sales No. E.16.IV.6]. Vienna, Australia: Author. http://www.unodc.org/documents/data-and-analysis/glotip/2016_Global_Report_on_Trafficking_in_Persons.pdf. Accessed 06 May 2017.

United States Department of State, Bureau of Consular Affairs. (2015). *Annual report on international parental child abduction (IPCA)*. Washington, DC: Author. https://travel.state.gov/content/dam/childabduction/complianceReports/(S_23872)FINALNCC-2015. Accessed 06 May 2017.

University of Minnesota, Human Rights Library. (n.d.). *Ratification of international human rights treaties—USA*. http://hrlibrary.umn.edu/research/ratification-USA.html. Accessed 18 May 2017.

Weine, S., Bahromov, M., Loue, S., & Owens, L. (2013). HIV sexual risk behaviors and multilevel determinants among male labor migrants from Tajikistan. *Journal of Immigrant and Minority Health, 15*(4), 700–710.

Weine, S. M., Bahromov, M., Loue, S., & Owens, L. (2012). Trauma exposure, PTSD and HIV sexual risk behaviors among labor migrants from Tajikistan. *AIDS & Behavior, 16*(6), 1659–1669.

Weine, S. M., Horgan, J., Robertson, C., Loue, S., Mohamed, A., & Noor, S. (2009). Community and family approaches to combating the radicalization of U.S. Somali refugee youth: A psychosocial perspective. *Dynamics of Asymmetric Conflict, 2*(3), 181–200.

World Medical Association. (2013). *Helsinki Declaration—Ethical principles for biomedical research involving human subjects*. http://www.wma.net/en/30publications/10policies/b3/index.html. Accessed 14 Mar 2017.

Wu, E., El-Bassel, N., Gilbert, L., Piff, J., & Sanders, G. (2004). Sociodemographic disparities in supplemental service utilization among male methadone patients. *Journal of Substance Abuse Treatment, 26*, 197–202.

Zabrocki, C., Weine, S., Chen, S., Brajkovic, I., Bahromov, M., Loue, S., et al. (2013). Sociostructural barriers, protective factors, and HIV risk among Central-Asian female migrants in Moscow. *Central Asian Journal of Global Health, 2*(1). https://doi.org/10.5195/cajgh.2013.31.

Legal References

Cases

Abdullahi v. Pfizer, 562 F.3d 163 (2d Cir. 2009).

International Conventions, Covenants, and Treaties

Abolition of Forced Labour Convention (ILO No. 105), 320 U.N.T.S. 291, entered into force Jan. 17, 1959.

Convention Concerning the Prohibition and Immediate Action for the Elimination of the Worst Forms of Child Labour (ILO No. 182), 2133 U.N.T.S.161, *entered into force* Nov. 19, 2000.

Convention on Elimination of All Forms of Discrimination Against Women, G.A. res. 34/180, 34 U.N. GAOR Supp. (No. 46) at 193, U.N. Doc. A/34/46, *entered into force* Sept. 3, 1981.

Convention on the Prevention and Punishment of the Crime of Genocide, 78 U.N.T.S. 277, *entered into force* Jan. 12, 1951.

Convention Against Torture and Cruel, Inhuman, or Other Degrading Treatment or Punishment, G.A. Res. 39/46, [annex, 39 U.N. GAOR Supp. (No. 51) at 197, U.N. Doc. A/39/51 (1984)], *entered into force* June 26, 1987.

International Convention on the Elimination of All Forms of Racial Discrimination, G.A. Res. 2106 (XX), Annex, 20 U.N. GAOR Supp. (No. 14) at 47, U.N. Doc. A/6014 (1966), 660 U.N.T.S. 195, *entered into force* January 4, 1969.

International Convention in the Prevention and Punishment of Crimes Against International Protected Persons, 1035 U.N.T.S. 167, 13 I.L.M. 41, *entered into force* Feb. 20, 1977.

International Convention for the Suppression of Terrorist Bombing, G.A. Res. 164, U.N. GAOR, 52nd Sess., Supp. No. 49, at 389, U.N. Doc. A/52/49 (1998), *entered into force* May 23, 2001.

International Convention Against the Taking of Hostages, G.A. Res. 146 (XXXIV), U.N. GAOR, 34th Sess., Supp. No. 46, at 245, U.N. Doc. A/34/46 (1979), *entered into force* June 3, 1983.

International Covenant on Civil and Political Rights, G.A. Res. 2200A (XXI), 21 U.N. GAOR Supp. (No. 16) at 52, U.N. Doc. A/6316 (1966), 999 U.N.T.S. 171, *entered into force* Mar. 23, 1976.

Optional Protocol to the Convention on the Rights of the Child on the Involvement of Children in Armed Conflicts, G.A. Res. 54/263, Annex I, 54 U.N. GAOR Supp. (No. 49) at 7, U.N. Doc. A/54/49, Vol. III (2000), *entered into force* February 12, 2002.

United Nations Millennium Declaration, G.A. Res. A/55/L.2, September 8, 2000.

Universal Declaration of Human Rights, G.A. Res. 217A (III), UN Doc. A/810 at 71 (1948).

Appendix A: State Laws Permitting Family-Related Discriminatory/Differential Treatment of LGBT Individuals on the Basis of Religious Belief

State	Provision (excerpted)	Source
Alabama	Section 4. The purposes of this act are as follows: (1) To prohibit governmental entities from discriminating or taking an adverse action against a child placing agency on the basis that the agency declines to make a child placement that conflicts, or under circumstances that conflict, with the sincerely held religious beliefs of the agency, provided the agency is otherwise in compliance with Minimum Standards for Child Placing Agencies. (2) To protect the exercise of religion of child placing agencies and to ensure that governmental entities will not be able to force those agencies, either directly or indirectly, to discontinue all or some of their child placing services because they decline to place a child for adoption or in a foster home that conflicts, or under circumstances that conflict, with their sincerely held religious beliefs, when otherwise the agency is in compliance with required Minimum Standards for Child Placing Agencies. (3) To provide relief to child placing agencies whose rights have been violated. Section 5. (a) The state may not refuse to license or otherwise discriminate or take an adverse action against any child placing agency that is licensed by or required to be licensed by the state for child placing services on the basis that the child placing agency declines to make, provide, facilitate, or refer for a placement in a manner that conflicts with, or under circumstances that conflict with, the sincerely held religious beliefs of the child placing agency provided the agency is otherwise in compliance with the requirements of the Alabama Child Care Act of 1971, Chapter 7, Title 38, Code of Alabama 1975, and the Minimum Standards for Child Placing Agencies.	H.B. 24, enacted May 2017. Alabama Code § 28-7C-1 et seq. (2017)

(continued)

Appendix A (continued)

State	Provision (excerpted)	Source
Kansas	Section 1. As used in sections 1 through 3, and amendments thereto: (a) "Benefit" means the following: (1) Recognition; (2) registration; (3) the use of facilities of the postsecondary educational institution for meetings or speaking purposes; (4) the use of channels of communication of the postsecondary educational institution; and (5) funding sources that are otherwise available to other student associations in the postsecondary educational institution. (b) "Postsecondary educational institution" shall have the same meaning as that term is defined in K.S.A. 74-3201b, and amendments thereto. (c) "Student" means any person who is enrolled on a full-time or part-time basis in a postsecondary educational institution. (d) "Religious student association" means an association of students organized around shared religious beliefs. Sec. 2. No postsecondary educational institution may take any action or enforce any policy that would deny a religious student association any benefit available to any other student association, or discriminate against a religious student association with respect to such benefit, based on such association's requirement that the leaders or members of such association: (a) Adhere to the association's sincerely held religious beliefs; (b) comply with the association's sincerely held religious beliefs; (c) comply with the association's sincere religious standards of conduct; or (d) be committed to furthering the association's religious missions, as such religious beliefs, observance requirements, standards of conduct or missions are defined by the religious student association, or the religion on which the association is based. Sec. 3. Any student or religious student association aggrieved by a violation of section 2, and amendments thereto, may bring a cause of action against the postsecondary educational institution for such violation and seek appropriate relief, including, but not limited to, monetary damages. Any student or religious student association aggrieved by a violation of section 2, and amendments thereto, also may assert such violation as a defense or counterclaim in any civil or administrative proceedings brought against such student or religious student association. Sec. 4. This act shall take effect and be in force from and after its publication in the statute book.	S.B. 175, enacted March 2016. Kansas Statutes Annotated § 60-5311-5313 (2016)

(continued)

Appendix A (continued)

State	Provision (excerpted)	Source

Kentucky	[unofficial copy; italics, bold, and underline in original]
	AN ACT relating to the expression of religious or political viewpoints in public schools and public postsecondary institutions.
	WHEREAS, the General Assembly is dedicated to enforcing the constitutional rights of its citizens, which are secured by the Constitutions of the United States of America and the Commonwealth of Kentucky;
	NOW, THEREFORE,
	Be it enacted by the General Assembly of the Commonwealth of Kentucky:
	Section 1. KRS 158.183 is amended to read as follows:
	(1) *Consistent with the Constitutions of the United States of America and the <u>Commonwealth of Kentucky,</u>* a student shall have the right to carry out an activity described in any of paragraphs (a) to *(i)*[(d)] of subsection (2) of this section, if the student does not:
	(a) Infringe on the rights of the school to:
	    Maintain order and discipline;
	    Prevent disruption of the educational process; and
	    Determine educational curriculum and assignments;
	(b) Harass other persons or coerce other persons to participate in the activity; or
	(c) Otherwise infringe on the rights of other persons.
	(2) *Consistent with the Constitutions of the United States of America and the <u>Commonwealth of Kentucky, and</u>* subject to the provisions of subsection (1) of this section, a student shall be permitted to voluntarily:
	(a) Pray *<u>or engage in religious activities</u>* in a public school, vocally or silently, alone or with other students to the same extent and under the same circumstances as a student is permitted to vocally or silently reflect, meditate,[or] speak on, *<u>or engage in</u>* nonreligious matters alone or with other students in the public school;
	(b) Express religious *<u>or political</u>* viewpoints in a public school to the same extent and under the same circumstances as a student is permitted to express viewpoints on nonreligious *<u>or nonpolitical</u>* topics or subjects in the school;
	(c) *<u>Express religious or political viewpoints in classroom, homework, artwork, and other written and oral assignments free from discrimination or penalty based on the religious or political content of the submissions;</u>*
	<u>(d)</u> Speak to and attempt to discuss religious *<u>or political</u>* viewpoints with other students in a public school to the same extent and under the same circumstances as a student is permitted to speak to and attempt to share nonreligious *<u>or nonpolitical</u>* viewpoints with other students. However, any student may demand that this speech or these attempts to share religious *<u>or political</u>* viewpoints not be directed at him or her;
		S.B. 17, enacted March 2017. Kentucky Revised Statutes Annotated §§ 158.183, 158.188, 158.186, 164.348 (2017)

(continued)

Appendix A (continued)

State	Provision (excerpted)	Source
	(e)[(d)] Distribute religious *or political* literature in a public school, subject to reasonable time, place, and manner restrictions to the same extent and under the same circumstances as a student is permitted to distribute literature on nonreligious *or nonpolitical* topics or subjects in the school;[and]	
	(f)[(e)] *Display religious messages on items of clothing to the same extent that a student is permitted to display nonreligious messages on items of clothing;*	
	(g) Access public secondary school facilities during noninstructional time as a member of a religious student organization for activities that may include prayer, Bible reading, or other worship exercises to the same extent that members of nonreligious student organizations are permitted access during noninstructional time;	
	(h) Use school media, including the public address system, the school newspaper, and school bulletin boards, to announce student religious *meetings to the same extent that a student is permitted to use school media to announce student nonreligious meetings;*	
	(i) Meet as a member of a religious student group during noninstructional time in the school day to the same extent that members of nonreligious student groups are permitted to meet, including before and after the school day; and	
	(j) Be absent, in accordance with attendance policy, from a public school to observe religious holidays and participate in other religious practices to the same extent and under the same circumstances as a student is permitted to be absent from a public school for nonreligious purposes.	
	(3) *Consistent with its obligations to respect the rights secured by the Constitutions of the United States of America and the Commonwealth of Kentucky, a local* board of education shall ensure that:	
	(a) 1. The selection of students to speak at official events is made without regard to the religious or political viewpoint of the student speaker;	
	The prepared remarks of the student are not altered before delivery, except in a viewpoint-neutral manner, unless requested by the student. However, student speakers shall not engage in speech that is obscene, vulgar, offensively lewd, or indecent; and	
	If the content of the student's speech is such that a reasonable *observer may perceive affirmative school sponsorship or endorsement of the student speaker's religious or political viewpoint, the school* shall communicate, in writing, orally, or both, that the student's *speech does not reflect the endorsement, sponsorship, position, or expression of the school;*	

(continued)

Appendix A (continued)

State	Provision (excerpted)	Source
	(b) Religious and political organizations are allowed equal access to public forums on the same basis as nonreligious and nonpolitical organizations; and	
	(c) No recognized religious or political student organization is hindered or discriminated against in the ordering of its internal affairs, selection of leaders and members, defining of doctrines and principles, and resolving of organizational disputes in the furtherance of its mission, or in its determination that only persons committed to its mission should conduct these activities.	
	(4) Consistent with its obligations to respect the rights secured by the Constitutions of the United States of America and the Commonwealth of Kentucky, a local board of education shall permit public schools in the district to sponsor artistic or theatrical programs that advance students' knowledge of society's cultural and religious heritage, as well as provide opportunities for students to study and perform a wide range of music, literature, poetry, and drama.	
	(5) No action may be maintained under KRS 158.181 to 158.187 unless the student has exhausted the following administrative remedies;	
	(a) The student or the student's parent or guardian shall state his or her complaint to the school's principal. The principal shall investigate and take appropriate action to ensure the rights of the student are resolved within seven (7) days of the date of the complaint;	
	(b) If the concerns are not resolved, then the student or the student's parent or guardian shall make a complaint in writing to the superintendent with the specific facts of the alleged violation;	
	(c) The superintendent shall investigate and take appropriate action to ensure that the rights of the student are resolved within thirty (30) days of the date of the written complaint; and	
	(d) Only after the superintendent's investigation and action may a student or the student's parent or legal guardian pursue any other legal action.	
	SECTION 2. A NEW SECTION OF KRS CHAPTER 158 IS CREATED TO READ AS FOLLOWS:	
	A teacher in a public school shall be permitted to:	
	(1) Teach about religion with the use of the Bible or other scripture, but without providing religious instruction, for the secular study of:	
	(a) The history of religion;	
	(b) Comparative religions;	
	(c) The Bible as literature;	
	(d) The role of religion in the history of the United States and other countries; and	
	(e) Religious influences on art, music, literature, and social studies; and	

(continued)

Appendix A (continued)

State	Provision (excerpted)	Source
	(2) Teach about religious holidays, including religious aspects, and celebrate the secular aspects of holidays. A teacher shall not observe holidays as religious events or promote such observance by students.	
	Section 3. KRS 158.186 is amended to read as follows: The Department of Education shall send *electronic or paper* copies of *Section 1 of this Act and* KRS *158.195*[158.181 to 158.187] to each local school board,[and] school-based decision making council*, and certified employee* in Kentucky on an annual basis. SECTION 4. A NEW SECTION OF KRS CHAPTER 164 IS CREATED TO READ AS FOLLOWS: *Consistent with its obligations to respect the rights secured by the Constitutions of the United States and the Commonwealth of Kentucky, a governing board of a public postsecondary education institution shall ensure that:* *(1) The expression of a student's religious or political viewpoints in classroom, homework, artwork, and other written and oral assignments is free from discrimination or penalty based on the religious or political content of the submissions;* *(2) (a) The selection of students to speak at official events is made in a viewpoint-neutral manner; and* *(b) The prepared remarks of the student are not altered before delivery, except in a viewpoint-neutral manner, unless requested by the student. However, student speakers shall not engage in speech that is obscene, vulgar, offensively lewd, or indecent; and (c) If the content of the student's speech is such that a reasonable observer may perceive affirmative institutional sponsorship or endorsement of the student speaker's religious or political viewpoint, the institution shall communicate, in writing, orally, or both, that the student's speech does not reflect the endorsement, sponsorship, position, or expression of the institution; (3) Religious and political organizations are allowed equal access to public forums on the same basis as nonreligious and nonpolitical organizations; (4) No recognized religious or political student organization is hindered or discriminated against in the ordering of its internal affairs, selection of leaders and members, defining of doctrines and principles, and resolving of organizational disputes in the furtherance of its mission, or in its determination that only persons committed to its mission should conduct such activities; and (5) There shall be no restrictions on the time, place, and manner of student speech that occurs in the outdoor areas of campus or is protected by the First Amendment of the United States Constitution, except for restrictions that are: (a) Reasonable; (b) Justified without reference to the content of the regulated speech; (c) Narrowly tailored to serve a compelling governmental interest; and (d) Limited to provide ample alternative options for the communication of the information.* On page 5, line 10–11, delete the following: "*A teacher shall not observe holidays as religious events or promote such observance by students.*"	

(continued)

Appendix A (continued)

State	Provision (excerpted)	Source
Mississippi	**SECTION 1.** This act shall be known and may be cited as the "Protecting Freedom of Conscience from Government Discrimination 13 Act." **SECTION 2.** The sincerely held religious beliefs or moral convictions protected by this act are the belief or conviction that: (a) Marriage is or should be recognized as the union of one man and one woman; (b) Sexual relations are properly reserved to such a marriage; (c) Male (man) or female (woman) refer to an individual's immutable biological sex as objectively determined by anatomy and genetics at time of birth. **SECTION 3.** (1) The state government shall not take any discriminatory action against a religious organization wholly or partially on the basis that such organization: (a) Solemnizes or declines to solemnize any marriage, or provides or declines to provide services, accommodations, facilities, goods or privileges for a purpose related to the solemnization, formation, celebration or recognition of any marriage, based upon or in a manner consistent with a sincerely held religious belief or moral conviction described in Section 2 of this act; (b) Makes any employment-related decision including, but not limited to, the decision whether or not to hire, terminate or discipline an individual whose conduct or religious beliefs are inconsistent with those of the religious organization, based upon or in a manner consistent with a sincerely held religious belief or moral conviction described in Section 2 of this act; or (c) Makes any decision concerning the sale, rental, occupancy of, or terms and conditions of occupying a dwelling or other housing under its control, based upon or in a manner consistent with a sincerely held religious belief or moral conviction described in Section 2 of this act. (2) The state government shall not take any discriminatory action against a religious organization that advertises, provides or facilitates adoption or foster care, wholly or partially on the basis that such organization has provided or declined to provide any adoption or foster care service, or related service, based upon or in a manner consistent with a sincerely held religious belief or moral conviction described in Section 2 of this act. (3) The state government shall not take any discriminatory action against a person who the state grants custody of a foster or adoptive child, or who seeks from the state custody of a foster or adoptive child, wholly or partially on the basis that the person guides, instructs or raises a child, or intends to guide, instruct, or raise a child based upon or in a manner consistent with a sincerely held religious belief or moral conviction described in Section 2 of this act.	H.B. 1523, enacted July 2016. Mississippi Code Annotated § 11-62-1 et seq. (2016)

(continued)

Appendix A (continued)

State	Provision (excerpted)	Source
	(4) The state government shall not take any discriminatory action against a person wholly or partially on the basis that the person declines to participate in the provision of treatments, counseling, or surgeries related to sex reassignment or gender identity transitioning or declines to participate in the provision of psychological, counseling, or fertility services based upon a sincerely held religious belief or moral conviction described in Section 2 of this act. This subsection (4) shall not be construed to allow any person to deny visitation, recognition of a designated representative for health care decision-making, or emergency medical treatment necessary to cure an illness or injury as required by law.	
	(5) The state government shall not take any discriminatory action against a person wholly or partially on the basis that the person has provided or declined to provide the following services, accommodations, facilities, goods, or privileges for a purpose related to the solemnization, formation, celebration, or recognition of any marriage, based upon or in a manner consistent with a sincerely held religious belief or moral conviction described in Section 2 of this act:	
	(a) Photography, poetry, videography, disc-jockey services, wedding planning, printing, publishing or similar marriage-related goods or services; or	
	(b) Floral arrangements, dress making, cake or pastry artistry, assembly-hall or other wedding-venue rentals, limousine or other car-service rentals, jewelry sales and services, or similar marriage-related services, accommodations, facilities or goods.	
	(6) The state government shall not take any discriminatory action against a person wholly or partially on the basis that the person establishes sex-specific standards or policies concerning employee or student dress or grooming, or concerning access to restrooms, spas, baths, showers, dressing rooms, locker rooms, or 93 other intimate facilities or settings, based upon or in a manner consistent with a sincerely held religious belief or moral conviction described in Section 2 of this act.	
	(7) The state government shall not take any discriminatory action against a state employee wholly or partially on the basis that such employee lawfully speaks or engages in expressive conduct based upon or in a manner consistent with a sincerely held religious belief or moral conviction described in Section 2 of this act, so long as:	
	(a) If the employee's speech or expressive conduct occurs in the workplace, that speech or expressive conduct is consistent with the time, place, manner and frequency of any other expression of a religious, political, or moral belief or conviction allowed; or	
	(b) If the employee's speech or expressive conduct occurs outside the workplace, that speech or expressive conduct is in the employee's personal capacity and outside the course of performing work duties.	

(continued)

Appendix A (continued)

State	Provision (excerpted)	Source
	(8) (a) Any person employed or acting on behalf of the state government who has authority to authorize or license marriages, including, but not limited to, clerks, registers of deeds or their deputies, may seek recusal from authorizing or licensing lawful marriages based upon or in a manner consistent with a sincerely held religious belief or moral conviction described in Section 2 of this act. Any person making such recusal shall provide prior written notice to the State Registrar of Vital Records who shall keep a record of such recusal, and the state government shall not keep a record of such recusal, and the state government shall not take any discriminatory action against that person wholly or partially on the basis of such recusal. The person who is recusing himself or herself shall take all necessary steps to ensure that the authorization and licensing of any legally valid marriage is not impeded or delayed as a result of any recusal. (b) Any person employed or acting on behalf of the state government who has authority to perform or solemnize marriages, including, but not limited to, judges, magistrates, justices of the peace or their deputies, may seek recusal from performing or solemnizing lawful marriages based upon or in a manner consistent with a sincerely held religious belief or moral conviction described in Section 2 of this act. Any person making such recusal shall provide prior written notice to the Administrative Office of Courts, and the state government shall not take any discriminatory action against that person wholly or partially on the basis of such recusal. The Administrative Office of Courts shall take all necessary steps to ensure that the performance or solemnization of any legally valid marriage is not impeded or delayed as a result of any recusal. **SECTION 4.** (1) As used in this act, discriminatory action includes any action taken by the state government to: (a) Alter in any way the tax treatment of, or cause any tax, penalty, or payment to be assessed against, or deny, delay, revoke, or otherwise make unavailable an exemption from taxation of any person referred to in Section 3 of this act; (b) Disallow, deny or otherwise make unavailable a deduction for state tax purposes of any charitable contribution made to or by such person; (c) Withhold, reduce, exclude, terminate, materially alter the terms or conditions of, or otherwise make unavailable or deny any state grant, contract, subcontract, cooperative agreement, guarantee, loan, scholarship, or other similar benefit from or to such person; (d) Withhold, reduce, exclude, terminate, materially alter the terms or conditions of, or otherwise make unavailable or deny any entitlement or benefit under a state benefit program from or to such person; (e) Impose, levy or assess a monetary fine, fee, penalty or injunction;	

(continued)

Appendix A (continued)

State	Provision (excerpted)	Source
	(f) Withhold, reduce, exclude, terminate, materially alter the terms or conditions of, or otherwise make unavailable or deny any license, certification, accreditation, custody award or agreement, diploma, grade, recognition, or other similar benefit, position, or status from or to any person; or	
	(g) Refuse to hire or promote, force to resign, fire, demote, sanction, discipline, materially alter the terms or conditions of employment, or retaliate or take other adverse H. B. No. 1523 employment action against a person employed or commissioned by the state government.	
	(2) The state government shall consider accredited, licensed or certified any person that would otherwise be accredited, licensed or certified, respectively, for any purposes under state law but for a determination against such person wholly or partially on the basis that the person believes, speaks or acts in accordance with a sincerely held religious belief or moral conviction described in Section 2 of this act.	
	SECTION 5. (1) A person may assert a violation of this act as a claim against the state government in any judicial or administrative proceeding or as defense in any judicial or administrative proceeding without regard to whether the proceeding is brought by or in the name of the state government, any private person or any other party. ***	
	SECTION 8. (1) This act shall be construed in favor of a broad protection of free exercise of religious beliefs and moral convictions, to the maximum extent permitted by the state and federal constitutions.	
	(2) The protection of free exercise of religious beliefs and moral convictions afforded by this act are in addition to the protections provided under federal law, state law, and the state and federal constitutions. Nothing in this act shall be construed to preempt or repeal any state or local law that is equally or more protective of free exercise of religious beliefs or moral convictions. Nothing in this act shall be construed to narrow the H. B. No. 1523 meaning or application of any state or local law protecting free exercise of religious beliefs or moral convictions. Nothing in this act shall be construed to prevent the state government from providing, either directly or through an individual or entity not seeking protection under this act, any benefit or service authorized under state law.	
	(3) This act applies to, and in cases of conflict supersedes, each statute of the state that impinges upon the free exercise of religious beliefs and moral convictions protected by this act, unless a conflicting statute is expressly made exempt from the application of this act. This act also applies to, and in cases of conflict supersedes, any ordinance, rule, regulation, order, opinion, decision, practice or other exercise of the state government's authority that impinges upon the free exercise of 232 religious beliefs or moral convictions protected by this act.	

(continued)

Appendix A (continued)

State	Provision (excerpted)	Source
	SECTION 9. As used in Sections 1 through 9 of this act, the following words and phrases shall have the meanings ascribed in this section unless the context clearly indicates otherwise: (1) "State benefit program" means any program administered or funded by the state, or by any agent on behalf of the state, providing cash, payments, grants, contracts, loans or in-kind assistance. (2) "State government" means: (a) The State of Mississippi or a political subdivision of the state; (b) Any agency of the state or of a political subdivision of the state, including a department, bureau, board, commission, council, court or public institution of higher education; (c) Any person acting under color of state law; and (d) Any private party or third party suing under or enforcing a law, ordinance, rule or regulation of the state or political subdivision of the state. (3) "Person" means: (a) A natural person, in his or her individual capacity, regardless of religious affiliation or lack thereof, or in his or her capacity as a member, officer, owner, volunteer, employee, manager, religious leader, clergy or minister of any entity described in this section; (b) A religious organization; (c) A sole proprietorship, or closely held company, partnership, association, organization, firm, corporation, cooperative, trust, society or other closely held entity operating with a sincerely held religious belief or moral conviction described in this act; or (d) Cooperatives, ventures or enterprises comprised of two (2) or more individuals or entities described in this subsection. (4) "Religious organization" means: (a) A house of worship, including, but not limited to, churches, synagogues, shrines, mosques and temples; (b) A religious group, corporation, association, school or educational institution, ministry, order, society or similar entity, regardless of whether it is integrated or affiliated with a church or other house of worship; and (c) An officer, owner, employee, manager, religious leader, clergy or minister of an entity or organization described in this subsection (4). (5) "Adoption or foster care" or "adoption or foster care service" means social services provided to or on behalf of children, including: (a) Assisting abused or neglected children; (b) Teaching children and parents occupational, homemaking and other domestic skills; (c) Promoting foster parenting; (d) Providing foster homes, residential care, group homes or temporary group shelters for children;	

(continued)

Appendix A (continued)

State	Provision (excerpted)	Source
	(e) Recruiting foster parents; (f) Placing children in foster homes; (g) Licensing foster homes; (h) Promoting adoption or recruiting adoptive parents; (i) Assisting adoptions or supporting adoptive families; (j) Performing or assisting home studies; (k) Assisting kinship guardianships or kinship caregivers; (l) Providing family preservation services; (m) Providing family support services; and (n) Providing temporary family reunification services.	
South Dakota	ENTITLED, An Act to provide certain protections to faith-based or religious child-placement agencies. BE IT ENACTED BY THE LEGISLATURE OF THE STATE OF SOUTH DAKOTA: Section 1. That chapter 26-6 be amended by adding a NEW SECTION to read: Terms used in this Act mean: (1) "Child-placement agency," a private organization that receives and places children in foster homes or for adoption, with or without compensation, as a regular activity of that organization or that performs those services as an adjunct to other regular activities; (2) "State benefit program," any program administered or funded by the state or by any agent on behalf of the state that provides cash, payments, grants, contracts, loans or in-kind assistance; (3) "State,": (a) The State of South Dakota or any political subdivision thereof; (b) Any agency of the State of South Dakota or of a political subdivision of the state including any department, bureau, board, commission, council, court, or public institution of higher education; (c) Any person acting under the authority of state law. Section 2. That chapter 26-6 be amended by adding a NEW SECTION to read: For the purposes of this Act, the term, adverse action, means any action that directly or indirectly adversely affects a child-placement agency or organization seeking to become a child-placement agency, places the child-placement agency or organization in a worse position than it was in before the action was taken, or is likely to deter a child-placement agency or organization from acting or refusing to act. The term includes, without limitation, the following: (1) Altering in any way the tax treatment of, or causing any tax, penalty, or payment to be assessed against, or denying, delaying, revoking, or otherwise making unavailable an exemption from taxation;	S.B. 149, enacted March 2017

Appendix A (continued)

State	Provision (excerpted)	Source
	(2) Disallowing, denying, or otherwise making unavailable a deduction for state tax purposes of any charitable contribution made to an organization;	
	(3) Denying an application for, refusing to renew, or canceling any benefit from a state benefit program or other funding;	
	(4) Declining to enter into, refusing to renew, or canceling a contract;	
	(5) Declining to issue, refusing to renew, or canceling a license;	
	(6) Imposing, levying, or assessing a monetary fine, fee, penalty, damages, award, or injunction;	
	(7) Taking any enforcement action;	
	(8) Discriminating against an organization in regard to participation in a state benefit program;	
	(9) Limiting the ability of a person to engage in child-placement services; or	
	(10) Taking any action that materially alters the terms or conditions of funding or a contract or license.	
	Section 3. That chapter 26-6 be amended by adding a NEW SECTION to read:	
	No child-placement agency may be required to provide any service that conflicts with, or provide any service under circumstances that conflict with any sincerely-held religious belief or moral conviction of the child-placement agency that shall be contained in a written policy, statement of faith, or other document adhered to by a child-placement agency.	
	If a child-placement agency declines to provide any services, the child-placement agency shall provide in writing information advising the applicant of the Department of Social Services website and a list of licensed child-placement agencies with contact information.	
	Section 4. That chapter 26-6 be amended by adding a NEW SECTION to read:	
	The state may not discriminate or take any adverse action against a child-placement agency or an organization seeking to become a child-placement agency on the basis, wholly or partly, that the child-placement agency has declined or will decline to provide any service that conflicts with, or provide any service under circumstances that conflict with the agency's written sincerely-held religious belief or moral conviction of the child-placement agency.	
	The state may not enter into a contract that is inconsistent with, would in any way interfere with, or would in any way require an organization to surrender any right created in this Act.	
	Section 5. That chapter 26-6 be amended by adding a NEW SECTION to read:	

(continued)

Appendix A (continued)

State	Provision (excerpted)	Source
	Any faith-based or religious child-placement agency or organization that seeks to become a child-placement agency is eligible, on the same basis as any other child-placement agency or organization, to receive a license or participate in a state benefit program. The state may not discriminate against a faith-based or religious organization on the basis, wholly or partly, of the organization's religious character or affiliation.	
	Section 6. That chapter 26-6 be amended by adding a NEW SECTION to read:	
	A faith-based or religious child-placement agency that enters into a contract with the state or participates in a state benefit program for child-placement services shall retain the agency's independence from the state, including the child-placement agency's control over the definition, development, practice, and expression of the agency's written religious beliefs and moral convictions; the agency's hiring and employment practices; and decisions as to whether any child-placement service conflicts with any sincerely-held religious belief or moral conviction of the agency.	
	Section 7. That chapter 26-6 be amended by adding a NEW SECTION to read	
	No provision of this Act may be construed to allow a child-placement agency to decline to provide a service on the basis of a person's race, ethnicity, or national origin. Due regard shall be afforded to the Indian Child Welfare Act (25 U.S.C. §§ 1901-1963), as amended to January 1, 2017, if that Act is applicable.	
	***	
	Section 11. That chapter 26-6 be amended by adding a NEW SECTION to read:	
	The provisions of this Act shall be construed in favor of a broad protection of free exercise of religious beliefs and moral convictions, to the maximum extent afforded by the federal and state constitutions. The protection of free exercise of religious beliefs and moral convictions afforded by this Act is in addition to the protections provided under federal law, state law, and the federal and state constitutions. Nothing in this section may be construed to:	
	(1) Preempt or repeal any state or local law that is equally or more protective of free exercise of religious beliefs or moral convictions;	
	(2) Narrow the meaning or application of any state or local law protecting free exercise of religious beliefs or moral convictions; or	
	(3) Prevent the state from providing, either directly or through an individual or entity not seeking protection under this Act, any benefit or service authorized under state law.	
	Section 12. That chapter 26-6 be amended by adding a NEW SECTION to read:	

Appendix A (continued)

State	Provision (excerpted)	Source
	The provisions of this Act apply to, and in cases of conflict, supersede any other provision of law that impinges upon the free exercise of religious beliefs and moral convictions protected pursuant to this Act, unless a conflicting law is expressly made exempt from the application of the provisions of this Act. Section 14. That chapter 26-6 be amended by adding a NEW SECTION to read: The provisions of this Act apply to any foster care or adoption placement for which a child-placement agency has received funding for that particular placement comprised in part of a federal subsidy only to the fullest extent allowed under federal law. Section 15. That chapter 26-6 be amended by adding a NEW SECTION to read: If a child-placement agency declines to provide any services under section 3 of this Act, the child-placement agency's decision does not limit the ability of another child placement agency to provide those services and shall not be a factor in determining whether a placement in connection with the service is in the best interest of the child.	
Tennessee	SECTION 1. Tennessee Code Annotated, Title 63, Chapter 22, is amended by adding the following new part: (a) No counselor or therapist providing counseling or therapy services shall be required to counsel or serve a client as to goals, outcomes, or behaviors that conflict with a sincerely held religious belief of the counselor or therapist; provided, that the counselor or therapist coordinates a referral of the client to another counselor or therapist who will provide the counseling or therapy. (b) The refusal to provide counseling or therapy services as described in subsection (a) shall not be the basis for: (1) A civil cause of action; or (2) Criminal prosecution. (c) For purposes of this section, "counseling or therapy services" means assisting an individual, who is seeking or engaged in the counseling relationship in a private practice setting, in a manner intended to facilitate normal human growth and development, using a combination of mental health and human development principles, methods, and techniques, to achieve mental, emotional, physical, social, moral, educational, spiritual, or career development and adjustment throughout the life span.	S.B. 1556, enacted March 2016. Tennessee Code Annotated §§ 63-22-301, 63-22-702, 63-22-110(b)(3) (2016)
Texas	Sec.A45.001.AALEGISLATIVE INTENT. It is the intent of the legislature to maintain a diverse network of service providers that offer a range of foster capacity options and that accommodate children from various cultural backgrounds. To that end, the legislature expects reasonable accommodations to be made by the state to allow people of diverse backgrounds and beliefs to be a part of meeting the needs of children in the child welfare system. Decisions regarding the placement of children shall continue to be made in the best interest of the child, including which person is best able to provide for the child's physical, psychological, and emotional needs and development.	H.B. 3859, enacted June 2017. Texas Human Resources Code Annotated § 45.001 et seq. (2017)

(continued)

Appendix A (continued)

State	Provision (excerpted)	Source
	Sec. A45.002. AADEFINITIONS. In this chapter:	
	(1)AA"Adverse action" means any action that directly or indirectly adversely affects the person against whom the adverse action is taken, places the person in a worse position than the person was in before the adverse action was taken, or is likely to deter a reasonable person from acting or refusing to act. An adverse action includes:	
	(A)AAdenying an application for, refusing to renew, or canceling funding;	
	(B)AAdeclining to enter into, refusing to renew, or canceling a contract;	
	(C)AAdeclining to issue, refusing to renew, or canceling a license;	
	(D)AAterminating, suspending, demoting, or reassigning a person; and	
	(E)AAlimiting the ability of a person to engage in child welfare services.	
	(2)AA"Catchment area" means a geographic service area for providing child protective services or child welfare services.	
	(3)AA"Child welfare services" means social services provided to or on behalf of children, including:	
	(A)AAassisting abused or neglected children;	
	(B)AAcounseling children or parents;	
	(C)AApromoting foster parenting;	
	(D)AAproviding foster homes, general residential operations, residential care, adoptive homes, group homes, or temporary group shelters for children;	
	(E)AArecruiting foster parents;	
	(F)AAplacing children in foster homes;	
	(G)AAlicensing foster homes;	
	(H)AApromoting adoption or recruiting adoptive parents;	
	(I)AAassisting adoptions or supporting adoptive families;	
	(J)AAperforming or assisting home studies;	
	(K)AAassisting kinship guardianships or kinship caregivers;	
	(L)AAproviding family preservation services;	
	(M)AAproviding family support services;	
	(N)AAproviding temporary family reunification services;	
	(O)AAplacing children in adoptive homes; and	
	(P)AAserving as a foster parent.	
	(4)AA"Child welfare services provider" means a person, other than a governmental entity, that provides, seeks to provide, or applies for or receives a contract, subcontract, grant, subgrant, or cooperative agreement to provide child welfare services. The person is not required to be engaged exclusively in child welfare services to be a child welfare services provider.	

(continued)

Appendix A (continued)

State	Provision (excerpted)	Source
	(5)AA"Governmental entity" means: (A)AAthis state or a municipality or other political subdivision of this state; (B)AAany agency of this state or of a municipality or other political subdivision of this state, including a department, bureau, board, commission, office, agency, council, and public institution of higher education; or (C)AAa single source continuum contractor in this state providing services identified under Section 264.126, Family Code. Sec.A45.003.AAAPPLICABILITY. (a) This chapter applies to any ordinance, rule, order, decision, practice, or other exercise of governmental authority. (b)AAThis chapter applies to an act of a governmental entity, in the exercise of governmental authority, granting or refusing to grant a government benefit to a child welfare services provider. Sec.A45.004.AACHILD WELFARE SERVICES PROVIDERS PROTECTED. A governmental entity or any person that contracts with this state or operates under governmental authority to refer or place children for child welfare services may not discriminate or take any adverse action against a child welfare services provider on the basis, wholly or partly, that the provider: (1)AAhas declined or will decline to provide, facilitate, or refer a person for child welfare services that conflict with, or under circumstances that conflict with, the provider's sincerely held religious beliefs; (2)AAprovides or intends to provide children under the control, care, guardianship, or direction of the provider with a religious education, including through placing the children in a private or parochial school or otherwise providing a religious education in accordance with the laws of this state; (3)AAhas declined or will decline to provide, facilitate, or refer a person for abortions, contraceptives, or drugs, devices, or services that are potentially abortion-inducing; or (4)AArefuses to enter into a contract that is inconsistent with or would in any way interfere with or force a provider to surrender the rights created by this chapter. Sec.A45.005.AASECONDARY SERVICES PROVIDERS AND REFERRALS. (a) A child welfare services provider may not be required to provide any service that conflicts with the provider's sincerely held religious beliefs. (b)AAA governmental entity or any person that operates under governmental authority to refer or place children for child welfare services shall: (1)AAensure that a secondary child welfare services provider is available in that catchment area to provide a service described by Subsection (a) to a child; or	

(continued)

Appendix A (continued)

State	Provision (excerpted)	Source
	(2) if there is an insufficient number of secondary services providers willing or available in that catchment area to provide that service, provide for one or more secondary services providers in a nearby catchment area. (c) A child welfare services provider who declines to provide a child welfare service as authorized by this section shall: (1) provide to the person seeking the service written information directing the person to: (A) the web page on the department's Internet website that includes a list of other licensed child welfare services providers; or (B) other information sources that identify other licensed child welfare services providers who provide the service being denied; (2) refer the applicant to another licensed child welfare services provider who provides the service being denied; or (3) refer the applicant to the department or to a single source continuum contractor to identify and locate a licensed child welfare services provider who provides the service being denied. Sec. A45.009. EFFECT ON RIGHTS; CONSTRUCTION OF LAW. (a) This chapter may not be construed to authorize a governmental entity to burden a person's free exercise of religion. (b) The protections of religious freedom afforded by this chapter are in addition to the protections provided under federal or state law and the constitutions of this state and the United States. (c) This chapter may not be construed to supersede any law of this state that is equally as protective of religious beliefs as, or more protective of religious beliefs than, this chapter. (d) This chapter may not be considered to narrow the meaning or application of any other law protecting religious beliefs. (e) This chapter may not be construed to prevent law enforcement officers from exercising duties imposed on the officers under the Family Code and the Penal Code. (f) This chapter may not be construed to allow a child welfare services provider to decline to provide, facilitate, or refer a person for child welfare services on the basis of that person's race, ethnicity, or national origin. (g) This chapter may not be construed to allow a child welfare services provider to deprive a minor of the rights, including the right to medical care, provided by Chapters 32, 263, and 266, Family Code. (h) This chapter may not be construed to prohibit the department from: (1) exercising its duty as the child's managing conservator to make decisions in the child's best interest; or (2) obtaining necessary child welfare services from an alternate child welfare services provider. Sec. A45.010. INTERPRETATION. This chapter shall be liberally construed to effectuate its remedial and deterrent purposes.	

Appendix B: State Laws Related to Emergency Hospitalization for Observation

State	Standard for emergency hospitalization for observation	Reference
Alabama	(a) When a law enforcement officer is confronted by circumstances and has reasonable cause for believing that a person within the county is mentally ill and also believes that the person is likely to be of immediate danger to self or others, the law enforcement officer shall contact a community mental health officer. The community mental health officer shall join the law enforcement officer at the scene and location of the person to assess conditions and determine if the person needs the attention, specialized care, and services of a designated mental health facility. If the community mental health officer determines from the conditions, symptoms, and behavior that the person appears to be mentally ill and poses an immediate danger to self or others, the law enforcement officer shall take the person into custody and, together with the community mental health officer, deliver the person directly to the designated mental health facility. At the designated mental health facility, a responsible employee of the facility who is on duty and in charge of admissions to the facility shall be informed by the community mental health officer that the person in custody appears to be mentally ill and is in need of examination and observation.	Alabama Code § 22-52-91(a) (1994)
	(b) No limitations shall be placed upon the respondent's liberty nor treatment imposed upon the respondent unless such limitations are necessary to prevent the respondent from doing substantial and immediate harm to himself or to others or to prevent the respondent from leaving the jurisdiction of the court. No respondent shall be placed in a jail or other facility for persons accused of or convicted of committing crimes.	Alabama Code § 22-52-7(b) (2006)

(continued)

Appendix B (continued)

State	Standard for emergency hospitalization for observation	Reference
Alaska	(a) A peace officer, a psychiatrist or physician who is licensed to practice in this state or employed by the federal government, or a clinical psychologist licensed by the state Board of Psychologist and Psychological Associate Examiners who has probable cause to believe that a person is gravely disabled or is suffering from mental illness and is likely to cause serious harm to self or others of such immediate nature that considerations of safety do not allow initiation of involuntary commitment procedures set out in AS 47.30.700, may cause the person to be taken into custody and delivered to the nearest evaluation facility. A person taken into custody for emergency evaluation may not be placed in a jail or other correctional facility except for protective custody purposes and only while awaiting transportation to a treatment facility. However, emergency protective custody under this section may not include placement of a minor in a jail or secure facility. The peace officer or mental health professional shall complete an application for examination of the person in custody and be interviewed by a mental health professional at the facility.	Alaska Statutes § 47.30.705(a) (2008)
Arizona	A. A written application for emergency admission shall be made to an evaluation agency before a person may be hospitalized in the agency. B. The application for emergency admission shall be made by a person with knowledge of the facts requiring emergency admission. The applicant may be a relative or friend of the person, a peace officer, the admitting officer or another responsible person. C. The application shall be upon a prescribed form and shall include the following: 1. A statement by the applicant that he believes on the basis of personal observation that the person is, as a result of a mental disorder, a danger to self or others, and that during the time necessary to complete the prepetition screening procedures set forth in sections 36-520 and 36-521 the person is likely without immediate hospitalization to suffer serious physical harm or serious illness or is likely to inflict serious physical harm upon another person. 2. The specific nature of the danger. 3. A summary of the observations upon which the statement of danger is based. 4. The signature of the applicant. D. A telephonic application may be made no more than twenty-four hours prior to a written application. A telephonic application shall be made by or in the presence of a peace officer unless the application is made by a health care provider who is licensed pursuant to title 32, chapter 13, 15, 17 or 19.1 and who is directly involved with the care of a patient who is in a health care facility licensed in this state. For an application made by a doctor or a nurse, the original signature of the applicant on a facsimile copy of the application is acceptable, does not have to be notarized and may be submitted as the written application.	Arizona Revised Statutes § 36-524 (2016)

(continued)

Appendix B (continued)

State	Standard for emergency hospitalization for observation	Reference
	E. If the person to be admitted is not already present at the evaluation agency and if the admitting officer, based upon review of the written or telephonic application and conversation with the applicant and peace officer, has reasonable cause to believe that an emergency examination is necessary, the admitting officer may advise the peace officer, that sufficient grounds exist to take the person into custody and to transport the person to the evaluation agency. The admitting officer shall not be held civilly liable for any acts committed by a person whom the admitting officer did not advise be taken into custody if the admitting officer has in good faith followed the requirements of this section.	
Arkansas	Whenever it appears that a person is of danger to himself or herself or others, as defined in 20-47-207, and immediate confinement appears necessary to avoid harm to the person or others	Arkansas Code Annotated § 20-47-210(a) (2016)
California	When a person, as a result of a mental health disorder, is a danger to others, or to himself or herself, or gravely disabled, a peace officer, professional person in charge of a facility designated by the county for evaluation and treatment, member of the attending staff, as defined by regulation, of a facility designated by the county for evaluation and treatment, designated members of a mobile crisis team, or professional person designated by the county may, upon probable cause, take, or cause to be taken, the person into custody for a period of up to 72 hours for assessment, evaluation, and crisis intervention, or placement for evaluation and treatment in a facility designated by the county for evaluation and treatment and approved by the State Department of Health Care Services. At a minimum, assessment, as defined in Section 5150.4, and evaluation, as defined in subdivision (a) of Section 5008, shall be conducted and provided on an ongoing basis. Crisis intervention, as defined in subdivision (e) of Section 5008, may be provided concurrently with assessment, evaluation, or any other service.	California Welfare & Institutions Code § 5150(a) (2016)
Colorado	(1) Emergency procedure may be invoked under either one of the following two conditions: (a) (I) When any person appears to have a mental illness and, as a result of such mental illness, appears to be an imminent danger to others or to himself or herself or appears to be gravely disabled, then a person specified in subparagraph (II) of this paragraph (a), each of whom is referred to in this section as the "intervening professional," upon probable cause and with such assistance as may be required, may take the person into custody, or cause the person to be taken into custody, and placed in a facility designated or approved by the executive director for a seventy-two-hour treatment and evaluation. (II) The following persons may effect a seventy-two-hour hold as provided in subparagraph	Colorado Revised Statutes § 27-5-105(1) (2016)

(continued)

Appendix B (continued)

State	Standard for emergency hospitalization for observation	Reference
	(I) of this paragraph (a): (A) A certified peace officer; (B) A professional person; (C) A registered professional nurse as defined in section 12-38-103 (11), C.R.S., who by reason of postgraduate education and additional nursing preparation has gained knowledge, judgment, and skill in psychiatric or mental health nursing; (D) A licensed marriage and family therapist, licensed professional counselor, or addiction counselor licensed under part 5, 6, or 8 of article 43 of title 12, C.R.S., who by reason of postgraduate education and additional preparation has gained knowledge, judgment, and skill in psychiatric or clinical mental health therapy, forensic psychotherapy, or the evaluation of mental disorders; or (E) A licensed clinical social worker licensed under the provisions of part 4 of article 43 of title 12, C.R.S. (b) Upon an affidavit sworn to or affirmed before a judge that relates sufficient facts to establish that a person appears to have a mental illness and, as a result of the mental illness, appears to be an imminent danger to others or to himself or herself or appears to be gravely disabled, the court may order the person described in the affidavit to be taken into custody and placed in a facility designated or approved by the executive director for a seventy-two-hour treatment and evaluation. Whenever in this article a facility is to be designated or approved by the executive director, hospitals, if available, shall be approved or designated in each county before other facilities are approved or designated. Whenever in this article a facility is to be designated or approved by the executive director as a facility for a stated purpose and the facility to be designated or approved is a private facility, the consent of the private facility to the enforcement of standards set by the executive director shall be a prerequisite to the designation or approval.	
Connecticut	(a) Any person who a physician concludes has psychiatric disabilities and is dangerous to himself or others or gravely disabled, and is in need of immediate care and treatment in a hospital for psychiatric disabilities, may be confined in such a hospital, either public or private, under an emergency certificate as hereinafter provided for not more than fifteen days without order of any court, unless a written application for commitment of such person has been filed in a probate court prior to the expiration of the fifteen days, in which event such commitment is continued under the emergency certificate for an additional fifteen days or until the completion of probate proceedings, whichever occurs first.	Connecticut General Statutes Annotated § 17a-502(a) (2016)

(continued)

Appendix B (continued)

State	Standard for emergency hospitalization for observation	Reference
Delaware	Any person who believes that another person's behavior is both the (a) product of a mental condition and is dangerous to self or dangerous to others may notify a peace officer or a credentialed mental health screener or juvenile mental health screener and request assistance for said person. Upon the observation by a peace officer or a credentialed mental health screener or juvenile mental health screener that such individual with an apparent mental condition likely constitutes a danger to self or danger to others, such person with an apparent mental condition shall be promptly taken into custody for the purpose of an emergency detention by any peace officer in the State without the necessity of a warrant.	Delaware Code Annotated tit. 16 § 5003 (2014)
District of Columbia	An accredited officer or agent of the Department of Mental Health of the District of Columbia, or an officer authorized to make arrests in the District of Columbia, or a physician or qualified psychologist of the person in question, who has reason to believe that a person is mentally ill and, because of the illness, is likely to injure himself or others if he is not immediately detained may, without a warrant, take the person into custody, transport him to a public or private hospital, or to the Department, and make application for his admission thereto for purposes of emergency observation and diagnosis. The application shall reveal the circumstances under which the person was taken into custody and the reasons therefor.	D.C. Code Annotated § 21-521 (2016)
Florida	(1)CRITERIA.—A person may be taken to a receiving facility for involuntary examination if there is reason to believe that the person has a mental illness and because of his or her mental illness: (a)1.The person has refused voluntary examination after conscientious explanation and disclosure of the purpose of the examination; or 2.The person is unable to determine for himself or herself whether examination is necessary; and (b)1.Without care or treatment, the person is likely to suffer from neglect or refuse to care for himself or herself; such neglect or refusal poses a real and present threat of substantial harm to his or her well-being; and it is not apparent that such harm may be avoided through the help of willing family members or friends or the provision of other services; or 2.There is a substantial likelihood that without care or treatment the person will cause serious bodily harm to himself or herself or others in the near future, as evidenced by recent behavior.	Florida Statutes § 394.463(1) (2017)

(continued)

Appendix B (continued)

State	Standard for emergency hospitalization for observation	Reference
Georgia	(a) Any physician within this state may execute a certificate stating that he or she has personally examined a person within the preceding 48 hours and found that, based upon observations set forth in the certificate, such person appears to be a mentally ill person requiring involuntary treatment. A physician's certificate shall expire seven days after it is executed. Any peace officer, within 72 hours after receiving such certificate, shall make diligent efforts to take into custody the person named in the certificate and to deliver him or her forthwith to the nearest available emergency receiving facility serving the county in which the patient is found, where he or she shall be received for examination. (*effective until June 30, 2018*) (d) Any psychologist, clinical social worker, licensed professional counselor, or clinical nurse specialist in psychiatric/mental health may perform any act specified by this Code section to be performed by a physician. Any reference in any part of this chapter to a physician acting under this Code section shall be deemed to refer equally to a psychologist, a clinical social worker, a licensed professional counselor, or a clinical nurse specialist in psychiatric/mental health acting under this Code section. For purposes of this Code section, the term "psychologist" means any person authorized under the laws of this state to practice as a licensed psychologist; the term "clinical social worker" means any person authorized under the laws of this state to practice as a licensed clinical social worker; the term "licensed professional counselor" means any person authorized under the laws of this state to practice as a licensed professional counselor; and the term "clinical nurse specialist in psychiatric/mental health" means any person authorized under the laws of this state to practice as a registered professional nurse and who is recognized by the Georgia Board of Nursing to be engaged in advanced nursing practice as a clinical nurse specialist in psychiatric/mental health. (*effective until June 30, 2018*) (a) Any physician within this state may execute a certificate stating that he has personally examined a person within the preceding 48 hours and found that, based upon observations set forth in the certificate, the person appears to be a mentally ill person requiring involuntary treatment. A physician's certificate shall expire seven days after it is executed. Any peace officer, within 72 hours after receiving such certificate, shall make diligent efforts to take into custody the person named in the certificate and to deliver him forthwith to the nearest available emergency receiving facility serving the county in which the patient is found, where he shall be received for examination. (*effective June 30, 2018*)	Georgia Code Annotated §§ 37-3-41(a), (d) (2016)

(continued)

Appendix B (continued)

State	Standard for emergency hospitalization for observation	Reference
	(d) Any psychologist, clinical social worker, or clinical nurse specialist in psychiatric/mental health may perform any act specified by this Code section to be performed by a physician. Any reference in any part of this chapter to a physician acting under this Code section shall be deemed to refer equally to a psychologist, a clinical social worker, or a clinical nurse specialist in psychiatric/mental health acting under this Code section. For purposes of this subsection, the term "psychologist" means any person authorized under the laws of this state to practice as a licensed psychologist, the term "clinical social worker" means any person authorized under the laws of this state to practice as a licensed clinical social worker, and the term "clinical nurse specialist in psychiatric/mental health" means any person authorized under the laws of this state to practice as a registered professional nurse and who is recognized by the Georgia Board of Nursing to be engaged in advanced nursing practice as a clinical nurse specialist in psychiatric/mental health. (*effective June 30, 2018*)	
	(a) A peace officer may take any person to a physician within the county or an adjoining county for emergency examination by the physician, as provided in Code Section 37-3-41, or directly to an emergency receiving facility if (1) the person is committing a penal offense, and (2) the peace officer has probable cause for believing that the person is a mentally ill person requiring involuntary treatment. The peace officer need not formally tender charges against the individual prior to taking the individual to a physician or an emergency receiving facility under this Code section. The peace officer shall execute a written report detailing the circumstances under which the person was taken into custody; and this report shall be made a part of the patient's clinical record.	Georgia Code Annotated § 37-3-42(a) (2016)
	(b) Any psychologist may perform any act specified by this Code section to be performed by a physician. Any reference in any part of this chapter to a physician acting under this Code section shall be deemed to refer equally to a psychologist acting under this Code section. For purposes of this subsection, the term "psychologist" means any person authorized under the laws of this state to practice as a licensed psychologist.	
Hawaii	(1) If a law enforcement officer has reason to believe that a person is imminently dangerous to self or others, the officer shall call for assistance from the mental health emergency workers designated by the director. Upon determination by the mental health emergency workers that the person is imminently dangerous to self or others, the person shall be transported by ambulance or other suitable means, to a licensed psychiatric facility for further evaluation and possible emergency hospitalization. A law enforcement officer may also take into custody and transport to any facility designated by the director any person threatening or attempting suicide.	Hawaii Revised Statutes § 334-59(a)(1), (3) (2016)

(continued)

Appendix B (continued)

State	Standard for emergency hospitalization for observation	Reference
	(3) Any licensed physician, advanced practice registered nurse, physician assistant, or psychologist who has examined a person and has reason to believe the person is: (A) Mentally ill or suffering from substance abuse; (B) Imminently dangerous to self or others; and (C) In need of care or treatment; may direct transportation, by ambulance or other suitable means, to a licensed psychiatric facility for further evaluation and possible emergency hospitalization. A licensed physician, an advanced practice registered nurse, or physician assistant may administer treatment as is medically necessary, for the person's safe transportation. A licensed psychologist may administer treatment as is psychologically necessary.	
Idaho	(1) No person shall be taken into custody or detained as an alleged emergency patient for observation, diagnosis, evaluation, care or treatment of mental illness unless and until the court has ordered such apprehension and custody under the provisions outlined in section 66-329, Idaho Code; provided, however, that a person may be taken into custody by a peace officer and placed in a facility, or the person may be detained at a hospital at which the person presented or was brought to receive medical or mental health care, if the peace officer or a physician medical staff member of such hospital or a physician's assistant or advanced practice registered nurse practicing in such hospital has reason to believe that the person is gravely disabled due to mental illness or the person's continued liberty poses an imminent danger to that person or others, as evidenced by a threat of substantial physical harm; provided, under no circumstances shall the proposed patient be detained in a nonmedical unit used for the detention of individuals charged with or convicted of penal offenses …. Whenever a person is taken into custody or detained under this section without court order, the evidence supporting the claim of grave disability due to mental illness or imminent danger must be presented to a duly authorized court within twenty-four (24) hours from the time the individual was placed in custody or detained. (2) If the court finds the individual to be gravely disabled due to mental illness or imminently dangerous under subsection (1) of this section, the court shall issue a temporary custody order requiring the person to be held in a facility, and requiring an examination of the person by a designated examiner within twenty-four (24) hours of the entry of the order of the court. Under no circumstances shall the proposed patient be detained in a nonmedical unit used for the detention of individuals charged with or convicted of penal offenses.	Idaho Code §§ 66-326(1), (2) (2013)

(continued)

Appendix B (continued)

State	Standard for emergency hospitalization for observation	Reference
Illinois	A person 18 years of age or older who is subject to involuntary admission on an inpatient basis and in need of immediate hospitalization may be admitted to a mental health facility pursuant to this Article.	405 Illinois Compiled Statutes 5/3-600 (2010)
Indiana	Sec. 1. (a) An individual may be detained in a facility for not more than seventy-two (72) hours under this chapter, excluding Saturdays, Sundays, and legal holidays, if a written application for detention is filed with the facility. The individual may not be detained in a state institution unless the detention is instituted by the state institution. (b) An application under subsection (a) must contain both of the following: (1) A statement of the applicant's belief that the individual is: (A) mentally ill and either dangerous or gravely disabled; and (B) in need of immediate restraint. (2) A statement by at least one (1) physician that, based on: (A) an examination; or (B) information given the physician; the individual may be mentally ill and either dangerous or gravely disabled.	Indiana Code Annotated § 12-26-5-1(b) (2016)
Iowa	1. If the applicant requests that the respondent be taken into immediate custody and the judge, upon reviewing the application and accompanying documentation, finds probable cause to believe that the respondent has a serious mental impairment and is likely to injure the respondent or other persons if allowed to remain at liberty, the judge may enter a written order directing that the respondent be taken into immediate custody by the sheriff or the sheriff's deputy and be detained until the hospitalization hearing.	Iowa Code §§ 229.22.11 (2016)
	1. The procedure prescribed by this section shall be used when it appears that a person should be immediately detained due to serious mental impairment, but an application has not been filed naming the person as the respondent pursuant to section 229.6, and the person cannot be ordered into immediate custody and detained pursuant to section 229.11. 2. a. (1) In the circumstances described in subsection 1, any peace officer who has reasonable grounds to believe that a person is mentally ill, and because of that illness is likely to physically injure the person's self or others if not immediately detained, may without a warrant take or cause that person to be taken to the nearest available facility or hospital as defined in section 229.11, subsection 1, paragraphs "b" and "c". A person believed mentally ill, and likely to injure the person's self or others if not immediately detained, may be delivered to a facility or hospital by someone other than a peace officer.	Iowa Code §§ 229.22.1-2a(1) (2016)

(continued)

Appendix B (continued)

State	Standard for emergency hospitalization for observation	Reference
Kansas	(a) Any law enforcement officer who has a reasonable belief formed upon investigation that a person is a mentally ill person and because of such person's mental illness is likely to cause harm to self or others if allowed to remain at liberty may take the person into custody without a warrant. *If the officer is in a crisis intervention center service area, as defined in section 2, and amendments thereto, the officer may transport the person to such crisis intervention center. If the officer is not in a crisis intervention service area, as defined in section 2, and amendments thereto, or does not choose to transport the person to such crisis intervention center, then* the officer shall transport the person to a treatment facility where the person shall be examined by a physician or psychologist on duty at the treatment facility, except that no person shall be transported to a state psychiatric hospital for examination, unless a written statement from a qualified mental health professional authorizing such an evaluation at a state psychiatric hospital has been obtained …. If a written statement is made by the physician or psychologist at the treatment facility that after preliminary examination the physician or psychologist believes the person likely to be a mentally ill person subject to involuntary commitment for care and treatment and because of the person's mental illness is likely to cause harm to self or others if allowed to remain at liberty, and if the treatment facility is willing to admit the person, the law enforcement officer shall present to the treatment facility the application provided for in subsection (b) of K.S.A. 59-2954*(b)*, and amendments thereto.	Kansas Statutes Annotated § 59-2953(a), as amended (2017)
Kentucky	(1) An authorized staff physician may order the admission of any person who is present at, or is presented at, a hospital. For the purposes of this subsection only, a hospital may include any acute care hospital that is licensed by the Commonwealth. Within twenty-four (24) hours (excluding weekends and holidays) of the admission under this section, the authorized staff physician ordering the admission of the individual shall certify in the record of the individual that in his opinion the individual should be involuntarily hospitalized. (2) Any individual who has been admitted to a hospital under subsection (1) of this section shall be released from the hospital within seventy-two (72) hours (excluding weekends and holidays) unless further detained under the applicable provisions of this chapter.	Kentucky Revised Statutes Annotated § 202A.031 (2004)
	(1) Following an examination by a qualified mental health professional and a certification by that professional that the person meets the criteria for involuntary hospitalization, a judge may order the person hospitalized for a period not to exceed seventy-two (72) hours, excluding weekends and holidays. For the purposes of this section, the qualified mental health professional shall be:	Kentucky Revised Statutes Annotated § 202A.028(1) (2017)

(continued)

Appendix B (continued)

State	Standard for emergency hospitalization for observation	Reference
	(a) A staff member of a regional community program for mental health or individuals with an intellectual disability; (b) An individual qualified and licensed to perform the examination through the use of telehealth services; or (c) The psychiatrist ordered, subject to the court's discretion, to perform the required examination.	
Louisiana	A. Any person of legal age may file with the court a petition which asserts his belief that a person is suffering from mental illness which contributes or causes that person to be a danger to himself or others or to be gravely disabled, or is suffering from substance abuse which contributes or causes that person to be a danger to himself or others or to be gravely disabled and may thereby request a hearing. D. (3) If the respondent refuses to be examined by the court appointed physician as herein provided, or if the judge, after reviewing the petition and an affidavit filed pursuant to R.S. 28:53.2 or the report of the treating physician or the court appointed physician, finds that the respondent is mentally ill or suffering from substance abuse and is in need of immediate hospitalization to protect the person or others from physical harm, or that the respondent's condition may be markedly worsened by delay, then the court may issue a court order for custody of the respondent, and a peace officer shall deliver the respondent to a treatment facility designated by the court.	Louisiana Revised Statutes Annotated §§ 28:54 (A), (D) (3) (2016)
	A.(1) A person who is mentally ill or a person who is suffering from substance abuse may be admitted and detained at a treatment facility for observation, diagnosis, and treatment for a period not to exceed fifteen days under an emergency certificate. (2) A person suffering from substance abuse may be detained at a treatment facility for one additional period, not to exceed fifteen days, provided that a second emergency certificate is executed.... B.(1) Any physician, psychiatric mental health nurse practitioner, or psychologist may execute an emergency certificate only after an actual examination of a person alleged to be mentally ill or suffering from substance abuse who is determined to be in need of immediate care and treatment in a treatment facility because the examining physician, psychiatric mental health nurse practitioner, or psychologist determines the person to be dangerous to self or others or to be gravely disabled. The actual examination of the person by a psychiatrist may be conducted by telemedicine utilizing video conferencing technology provided that a licensed health care professional who can adequately and accurately assist with obtaining any necessary information including but not limited to the information listed in Paragraph (4) of this Subsection shall be in the examination room with the patient at the time of the video conference	Louisiana Revised Statutes Annotated § 28:53 (2016)

(continued)

Appendix B (continued)

State	Standard for emergency hospitalization for observation	Reference
Maine	1. Law enforcement officer's power. If a law enforcement officer has probable cause to believe that a person may be mentally ill and that due to that condition the person presents a threat of imminent and substantial physical harm to that person or to other persons, or if a law enforcement officer knows that a person has an advance health care directive authorizing mental health treatment and the officer has probable cause to believe that the person lacks capacity, the law enforcement officer: A. May take the person into protective custody; and B. If the law enforcement officer does take the person into protective custody, shall deliver the person immediately for examination by a medical practitioner as provided in section 3863 or, for a person taken into protective custody who has an advance health care directive authorizing mental health treatment, for examination as provided in Title 18-A, section 5-802, subsection (d) to determine the individual's capacity and the existence of conditions specified in the advance health care directive for the directive to be effective. When formulating probable cause, the law enforcement officer may rely upon information provided by a 3rd-party informant if the officer confirms that the informant has reason to believe, based upon the informant's recent personal observations of or conversations with a person, that the person may be mentally ill and that due to that condition the person presents a threat of imminent and substantial physical harm to that person or to other persons.	Maine Revised Statutes Annotated, title 34-B § 3862 (2009)
	A person may be admitted to a psychiatric hospital on an emergency basis according to the following procedures. 1. Application. Any health officer, law enforcement officer or other person may apply to admit a person to a psychiatric hospital, subject to the prohibitions and penalties of section 3805, stating: A. The applicant's belief that the person is mentally ill and, because of the person's illness, poses a likelihood of serious harm; and B. The grounds for this belief.	Maine Revised Statutes Annotated, title 34-B § 3863 (2009)
Maryland	(a) Petition authorized. -- A petition for emergency evaluation of an individual may be made under this section only if the petitioner has reason to believe that the individual: (1) Has a mental disorder; and (2) The individual presents a danger to the life or safety of the individual or of others. (b) Petitioners; basis for petition. -- (1) The petition for emergency evaluation of an individual may be made by: (i) A physician, psychologist, clinical social worker, licensed clinical professional counselor, clinical nurse specialist in psychiatric and mental health nursing, psychiatric nurse practitioner, licensed clinical marriage and family therapist, or health officer or designee of a health officer who has examined the individual;	Maryland Code Annotated, Health-General § 10-622(a) (2016)

(continued)

Appendix B: State Laws Related to Emergency Hospitalization for Observation 295

Appendix B (continued)

State	Standard for emergency hospitalization for observation	Reference
	(ii) A peace officer who personally has observed the individual or the individual's behavior; or (iii) Any other interested person. (2) An individual who makes a petition for emergency evaluation under paragraph (1)(i) or (ii) of this subsection may base the petition on: (i) The examination or observation; or (ii) Other information obtained that is pertinent to the factors giving rise to the petition.	
Massachusetts	Section 12. (a) Any physician who is licensed pursuant to section 2 of chapter 112 or qualified psychiatric nurse mental health clinical specialist authorized to practice as such under regulations promulgated pursuant to the provisions of section 80B of said chapter 112 or a qualified psychologist licensed pursuant to sections 118 to 129, inclusive, of said chapter 112, or a licensed independent clinical social worker licensed pursuant to sections 130 to 137, inclusive, of chapter 112 who, after examining a person, has reason to believe that failure to hospitalize such person would create a likelihood of serious harm by reason of mental illness may restrain or authorize the restraint of such person and apply for the hospitalization of such person for a 3?day period at a public facility or at a private facility authorized for such purposes by the department. If an examination is not possible because of the emergency nature of the case and because of the refusal of the person to consent to such examination, the physician, qualified psychologist, qualified psychiatric nurse mental health clinical specialist or licensed independent clinical social worker on the basis of the facts and circumstances may determine that hospitalization is necessary and may apply therefore. In an emergency situation, if a physician, qualified psychologist, qualified psychiatric nurse mental health clinical specialist or licensed independent clinical social worker is not available, a police officer, who believes that failure to hospitalize a person would create a likelihood of serious harm by reason of mental illness may restrain such person and apply for the hospitalization of such person for a 3?day period at a public facility or a private facility authorized for such purpose by the department. An application for hospitalization shall state the reasons for the restraint of such person and any other relevant information which may assist the admitting physician or physicians. Whenever practicable, prior to transporting such person, the applicant shall telephone or otherwise communicate with a facility to describe the circumstances and known clinical history and to determine whether the facility is the proper facility to receive such person and also to give notice of any restraint to be used and to determine whether such restraint is necessary.	Massachusetts General Laws Annotated chapter 123 § 12(a) (2017)

(continued)

Appendix B (continued)

State	Standard for emergency hospitalization for observation	Reference
Michigan	(1) If a peace officer observes an individual conducting himself or herself in a manner that causes the peace officer to reasonably believe that the individual is a person requiring treatment, the peace officer may take the individual into protective custody and transport the individual to a preadmission screening unit designated by a community mental health services program for examination under section 429 or for mental health intervention services.	Michigan Compiled Laws § 330.1427(1) (2017)
	If it appears to the court that the individual requires immediate assessment because the individual presents a substantial risk of significant physical or mental harm to himself or herself in the near future or presents a substantial risk of significant physical harm to others in the near future, the court may order the individual hospitalized and may order a peace officer to take the individual into protective custody and transport the individual to a preadmission screening unit designated by the community mental health services program. If the preadmission screening unit authorizes hospitalization, the peace officer shall transport the individual to a hospital designated by the community mental health services program, unless other arrangements are provided by the preadmission screening unit. If the examinations and clinical certificates of the psychiatrist, and the physician or the licensed psychologist, are not completed within 24 hours after hospitalization, the individual shall be released.	Michigan Compiled Laws § 330.1438 (2017)
Minnesota	(a) Any person may be admitted or held for emergency care and treatment in a treatment facility, except to a facility operated by the Minnesota sex offender program, with the consent of the head of the treatment facility upon a written statement by an examiner that: (1) the examiner has examined the person not more than 15 days prior to admission; (2) the examiner is of the opinion, for stated reasons, that the person is mentally ill, developmentally disabled, or chemically dependent, and is in danger of causing injury to self or others if not immediately detained; and (3) an order of the court cannot be obtained in time to prevent the anticipated injury. (b) If the proposed patient has been brought to the treatment facility by another person, the examiner shall make a good faith effort to obtain a statement of information that is available from that person, which must be taken into consideration in deciding whether to place the proposed patient on an emergency hold. The statement of information must include, to the extent available, direct observations of the proposed patient's behaviors, reliable knowledge of recent and past behavior, and information regarding psychiatric history, past treatment, and current mental health providers. The examiner shall also inquire into the existence of health care directives under chapter 145, and advance psychiatric directives under section 253B.03, subdivision 6d.	Minnesota Statutes § 253B.05(1)(a) (2017)

(continued)

Appendix B (continued)

State	Standard for emergency hospitalization for observation	Reference
	(a) A peace or health officer may take a person into custody and transport the person to a licensed physician or treatment facility if the officer has reason to believe, either through direct observation of the person's behavior, or upon reliable information of the person's recent behavior and knowledge of the person's past behavior or psychiatric treatment, that the person is mentally ill or developmentally disabled and in danger of injuring self or others if not immediately detained. A peace or health officer or a person working under such officer's supervision, may take a person who is believed to be chemically dependent or is intoxicated in public into custody and transport the person to a treatment facility.	Minnesota Statutes § 253B.05(2) (2017)
Mississippi	(5) (a) Whenever a licensed psychologist, nurse practitioner or physician assistant who is certified to complete examinations for the purpose of commitment or a licensed physician has reason to believe that a person poses an immediate substantial likelihood of physical harm to himself or others or is gravely disabled and unable to care for himself by virtue of mental illness, as defined in Section 41-21-61(e), then the physician, psychologist, nurse practitioner or physician assistant may hold the person or may admit the person to and treat the person in a licensed medical facility, without a civil order or warrant for a period not to exceed seventy-two (72) hours ….	Mississippi Code Annotated § 41-21-67(5)(a) (2016)
Missouri	1. An application for detention for evaluation and treatment may be executed by any adult person, who need not be an attorney or represented by an attorney, including the mental health coordinator, on a form provided by the court for such purpose, and must allege under oath that the applicant has reason to believe that the respondent is suffering from a mental disorder and presents a likelihood of serious harm to himself or to others. The application must specify the factual information on which such belief is based and should contain the names and addresses of all persons known to the applicant who have knowledge of such facts through personal observation. 2. The filing of a written application in court by any adult person, who need not be an attorney or represented by an attorney, including the mental health coordinator, shall authorize the applicant to bring the matter before the court on an ex parte basis to determine whether the respondent should be taken into custody and transported to a mental health facility. The application may be filed in the court having probate jurisdiction in any county where the respondent may be found. If the court finds that there is probable cause, either upon testimony under oath or upon a review of affidavits, to believe that the respondent may be suffering from a mental disorder and presents a likelihood of serious harm to himself or others, it shall direct a peace officer to take the respondent into custody and transport him to a mental health facility for detention for evaluation and treatment for a period not to exceed ninety-six hours unless further detention and treatment is authorized pursuant to this chapter. Nothing herein shall be construed to prohibit the court, in the exercise of its discretion, from giving the respondent an opportunity to be heard.	Missouri Annotated Statutes §§ 632-305 (1)-(3) (2016)

(continued)

Appendix B (continued)

State	Standard for emergency hospitalization for observation	Reference
	3. A mental health coordinator may request a peace officer to take or a peace officer may take a person into custody for detention for evaluation and treatment for a period not to exceed ninety-six hours only when such mental health coordinator or peace officer has reasonable cause to believe that such person is suffering from a mental disorder and that the likelihood of serious harm by such person to himself or others is imminent unless such person is immediately taken into custody. Upon arrival at the mental health facility, the peace officer or mental health coordinator who conveyed such person or caused him to be conveyed shall either present the application for detention for evaluation and treatment upon which the court has issued a finding of probable cause and the respondent was taken into custody or complete an application for initial detention for evaluation and treatment for a period not to exceed ninety-six hours which shall be based upon his own personal observations or investigations and shall contain the information required in subsection 1 of this section.	
Montana	(1) When an emergency situation as defined in 53-21-102 exists, a peace officer may take any person who appears to have a mental disorder and to present an imminent danger of death or bodily harm to the person or to others or who appears to have a mental disorder and to be substantially unable to provide for the person's own basic needs of food, clothing, shelter, health, or safety into custody only for sufficient time to contact a professional person for emergency evaluation. If possible, a professional person should be called prior to taking the person into custody. (2) If the professional person agrees that the person detained is a danger to the person or to others and that an emergency situation as defined in 53-21-102 exists, then the person may be detained and treated until the next regular business day. At that time, the professional person shall release the detained person or file findings with the county attorney who, if the county attorney determines probable cause to exist, shall file the petition provided for in 53-21-121 through 53-21-126 in the county of the respondent's residence. In either case, the professional person shall file a report with the court explaining the professional person's actions.	Montana Code Annotated § 53-21-128 (1)-(2) (2013)

(continued)

Appendix B (continued)

State	Standard for emergency hospitalization for observation	Reference
Nebraska	(1) A law enforcement officer who has probable cause to believe that a person is mentally ill and dangerous or a dangerous sex offender and that the harm described in section 71-908 or subdivision (1) of section 83-174.01 is likely to occur before mental health board proceedings under the Nebraska Mental Health Commitment Act or the Sex Offender Commitment Act may be initiated to obtain custody of the person may take such person into emergency protective custody, cause him or her to be taken into emergency protective custody, or continue his or her custody if he or she is already in custody. Such person shall be admitted to an appropriate and available medical facility, jail, or Department of Correctional Services facility as provided in subsection (2) of this section. Each county shall make arrangements with appropriate facilities inside or outside the county for such purpose and shall pay the cost of the emergency protective custody of persons from such county in such facilities. A mental health professional who has probable cause to believe that a person is mentally ill and dangerous or a dangerous sex offender may cause such person to be taken into custody and shall have a limited privilege to hold such person until a law enforcement officer or other authorized person arrives to take custody of such person.	Nebraska Revised Statutes § 71-919(1)
Nevada	Except as otherwise provided in subsection 2, an application for the emergency admission of a person alleged to be a person with mental illness for evaluation, observation and treatment may only be made by an accredited agent of the Department, an officer authorized to make arrests in the State of Nevada or a physician, physician assistant, psychologist, marriage and family therapist, clinical professional counselor, social worker or registered nurse. The agent, officer, physician, physician assistant, psychologist, marriage and family therapist, clinical professional counselor, social worker or registered nurse may: Without a warrant: (a) Take a person alleged to be a person (1) with mental illness into custody to apply for the emergency admission of the person for evaluation, observation and treatment; and (2) Transport the person alleged to be a person with mental illness to a public or private mental health facility or hospital for that purpose, or arrange for the person to be transported by: (I) A local law enforcement agency;	Nevada Revised Statutes § 433A.160 (2015)

(continued)

Appendix B (continued)

State	Standard for emergency hospitalization for observation	Reference
	(II) A system for the nonemergency medical transportation of persons whose operation is authorized by the Nevada Transportation Authority;	
	(III) An entity that is exempt pursuant to NRS 706.745 from the provisions of NRS 706.386 or 706.421; or	
	(IV) If medically necessary, an ambulance service that holds a permit issued pursuant to the provisions of chapter 450B of NRS, only if the agent, officer, physician, physician assistant, psychologist, marriage and family therapist, clinical professional counselor, social worker or registered nurse has, based upon his or her personal observation of the person alleged to be a person with mental illness, probable cause to believe that the person has a mental illness and, because of that illness, is likely to harm himself or herself or others if allowed his or her liberty.	
	(b) Apply to a district court for an order requiring:	
	(1) Any peace officer to take a person alleged to be a person with mental illness into custody to allow the applicant for the order to apply for the emergency admission of the person for evaluation, observation and treatment; and	
	(2) Any agency, system or service described in subparagraph (2) of paragraph (a) to transport the person alleged to be a person with mental illness to a public or private mental health facility or hospital for that purpose. The district court may issue such an order only if it is satisfied that there is probable cause to believe that the person has a mental illness and, because of that illness, is likely to harm himself or herself or others if allowed his or her liberty.	
	2. An application for the emergency admission of a person alleged to be a person with mental illness for evaluation, observation and treatment may be made by a spouse, parent, adult child or legal guardian of the person. The spouse, parent, adult child or legal guardian and any other person who has a legitimate interest in the person alleged to be a person with mental illness may apply to a district court for an order described in paragraph (b) of subsection 1.	
	3. The application for the emergency admission of a person alleged to be a person with mental illness for evaluation, observation and treatment must reveal the circumstances under which the person was taken into custody and the reasons therefor.	
	4. Except as otherwise provided in this subsection, each person admitted to a public or private mental health facility or hospital under an emergency admission must be evaluated at the time of admission by a psychiatrist or a psychologist. If a psychiatrist or a psychologist is not available to conduct an evaluation at the time of admission, a physician may conduct the evaluation. Each such emergency admission must be approved by a psychiatrist.	

(continued)

Appendix B (continued)

State	Standard for emergency hospitalization for observation	Reference
	Except as otherwise provided in this section, the administrative officer of a facility operated by the Division or of any other public or private mental health facility or hospital shall not accept an application for an emergency admission under NRS 433A.160 unless that application is accompanied by a certificate of a licensed psychologist, a physician, a physician assistant under the supervision of a psychiatrist, a clinical social worker who has the psychiatric training and experience prescribed by the Board of Examiners for Social Workers pursuant to NRS 641B.160, an advanced practice registered nurse who has the psychiatric training and experience prescribed by the State Board of Nursing pursuant to NRS 632.120 or an accredited agent of the Department stating that he or she has examined the person alleged to be a person with mental illness and that he or she has concluded that the person has a mental illness and, because of that illness, is likely to harm himself or herself or others if allowed his or her liberty. The certificate required by this section may be obtained from a licensed psychologist, physician, physician assistant, clinical social worker, advanced practice registered nurse or accredited agent of the Department who is employed by the public or private mental health facility or hospital to which the application is made.	Nevada Revised Statutes § 433A.170 (2015)
New Hampshire	A person shall be eligible for involuntary emergency admission if he is in such mental condition as a result of mental illness to pose a likelihood of danger to himself or others. I. As used in this section "danger to himself" is established by demonstrating that: (a) Within 40 days of the completion of the petition, the person has inflicted serious bodily injury on himself or has attempted suicide or serious self-injury and there is a likelihood the act or attempted act will recur if admission is not ordered; (b) Within 40 days of the completion of the petition, the person has threatened to inflict serious bodily injury on himself and there is likelihood that an act or attempt of serious self-injury will occur if admission is not ordered; or (c) The person's behavior demonstrates that he so lacks the capacity to care for his own welfare that there is a likelihood of death, serious bodily injury, or serious debilitation if admission is not ordered. (d) The person meets all of the following criteria:	New Hampshire Revised Statutes Annotated § 135-C:27 (1986)

(continued)

Appendix B (continued)

State	Standard for emergency hospitalization for observation	Reference
	(1) The person has been determined to be severely mentally disabled in accordance with rules authorized by RSA 135-C:61 for a period of at least one year;	
	(2) The person has had at least one involuntary admission, within the last 2 years, pursuant to RSA 135-C:34-54;	
	(3) The person has no guardian of the person appointed pursuant to RSA 464-A;	
	(4) The person is not subject to a conditional discharge granted pursuant to RSA 135-C:49, II;	
	(5) The person has refused the treatment determined necessary by a mental health program approved by the department; and	
	(6) A psychiatrist at a mental health program approved by the department has determined, based upon the person's clinical history, that there is a substantial probability that the person's refusal to accept necessary treatment will lead to death, serious bodily injury, or serious debilitation if admission is not ordered.	
	II. As used in this section "danger to others" is established by demonstrating that within 40 days of the completion of the petition, the person has inflicted, attempted to inflict, or threatened to inflict serious bodily harm on another.	
	I. The involuntary emergency admission of a person shall be to the state mental health services system under the supervision of the commissioner. The admission may be ordered upon the certificate of a physician or APRN, as defined in RSA 135-C:2, II-a, who is approved by either a designated receiving facility or a community mental health program approved by the commissioner, provided that within 3 days of the completion of the petition the physician or APRN has conducted, or has caused to be conducted, a physical examination if indicated and circumstances permit, and a mental examination ….	New Hampshire Revised Statutes Annotated § 135-C-28 (2009)
	II. Upon request for involuntary emergency admission by a petitioner, if the person sought to be admitted refuses to consent to a mental examination, a petitioner or a law enforcement officer may sign a complaint which shall be sworn to before a justice of the peace. The complaint shall be submitted to the justice of the peace with the petition. The petition shall state in detail the acts or actions of the person sought to be admitted which the petitioner has personally observed or which have been personally reported to the petitioner and in his or her opinion require a compulsory mental examination. If the justice of the peace finds that a compulsory mental examination is necessary, the justice may order the examination.	

(continued)

Appendix B (continued)

State	Standard for emergency hospitalization for observation	Reference
	III. When a peace officer observes a person engaging in behavior which gives the peace officer reasonable suspicion to believe that the person may be suffering from a mental illness and probable cause to believe that unless the person is placed in protective custody the person poses an immediate danger of bodily injury to himself or others, the police officer may place the person in protective custody. Any person taken into protective custody under this paragraph shall be transported directly to an emergency room of a licensed general hospital or to another site designated by the community mental health program serving the area, for the purpose of determining if an involuntary emergency admission shall be ordered in accordance with RSA 135-C:28, I. The period of protective custody shall end when a physician or APRN makes a determination as to whether involuntary emergency admission shall be ordered or at the end of 6 hours, whichever event occurs first.	
New Jersey	6.A State or local law enforcement officer shall take custody of a person and take the person immediately and directly to a screening service if: (a) On the basis of personal observation, the law enforcement officer has reasonable cause to believe that the person is in need of involuntary commitment to treatment; (b) A mental health screener has certified on a form prescribed by the division that based on a screening outreach visit the person is in need of involuntary commitment to treatment and has requested the person be taken to the screening service for a complete assessment; (c) The court orders that a person subject to an order of conditional discharge issued pursuant to subsection c. of section 15 of P.L.1987, c.116 (C.30:4-27.15) who has failed to follow the conditions of the discharge be taken to a screening service for an assessment; or (d) An outpatient treatment provider has certified on a form prescribed by the division that the provider has reasonable cause to believe the person is in need of evaluation for commitment to treatment. The involvement of the law enforcement authority shall continue at the screening service as long as necessary to protect the safety of the person in custody and the safety of the community from which the person was taken.	New Jersey Statutes Annotated § 30:4-27.6 (2009)

(continued)

Appendix B (continued)

State	Standard for emergency hospitalization for observation	Reference
New Mexico	A. A peace officer may detain and transport a person for emergency mental health evaluation and care in the absence of a legally valid order from the court only if: (1) the person is otherwise subject to lawful arrest; (2) the peace officer has reasonable grounds to believe the person has just attempted suicide; (3) the peace officer, based upon his own observation and investigation, has reasonable grounds to believe that the person, as a result of a mental disorder, presents a likelihood of serious harm to himself or others and that immediate detention is necessary to prevent such harm. Immediately upon arrival at the evaluation facility, the peace officer shall be interviewed by the admitting physician or his designee; or (4) a licensed physician or a certified psychologist has certified that the person, as a result of a mental disorder, presents a likelihood of serious harm to himself or others and that immediate detention is necessary to prevent such harm. Such certification shall constitute authority to transport the person. C. An evaluation facility may accept for an emergency based admission any person when a licensed physician or certified psychologist certifies that such person, as a result of a mental disorder, presents a likelihood of serious harm to himself or others and that immediate detention is necessary to prevent such harm. Such certification shall constitute authority to transport the person.	New Mexico Statutes Annotated § 43-1-10(A), (C) (2011)
New York	(a) The director of any hospital maintaining adequate staff and facilities for the observation, examination, care, and treatment of persons alleged to be mentally ill and approved by the commissioner to receive and retain patients pursuant to this section may receive and retain therein as a patient for a period of fifteen days any person alleged to have a mental illness for which immediate observation, care, and treatment in a hospital is appropriate and which is likely to result in serious harm to himself or others. "Likelihood to result in serious harm" as used in this article shall mean: 1. substantial risk of physical harm to himself as manifested by threats of or attempts at suicide or serious bodily harm or other conduct demonstrating that he is dangerous to himself, or 2. a substantial risk of physical harm to other persons as manifested by homicidal or other violent behavior by which others are placed in reasonable fear of serious physical harm. The director shall cause to be entered upon the hospital records the name of the person or persons, if any, who have brought such person to the hospital and the details of the circumstances leading to the hospitalization of such person. The director shall admit such person pursuant to the provisions of this section only if a staff physician of the hospital upon examination of such person finds that such person qualifies under the requirements of this section. Such person shall not be retained for a period of more than forty-eight hours unless within such period such finding is confirmed after examination by another physician who shall be a member of the psychiatric staff of the hospital	New York Mental Hygiene Code § 9.39(a) (2015)

(continued)

Appendix B (continued)

State	Standard for emergency hospitalization for observation	Reference
North Carolina	(a) Anyone, including a law enforcement officer, who has knowledge of an individual who is subject to inpatient commitment according to the criteria of G.S. 122C-261(a) and who requires immediate hospitalization to prevent harm to self or others, may transport the individual directly to an area facility or other place, including a State facility for the mentally ill, for examination by a physician or eligible psychologist in accordance with G.S. 122C-263(c).	North Carolina General Statutes § 122C-262(a) (1995)
North Dakota	"Mental health professional" means: (a). A psychologist with at least a master's degree who has been either licensed or approved for exemption by the North Dakota board of psychology examiners. (b). A social worker with a master's degree in social work from an accredited program. (c). An advanced practice registered nurse. (d). A registered nurse with a minimum of two years of psychiatric clinical experience under the supervision of an expert examiner. (e). A licensed addiction counselor. (f). A licensed professional counselor with a master's degree in counseling from an accredited program who has either successfully completed the advanced training beyond the master's degree as required by the national academy of mental health counselors or a minimum of two years of clinical experience in a mental health agency or setting under the supervision of a psychiatrist or psychologist. (g). A physician assistant.	North Dakota Century Code § 25.03-1-02 (2017).
	1. When a peace officer, physician either in person or directing an emergency medical services professional, psychiatrist, physician assistant, psychologist, advanced practice registered nurse, or mental health professional has reasonable cause to believe that an individual is a person requiring treatment and there exists a serious risk of harm to that individual, others, or property of an immediate nature that considerations of safety do not allow preliminary intervention by a magistrate, the peace officer, physician either in person or directing an emergency medical services professional, psychiatrist, physician assistant, psychologist, advanced practice registered nurse, or mental health professional, using the screening process set forth in section 25-03.1-04, may cause the individual to be taken into custody and detained at a treatment facility as provided in subsection 3, and subject to section 25-03.1-26, except that if emergency conditions exist that prevent the immediate conveyance of the individual to a public treatment facility, a private facility that has adequate resources and capacity to hold that individual may hold the individual in anticipation of conveyance to a public treatment facility for up to twenty- three hours: (a). Without conducting an immediate examination required under section 25-03.1-26; and (b). Without following notice and hearing requirements for a transfer to another treatment facility required under subsection 3 of section 25-03.1-34.	North Dakota Century Code § 25.03-1-25.1-.2 (2017)

(continued)

Appendix B (continued)

State	Standard for emergency hospitalization for observation	Reference
	2. If a petitioner seeking the involuntary treatment of a respondent requests that the respondent be taken into immediate custody and the magistrate, upon reviewing the petition and accompanying documentation, finds probable cause to believe that the respondent is a person requiring treatment and there exists a serious risk of harm to the respondent, others, or property if allowed to remain at liberty, the magistrate may enter a written order directing that the respondent be taken into immediate custody and be detained as provided in subsection 3 until the preliminary or treatment hearing, which must be held no more than seven days after the date of the order	
Ohio	Any psychiatrist, licensed clinical psychologist, licensed physician, health officer, parole officer, police officer, or sheriff may take a person into custody, or the chief of the adult parole authority or a parole or probation officer with the approval of the chief of the authority may take a parolee, an offender under a community control sanction or a post-release control sanction, or an offender under transitional control into custody and may immediately transport the parolee, offender on community control or post-release control, or offender under transitional control to a hospital or, notwithstanding section 5119.33 of the Revised Code, to a general hospital not licensed by the department of mental health and addiction services where the parolee, offender on community control or post-release control, or offender under transitional control may be held for the period prescribed in this section, if the psychiatrist, licensed clinical psychologist, licensed physician, health officer, parole officer, police officer, or sheriff has reason to believe that the person is a mentally ill person subject to court order under division (B) of section 5122.01 of the Revised Code, and represents a substantial risk of physical harm to self or others if allowed to remain at liberty pending examination	Ohio Revised Code Annotated § 5122.10 (2013)
Oklahoma	A. Any person who appears to be or states that such person is mentally ill, alcohol-dependent, or drug-dependent to a degree that immediate emergency action is necessary may be taken into protective custody and detained as provided pursuant to the provisions of this section. Nothing in this section shall be construed as being in lieu of prosecution under state or local statutes or ordinances relating to public intoxication offenses. B. 1. Any peace officer who reasonably believes that a person is a person requiring treatment as defined in Section 1-103 of this title shall take the person into protective custody. The officer shall make every reasonable effort to take the person into custody in the least conspicuous manner.	43A Oklahoma Statutes § 5-207 (2016)
Oregon	A peace officer may take into custody a person who the officer has probable cause to believe is dangerous to self or to any other person and is in need of immediate care, custody or treatment for mental illness. As directed by the community mental health program director, a peace officer shall remove a person taken into custody under this section to the nearest hospital or nonhospital facility approved by the Oregon Health Authority.	Oregon Revised Statutes §426.228(1) (2015)

(continued)

Appendix B: State Laws Related to Emergency Hospitalization for Observation 307

Appendix B (continued)

State	Standard for emergency hospitalization for observation	Reference
Pennsylvania	(a) Persons Subject--Whenever a person is severely mentally disabled and in need of immediate treatment, he may be made subject to involuntary emergency examination and treatment. A person is severely mentally disabled when, as a result of mental illness, his capacity to exercise self-control, judgment and discretion in the conduct of his affairs and social relations or to care for his own personal needs is so lessened that he poses a clear and present danger of harm to others or to himself. (b) Determination of Clear and Present Danger.--(1) Clear and present danger to others shall be shown by establishing that within the past 30 days the person has inflicted or attempted to inflict serious bodily harm on another and that there is a reasonable probability that such conduct will be repeated. If, however, the person has been found incompetent to be tried or has been acquitted by reason of lack of criminal responsibility on charges arising from conduct involving infliction of or attempt to inflict substantial bodily harm on another, such 30-day limitation shall not apply so long as an application for examination and treatment is filed within 30 days after the date of such determination or verdict. In such case, a clear and present danger to others may be shown by establishing that the conduct charged in the criminal proceeding did occur, and that there is a reasonable probability that such conduct will be repeated. For the purpose of this section, a clear and present danger of harm to others may be demonstrated by proof that the person has made threats of harm and has committed acts in furtherance of the threat to commit harm. (2) Clear and present danger to himself shall be shown by establishing that within the past 30 days: (i) the person has acted in such manner as to evidence that he would be unable, without care, supervision and the continued assistance of others, to satisfy his need for nourishment, personal or medical care, shelter, or self-protection and safety, and that there is a reasonable probability that death, serious bodily injury or serious physical debilitation would ensue within 30 days unless adequate treatment were afforded under this act; or (ii) the person has attempted suicide and that there is the reasonable probability of suicide unless adequate treatment is afforded under this act. For the purposes of this subsection, a clear and present danger may be demonstrated by the proof that the person has made threats to commit suicide and has committed acts which are in furtherance of the threat to commit suicide; or (iii) the person has substantially mutilated himself or attempted to mutilate himself substantially and that there is the reasonable probability of mutilation unless adequate treatment is afforded under this act. For the purposes of this subsection, a clear and present danger shall be established by proof that the person has made threats to commit mutilation and has committed acts which are in furtherance of the threat to commit mutilation.	50 Pennsylvania Consolidated Statutes Annotated § 7301 (1976)

(continued)

Appendix B (continued)

State	Standard for emergency hospitalization for observation	Reference
Rhode Island	*(a) Applicants.* (1) Any physician, who after examining a person, has reason to believe that the person is in need of immediate care and treatment, and is one whose continued unsupervised presence in the community would create an imminent likelihood of serious harm by reason of mental disability, may apply at a facility for the emergency certification of the person thereto. The medical director, or any other physician employed by the proposed facility for certification may apply under this subsection if no other physician is available and he or she certifies this fact. If an examination is not possible because of the emergency nature of the case and because of the refusal of the person to consent to the examination, the applicant on the basis of his or her observation may determine, in accordance with the above, that emergency certification is necessary and may apply therefor. In the event that no physician is available, a qualified mental health professional or police officer who believes the person to be in need of immediate care and treatment, and one whose continued unsupervised presence in the community would create an imminent likelihood of serious harm by reason of mental disability, may make the application for emergency certification to a facility. Application shall in all cases be made to the facility which in the judgment of the applicant at the time of application would impose the least restraint on the liberty of the person consistent with affording him or her the care and treatment necessary and appropriate to his or her condition.	Rhode Island General Laws § 40.1-5-7(a) (1) (1987)
	(9) "Mental health professional" means a psychiatrist, psychologist, or social worker and such other persons, including psychiatric nurse clinicians, as may be defined by rules and regulations promulgated by the director.	Rhode Island General Laws § 40.1-5-2(9) (2014)
South Carolina	If a person believed to be mentally ill and because of this condition likely to cause serious harm if not immediately hospitalized cannot be examined by at least one licensed physician pursuant to Section 44-17-410 because the person's whereabouts are unknown or for any other reason, the petitioner seeking commitment pursuant to Section 44-17-410 shall execute an affidavit stating a belief that the individual is mentally ill and because of this condition likely to cause serious harm if not hospitalized, the ground for this belief and that the usual procedure for examination cannot be followed and the reason why. Upon presentation of an affidavit, the judge of probate for the county in which the individual is present may issue an order requiring a state or local law enforcement officer to take the individual into custody for a period not exceeding twenty-four hours. The order expires seventy-two hours after it was issued, and if the person is not taken into custody within those seventy-two hours, the order is no longer valid. During the person's detention the person must be examined by at least one licensed physician as provided for in Section 44-17-410(2).	South Carolina Code § 44-17-430 (2015)

(continued)

Appendix B (continued)

State	Standard for emergency hospitalization for observation	Reference
	A person may be admitted to a public or private hospital, mental health clinic, or mental health facility for emergency admission upon: (1) written affidavit under oath by a person stating: (a) a belief that the individual is a person with a mental illness as defined in Section 44-23-10(21) and because of this condition there is the likelihood of serious harm as defined in Section 44-23-10(13) to himself or others if not immediately hospitalized; (b) the specific type of serious harm thought probable if the person is not immediately hospitalized and the factual basis for this belief; (2) a certification in triplicate by at least one licensed physician stating that the physician has examined the person and is of the opinion that the person is mentally ill and because of this condition is likely to cause harm to himself through neglect, inability to care for himself, or personal injury, or otherwise, or to others if not immediately hospitalized. The certification must contain the grounds for the opinion. A person for whom a certificate has been issued may not be admitted on the basis of that certificate after the expiration of three calendar days after the date of the examination; (3) within forty-eight hours after admission, exclusive of Saturdays, Sundays, and legal holidays, the place of admission shall forward the affidavit and certification to the probate court of the county in which the person resides or, in extenuating circumstances, where the acts or conduct leading to the hospitalization occurred. Within forty-eight hours of receipt of the affidavit and certification exclusive of Saturdays, Sundays, and legal holidays, the court shall conduct preliminary review of all the evidence to determine if probable cause exists to continue emergency detention of the patient. If the court finds that probable cause does not exist, it shall issue an order of release for the patient. Upon a finding of probable cause, the court shall make a written order detailing its findings and may order the continued detention of the patient.	South Carolina Code § 44-17-410 (2005)
South Dakota	Petition asserting need for immediate intervention of mentally ill person--Contents. If any person is alleged to be severely mentally ill and in such condition that immediate intervention is necessary for the protection from physical harm to self or others, any person, eighteen years of age or older, may complete a petition stating the factual basis for concluding that such person is severely mentally ill and in immediate need of intervention. The petition shall be upon a form and be verified by affidavit. The petition shall include the following: (1) A statement by the petitioner that the petitioner believes, on the basis of personal knowledge, that such person is, as a result of severe mental illness, a danger to self or others; (2) The specific nature of the danger;	South Dakota Codified Laws § 27A-10-1 (2000)

(continued)

Appendix B (continued)

State	Standard for emergency hospitalization for observation	Reference
	(3) A summary of the information upon which the statement of danger is based; (4) A statement of facts which caused the person to come to the petitioner's attention; (5) The address and signature of the petitioner and a statement of the petitioner's interest in the case; and (6) The name of the person to be evaluated; the address, age, marital status, and occupation of the person and the name and address of the person's nearest relative.	
Tennessee	IF AND ONLY IF (1) a person has a mental illness or serious emotional disturbance, AND (2) the person poses an immediate substantial likelihood of serious harm under § 33-6-501 because of the mental illness or serious emotional disturbance, THEN (3) the person may be detained under § 33-6-402 to obtain examination for certification of need for care and treatment.	Tennessee Code Annotated § 33-6-401 (2016)
	If an officer authorized to make arrests in the state, a licensed physician, a psychologist authorized under § 33-6-427(a), or a professional designated by the commissioner under § 33-6-427(b) has reason to believe that a person is subject to detention under § 33-6-401, then the officer, physician, psychologist, or designated professional may take the person into custody without a civil order or warrant for immediate examination under § 33-6-404 for certification of need for care and treatment.	Tennessee Code Annotated § 33-6-402 (2016)
	IF AND ONLY IF (1) a person has a mental illness or serious emotional disturbance, AND (2) the person poses an immediate substantial likelihood of serious harm, under § 33-6-501, because of the mental illness or serious emotional disturbance, AND (3) the person needs care, training, or treatment because of the mental illness or serious emotional disturbance, AND (4) all available less drastic alternatives to placement in a hospital or treatment resource are unsuitable to meet the needs of the person, THEN (5) the person may be admitted and detained by a hospital or treatment resource for emergency diagnosis, evaluation, and treatment under this part.	Tennessee Code Annotated § 33-6-403 (2016)

(continued)

Appendix B (continued)

State	Standard for emergency hospitalization for observation	Reference
Texas	(a) A peace officer, without a warrant, may take a person into custody if the officer: 　(1) has reason to believe and does believe that: 　　(A) the person is a person with mental illness; and 　　(B) because of that mental illness there is a substantial risk of serious harm to the person or to others unless the person is immediately restrained; and 　(2) believes that there is not sufficient time to obtain a warrant before taking the person into custody. (b) A substantial risk of serious harm to the person or others under Subsection (a)(1)(B) may be demonstrated by: 　(1) the person's behavior; or 　(2) evidence of severe emotional distress and deterioration in the person's mental condition to the extent that the person cannot remain at liberty. (c) The peace officer may form the belief that the person meets the criteria for apprehension: 　(1) from a representation of a credible person; or 　(2) on the basis of the conduct of the apprehended person or the circumstances under which the apprehended person is found. (d) A peace officer who takes a person into custody under Subsection (a) shall immediately transport the apprehended person to: 　(1) the nearest appropriate inpatient mental health facility; or 　(2) a mental health facility deemed suitable by the local mental health authority, if an appropriate inpatient mental health facility is not available. (e) A jail or similar detention facility may not be deemed suitable except in an extreme emergency. (f) A person detained in a jail or a nonmedical facility shall be kept separate from any person who is charged with or convicted of a crime.	Texas Health & Safety Code § 573.001(a)-(f) (2015)
	(a) An adult may file a written application for the emergency detention of another person. (b) The application must state: 　(1) that the applicant has reason to believe and does believe that the person evidences mental illness; 　(2) that the applicant has reason to believe and does believe that the person evidences a substantial risk of serious harm to himself or others; 　(3) a specific description of the risk of harm; 　(4) that the applicant has reason to believe and does believe that the risk of harm is imminent unless the person is immediately restrained; 　(5) that the applicant's beliefs are derived from specific recent behavior, overt acts, attempts, or threats;	Texas Health & Safety Code § 573.011 (1991)

(continued)

Appendix B (continued)

State	Standard for emergency hospitalization for observation	Reference
	(6) a detailed description of the specific behavior, acts, attempts, or threats; and (7) a detailed description of the applicant's relationship to the person whose detention is sought. (c) The application may be accompanied by any relevant information.	
Utah	An adult may be temporarily, involuntarily committed to a local mental health authority upon: (i) written application by a responsible person who has reason to know, stating a belief that the individual is likely to cause serious injury to self or others if not immediately restrained, and stating the personal knowledge of the individual's condition or circumstances which lead to that belief; and (ii) a certification by a licensed physician or designated examiner stating that the physician or designated examiner has examined the individual within a three-day period immediately preceding that certification, and that the physician or designated examiner is of the opinion that the individual has a mental illness and, because of the individual's mental illness, is likely to injure self or others if not immediately restrained.	Utah Code Annotated § 62A-15-629(1)(a) (2011)
	(2) If a duly authorized peace officer observes a person involved in conduct that gives the officer probable cause to believe that the person has a mental illness, as defined in Section 62A-15-602, and because of that apparent mental illness and conduct, there is a substantial likelihood of serious harm to that person or others, pending proceedings for examination and certification under this part, the officer may take that person into protective custody. The peace officer shall transport the person to be transported to the designated facility of the appropriate local mental health authority pursuant to this section, either on the basis of the peace officer's own observation or on the basis of a mental health officer's observation that has been reported to the peace officer by that mental health officer. Immediately thereafter, the officer shall place the person in the custody of the local mental health authority and make application for commitment of that person to the local mental health authority. The application shall be on a prescribed form and shall include the following: (a) a statement by the officer that the officer believes, on the basis of personal observation or on the basis of a mental health officer's observation reported to the officer by the mental health officer, that the person is, as a result of a mental illness, a substantial and immediate danger to self or others; (b) the specific nature of the danger; (c) a summary of the observations upon which the statement of danger is based; and (d) a statement of facts which called the person to the attention of the officer.	Utah Code Annotated § 62A-15-629(2) (2011)

(continued)

Appendix B (continued)

State	Standard for emergency hospitalization for observation	Reference
Vermont	(a) Upon written application by an interested party made under the pains and penalties of perjury and accompanied by a certificate by a licensed physician who is not the applicant, a person shall be held for admission to a hospital for an emergency examination to determine if he or she is a person in need of treatment. The application and certificate shall set forth the facts and circumstances that constitute the need for an emergency examination and that show that the person is a person in need of treatment.	Vermont Statutes Annotated title 18 § 7504(a) (2014)
	(a) In emergency circumstances where certification by a physician is not available without serious and unreasonable delay, and when personal observation of the conduct of a person constitutes reasonable grounds to believe that the person is a person in need of treatment, and he or she presents an immediate risk of serious injury to himself or herself or others if not restrained, a law enforcement officer or mental health professional may make an application, not accompanied by a physician's certificate, to any Superior judge for a warrant for an emergency examination.	Vermont Statutes Annotated title 18 § 7505 (a) (2014)
Virginia	A. Any magistrate shall issue, upon the sworn petition of any responsible person, treating physician, or upon his own motion, an emergency custody order when he has probable cause to believe that any person (i) has a mental illness and that there exists a substantial likelihood that, as a result of mental illness, the person will, in the near future, (a) cause serious physical harm to himself or others as evidenced by recent behavior causing, attempting, or threatening harm and other relevant information, if any, or (b) suffer serious harm due to his lack of capacity to protect himself from harm or to provide for his basic human needs, (ii) is in need of hospitalization or treatment, and (iii) is unwilling to volunteer or incapable of volunteering for hospitalization or treatment .... When considering whether there is probable cause to issue an emergency custody order, the magistrate may, in addition to the petition, consider (1) the recommendations of any treating or examining physician or psychologist licensed in Virginia, if available, (2) any past actions of the person, (3) any past mental health treatment of the person, (4) any relevant hearsay evidence, (5) any medical records available, (6) any affidavits submitted, if the witness is unavailable and it so states in the affidavit, and (7) any other information available that the magistrate considers relevant to the determination of whether probable cause exists to issue an emergency custody order. **[pertains to emergency custody]**	Virginia Code Annotated § 37-2-808(A) (2016)

(continued)

Appendix B (continued)

State	Standard for emergency hospitalization for observation	Reference
	B. Any person for whom an emergency custody order is issued shall be taken into custody and transported to a convenient location to be evaluated to determine whether the person meets the criteria for temporary detention pursuant to § 37.2-809 and to assess the need for hospitalization or treatment. The evaluation shall be made by a person designated by the community services board who is skilled in the diagnosis and treatment of mental illness and who has completed a certification program approved by the Department. **[pertains to determination of temporary detention, following emergency custody]**	Virginia Code Annotated § 37.2-809(B) (2016)
Washington	(1) When a designated mental health professional receives information alleging that a person, as the result of a mental disorder, presents an imminent likelihood of serious harm, or is in imminent danger because of being gravely disabled, after investigation and evaluation of the specific facts alleged and of the reliability and credibility of the person or persons providing the information if any, the designated mental health professional may take such person, or cause by oral or written order such person to be taken into emergency custody in an evaluation and treatment facility for not more than seventy-two hours as described in RCW 71.05.180. (2) A peace officer may take or cause such person to be taken into custody and immediately delivered to a triage facility, crisis stabilization unit, evaluation and treatment facility, or the emergency department of a local hospital under the following circumstances: (a) Pursuant to subsection (1) of this section; or (b) When he or she has reasonable cause to believe that such person is suffering from a mental disorder and presents an imminent likelihood of serious harm or is in imminent danger because of being gravely disabled. (*effective until April 1, 2018*) (1) When a designated crisis responder receives information alleging that a person, as the result of a mental disorder, presents an imminent likelihood of serious harm, or is in imminent danger because of being gravely disabled, after investigation and evaluation of the specific facts alleged and of the reliability and credibility of the person or persons providing the information if any, the designated crisis responder may take such person, or cause by oral or written order such person to be taken into emergency custody in an evaluation and treatment facility for not more than seventy-two hours as described in RCW 71.05.180.	Revised Washington Code § 71.05.153 (2015)

(continued)

Appendix B (continued)

State	Standard for emergency hospitalization for observation	Reference
	(2) When a designated crisis responder receives information alleging that a person, as the result of substance use disorder, presents an imminent likelihood of serious harm, or is in imminent danger because of being gravely disabled, after investigation and evaluation of the specific facts alleged and of the reliability and credibility of the person or persons providing the information if any, the designated crisis responder may take the person, or cause by oral or written order the person to be taken, into emergency custody in a secure detoxification facility or approved substance use disorder treatment program for not more than seventy-two hours as described in RCW 71.05.180, if a secure detoxification facility or approved substance use disorder treatment program is available and has adequate space for the person. (3)(a) Subject to (b) of this subsection, a peace officer may take or cause such person to be taken into custody and immediately delivered to a triage facility, crisis stabilization unit, evaluation and treatment facility, secure detoxification facility, approved substance use disorder treatment program, or the emergency department of a local hospital under the following circumstances: (i) Pursuant to subsection (1) or (2) of this section; or (ii) When he or she has reasonable cause to believe that such person is suffering from a mental disorder or substance use disorder and presents an imminent likelihood of serious harm or is in imminent danger because of being gravely disabled. (*effective April 1, 2018–July 1, 2026*)	
West Virginia	(a) Any adult person may make an application for involuntary hospitalization for examination of an individual when the person making the application has reason to believe that the individual to be examined is addicted, as defined in section eleven, article one of this chapter, or is mentally ill and, because of his or her addiction or mental illness, the individual is likely to cause serious harm to himself, herself or to others if allowed to remain at liberty while awaiting an examination and certification by a physician or psychologist.	West Virginia Code § 27-5-2(a) (2016)
Wisconsin	(ag) The purpose of this section is to provide, on an emergency basis, treatment by the least restrictive means appropriate to the individual's needs, to individuals who meet all of the following criteria: 1. Are mentally ill, drug dependent, or developmentally disabled. 2. Evidence one of the standards set forth in par. (ar) 1. to 4. 3. Are reasonably believed to be unable or unwilling to cooperate with voluntary treatment. (ar) A law enforcement officer or other person authorized to take a child into custody under ch. 48 or to take a juvenile into custody under ch. 938 may take an individual into custody if the officer or person has cause to believe that the individual is mentally ill, is drug dependent, or is developmentally disabled, that taking the person into custody is the least restrictive alternative appropriate to the person's needs, and that the individual evidences any of the following:	Wisconsin Statutes Annotated § 51.15(1)(a) (2017)

(continued)

Appendix B (continued)

State	Standard for emergency hospitalization for observation	Reference
	1. A substantial probability of physical harm to himself or herself as manifested by evidence of recent threats of or attempts at suicide or serious bodily harm.	
	2. A substantial probability of physical harm to other persons as manifested by evidence of recent homicidal or other violent behavior on his or her part, or by evidence that others are placed in reasonable fear of violent behavior and serious physical harm to them, as evidenced by a recent overt act, attempt or threat to do serious physical harm on his or her part.	
	3. A substantial probability of physical impairment or injury to himself or herself or other individuals due to impaired judgment, as manifested by evidence of a recent act or omission. The probability of physical impairment or injury is not substantial under this subdivision if reasonable provision for the individual's protection is available in the community and there is a reasonable probability that the individual will avail himself or herself of these services or, in the case of a minor, if the individual is appropriate for services or placement under s. 48.13 (4) or (11) or 938.13 (4). Food, shelter or other care provided to an individual who is substantially incapable of obtaining the care for himself or herself, by any person other than a treatment facility, does not constitute reasonable provision for the individual's protection available in the community under this subdivision.	
	4. Behavior manifested by a recent act or omission that, due to mental illness, he or she is unable to satisfy basic needs for nourishment, medical care, shelter, or safety without prompt and adequate treatment so that a substantial probability exists that death, serious physical injury, serious physical debilitation, or serious physical disease will imminently ensue unless the individual receives prompt and adequate treatment for this mental illness. No substantial probability of harm under this subdivision exists if reasonable provision for the individual's treatment and protection is available in the community and there is a reasonable probability that the individual will avail himself or herself of these services, if the individual may be provided protective placement or protective services under ch. 55, or, in the case of a minor, if the individual is appropriate for services or placement under s. 48.13 (4) or (11) or 938.13 (4). The individual's status as a minor does not automatically establish a substantial probability of death, serious physical injury, serious physical debilitation or serious disease under this subdivision. Food, shelter or other care provided to an individual who is substantially incapable of providing the care for himself or herself, by any person other than a treatment facility, does not constitute reasonable provision for the individual's treatment or protection available in the community under this subdivision.	

(continued)

Appendix B (continued)

State	Standard for emergency hospitalization for observation	Reference
	(b) The officer's or other person's belief shall be based on any of the following: 1. A specific recent overt act or attempt or threat to act or omission by the individual which is observed by the officer or person. 51.15(1)(b)2. 2. A specific recent overt act or attempt or threat to act or omission by the individual which is reliably reported to the officer or person by any other person, including any probation, extended supervision and parole agent authorized by the department of corrections to exercise control and supervision over a probationer, parolee or person on extended supervision.	
Wyoming	(a) When a law enforcement officer or examiner has reasonable cause to believe a person is mentally ill pursuant to W.S. 25-10-101, the person may be detained. (b) Immediately after detaining the person, the officer shall contact an examiner. A preliminary examination of the person shall be conducted by an examiner within twenty-four (24) hours after the detention. If a preliminary examination is not conducted within twenty-four (24) hours the detained person shall be released. If the examiner giving the preliminary examination finds that the person: (i) Is not mentally ill, the person shall be released immediately; (ii) Was mentally ill, but is no longer dangerous to himself or others, the person shall be released immediately; or (iii) Is mentally ill, the person may be detained for seventy-two (72) hours excluding Saturdays, Sundays and legal holidays. (c) No person shall be detained for more than seventy-two (72) hours, excluding Saturdays, Sundays and legal holidays, without a hearing under subsections (h) through (k) of this section.	Wyoming Statutes Annotated § 25-10-109(a)-(c) (2016)

Includes provisions that utilize the following terms: detention, emergency admission, hold, pickup, temporary detention, and others

Index

A
Abandonment, 4, 58, 138, 142, 143, 212, 218
Abuse, 2, 18, 47, 71, 83, 105, 136, 158, 171, 186, 207–225, 239, 260
Access to care, 171, 172, 174
Accredited representatives, 136, 218, 248–250
Admissibility, 117–119, 224
Adoption, 29, 30, 68, 94, 133, 136–139, 142, 246, 253–255, 265, 271, 275, 276, 279, 280
Advance directives, 177–179
Advocacy, 46, 81, 103, 123–125, 153, 155, 158, 183–185, 201, 249, 254
African Americans, 187
Americans with Disabilities Act, 69, 160, 161, 174, 200–201
Amish, 154
Archival data, 96
Assault and battery, 58, 66
Asylum, 173, 241–243, 246, 247
Authorship, 96–97
Autonomy, 6, 82, 83, 184, 208, 222, 224

B
Beneficence, 1, 2, 82, 88, 184
Boundary crossing, 3
Boundary violation, 2, 3
Breach of confidentiality, 65–67, 71
Breach of contract, 57, 66, 68, 70

C
Capacity, 6–8, 21, 22, 27, 46, 61, 83, 90, 106, 135, 146, 176–179, 199, 222, 224, 225, 237, 250, 254, 256, 272, 275, 279, 294, 301, 305, 307, 313
Case management, 87, 197, 247
Certificate of confidentiality, 93, 94
Child, 2, 18, 48, 57, 81, 104, 134, 155, 171, 186, 207–214, 233, 253
Child abuse, 11, 19, 25, 28–30, 33–35, 39, 41, 48, 49, 71, 92, 158, 186–188, 190–192, 207–210, 214, 222, 260
Child custody, 30, 35, 40, 105, 106, 141
Child endangerment, 190, 191
Child neglect, 108, 190–192, 209
Children's Health Insurance Program (CHIP), 245, 246
Civil lawsuits, 52, 70, 93, 109, 170
Civil Rights, 19, 20, 22, 69, 122, 157, 161, 200
Client-social worker privilege, 40
Cloture, 121
Code of Ethics of the National Association of Social Workers, 2–4, 7, 17, 26, 85, 91, 193, 255
Coercion, 87, 157, 184, 185, 199, 211, 220, 221
Communications, 3, 4, 17, 21, 22, 25–29, 31–34, 36–41, 62, 63, 66, 67, 88, 90–92, 124, 164, 176, 236, 266, 270
Competence, 6, 8, 28, 45, 51, 63, 83, 103, 176, 197, 224, 256, 260
Confidentiality, 8, 17–41, 47, 49, 57, 65–68, 71, 73, 75, 86, 89–96, 126, 162–164, 169–171, 193, 197, 199

Confidentiality of Alcohol and Drug Abuse Patient Records Act, 23–25
Conflict of interest, 3, 4, 249
Consent, 4–13, 17, 20, 22, 24–27, 29, 31–33, 35–37, 40, 41, 47, 48, 52, 58, 59, 66, 67, 73, 75, 82, 83, 85–88, 90, 94, 96, 126, 135, 138, 141, 146–149, 158, 163, 171, 174–177, 218, 221, 224, 260, 261, 286, 295, 296, 302, 308
Constitutional claims, 69
Contract, 4–6, 9, 66, 68, 145, 172, 237, 238, 275–277, 280, 281
Conventions, 107, 122, 137, 138, 255, 257, 258
Conversion therapy, 61
Copyright, 94, 96, 97
Court structure, 109
Covenant, 82, 255–258
Criminal prosecution, 40, 71, 93, 188, 279
Custody proceedings, 67, 74, 108, 139–142

D

Data archives, 95, 96
Data ownership, 89, 94–96
Data sharing, 89, 94–96
Data storage, 94–96
Declaration, 81, 135, 149, 255–258
Defamation, 58, 66
Deportation, 162, 173, 174, 243, 245, 250, 261
Deposition, 70, 110
Disability, 8, 40, 46, 63, 69, 82, 106, 141, 146, 155, 158–162, 173, 174, 178, 200–201, 211, 216, 221, 257, 286, 290, 293, 308
Disciplinary proceedings, 10, 33, 45–53
Disclosure, 8, 12, 17–41, 64, 66, 70, 71, 73, 75, 85, 90, 92, 96, 158, 163, 164, 171, 199, 224, 287
Discovery, 27, 70, 110, 157
Discrimination, 40, 81, 111, 157, 160, 161, 200, 257, 258, 267, 270, 271
Dispute resolution, 103, 106–108, 127, 159
Distributive justice, 82, 89
Divorce, 9, 40, 67, 71, 74, 104, 105, 108, 110, 135, 140–152
Documentation, 5, 12, 18, 72, 74, 75, 125, 169–171, 218, 234, 291, 306
Domestic partnership, 135, 136
Drug court, 193–200
Dual relationship, 2–4, 47, 64, 75, 126
Due process, 52, 69, 143, 159, 187, 194
Durable power of attorney for health care (DPAHC), 178, 179
Duty to protect, 37, 38, 92, 214
Duty to warn, 21, 31, 37–39, 66, 91, 92, 164

E

Education Amendment Act of 1972, 157, 158, 162
Education records, 162, 163
Elder abuse, 92, 94, 126, 218–221
Elder neglect, 35, 39, 92, 218–223
Electronic transmissions, 19, 65, 67, 73, 91
Elementary and Secondary Education Act of 1965, 155
Emancipated minor, 10, 144, 145, 149, 176
Emergency hospitalization, ix, 186, 283, 289, 290
Emergency Medical Treatment and Active Labor Act (EMTALA), 171, 175
Employment, 5, 40, 66, 69, 111, 126, 141, 145, 157, 159, 160, 198, 200, 201, 233, 236–238, 240, 241, 245, 254, 259, 271, 274, 278
Empowerment, 185, 224, 254, 256
English proficiency, 155, 233
Engrossed bill, 120
Enhanced interrogation, 259
Enrolled bill, 120
Equal Access Act, 156
Equal protection, 69, 154
Ethics, 1–4, 7, 17, 26, 40, 45, 49–51, 53, 74, 85, 91, 104, 139, 169, 178, 193, 224, 255–261
Ethics audit, 74–76
Evaluation research, 60, 85, 91, 124
Every Student Succeeds Act, 155, 156
Evidence-based practices, 59–61, 72
Expert testimony, 112, 116–120, 224, 247
Expert witness/extrajudicial medical removal, 70, 103, 104, 108–119, 139, 142, 174, 224, 247–248

F

Family Educational Rights and Privacy Act (FERPA), 162–164
Federal Rule of Evidence 702, 118, 119
Fetus, 186–192
Fiduciary relationship, 1–5
Filibuster, 121
Forensic social work
    definition, 103–105
    functions, 103, 124
Fourteenth Amendment, 69, 139, 154, 214
Fraud, 29, 31, 47, 48, 67, 71, 242, 249

G

Gatekeeping, 49–51, 119
Grandparenting, 45, 135
Green card, *see* Permanent residence

H

Health Insurance Portability and
  Accountability Act of 1996 (HIPAA),
  19–25, 90, 163, 169
HIV, 39, 81, 93, 117, 141, 163, 174, 215, 253, 260
Homosexuality, 61

I

Illegal Immigration Reform and Immigrant
  Responsibility Act of 1996 (IIRAIRA),
  173, 243
Immigrants, 137, 138, 173, 218, 233–250, 254
Impairment, 46, 49–51, 160, 161, 171, 200,
  220, 244, 291, 316
Improving America's Schools Act, 155
Individuals with Disabilities Education Act
  (IDEA), 158–161
Information, 2, 17, 47, 62, 83, 111, 136, 155,
  170, 199, 209, 237, 253
Informed consent, 4–10, 13, 26, 58, 73, 75,
  82, 83, 85, 86, 88, 94, 96, 126, 175,
  176, 261
Informed consent to treatment, 7, 171, 175
Intake, 39
Intercountry adoption, 136–139
International Convention on the Elimination of
  All Forms of Racial Discrimination, 257
International Covenant on Civil and Political
  Rights, 82, 256–258
International social work, 253–261
Internet, 62–64, 67, 282
Internet-based services, 62, 63
Interpreter, 7, 159, 243
Interrogatories, 70, 110, 259
Involuntary emergency inpatient
  commitment, 186
Involuntary outpatient civil commitment, 183–185

J

Jail, 123, 125, 188, 193, 196, 198, 199, 213,
  283, 284, 299, 311
Justice, 30, 34, 71, 82, 89, 103–108, 127, 163,
  194–198, 200, 217, 223, 240, 242, 254,
  256, 273, 302
Juvenile Justice and Delinquency Prevention
  Act of 1974, 119

L

Least restrictive environment (LRE), 158
Legislation, 19, 23, 38, 39, 119–122, 155, 156,
  160, 177, 184, 219, 257

Liability, 38–41, 48, 57–76, 187, 209
Licensing
  boards, 45–53, 126
  revocation, 52
  suspension, 10, 52
Living will, 179
Lobbying, 122, 123

M

Major life activity, 160, 161
Malfeasance, 57
Malpractice, 4, 8, 26, 29, 35, 40, 57–66, 68,
  170, 175
Managed care, 9
Mandatory reporting, 49, 222
Marriage, 10, 18, 46–49, 52, 133–135, 140,
  145–149, 237, 242, 271–273, 286, 294,
  299, 300
Mediation, 106, 107, 127, 139, 159, 195
Medicaid, 47, 71, 85, 95, 106, 172–174, 178,
  223, 244–247
Medicare, 85, 95, 106, 172, 174, 178, 247
Mental health court, 126, 193–200
Minors
  emancipated, 10, 144, 145, 148, 176
  and guardians, 10–12, 145, 147
  mature, 10, 11, 146, 176
  and mental health services, 10–12
Motion for summary judgment, 157

N

Negligence, 58, 68, 71, 73
Negligent infliction of emotional distress, 66
Negligent supervision, 65, 66, 261
No Child Left Behind Act, 155
Nonfeasance, 57
Nonimmigrants, 234–240
Nonmaleficence, 1, 2, 82, 88
Nuremberg Code, 81, 82, 86, 258

O

Older Americans Act of 1965, 225

P

Parental consent, 10–13, 158, 163
Partner violence, 81, 92, 158, 164, 212,
  215–219, 253
Patient rights, 171–177
Payment, 6, 9, 11, 19–21, 30, 58, 74, 75, 85,
  87, 90, 172, 174, 273, 275, 276

Permanent residence, 237, 242
Personal Responsibility and Work Opportunity reconciliation Act of 1996 (PRWORA), 173, 243–245
Personal services agreement, 5
Pocket veto, 121
Power, 2, 40, 63, 83, 86, 87, 109, 178, 179, 185, 220, 222, 224, 294
Practice guidelines, 126, 127
Practice standards, 19, 126
Pregnancy, 10, 117, 142, 173, 186–193, 216
Prison, 58, 81, 104, 123, 125, 188, 189, 193, 194, 196, 198, 199
Privacy, 17–19, 23, 24, 37, 39, 41, 57, 65, 73, 75, 82, 85, 89–94, 162–164, 170, 171
Private practice, 4, 19, 69, 169, 172, 279
Privilege (legal), 39, 40, 126, 218, 224
Protected health information (PHI), 19, 20, 24, 25, 90, 163
Psychologists, 1, 18, 37, 91, 164, 186, 259, 284, 287, 289, 290, 292, 293, 294–297, 299–301, 304–306, 308, 310, 313, 315
Psychotherapy, 20–22, 26, 28, 46, 62, 103, 286
Public benefits, 173, 245, 247
Public charge, 245–246
Public support, 243–246

Q
Qualitative data, 96
Quantitative data, 95, 96

R
Race, 84, 141, 154, 159, 193, 213, 241, 242, 257, 278, 282
Ratification, 255, 258
Records, 11, 12, 18, 21, 23–27, 30, 36, 39–41, 47, 48, 51, 64, 65, 67, 68, 70, 71, 73–75, 90, 93, 94, 111, 119, 123, 135, 159, 160, 162, 163, 169–171, 218, 241, 255, 273, 289, 292, 313
Reentry social worker, 124, 125
Refugee, 84, 173, 233, 254, 255
Refusal of treatment, 175–177
Release of information, 37, 75, 162–164
Reliability (of evidence), 114, 118, 314
Removal proceedings, 242–243, 247
Research, 13, 18, 59, 81–101, 112, 185, 208, 254
Respect for persons, 6, 82–88, 184
Respondent superior, 48, 64, 66
Restorative justice, 106–108, 127, 195
Risk management, 72–74, 169

S
Sanctions, 8, 157, 194, 197, 208, 274, 306
School, 3, 37, 91, 145, 147, 148, 153–167, 174, 212, 235, 244, 246, 253, 267–270, 275, 281
Self-determination, 7, 82, 179, 184, 185, 222, 256
Self-neglect, 222
Sexual harassment, 110, 157, 162, 164, 211, 221
Social Security Act, 171, 172, 244
Social Worker-Client Agreement, 5, 6
Social worker-client privilege, 25–35, 217, 218
Special education, 158–162
Special interest group, 121, 122
Standard of care, 38, 57, 59–61, 71, 92, 126
Stay-put rule, 159
Subpoena, 25, 33, 34, 36, 40, 41, 67, 70, 71, 92, 93, 163, 169, 171, 218, 224
Substance abuse, 19, 23, 49, 52, 127, 188–195, 290, 293
Suicide, 57, 73, 184, 207, 216, 289, 301, 304, 307, 316
Supervision, 33, 45, 47, 48, 51, 52, 61, 62, 64–66, 73–75, 140, 142, 148, 153, 158, 170, 194, 197, 198, 261, 297, 301, 302, 305, 307, 317
Supervisory liability, 64
Supplemental Nutrition Program for Women, Infants, and Children (WIC), 244, 246
Surrogate, health care, 176–178

T
Teacher, 3, 155–158, 237, 269, 270
Termination of parental rights, 40, 105, 139–150
Therapeutic contract, 5
Therapeutic jurisprudence, 106–108, 127, 195, 197, 199
Therapeutic misconception, 85
Title IX of the Education Amendment of 1972, 157, 158, 162
Tort, 38, 65–68
Treatment goals, 6, 199
Treaty, 235, 239
Trial, 28, 35, 41, 60, 70, 87, 103, 110–112, 118, 119, 157

U
Understanding, 6, 7, 9, 13, 19, 36, 61, 64, 81, 83, 84, 88, 95, 96, 103, 107, 113, 119, 125, 156, 208, 209, 217, 254, 257
United Nations Millennium Declaration, 256
Universal Declaration of Human Rights, 255–257

V

Violence, 27, 35, 38, 81, 86, 91, 92, 140, 157, 158, 164, 210, 212, 215, 219, 221, 240, 242, 244, 245, 253, 255

Visas, 240

Vocational Rehabilitation Act of 1973, 161, 162

Voir dire, 112

Voluntariness, 86, 87

Vulnerability, 83, 84, 87

W

Witness, 52, 70, 92, 103, 104, 108, 110–117, 142, 162, 175, 176, 179, 216, 223, 224, 238–241, 243, 247–248, 313

Index to Legal Cases

A
Abdullahi v. Pfizer, 81, 258
Alfred v. Alaska, 27
Anderson v. Anderson, 135
Andrews v. Board of Social Work Licensure, 10
Ankrom v. State, 188
Application of Halko, 177
Arkansas Department of Human Services v. Collier, 188

B
Brady v. Hopper, 38
Bragdon v. Abbott, 174
Braschi v. Stahl, 134
Brown v. Board of Education, 154
Bryant v. Oakpointe Villa Nursing Centre, 58
B.S. v. Somerset County, 69
Burr v. Board of County Commissioners, 67

C
Caban v. Mohammed, 140
Carney v. Carney, 141
Carothers v. County of Cook, 201
City of New York v. Antoinette R., 177
City of Newark v. J.S., 177
Cochran v. Commonwealth, 189
Collins v. Texas, 191
Commonwealth v. Kemp, 191
Commonwealth v. Oliveira, 30
Commonwealth v. Pellegrini, 189
Commonwealth v. Pelosi, 30
Commonwealth v. Welch, 189
Cruz v. Central Iowa Hospital Corporation, 175

Cruzan v. Director, Missouri Department of Health, 178
Currier v. Doran, 64
Custody of a Minor, 176, 177

D
Daubert v. Merrell Dow Pharmaceuticals, 117, 118
Davis v. Lhim, 38, 92
DeShaney v. Winnebago County Department of Social Services, 214
Doe v. District of Columbia, 214
Doe v. Harbor Schools, Inc., 3
Doe v. Maryland Board of Social Workers, 41
Doe v. Roe, 141

E
Earle v. Kuklo, 38, 92
Ewing v. Goldstein, 38, 92
Ewing v. Northridge Hospital Medical Center, 38, 92

F
Fiore v. Bureau of Professional and Occupational Affairs, State Board of Social Workers, Marriage and Family Therapists and Professional Counselors, 48
Friederwitzer v. Friederwitzer, 142
Frye v. United States General Electric v. Joiner, 117, 118

G
General Electric v. Joiner, 118
Green v. Ross, 39
Grzan v. Charter Hospital of Northwest Indiana et al, 58, 59, 65

H
Haldeman v Golden, 69
Herron v. State, 189

I
In re Baby Boy Blackshear, 191
In re Brian T, 143
In re Claire C. Conroy, 176
In re Emmanuel, 144
In re Isaiah J., 143
In re Justin F., 143
In re Karen Quinlan, 177
In re Nicholas H., 134
In re Paul M., Jr., 143
In re Sean H., 143
In re Unborn Child, 190
In re Unborn Child Julie Starks, 191
In re Valerie, 188
In re V.R., 191
In re Yetter, 176

J
Jablonski v. United States, 38, 92
Jaffee v. Redmond, 26
Jehovah's Witnesses of Washington v. King County Hospital, 176
Jensen v. Anderson County Department of Social Services, 214
J.K. v. Arizona Board of Regents, 157, 158
Johnson v. State, 188

K
Kilmon v. State, 189
Kumho Tire Co. v. Carmichael, 119

L
Lassiter v. Department of Social Service, 144
Lehr v. Robertson, 140
Loughlin et al. v. Vance County Department of Social Services et al., 69
Loveheart v. Long, 143
Loving v. Virginia, 134

M
MacDonald v. Clinger, 3, 66
Marisol v. Giuliani, 69, 214
Martino v. Family Service Agency of Adams County, 1, 3, 66–68
Mathews v. Eldridge, 144
Matter of Ahleman
Matter of Bass, 48, 52
Matter of Currie, 48, 52
Matter of James, 48, 52
Matter of King, 52
Matter of Licensure of Penny v. State of Wyoming, 48
Matter of Nedoba, 48, 52
Matter of Smith, 190
Matter of Tartakoff v. New York State Education Department, 48, 52
McIntosh v. Milano, 38, 92
Meyer v. Nebraska, 139, 154
Michael H. v. Gerald D, 140
Montejo v. Martin Memorial Hospital, 174, 175
Moore v. Department of Human Resources, 68
M.R. v. Cox, 65

N
N.D. v. Copeland, 35
Nelson v. Green, 41
New Jersey Department of Children and Families v. A.L., 190
Noval v. Kaiser Foundation Health Plan, Inc., 3

O
Obergefell v. Hodges, 133

P
Palmore v. Sidoti, 141
Penninger v. Oklahoma, 32
Penny v. State of Wyoming, 67
People v. Bedenkop, 189
People v. Cavaiana, 213
People v. Hardy, 189
People v. Morabito, 190
People v. Newman, 93
Phelan v. Torres, 69
Pierce v. Society of Sisters, 154
Pineda v. Ford Motor Co., 112
Plyler v. Doe, 154

Q
Quilloin v. Wolcott, 140

R

Reinesto v. Superior Court, 188
Reyes v. Superior Court of San Bernardino County, 188
Roy v. Hartogs, 3
Rubano v. DiCenzo, 134

S

San Antonio v. Rodriguez, 154
Santosky v. Kramer, 144
Schaefer v. Wilcock, 69
Schloendorff v. Society of New York Hospital, 175
Sheriff v. Encoe, 190
Simpson v. University of Colorado, 158
St. John v. Pope, 59
Stanley v. Illinois, 140
State ex rel. Holcombe v. Armstrong, 177
State ex. rel. M.E.C., 192
State v. Aiwohi, 189
State v. Amanda H., 190
State v. Arandus, 190
State v. Brown, 213
State v. Dunn, 192
State v. Gethers, 188
State v. Grover, 213
State v. Grubbs, 188
State v. Hurd, 213
State v. Inzar, 191
State v. Louk, 192
State v. Luster, 189
State v. McKnight, 191
State v. R.R., 112, 117
State v. Taylor, 111
State v. Wade, 190
Summers v. Altarum Institute Corp, 201

T

Tarasoff v. Regents of the University of California, 37, 66, 91, 92, 164
T.E.P. v. Leavitt, 134
Thompson v. County of Alameda, 38, 92
Tony L. By and Through Simpson v. Childer, 214
Truth v. Kent School District, 156
Turner v. Safley, 134
Tylena M. v. Heartshare Children's Services, 66

U

United States v. Hicks, 112
United States v. Vaughn, 188

V

V.B.T. v. Family Services of Western Pennsylvania, 33
Vonner v. State of Louisiana, 64

W

Weisbeck v. Hess, 3
Whitner v. State, 191
Wisconsin ex. rel. Angela M.W. v. Kruzicki, 192
Wisconsin v. Yoder, 154

Z

Zavatsky v. Anderson, 69

Printed by Printforce, the Netherlands